A Cheerful and Comfortable Faith

A Cheerful and Comfortable Faith

Anglican Religious Practice in the
Elite Households of
Eighteenth-Century Virginia

LAUREN F. WINNER

Yale
UNIVERSITY PRESS

New Haven & London

Yale University Press books may be purchased in quantity for educational, business,
or promotional use. For information, please e-mail sales.press@yale.edu (U.S. office)
or sales@yaleup.co.uk (U.K. office).

Set in Adobe Caslon type by Keystone Typesetting, Inc.
Printed in the United States of America by Sheridan Books, Ann Arbor, Michigan.

Library of Congress Cataloging-in-Publication Data

Winner, Lauren F.
A cheerful and comfortable faith : Anglican religious practice in the elite households of
eighteenth-century Virginia / Lauren F. Winner.
p.   cm.
Includes bibliographical references and index.

ISBN 978-0-300-12469-9 (cloth : alk. paper)
1. Episcopal Church—Virginia—History—18th century. 2. Virginia—Religious life and customs.
I. Title.
BX5917.V8W56 2010
283′.75509033—dc22
2010003115

A catalogue record for this book is available from the British Library.

This paper meets the requirements of ANSI/NISO Z39.48-1992 (Permanence of Paper).

10 9 8 7 6 5 4 3 2 1

For
Dennis Winner
and in memory of
Linda Cogdill Winner
with gratitude

Contents

Illustrations

A Cheerful and Comfortable Faith

1

Elizabeth Boush's Sacrifice of Isaac (1768–1769) suggests that girls learned biblical stories as they were learning to embroider. Collection of the Museum of Early Southern Decorative Arts, Old Salem Museums and Gardens.

Kitchenware That Wants You to Love Your Neighbor

Household Religious Practice in Anglican Virginia

Her Religion was Pure Fervent Cheerful and of the Church of England.
—From the grave marker of Lettice Turberville (1707–1732), at the
Turberville estate, Hickory Hill, Westmoreland County, Virginia

This book was conceived one afternoon almost a decade ago, as I wandered through the rooms of the Museum of Early Southern Decorative Arts. I had narratives in which to place most of the objects I saw there: salt-glazed stoneware had become popular on the Eastern seaboard in the eighteenth century because it was sturdier than delft; South Carolina produced more silverwork than its poorer neighbor North Carolina; Moravians in backcountry Carolina, because of design sensibilities they brought with them from Europe and because of trade encounters with sophisticates in Charleston and Philadelphia, prized furniture that was more elaborately upholstered than that of many other backcountry dwellers.[1] Yet there was one object, a piece of embroidery made in 1768 and 1769 by a Virginia girl named Elizabeth Boush, that I could not explain. The needlework featured a biblical scene, the Sacrifice of Isaac. What, I wondered, had the girl who made this needlework thought about the story she so artfully rendered in silk? And what did her parents and teacher hope she was learning, not only about sewing but also about God and her duties to God, as she sewed this dramatic scene? I had been taught that "religious instruction for children . . . appears to have been largely nonexistent in most Anglican planter families."[2] Yet here was an object that seemed to testify to a sort of religious instruction. Nothing I knew about girls' religious education in the colonial South or, indeed, about southern Anglicanism more broadly, helped me interpret Boush's needlework.

So this book began as an effort to understand that piece of embroidery and a handful of other objects—objects like the Randolph family's baptismal gown, William Byrd's prayer book, and the Mason family Bible. My previously held conception of the gentry household as more or less secular did not account for these objects; nor did the categories of "display" and "refinement" seem to fully illuminate them. (Refinement, after all, is usually a gloss on other activities, not something by itself; refinement serves other purposes, and some of those purposes may be religious.) *A Cheerful and Comfortable Faith* is my effort to understand those objects; more specifically, it is my effort to understand the religious practices those objects imply, the religious practices in which those objects were produced or used.

In this book I shall argue that in the highly laicized environment that was Virginia's Anglican church, laypeople not only (as has been well established) adapted English forms of church governance to the new Virginia environment. In the absence of a strong clergy—and thus in a religious environment where clerically dominated forms of religion such as preaching and the Eucharist could not occupy a central place in everyday piety—laypeople engaged in vital religious practices in the household, a space where ordinary men and women, not clerics, presided. The religious practices in elite households were quotidian rather than rapturous, a part of ordinary life rather than characterized by rupture from it. Indeed, sometimes the gentry's household religious practices subtly but unambiguously underwrote the other orders of their households—hierarchical orders of slavery and of rigid gender roles, for example. As Elizabeth Boush's needlework—with its expensive silk thread and its implication of both refined education and plenty of leisure time—suggests, the "religious" meanings of practices and objects cannot be separated from their social and economic meanings. In the religious practices I shall investigate, theology and ritual combined with social and economic location to produce a coherent religious experience that was exceptionally well suited to the prerogatives and prerequisites of elite slaveowners. Virginia gentry's Anglicanism was a religion at ease with the world, and it helped the gentry articulate and sustain its own comfortable place in that world.

Around the same time that I first encountered Elizabeth Boush's needlework, I read an essay on baptism by the Anglican reformer Thomas Cranmer. Cranmer wrote confidently that "the very true doctrine of Christ and his pure church from the beginning is plain, certain, without wrinkles, without any inconvenience or absurdity, so cheerful and comfortable to all Christian people."[3] The phrase "cheerful and comfortable" kept coming back to me as I studied the Virginia gentry and its religious practices. The word *comfortable* meant something slightly different in the sixteenth century than it does today. It did not principally mean cozy. Its primary meaning was "comfort-giving," "solacing," "cheering"—as in the Book of Common Prayer's instruction before the reading of Scripture, "Hear what comfortable words."[4] It is in the slippage between these two meanings of *comfortable*—"comfort-giving" and "solacing," versus "at ease," "cozy"—that I find the phrase "cheerful and comfortable" a useful interpretation of the household religious practices of Virginia's Anglican gentry. The dominant note *A Cheerful and Comfortable Faith* strikes is this: the religiosity of the gentry was "comfortable" in today's meaning of the term. Its preachers didn't dwell overmuch on hellfire, its pious disciplines weren't arduous, its theology was by and large assuring, optimistic, and not unduly speculative. It was, in contemporary phrasing, amiable.[5] It was a religion at ease with the world; it did not demand that practitioners be unsettled, nor did it urge them to break from the world. In this way, the household religious practices of Virginia's gentry made good sense for people who led (in today's terms) cheerful and comfortable lives. Yet this study also suggests, contrapuntally, that if we listen carefully, we can hear that the gentry's Anglicanism was also "comfortable" in Cranmer's sense. There were occasional tensions in the well-appointed and elegant gentry houses, and, in the face of those tensions, Anglican gentry turned to religious practice as a source of comfort. The gentry's Anglican practice mediated social tensions— the gentry deployed religious practice, as we shall see most especially in the consideration in Chapter 3 of prayer, in managing the tensions of slavery. And, as we shall see most explicitly in the consideration of death in Chapter 5, Anglican practice responded to existential tensions as well. This study of gentry religious practice, then, shines a light on the comfort of elites' domestic lives, but it also acknowledges the dissonance in gentry households, and illustrates how household religious practice served the gentry both in moments of ease and moments of disquiet.[6]

Anglicanism in Colonial Virginia: Rhys Isaac and His Revisers

To venture a description of religion in early Virginia is to wade into a historical literature that is well established. In 1982 the terms of scholarly discussion of Anglicanism in colonial Virginia were set by Rhys Isaac, whose Pulitzer Prize–winning *The Transformation of Virginia* traced the religious and politi-

cal upheavals that upended Virginia society in the second half of the eighteenth century. In an anthropologically inflected study—its main metaphor is
"dramaturgy"—Isaac argued that buttressing social hierarchy was a primary
function (a term I use advisedly, for if ever there was a functionalist reading of
religion, it is Isaac's) of the Anglican Church. Isaac was interested in the
Church of England insofar as Anglicanism bolstered, and then ultimately
failed to sustain, the dominance of the gentry. Concerned not with Anglican
religious practice per se, but with the ways that Anglican religious performance supported the social order, he saw Anglicanism as merely a phase of
colonial Virginia's religion—a step between unchurched near-anarchy and
evangelical success.[7]

A generation of scholarship on colonial Virginia followed Isaac's lead,
and as a result, historical narratives about early America, when they discussed
religion in Virginia at all, often assumed that before the Great Awakening,
Virginia was an essentially irreligious place and, according to one scholar,
became "increasingly secular" over the course of the eighteenth century. In
particular, "religious values rarely intruded into family life and childrearing,
especially in Anglican planter households."[8] A recent synthesis of early
American history captures the prevailing view in the thesis sentence of the
one paragraph devoted to Anglicanism in the colonial South: southern Anglicans were "either lax in religious observance, torn by dissension, or unchurched altogether."[9]

The Virginians who populate *A Cheerful and Comfortable Faith* were
neither "secular" nor "lax in religious observance." To the contrary, religious
practices punctuated life in elite households; elites' piety overtly and self-
consciously figured into their day-to-day routines. The scholarship that suggests otherwise, I propose, is based on a limited view in which only religion
that mandates a sharp break with the world counts as such. This may have
been the view of clerics in Puritan New England and of the Baptist revivalists
who stormed Virginia in the second half of the eighteenth century, and it may
have become equally orthodox among some historians of American religion.
But religion has always come in a more quotidian form too, and it is not any
less "religious" as a result—just religious in a different key.

In offering this corrective to the view that Virginians were "secular" until
the evangelicals brought religion south, I am adding to an exciting and over-
due reevaluation of Virginia Anglicanism. Two scholars hinted at this reevaluation in studies of the early-national and antebellum South. Jan Lewis, in
The Pursuit of Happiness, noted that it would be a mistake to imagine that
after Disestablishment, in the fires of the Second Great Awakening, white

Virginians suddenly "became profoundly religious." Rather, they "became religious in a different way" than they had been before. Similarly, in the beginning of her study *Southern Cross,* Christine Heyrman suggestively observed that in the decades before the Revolution, "Many southern whites found spiritual satisfaction in hearing intoned the familiar, stately cadences of the Book of Common Prayer. . . . [They] took consolation from carefully crafted sermons emphasizing the reasonableness of Christianity, the benevolence of God, and the moral capacity of humankind. And they drew assurance from frequent allusions to the divine origin of a social hierarchy that set rich over poor, men over women, and white over black." Lewis's and Heyrman's insights about the vitality of pre-Revolutionary Anglicanism have been fleshed out and most forcefully articulated in studies of colonial Virginia's Anglicanism by John Nelson, Edward L. Bond, Albert Zambone, and Patrick Butler (and, mutatis mutandis, by Louis Nelson and Nicholas Beasley, from whose studies of Anglicanism in South Carolina and the West Indies scholars of Virginia will learn a great deal).[10] These scholars admit that historians of Puritan New England have far more written sources with which to work than do scholars of the Anglican South. But the fact that Virginia's Anglicans wrote less and preserved less of what they wrote than their contemporaries in Massachusetts and Connecticut does not mean they were less religious. As these recent revisions of standard wisdom have shown, the Anglican Church was a vital presence in Virginia. The churches provided for all manner of social and civil needs, chief among them caring for the poor. Clergymen were more competent, better educated, and less profligate than previous portraits suggest. The liturgical forms of corporate worship, far from being tedious and empty, solaced and indeed spiritually sustained Virginia Anglicans. Virginians were not, this recent literature makes clear, indifferent to religion; they were not whited sepulchers just waiting for evangelical revivalists to "awaken" them to the importance of Christianity.

I thought, when I began writing this book, that I was setting out to "revise Rhys Isaac." Eventually I realized that I actually had a humbler goal: to riff on the sentence in *The Transformation of Virginia* that most captured my imagination. Because Isaac set up the Anglicans in order to knock them down, he did not inquire deeply into habits of Anglican religious practice—but he did note, almost in passing, that "Christian formulas were scattered throughout the daily routines of Anglo-Virginians." *A Cheerful and Comfortable Faith* may be read as an extended exegesis on that one sentence—an investigation of those "Christian formulas" and what, exactly, they formulated for Virginia's gentry.[11]

Aspects of Anglicanism in Seventeenth-Century Virginia: Religious Establishment, Clerical Vicissitudes, and a Strong Laity

Anglicanism came to Virginia with the first English settlers. Under an "olde saile" hung from a few trees, those first settlers gathered with their parson Robert Hunt for "daily Common Prayer morning and evening," and at a "Pulpit a bar of wood nailed to two neighbouring trees," Hunt preached two sermons every Sunday. Indeed, Virginia's earliest documents reflected the assumption that the Church of England would have a presence in the colony: although the drafters of the colony's charters did not specifically discuss the establishment of the Church of England, they did acknowledge "the glory of [God's] divine majesty," and they included language, which would become ubiquitous in English colonial charters, about the "propagating of *Christian* Religion to such people as yet live in Darkness and miserable Ignorance of the true Knowledge and Worship of God." The second Virginia charter instantiated the colony's Anglican identity in part through anti-Catholic sentiment— "we should be loath, that any Person should be permitted to pass, that we suspected to affect the superstitions of the Church of *Rome;* We do hereby DECLARE, that it is our Will and Pleasure, that none be permitted to pass in any Voyage from time to time to be made into the said Country, but such, as first shall have taken the Oath of Supremacy" (in which a person swore to uphold the English monarch as the head of the Church of England). In addition to these charters, other founding documents tied Virginia to Anglicanism, specifying that the leaders of the colony were to "provide, that the true Word and Service of God be preached, planted, and used, not only in the said Colonies, but also, as much as might be, among the Savages bordering upon them, according to the Rites and Doctrine of the Church of *England.*" In 1619, at its first meeting, Virginia's General Assembly formally established the church, declaring that "all ministers shall duely read divine service, and exercise their ministerial function according to the Ecclesiastical Lawes and orders of the church of England." During the next decades, the Assembly spelled out what that establishment meant: liturgy to be recited "according to the booke of common prayer"; fines to be paid by those who skipped divine service on Sundays; a system of taxation to support the clergy; what the clergy were to do (catechize the youth, visit "the dangerouslie sick") and what they were to avoid ("giv[ing] themselves to excesse in drinking or ryott, spending the time idelie by day or by night, playing at dice, cards, or any other unlawful game"). In short, as a 1632 law put it, there was to "be an uniformity in our church as neere as may be to the canons in England; both in substance and circumstance, and that all persons yeild readie obedience unto them under paine of censure."[12]

The men who drafted that 1632 law were prescient when they called for uniformity to the English church "as neere as may bee." From the start, the church in Virginia could only "neerely" approximate the English church, for the colonists did not have the resources to create the church they had known in England. Most significant, for most of the seventeenth century, Virginia experienced a severe clergy shortage: in 1661, some twenty-six thousand Virginians relied upon the ministrations of twelve Anglican clerics. This led to what Edward Bond calls a "crisis in pastoral care." It was a crisis contemporary Virginians noted: in 1686/7, William Fitzhugh, a lawyer and devout Anglican who had migrated to Virginia in the early 1670s, lamented the "want of spirituall help & comforts" to be found in Virginia.[13] In the absence of a strong clergy, laity, especially elite laity, took charge of church life—and in doing so they sometimes broke with English precedent. Their most significant innovation was the evolution of the vestry system, which was in place in Virginia by the mid-seventeenth century. Virginia vestries, or boards of laymen who governed the church, had more power than their counterparts in England. In particular, vestries in Virginia claimed the right to select clergy for their parishes.[14] Clergy served at the whim of the vestries, and should a parson displease a powerful layman in his parish, he could find himself out of a job. Governor Alexander Spotswood captured the lay appropriation of ecclesiastical authority when he referred to the vestry of St. Anne's Parish as "the Twelve Bishops."[15]

Beginning in the last quarter of the seventeenth century—about the time that Fitzhugh lamented the absence of "spirituall help" in Virginia—church officials in England began to take a more active interest in the spiritual affairs of the colonies. The colonies fell under the ecclesial oversight of the bishop of London, and in 1675 Charles II named Henry Compton to that post. Compton was more interested in the state of the colonial churches than had been his predecessors—as he wrote in March 1676, "As the care of your churches . . . lies upon me as your diocesan, so to discharge that trust, I shall omit no occasions of promoting their good and interest." Compton was worried, among other things, about the power the lay members of vestries in Virginia claimed: they "pretend an Authority to be intrusted with the sole management of Church Affaires, & to exercise an arbitrary power over the Ministers themselves." Compton set about improving both the number and quality of clergy in Virginia, and the colony began to have what Bond has termed "a more distinctly Anglican tenor" after 1675.[16]

The strength of the clergy ebbed and flowed over the course of the late seventeenth and eighteenth centuries. In 1689 James Blair was appointed commissary, or representative of the bishop of London. Until 1776 there would be a commissary in Virginia, helping keep the church connected to the ecclesiastical nerve center in England; this strengthened the colonial church in part because the commissary reminded the bishop that he needed to help provide Virginia with an able clergy. After about 1730 Virginia also began to produce more of its own ministers—the College of William and Mary was founded in 1693, in part as a training school for clergy, and Virginia began to send some of its own men to London to be ordained. From the 1750s until 1774 most parishes were staffed with a parson (although the early to mid-1760s saw a temporary increase in vacant pulpits), and most of these parsons were competent—reasonably well educated, sufficiently pious, diligent. Although for many years, scholars enjoyed caricaturing Virginia clergy as dissolute, the historian John Nelson recently determined that only about ten percent got into serious trouble—with liquor, with women, or simply for neglecting the parish. Many clergymen were described by contemporaries with such phrases as "a man of great caution, [and] good understanding" and "agreeable companion and worthy divine." Yet even as the numbers of able clergy increased, a thoroughgoing laicism continued to characterize Virginia Anglicanism. Gentry may have been glad to receive the "spirituall help" that a respectable clergy could provide, but the elite laymen who had been running Virginia's churches during the decades of clergy shortage were not keen to hand over the reins of power to ministers. In Nelson's conclusion, laity "from early on were fundamentally important in shaping and managing the institution" and throughout the eighteenth century, the church could be described as a "decentralized, lay-dominated establishment."[17]

Encountering the Church in Three Places: In the Parish-County, at Church on Sunday, and in "Private Houses"

Elite laity would have regularly encountered Anglicanism in three central loci: the parish-county, the parish church and chapels of ease, and the household. "Parish-county," a term coined by John Nelson, aptly designates the basic unit of local government of colonial Virginia. The parish and the county shared the tasks of governance, and, in fact, Virginians paid higher taxes to support the parish than they did to support the county. Their tithes did not go only to purchase communion wine. Much of the money Virginians paid as tithes flowed back into the community, as the parish, led by the vestry, was responsible for all manner of civil and social maintenance. The vestry oversaw poor relief, disbursing funds for the poor of the parish and employing economically marginal men and women to care for the sick. Vestries bound out children and oversaw apprentice relationships. They were charged with the quadrennial ritual of "processioning" the parish (that is, walking the parish and checking on boundaries and borders, and brokering any property disputes). Vestries also assisted the county in constructing roads and bridges. In some parishes, vestries ran free schools "for the Education of poor Children." The parish was thus a basic unit of civil society, and every time people left their houses and found society functioning—property lines agreed upon, the poor fed and clothed—they were encountering the work of their church, the established church.[18]

Virginians also encountered the church, sensibly enough, at church. In 1662 the Assembly passed legislation requiring that churches be built in each parish. Many Virginia parishes were large—the average Tidewater parish was twenty to forty miles long, and five to ten miles wide—and it was difficult for people to get to church. In response to that geographical reality, vestries built multiple church buildings in each parish, "mother churches" and "chapels of ease" (smaller church buildings that dotted Virginia's parishes, so named because they made it easier for parishioners who lived far away from the central church buildings to get to corporate worship). Despite the construction of conveniently located chapels of ease, Virginia laity did not, in fact, attend church every Sunday; indeed, attendance was legally required only once a month. Parishioners were often deterred by bad weather. If the cleric was not going to be present, and the service taken instead by a lay reader, families skipped. Nonetheless, the historians Patricia Bonomi and Peter Eisenstadt have concluded that Virginians attended more often than required—they found that just over half of adult Anglican parishioners in Virginia attended Sunday services "regularly." Some churches found that attendance was so high that (as the pastor of Accomack Parish wrote) the "churches cannot contain all that come," and (as the parson of St. Paul's informed the bishop of London) there were "Often more [people] than pews for."[19]

Two letters from Maria Taylor Byrd to her son, William Byrd III, who was away from home serving the Second Virginia Regiment during the Seven Years' War, capture what the gentry experienced when they attended church on Sunday. In the first letter, written September 23, 1759, Maria Byrd takes her son to task for not informing her directly of an anticipated promotion:

The very last sermon Sunday Wayles comes to our pew before church began & says Madam I give you joy of Mr Byrd's being made governour of Pittsburge. . . . & I can tell you farther says he, he is soon to have a Regiment upon the Establishment. Pray Sir says I how might you hear this? He said Mr Pride that lives at York told him: but surely if there were any foundation for these rumours you would have inform'd me.[20]

In the second letter, written May 13, 1760, Maria Byrd comments on recent conversations with friends about parish politics. Westover Parish's parson, William Davis, had recently gone to serve a stint as wartime chaplain, and several members of the parish were disgruntled:

> There is in this parish of those that go syldomest to church much murmuring at Mr. Davises absince; here came Col. Harrison the other day accompany'd by Will Randolph & they advised me to write to Parson Fenney to get him to preach at our churches some times, & accordingly I wrote to him & he has given me his promise that he will. Mr. Wayles is extremely kind in doing what he can in that respect, he has engaged Parson Mosson already & designs likewise to get Parson Duglish, he says to make us laugh. Some of the abovemention'd perishioners the gentlemen told me with concern, are resolved the next Assembly to get the vestrymen desolv'd that agreed to Mr. Davis's making a campaign. I cant find any reason for their discontent as the churches in this parish have been well attended hitherto. Mr. Thomas Davis preached at our church on Sunday last & is to give us a sermon again on Thursday & has published giving the Sacrament this month, so I cant think what the people would have more.[21]

In addition to making clear that some people attended church more than others—one has the impression that Maria Taylor Byrd was a regular, but some members of Westover Parish went to church "syldom"—Byrd's letters also capture how the social and the divine mingled together on Sunday mornings. Church was an opportunity for socializing. Maria Byrd was able to learn important information about her son from her neighbor at church. Indeed, parishioners often gathered as much as thirty minutes before the service began. Men and women mingled on the church steps, chatting and chewing the fat—or, more properly, the tobacco—before the service. Church was an especially important place of conversation and visiting for elite women, who had fewer opportunities than their husbands and fathers to leave home and socialize.

Church not only provided a chance for neighborly conversation; church also staged social hierarchy. Elite parishioners displayed their wealth as they arrived on Sundays, riding up to church in elegant carriages; as Lucy Grymes

Nelson's daughter recalled being told, her mother always attended church as a girl, and "The coach was brought to the door at church time for her parents being wealthy always had carriages at command." Once inside, churchgoers sat "according to their several ranks and degrees." Enslaved Afro-Virginians and free Virginians of humble means often sat on benches in the back of the church, or along the sides of the sanctuary, or even stood through the service. Gentry purchased the best pews up front, or sat in separate galleries they paid to build. An oft-quoted passage from the diary of Philip Fithian, a New Jersey Presbyterian who worked as a tutor at the Westmoreland County estate of Robert and Ann Carter in 1773 and 1774, has influenced how historians imagine church life in colonial Virginia: "It is not the Custom for Gentlemen to go into church till Service is beginning when they enter in a Body, in the same manner as they come out." This passage has been made famous by Rhys Isaac, who used Fithian's observation of church on a Sunday morning in Cople Parish to bolster his argument about social hierarchy and the churches. "Pride of rank accompanied the gentry even as they took their places within" the church, explained Isaac, "so that we may picture them tramping booted to their pews at the front." Byrd's letter demonstrates that not in all times and places did the gentlemen linger outside of church till the service was starting and then ostentatiously troop in en masse. Maria Byrd was seated in church; perhaps all the other elite men were outside waiting to parade in, but John Wayles (the successful lawyer, debt collector, and slave-trade agent who fathered both Martha Wayles Jefferson and Sally Hemings) was inside chatting with Byrd.[22]

If social hierarchy was inscribed into the church pews, church architecture and décor could also bespeak divinity. In Christ Church, Lancaster County, cherubim gazed up at parishioners from baptismal fonts, turning worshipers' attention from the social to the supernatural. In Poplar Spring Church, Mattapony Church, and Lamb's Creek Church, parishioners were greeted by murals with angels, and they made an impression on worshipers; in 1867 Eliza Hansford wrote from Kentucky to a relative at Lamb's Creek Church, saying "You tell me of the desecration of that dear old Church. Yes, I venerate [it] and deeply grieve at the destruction; there is not a part but I well remember. . . . The belief [the creed], the Lord's Prayer and the Ten Commandments, with the representation of Angels floating in the clouds, all are present in my memory." Lamb's Creek was not the only church whose walls were adorned with religious writing. The indentured servant Richard Cooke painted the creed, the Lord's Prayer, and the Decalogue in gold leaf on the chancel of Poplar Spring Church, and in Yeocomico Church in Westmore-

2

Altar pieces donated by wealthy members of the parish—such as the tablets given to St. Mary's White Chapel by David Fox and William Fox—called to mind both God and the elite individual who gave the gift. Photograph by Charles Lawson, Courtesy of St. Mary's Whitechapel, Lancaster, VA.

land County, framed canvases with the same three texts hung in the chancel. The reredos in the chancel at Mattapony Church included those three texts, and the tetragrammaton. Tablets of the Ten Commandments, the Creed, and the Lord's Prayer adorned the walls of St. Mary's White Chapel. Parishioners left bequests for the ornamentation in their wills—Elizabeth Churchill of Middlesex County left her church £125 for altar pieces, which probably featured the Decalogue. A parishioner in Southwark Parish left money for the purchase of an altar piece "for the lower church. . . . I would have Moses and Aaron drawn at full length holding up between them the Ten commandments and if money enough I would have the Lord's prayer in a small Fraim to hang on the right hand over the great Pew and the creed in another small Fraim to Hang in the Left Hand over the other great Pew."[23]

As Louis Nelson has argued in his analysis of Anglican church architecture in colonial South Carolina, these many material cues helped parishioners

The Letters to be wrought on ye Pulpette Cloath are

× ℋ ×

× 𝓝 × 𝓟 ×

3
In 1694 the vestry of Kingston Parish decided to order an embroidered "Pulpette Cloath." Text from the Kingston Parish Vestry Book reproduced by Carole Baker.

"sense the sacred," focusing their thoughts on worship, and signaling that "the church [was] a space created by man but occupied by God and the heavenly host." When the church ornaments were bequests or donations, altar pieces could further imbricate the social and the divine; when parishioners at St. Mary's White Chapel looked at their altar pieces and saw the Ten Commandments, the Creed, and the Lord's Prayer, they may have thought of God, or they may have thought of David Fox and William Fox, who donated the pieces in 1702 and 1718—or perhaps they thought of both, thanking God for the Foxes (or whinging to God about them, if they had found the Foxes irksome). The vestry of Kingston Parish ordered an altar cloth embroidered with the parish initials. This cloth, which was green, might have reminded people of the liturgical season, or it may have filled worshipers with pride in their community and solidified their sense of identifying with the community (a sense of identification that could loop back to the divine, since the community was the body of Christ). Sometimes church decoration inspired not thoughts of divinity but sinful actions: Lawrence Washington (George Washington's grandfather) left pulpit cloths and cushions—green velvet, with silk fringe and gold embroidery—to each of the two churches in Washington Parish. Seventeen years later, a peddler stole part of Washington's gift and in turn sold the goods, which were then turned into a pair of pants.[24]

These material cues reminded parishioners that they were in church not just to meet neighbors but also to meet God, through prayer, and, as Byrd's letter attests, through sacraments and sermons. In this space that conveyed both social and sacred lessons, a parson or a lay reader led the congregation in the Divine Office. Three or four times a year, the parson would celebrate communion. More typically, he recited Morning Prayer, the Litany, and Ante-Communion (the beginning of the communion service, concluding before consecration of the bread and wine). Psalms were lined out by the clerk and repeated by the congregation; most singing in Virginia churches was a cappella, as only half a dozen or so churches boasted organs. The service included a sermon. It appears that the sermon could range from fourteen minutes to an hour, but evidence does not permit a confident estimate of Virginia sermons' average length. The theological orientation of the sermon varied with the preacher; congregants might hear anything ranging from a heartfelt meditation on the meaning of Christ's blood to a Latitudinarian exhortation to sober living. Jacob Blosser has recently demonstrated that parishioners did not necessarily pay rapt attention to the prayers and homilies. Parsons complained that parishioners were often "absent in Mind," distracted or bored, even chatting, flirting with one another, or snoozing instead of actively and respectfully engaging the liturgy.[25]

Byrd's 1760 letter attests that elite men and women took an active interest and active role in what happened on Sunday mornings. In Parson Davis's absence, Byrd herself wrote to Alexander Finnie of Martin's Brandon Parish in Prince George's County to request that he come preach, and John Wayles engaged David Mossom, parson of nearby St. Peter's Parish in New Kent County, and was seeking William Douglas of St. James Northam Parish, Goochland County, "to make us laugh" (whether because the likes of Byrd and Wayles found Douglas's delivery or evangelical theology risible or because he had a good sense of humor Byrd does not say). Byrd's letter also suggests that Sunday church was a map on which elite Virginians jockeyed with one another. According to Byrd's account, some men who rarely went to church were so irate about their parson's having headed to the front that they were trying to remove from the vestry those men who had agreed to the parson's military service. But was the parson's wartime chaplaincy the real reason these infrequent worshipers interfered in the makeup of the vestry? Perhaps the parson's military service was just an excuse that allowed them to take action against men who had done them wrong in a business deal or been rude to their wives at a dinner party.[26]

Finally, the most mundane point: church was the stuff of ordinary intercourse, of correspondence between a mother and a son who was at war. Had William been home, he and Maria probably would have gossiped about the parish goings on around the dining room table. As it was, Maria sat at her table or desk, and wrote to her son about these parochial dramas.[27] This casual conversation was one way church entered the homes of elite Anglicans.

And that is the third place elite Virginians encountered the church: in their own houses. Yes, the church building was one site of religious engagement, but in the context of Virginia's high degree of lay autonomy, the household also emerges as an important place of religious practice. Through the eighteenth century, even as the clergy took on greater prominence and the institutional church more vigor than either had in the seventeenth century, a vital tradition of lay religious practice flourished in elite households; those household expressions of Anglican piety are the focus of this book. In the household, we see the regular workings out—the "lived religion"—of Virginia Anglicanism's persistent laicism. In the household, laypeople constructed and maintained religious practice, and they exercised religious authority. Indeed, for many men and women, the household was the site of more intensive or more sustained religious engagement than the nearest chapel of ease.

Religion Inside the Great House

The houses of the eighteenth-century Virginia oligarchy are the central setting for *A Cheerful and Comfortable Faith*. The "great houses" that occupy such a conspicuous place in Americans' cultural imagination were situated in a larger territory that contributed to household culture. The main house was flanked by outbuildings—kitchens, smokehouses, barns and tobacco houses, and "negro quarters" or "outhouses for the reception of Negroes." The land surrounding all these buildings had been improved—waterways drained and dammed, land cleared and fenced. Gardens, often laid out geometrically and enclosed by a fence, were both functional and aesthetically pleasing. The careful landscaping was taken to be a material demonstration of the owner's superior intelligence, and gentlemen like William Byrd and John Custis took great interest and pride in their gardens, which reassured them that they were controlling nature and bringing civilization to the Virginia wilderness. The houses were situated to give the planters good views, and to allow them to be seen: as Philip Fithian noted when he visited John Tayloe's plantation "From this house there is a good prospect of the River Rapahannock. We can also from the chambers easily see the town Hobbes-Hole & the ships which lie there." In other words, Tayloe's plantation had a view that spanned almost five miles.[28]

And then there was the house itself. The houses were large—Wilton House, for example, boasted more than five thousand square feet of living space—and their layout symmetrical. While most Virginia houses were made of wood, the grandest were brick—for example, William Jordan's Richmond County "two-story brick house with a central passage and four rooms on each floor." The rooms would be wainscoted, the walls "elegantly papered." The gentry's houses tended to have many windows, which made possible extended pursuits of leisure activities like reading and embroidery that required good light.[29]

The floor plan of gentry houses changed dramatically over the course of the eighteenth century; these changes reflected and fostered changes in how gentry used domestic space, and how they conceived of the public and the private within their households. In the early decades, even the houses of wealthiest Virginians typically had only two rooms on the ground floor, a large hall one entered from the outside of the house and a small parlor or chamber one could enter only from the hall. Later in the century, many gentry built houses that were two rooms deep, with a central passage dividing the ground floor into two halves. The central passage separated more public rooms from more private spaces and was itself a sort of in-between space, in which people sometimes sat and visited, especially in the hot summers, as the halls were often the draftiest, most comfortable places in the house. During the middle of the eighteenth century, elite men and women redefined and increasingly differentiated rooms and room use. For example, the "dining room" began to appear in gentry households in the 1720s, and by the 1770s it was often the best room in the house—the largest, the room with the most windows. During the same decades gentry began to design and differentiate a second room for dining, a room variously called the "small dining room" or the "dining-Room for the Children." This space was used for more intimate family meals, allowing gentry to reserve the primary dining room for formal entertainment: as John Mason recalled, Gunston Hall, the estate Mason's father built, featured "a small dining room commonly used as such by the family and a larger one at the other end of the house which was used when there was company."[30]

The domestic life within these houses has often been assumed to be "secular," but one who enters looking for religious practices notices visual hints of a vital religiosity everywhere. Visual representations of scriptural stories kept scenes from the Bible ever before residents: a Delft tile depicting David slaying Goliath would have, with seventeen or twenty-three other such tiles, framed a fireplace in a house like Westover or Mason's Gunston Hall. Engravings, paintings, and other biblical art—such as a painting Governor Spotswood owned of "The History of the Woman Taken in Adultery," Sarah Green's rendering of Solomon's Temple, and Thomas Thompson's seven "Scripture pieces"—hung on interior walls. As a 1748 article in *Universal Magazine* explained, "Pictures speak ALL languages," and works of biblical art "impress on the mind, such clear, strong, lively apprehensions of what they represent." These images, which gentry, their guests, and their slaves saw every

4
Religious activities, ranging from baptism to prayer to catechesis to funeral gatherings, punctuated life at the Masons' estate, Gunston Hall, and at other "great houses" of the Virginia gentry. Library of Congress, Prints and Photographs Division, Historic American Buildings Survey.

day, formed people's imaginations along the contours of particular scriptural narratives. Hints about household religiosity are not limited to purely decorative artwork. Alimentary items like plates bore religious messages: a charger on which was painted Adam and Eve, a teapot glazed with words from the Twenty-third Psalm, iron and brass spoons and pots whose handles bore messages like "the wages of sin are death" and "love thy neighbor." These images and objects are clues to the quotidian religiosity of the eighteenth-century Virginia gentry.[31]

In each of the five chapters of the present study I examine a religious practice that Anglican gentry undertook in domestic space. Specifically, I consider baptism, the production of religious needlework, prayer, the organization of meals around the liturgical calendar, and practices of death and mourning. Domestic religious performance served both public and private needs, individual and communal needs—and religious activities traversed the public-private divide that was increasingly written into gentry houses during the eighteenth century. Some activities—like hosting Twelfth Night parties or displaying needlework in passageways—brought religion into the more public spaces of gentry's houses. Other religious engagements were, in the estimation of their practitioners, better suited to more private spaces. For

5
The engravings, embroidery, paintings, and tiles that hung in great Virginia estates often featured biblical scenes. Collection of the Museum of Early Southern Decorative Arts, Old Salem Museums and Gardens.

example, William Byrd II often read his Bible and said his prayers in his library, which he built as a freestanding outbuilding in 1709 (and to which he added locks a year later). Females had less access to private space in households, but women and girls seeking time and space for individual religious reflection could sometimes creatively find that space: for example, as a girl, Rebecca Burwell found a quiet "spot in the garret where she erected a little altar to worship at, there with her collection of sacred books." (This "garret" would have been an attic space of some kind, and the contrast between Burwell's "garret" and Byrd's freestanding library illustrates the extent to which men had greater access than did women and girls to private space within the household.)[32]

The household was, as numerous scholars have noted, not impermeably bounded. Rather it was porous, and household practices, including household religious practices, need not be read as "private" practices, tacitly or explicitly contrasted to "public" practices (categories that, in any event, are ideological rather than descriptive, and whose modern meanings were constituted during the very century that I am considering).[33] Although there was a private dimension to the practices of the household, household life had a public aspect. Most germane to this study are the ways that household religiosity connected practitioners to the "public" institution of the Church of

England. The religious practices we find flourishing in the household—baptism, catechesis, prayer guided by the church's liturgy—are *practices of the church*, albeit often modified to suit the domestic context. In other words, rather than abandoning church forms and creating wholly new religious practices, the gentry adapted established liturgical forms to the laicized environment of their households. Indeed, all five of the practices considered here defined Anglicans as such, to one degree or another. What is the correct rite of Christian initiation? Which holidays ought Christians observe? What should one eat at a postmortem meal? How best to pray—liturgically or free-form? These questions were, in England, flash points between Anglican churchmen and Puritans, and in Virginia, Anglicans' answers to those questions defined them against dissenters (Baptists, Methodists, Presbyterians, Quakers). In this way, although the laity's control over religious practices sometimes rankled clerics, the seemingly "private" religiosity of the household helped connect the gentry to the institution of the church (and, in the context of a colonial, established church, to the state). Indeed, as I will suggest in the epilogue, the vitality and the ecclesiastical character of these household practices helped sustain gentry's Anglican (or Episcopal) identity in the post-Disestablishment years when the institutional church foundered.[34]

A Few Words on Method: Characters and Sources

It is no doubt already obvious that this study does not consider the household religious practices of all Anglican laity in Virginia. My focus is primarily on a small group of elite men and women who lived east of the Blue Ridge, whose surnames will be familiar to students of Virginia history: Byrd, Carter, Washington, Mason, Randolph. Where the sources suggest, I also include members of what might be termed the lesser gentry. (When the religious affiliation of the people under consideration is not obvious, I have included discussion of their ties to Anglicanism in the notes.) My interest here is not so much how Anglican elites, with their grand, imposing church buildings and their socially ranked parades into church each Sunday morning, shored up the social hierarchy of their society. (Durkheim long ago made it clear that those in power will use whatever religion is at hand to help keep society running on its rails.) I have instead pursued the daily, familial, and even intimate religious experiences of the Virginia gentry (which were of course inflected by, but not reducible to, power and political jockeying). Scholars of "lived religion" have tended to focus on people who are somehow marginalized. I have tried here to take seriously the lived religion of elites, and I hope to demonstrate that the

6

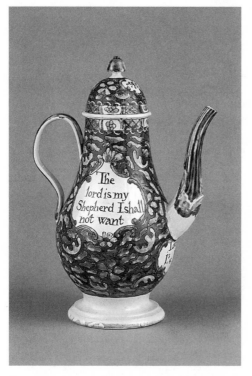

Teapots (6), coffeepots (7),
chargers (8), and spoons (9) were
among the ordinary, utilitarian
objects that sometimes conveyed
religious messages in elite Virginia
households. Colonial Williamsburg Foundation (6–8); courtesy of
Sara Pennell (9).

7

8

9

Anglican gentry in eighteenth-century Virginia led religious lives at least as rich and complicated as those of working-class Italian Catholics in twentieth-century Harlem or Vodou practitioners in twentieth-century Brooklyn.[35]

A Cheerful and Comfortable Faith is not a study of the religious practices of enslaved Afro-Virginians. Nonetheless, the enslaved men and women who provided the labor in elite households are important to this study in at least four ways. First, most obviously, enslaved men and women did the work that made the gentry's religious practices possible. Sometimes that is quite literally true—slaves prepared the food that gentry ate on festival occasions. More broadly, the religious practices described here are, to varying extents, leisure pursuits. William Byrd had time to translate Scripture and Elizabeth Boush had time to produce biblical ornamental needlework because they were not out seeding the back forty. Second, enslaved men and women appear in this story as objects over which the gentry tried to work out their own concerns. For example, gentry's ongoing efforts to negotiate their authority vis-à-vis clergy were worked out in part through gentry's debate with clergy about whether clergy should baptize slaves. Third, enslaved men and women are implicated in occasional efforts by elite Anglicans to use religious practice as a tool to delineate their place as slaveholders and to draw distinctions between themselves and the enslaved men and women in their midst. For example, members of the gentry used religious practice to draw boundaries between themselves and their slaves when they embraced an elaborate set of mourning practices for themselves while also trying to curtail Afro-Virginians' mourning rites. Finally, slaves are present in this narrative as subjects, too. Although the gentry delimited Afro-Virginians' religious practices, enslaved men and women made their own religious choices, determining to be baptized (or not), choosing how and when to pray. Sometimes they turned their assigned role in gentry's religious practices to their own purposes. For example, a dying elite man may have wanted his slaves arrayed around his deathbed because the slaves' presence allowed him, at the end of life, to reflect on his accomplishments and bask in his wealth. But as we shall see in Chapter 5, enslaved men and women had their own reasons for being present and attentive at gentry deathbeds.

Elite women are also important to this account of gentry religious life. Many historians before me have astutely analyzed women's engagement with Anglicanism in colonial Virginia. Patricia Bonomi has suggested that, although women outnumbered men in church attendance in New England's Puritan churches and Virginia's Baptist churches, this "feminization" of the pews did not obtain in Anglican Virginia: men and women appear to have attended public worship in roughly equal numbers. Joan Gundersen has demonstrated that although women had no formal role in church governance or liturgical leadership, they "were active lay participants, especially where church and family roles intersected." In particular, Gundersen argues that women oversaw the celebration of religious life-cycle events in the home (baptism, marriage, and funerals), and that they actively participated in children's religious education. My focus on household religiosity is clearly indebted to Gundersen's work. Other historians have fruitfully contrasted the kinds of selfhood that different early American Christian traditions made possible for women. Martha Saxton has found that Puritanism, with its insistence on scrutinizing the self, encouraged women to act as moral agents in a way that Anglicanism did not. Catherine Kerrison has contrasted the Anglican devotional literature that early eighteenth-century southern women read with the evangelical literature that gained currency later in the century and found, similarly, that evangelicalism, more than Anglicanism, allowed southern women to forge individuated selves.[36]

In *A Cheerful and Comfortable Faith*, I suggest that gentry women had a greater opportunity for active participation in religious ritual than women had in communities where religious ritual unfolded principally in church buildings and where religious subjectivity was more strictly ordered around preaching and the celebration of sacraments. In colonial Virginia, the household was not a "woman's sphere" or a female preserve.[37] Women's authority in the household—even regarding arenas in which we might assume they had large measures of control, such as cooking—was contested, contextual, and not to be taken for granted. Nonetheless, women are important characters in this story of household religiosity.[38] Some of the religious practices women undertook in the household, such as the production of religious needlework, disciplined them, teaching them gendered lessons about their place in the hierarchies that structured slave society. Nevertheless, within the domestic confines (and the confines of patriarchy), women shaped a religious life for themselves, and in part, for their families. They imbued gendered domestic work like embroidery with religious significance. Indeed, the domestic religion described in this book—especially women's domestic religious performance—may have glossed the cruelties of slavery with practices that made household routines appear moral or blessed.

The gentry family itself is a central character in this study. During the eighteenth century, the Virginia gentry family was transformed from a fragile institution to a self-conscious, self-perpetuating elite that passed down vast wealth and positions of political leadership from generation to generation.

The disastrous demographics of the seventeenth century had stabilized, and members of the gentry employed a variety of strategies to reify their individual families, and to strengthen the institutional power of gentry families writ large. For example, gentry families adopted particular naming patterns that asserted the ongoing connections of grandparents and cousins. Land use and architectural patterns also bolstered the Virginia oligarchy; gentry families increasingly lived near one another, in enclaves that kept them separate from middling families. The College of William and Mary was also enmeshed in this development of the family: as Thad Tate has argued, the college was founded only after demographics made it possible for families to worry about how they would educate the family's (and the colony's) next generation of leaders.[39] Similarly, I read household religious practice as, in part, a family strategy. Religious ritual was deployed in demarcating and upholding the gentry family, as when, for example, gentry tried to assert the familial unit at baptism, a ritual whose liturgy, as I explore in Chapter 1, subtly questioned the coherence of the family. At the end of life as well as at the beginning, mourning practices reified and drew boundaries around the gentry family. Elites' mourning practices perpetuated the memory of ancestors, and fostered, among the living, an ongoing identification with a family unit that reached back to include the dead. Religious practice thus outlined the spiritual geography of this gathering community of elites, marked out the imaginary boundaries of belonging, and mapped the family's way forward to a confident future.

A final group deserves special mention: clergy. Clerics occupied an ambiguous place in Virginia society—as Joan Gundersen has written, "Ordination brought a certain acceptance by the upper class, but not necessarily membership in it." Parsons had complicated relationships with the elite laity whom they ostensibly shepherded through the spiritual life. Some clergy had worked in elite households as tutors before going to England for ordination; other clergy married into elite families. And, of course, clergy had to answer to the elite men who served on parish vestries. Sometimes clergy and elite laity had cordial social relationships; William Byrd, for example, regularly had parsons to dine. Such meals both forged real, meaningful friendships, and reminded local clergy who, as it were, buttered their bread. Clergy were implicated in elite laypeople's household religious practice in at least two ways. First, insofar as laity participated in the sacramental and liturgical life of the church, their spiritual lives were shaped by the work of clergy. Surviving sermons can be useful indexes of the theology that shaped laypeople's religious imaginations. Second—and not unrelated to laypeople's dependence on clergy for sacramental celebration—one can discern real conflict between clergymen and elite laity. They disagreed about many particulars of ritual practice—where people should be buried, for example, and what food people should eat on holidays. Laypeople's construction of household religious practices—religious practices, that is, largely out of the purview of the clergy—may be seen as part of an ongoing struggle between elite laity and clergy for authority in the religious sphere, and tensions between clergy and laity are shot through this account.[40]

Finally, a word about sources is in order. As is often lamented, the letters, diaries, and other literary sources that scholars of daily life and religion in New England have mined are in short supply for eighteenth-century Virginia. Actually, the absence of this kind of literary evidence—especially the absence of the kind of self-revealing religiously inflected diaries on which scholars of Puritan New England rely—is itself evidence about the way Virginia's Anglican religious culture differed from other Protestant communities in the colonies. The dearth of pious diaries does not tell us that Anglicans were "less religious" than Puritans. After all, as scholars of Puritanism have long understood, it was a particular Calvinist notion of sin and grace that prompted Puritans to keep all those diaries.[41] The absence of similar diaries in Virginia archives does not suggest that Virginians were irreligious. Rather, it suggests that neither Anglican theology nor Anglican preaching inspired people to take up religious practices keyed to scrutinizing the self for marks of election or damnation, sin or grace. Puritans were at war, and their spiritual practices were meant to provoke battle—battle with the devil, with sin, with themselves. But not all religious systems are keyed to struggle. For elite Anglicans, being religious was more a matter of fostering comfort with one's self and the world, and as Puritan practice reflects Puritans' struggle and spiritual warfare, gentry Anglicans' practices (and the resulting textual and material evidence of those practices) reflect their quest for comfort and ease.

The historian interested in the texture of people's everyday lives cannot let the absence of a rich trove of diaries and letters prove an intractable problem. Given the paucity of traditional literary sources, I have tried to expand the range of sources that can be asked to yield information about the gentry's household religious practice, not only looking into the familiar diaries of William Byrd and Landon Carter but also reading cookbooks and amethyst rings. At times, I feel I've read the available sources a bit too hard; at times my readings feel speculative; at times they veer toward the antiquarian. Nonetheless, I offer *A Cheerful and Comfortable Faith* as one plausible reconstruction of the household religious practices of the Virginia gentry.

Material artifacts figure significantly in this study. In keeping with my focus on lived religion in elite households, I look not at communion chalices and kneelers but at objects from Anglicans' kitchens and gardens. Some of the objects—a baptismal bowl, a tombstone—were props in the celebration and commemoration of the life cycle. Other objects—such as William Beale's Shrove Tuesday pancakes—made possible the observance of an annual liturgical calendar. Some of the objects still exist and can be visited today in museums; others, like the pancakes, come down to us only in the written record.

Material objects constitute part of a larger world of practice. Objects invite the study of religious practice because objects imply practices and practitioners: a piece of needlework implies a needleworker (and, when displayed, it implies a viewer). A Shrove Tuesday pancake implies an eater (and it implies a cook; in the context of elite Virginians, it implies an enslaved cook and a relationship between religious festivity and the labor system that made that festivity possible). Material objects are not merely second-best sources to be considered in the absence of literary evidence. More than words in a diary, which authors likely considered, questioned, and consciously decided on, objects that were used in religious activities may testify to religious practices and religious meanings that practitioners took for granted (and thus did not worry over in their diaries). Examining objects can help decenter a broadly Protestant methodological assumption that has long marked the study of American religion—the idea that materiality profanes religion and that words are the principal source for any investigation of the religion of people who worship the Word.[42] As Vanessa Ochs has noted, when considering religious practice, objects are not necessarily "more eloquent, more instructive, or more essential" than texts or beliefs, but they certainly are "equally eloquent and pivotal."[43]

Our exploration of Anglican gentry's household religious practice begins with a most eloquent baptismal bowl.

CHAPTER ONE

With Cold Water and Silver Bowls
Becoming an Anglican in Eighteenth-Century Virginia

Children shd enquire of their Parents wn they See a Child washed with Water,
& Say, wt is the meaning of yt washing?
—Charles Clay, Anglican parson in St. Anne's Parish and
Manchester Parish, Virginia

In 1773, shortly after his wife, Ann, died, George Mason IV wrote his will. There he confirmed his son's ownership of "a large silver Bowl given him [George Mason V] by my Mother, in which all my children have been christened, and which I desire remain in the family unaltered for that purpose."[1] This bowl is worth lingering over, for it reveals something important about the ritual in which it was used—Anglican baptism as practiced by gentry like the Masons. Indeed, the Masons' bowl may be taken as a synecdoche not just for household baptism but for elite Virginians' household religious practice writ large.

Mason's short testamentary discussion sets the bowl in a familial context and a liturgical context. Mason explained that the bowl was used for baptism, for washing Mason's children clean of sin and conferring Christian identity on each child. Baptism was one of Anglicanism's two sacraments, those mysterious rites that were, in the prayer book's language, "an outward and visible sign of an inward and spiritual grace."[2] Sacraments—events in which the terrestrial and the spiritual worlds met in some especially vital way—required, by their nature, material objects. In Holy Communion, those material objects were bread and wine. In baptism, the material object was water, and Mason's bowl was the baptismal equivalent of a communion chalice, holding, and beautifying, the water.

Mason's will also identifies the bowl as a family treasure, passed through the generations: George Mason II purchased the bowl, which was made around 1700 by Isaac Dighton, a French Huguenot living in London. Mason II passed it to his son, George Mason III; it was Mason III's widow, Ann

1.1

George and Ann Mason's children were christened in this silver monteith. In his will, Mason stated that he wished the bowl to "remain in the family unaltered for that purpose." Courtesy of the Board of Regents of Gunston Hall.

Thomson Mason, who gave the bowl to her grandson, George Mason V. In stating his wishes that the bowl remain "unaltered," Mason IV signaled his deep connection to the bowl. By the 1770s, when Mason wrote his will, the particular form of this bowl, the monteith, had been out of fashion for more than a generation, but Mason did not want his son to follow the common practice of melting down outmoded silver objects and reshaping them into more modish forms.[3] The bowl's importance derived not just from its monetary value but from its place in a chain of family transmission and its use in a religious ritual. It was an object handed down from parents to children, and it was an object intimately associated with each of Mason's children, the four daughters and eight sons who were baptized in the water it held.

If Mason's will gives some indication of how and why he valued the bowl, the bowl itself—the material of which it is made, its shape, the ornaments that decorate it—suggests something about the meanings of baptism to families like the Masons. To begin, the bowl is silver, an exceptionally valuable and symbolic commodity in the eighteenth century. Silver signaled gentility; in the estimation of the historian Richard Bushman, it was "perhaps the surest way to assert cultural authority and superiority in colonial society." The Mason bowl spoke to George Mason's guests, and to the Mason family themselves, about the Masons' elegance, about their position in a (local) social hierarchy, and about their participation in a (transatlantic) market of luxury goods. But social status is only one meaning we can find in the bowl's silver gleam. Silver also had a strong association with divinity. Its beauty hinted at the beauty of God, and, to quote Bushman again, a silver object "trailed clouds of glory as it performed its duties." Silver was used at the altar because of its divine connotations, and in turn its use in the sacraments of baptism and Holy Communion further instructed people that silver was the right material to use in rituals where "divinity was embodied in external forms."[4]

Silver's association with divinity is made explicit by the cherubim that decorate the top of Mason's bowl. Perhaps those angels first suggested to the Masons that this bowl would be appropriate for use in baptism. Cherubim crop up elsewhere in both ecclesial architecture and household decorative arts of the period; the baptismal font at Christ Church, Lancaster Country, Virginia, for example, was a gray marble bowl decorated with the heads of four cherubs. Especially in the context of baptism, cherubs held a double meaning. First, cherubim connoted death. Angels were said to be present at the deathbeds of faithful Christians, ushering the dying heavenward; that association was underscored by cherubim's appearance on English tombstones since at least the early eighteenth century. When found on a baptismal font or christening bowl, cherubs, with their associations with mortality, signaled that baptism was a kind of death—a going down into a tomb of water. Of course, the "death" of baptism was a death that culminated in regeneration and, ultimately, resurrection—a point first made by Paul, who reminded the early Christians in his care that "buried with him in baptism, wherein also ye are risen with him through the faith of the operation of God, who hath raised him from the dead" (Rom 6:3–4). And like baptism itself, cherubs betokened rising up out of death. They reminded faithful Christians that baptism was the first step in a life that ended in heaven; after death, Christians would arrive at God's heavenly kingdom, where they would be greeted by choirs of angels. As the English churchman John Scott put the matter, "In our Baptism, wherein we gave up our names to Christ, we became denizens and freemen of heaven. All the difference between [the saints] and us is only this, that we are abroad and they are at home." The bowl's silver and the smiling angels, then, pointed to the presence of God at baptism, and to baptism's power to propel the Mason children heavenward. Baptism's heavenly prom-

1.2
Cherubs decorated the baptismal font at Christ Church, Lancaster County, Virginia.
Photograph by John H. Whitehead III, courtesy of the Foundation for Historic Christ
Church.

ises were especially salient given colonial Virginia's high infant mortality
rates. When Richard and James Mason, twins, died within a day of their
premature birth, Ann and George Mason may have taken some comfort in
the fact that the boys had been baptized as soon as they were born.[5]

If Anglican infant baptism thus served the emotional needs of parents of
ill or dead children, Anglican baptism was, in other ways, in tension with the
prerogatives of the gentry family. During the eighteenth century, kinship ties
were crucially important to the Virginia oligarchy. In Allan Kulikoff's phrasing, "Groups of relations increasingly separated themselves from unrelated
neighbors." The family was not just an affective unit; it was also a political and
economic unit. In order to consolidate their wealth, elite families intermarried. Political offices were generally reserved for elite men—who had other
people to do their labor for them, and could thus devote themselves to public
service.[6] Eighteenth-century elites were beginning to look at their children as
sources of pleasure (a new idea about children that emerged in the mid-

eighteenth century), but they also saw their children as future leaders of a political and economic dynasty.[7]

This notion of family, and children's place in the family, was in tension with the notion of family that Anglican infant baptism staged. Anglican infant baptism ritually and physically removed the baby from his or her parents; the liturgy spoke of the baby's "adoption" by God "the Father." Indeed, parents had no formal role in the baptismal liturgy. The ritual implied that one's membership in the church took priority over membership in one's family. In a culture in which the institution of "domestic patriarchalism" was both crucial to social order and yet not to be taken for granted,[8] this ritual removal of babies from parents was subtly transgressive. The Masons' baptismal bowl seemed to betoken a recognition, and rejection, of the potentially destabilizing effects of baptism: the initials "GM" were pounced in silver on the side of the bowl, and the Mason family crest was also emblazoned on the bowl.[9] In choosing to baptize their babies not in the font at their parish church but in a bowl emblazoned with the Mason crest and initials, the Masons were ritually contradicting the implications of the liturgy: the initials and crest insisted that the claims that the Church and God had on the newly baptized Mason children would not trump, and were perhaps even subordinate to, the claims of the Mason family.

The most striking feature of the bowl is not its silver shine or the family crest but its shape. The form of the monteith is defined in Nathan Bailey's *An universal etymological English dictionary* (1721) as "a scollop'd Bason to cool Glasses in." Introduced into England in the 1680s, the monteith supposedly took its name from an eccentrically dressed Scotsman. As the great Oxford antiquarian Anthony Wood explained in 1683, "This yeare in the summer time came up a vessel or bason notched at the brims to let drinking glasses hang there by the foot so that the body or drinking place might stand in the water to coole them. Such a bason was called a 'Monteigh' from a fantastical Scot called 'Monsieur Monteigh' who at that time or a little before, wore the bottom of his cloak or coate so notched U U U U."[10] George Mason declared in his will that his son should continue using the bowl in family baptisms, but in fact the bowl (as its monteith shape suggests) had another purpose. When it wasn't holding the water that cleansed the Masons' children from sin, it held water to chill wine goblets. A bowl used both to chill wine glasses and to baptize babies poses something of a riddle, confounding some of our presuppositions about what religion is and how it works. How can something so worldly as a wineglass-cooler be used for something so holy as baptism?[11] A sharp dichotomy between the category of the "sacred" and the category of the

1.3
The initials *GM* were pounced on the side of the Masons' bowl. Courtesy of the Board of Regents of Gunston Hall.

"profane" has long structured how scholars theorize religion. In a society in which the sacred is set apart from the secular, a bowl like the Masons' does not make much sense. In a society that draws a sharp boundary between the things of God and the things of man, punch bowls do not sit on altars, and baptismal bowls are not used at parties. If we look without such presuppositions at the Masons' bowl, however, we can begin to see a form of religion and a form of society in which baptizing and tippling were close kin. In the process we can begin to see that the sacred and the secular can both pray and party together—that the much-vaunted divide between the sacred and the profane does not obtain at all times and in all places. In a sense, the rest of this book is devoted to describing and illuminating a religious culture in which a monteith christening bowl makes sense. Yes, this monteith was the christening bowl that Mason named in its will. But it was also a "Bason to cool Glasses in." The bowl's doubleness suggests the ways that religion and ordinary life were intertwined in the households of Virginia's Anglican gentry. "Lived religion" was in no way set apart from living itself.[12]

For scholars of early Virginia, the terms *holy* and *profane* probably call to mind, first and foremost, Dell Upton's influential study of Anglican church architecture, *Holy Things and Profane.* Upton took his title from a silver communion chalice and paten used in James City Parish beginning in the mid-seventeenth century. The chalice and paten were inscribed "Mixe not holy thinges with profane." Upton suggests that church life in Virginia alternately abided by and flouted that injunction. "A certain social order and a certain religious order were melded in the parish churches of Virginia," argues Upton. Thus the distinctions between the holy and the profane, the sacred and the secular, and the religious and the everyday may serve scholars elsewhere (including perhaps colonial New England), but they obscure more than they illuminate in colonial Virginia. No one in the Mason household would fail to see this christening bowl as a monteith, this monteith as a christening bowl—because in the households of many elite Virginians holy and profane things were mixed with a vengeance, and without a hint of shame.[13]

The bowl's doubleness suggests the theology of baptism that obtained at Gunston Hall. Inherent in baptism were the questions *Who is the church?* and *What is the relationship of that church and its members to the rest of the world?* As we shall see, for some Christian communities in early America, baptism dramatically interrupted daily life, dislodging the baptized person from the world around her. But at Gunston Hall, baptism was neither dramatic nor an interruption. There, religious meanings and religious practices were inte-

1.4

1.5

grated elegantly into daily life. The Christian life into which George and Ann Mason's children were inaugurated was wholly compatible with life in the world—with worldly success and worldly pleasure. Silver's signification of divinity was in no way in tension with its signification of worldly status and hierarchy. The cherubic reminders of eternal life did not impede the enjoyment in this life of chilled wine; nor did entering the church mean one was pulled out of the obligations and amusements of the world. This is not to say that religious meaning always dissolved into evanescence: baptism was special, a rite of passage to be both named and noticed. But after the ritual was over, the ordinary life out of which it emerged—a life in which the logics of religion, family, and society were knit together—took over again. The bowl that had once held water that cleansed children from sin returned to the dinner table, where it was transformed, quite unmiraculously, back into a monteith holding water used to chill upside-down wine glasses.

Baptism was a source of real controversy in early Virginia, and in this chapter I will illuminate the meanings of baptism by considering some of these controversies. First, I will consider the conflicts baptism occasioned between clergy and elite laity, particularly conflicts over who should be baptized, and where. Then I will look beyond the bounds of Anglicanism to two other Protestant communities that practiced different forms of baptism. Virginia's Quakers and Baptists spurned Anglican baptismal rituals and, in the legislature and at the pulpit, Anglicans denounced these dissenters' practices and defended their own rites in turn. These conflicts reveal just how singular the elite Anglican interpretation of baptism was in the context of early Virginia Christianity.

Baptismal Battles: Conflict between Clergy and Elite Laity over Baptism

In reference to baptism, clergy and elite laity tussled over three central questions: where should baptism occur, who should serve as children's godparents, and who should be baptized? First was the debate over the proper location of baptism. Many Virginia gentry preferred to have their children baptized at home, not in church. Despite a 1632 law that declared that "all preachinge, administringe of the communion baptizinge of children and marriages, shall be done in the church except in cases of necessitie," members of the gentry

Facing page: The Masons were not the only family to baptize in bowls designed for other functions. The Dandridge family, for example, is said to have used these two porcelain punch bowls for baptism. Courtesy of the Mount Vernon Ladies' Association.

like Mason often insisted that parsons come to their homes to perform baptism. That such a law was necessary, of course, indicates that these celebrations were routinely happening somewhere besides church, and the law proved difficult to enforce. As James Blair, Commissary of Virginia, complained in 1719, "We are obliged to Baptize[,] Church women, marry, and bury at private houses."[14] An argument about baptism between Landon Carter, patriarch of Sabine Hall in Richmond County, and his parson, Isaac Giberne, illustrates the clash between ministers' sacramental prerogative and the wishes of elite gentry. To the extreme displeasure of Landon Carter, Giberne refused to baptize a Carter child at home: "By the whim of our Minister all children must be christened in Church," wrote Carter in his diary. "I wrote to him yesterday that we should be there unless it was bad weather and asked if he could not, should it prove bad weather, perform that service at home. . . . His answer acknowledges he had done so for others but as he had gained nothing but censure in such compliances, imagining I hinted at them, he was determined in preserving in his resolution in baptizing no Children out of the church."[15] There were, as this vignette makes clear, practical reasons for domestic baptism. Carter offered the weather as a reason to hold the baptism at home; generally, poor traveling conditions and the size of parishes argued for household baptism. But more than convenience was at stake in Carter and Giberne's spat. For the gentry who insisted that clergymen baptize "at private houses," entering the church through baptism did not require leaving the family or the social order represented by their great houses. Household baptism quietly asserted that the household, not the church, was the locus of Christian practice. It quietly asserted that the community into which the new Christian was being inducted was not the whole parish but a more select group, friends and family who were gathered together not in pews but in a grandee's great hall, around an elegant silver bowl. Carter and Giberne's argument may be read as an episode in the ongoing struggle for authority between clergy and lay elites unwilling to cede ecclesial control to ministers. Baptism was one of two moments in church life—the other being the celebration of Holy Communion—that could not proceed without an ordained person. (If a newborn's life was in peril, a layperson could baptize, but this exception was not abused.) In bucking the rubrics of the prayer book and trying to insist on domestic baptism, elite laity attempted to reassert a bit of control in the one arena where, ultimately, even grandees were dependent upon the largesse of clerics.

The intersection of practicality and social prerogative in domestic baptism may be seen in a dialogue that Philip Fithian recorded in his diary in

September 1774. "Yesterday the Inspector, whom I have named & described before, desired the Parson to wait on them in his family and christen his Child—Is the child sick? No Sir—Why then today? it is the Mothers Desire sir—Why was it not brought to Church? The Mother is unwell, Sir—The Parson excused himself & promised to come some Days hence, but the long winded officer, inured to Stubbornness, hung on, & without moderation or Apology demanded his presence!—And prevail'd.—" Here we see an obvious practical rationale for domestic baptism: recently delivered mothers did not want to trek to church. But we also see that domestic baptism carried class connotations. The man who insisted on domestic baptism in Fithian's story was the tobacco inspector. Tobacco inspectors were charged with determining whether tobacco was "good, sound, well-conditioned, and merchantable, and free from trash, sand, and dirt." If it was, it could be exported; trashy tobacco was destroyed. The enforcement of tobacco inspection acts meant that farmers who grew top-notch tobacco ultimately made more money, because they were not undercut by a market flooded with cheap leaves, but farmers whose tobacco was not top grade had reason to dislike the inspectors. Tobacco inspectors thus were significant, but ambiguous, figures in Virginia society; they had a bit of power, but they were not typically members of the gentry's inner circle. The inspector whose dialogue with the parson Fithian quotes had figured in Fithian's journal before. Fithian found him "rather Dull" and criticized him for inaccurately aping genteel etiquette: he "seems unacquainted with company for when he would, at Table, drink to our Health, he held the Glass of Porter fast with both his Hands, and then gave an insignificant nod to each one at the Table, in Hast, & with fear, & then drank like an Ox." The inspector was, in other words, someone who affected genteel standards but had not quite mastered them yet. We may read his desire for domestic baptism on this register: sensing that domestic baptism was something the gentry demanded, something that marked the elite as such, the inspector importunately goaded the parson (who probably grew a bit of his own tobacco) into baptizing his child at home.[16]

In addition to challenging clergy about the venue for baptism, the gentry also disputed particulars of the ritual itself. Specifically, they wanted, in contravention of the prayer book's rubrics, to serve as godparents for their own children. Parents had no part in the baptismal liturgy. The person saying the prayers and pouring the water was the minister; the one washing away sin was God; the ones making promises on behalf of the baptized child were godparents. As we have seen, baptism was a moment at which children were ritually taken away from parents; God, the "most merciful Father" "adopts" the child, and the godparents oversaw that adoption. Barred from the ritual, some Virginia laypeople demanded to serve as godparents for their own children: as the clergyman Thomas Dell reported to Bishop Gibson on June 1, 1724, parents in his parish "plead ymselves ye fittest to stand for yr own Children in Opposition to ye Canon of ye xch." In 1764 William Robinson, then the commissary, informed the bishop that the governor, Francis Fauquier, was trying to require a minister to "suffer parents to stand as sureties for their own Children in Baptism." When the minister insisted that "he could not admit any thing so contrary to the laws of the Church," the governor replied that canon law "signified nothing, for he the Governor thought it right that parents should be sureties for their own children." Governor Fauquier was taking the issue as an opportunity to demonstrate that gubernatorial authority trumped ecclesial authority, but he may also have been speaking as a father (he and his wife Catherine had two sons). Like the initials and crest on the Mason monteith, the efforts of parents to serve as godparents for their own children challenged the sacrament's disruption of the gentry family.[17]

Clergy and elite laity also argued about whom to baptize. Specifically, they often disagreed about the wisdom and propriety of baptizing slaves. From the arrival of the first Africans to Virginia, in 1619, English colonists were of two minds about evangelizing Afro-Virginians. Part of the motive for English settlement was to share the saving Gospel of (Protestant) Christianity with Native American "infidels," and that impulse extended to the African "heathens" now in the colonists' midst. Yet there was deep ambivalence about baptizing enslaved Afro-Virginians. Because of a long-standing equation of Christianity with the rights of the English as freemen, baptizing enslaved men and women raised the question of whether Christianity always entailed freedom. Could an Anglo-Virginian continue to own an Afro-Virginian after the slave was baptized, or was the slaveowner obligated to free his brother or sister in Christ?[18] Slaveowners' fears that "children that are slaves by birth, and by the charity and piety of their owners made pertakers of the blessed sacrament of baptisme, should by vertue of their baptisme be made ffree" were addressed by the Virginia legislature in 1667 with the passage of "An act declaring that baptisme of slaves doth not exempt them from bondage," which stated plainly that "conferring of baptisme doth not alter the condition of the person as to his bondage or ffreedome." Ostensibly, the law should have done the trick: slaveowners, now assured that baptism did not entail freedom, could have consented to let their slaves be baptized. But the law did not, in fact, set the gentry's minds at ease. Slaveowning Anglicans knew that slave baptism represented, if not legal freedom, a kind of social, cultural, and religious leveling, and they did not like it. They were discomforted by the symbolism of meeting slaves at the communion table, and they worried that they would have to spend time in Heaven with slaves. They also worried that slaves who were baptized wouldn't work as hard as non-Christian slaves.[19]

Despite gentry opposition, many clergy tried to evangelize slaves. On the whole, they did not make many converts, and the clergy blamed their failures on the resistance they met from slaveowners. John Bagg, minister of St. Ann's Parish, reported that "the owners Generaly [do] not approv[e]" of slave baptism, "being led away by the notion of their being and becoming worse slaves when Christians." Zachary Brooke, parson in St. Paul's Parish in Hanover County, explained to the bishop of London that slaves were baptized only "when their Masters desire it." The gentry in Thomas Baker's parish complained that "since we got to baptizing them [slaves] they are become insolent & Idle, Runaways, &c.; that they were never so till Baptism cam in Fashion amongst 'em." One minister complained that his efforts to baptize slaves earned him the displeasure of the "Great Ones," who castigated him as a "Negro Parson."[20]

Clergy insisted that baptism would make slaves more obedient, not less. Thomas Bacon, an Anglican pastor in Maryland who devoted terrific energy to evangelizing slaves, argued with nervous planters from the pulpit. "We are all apt to complain of bad servants—and truly, so far as there is justice and reason in this complaint, I am of opinion the fault is, in a great measure, our own: we do not take the proper methods of making them good. For what, in the name of GOD, can we expect from poor ignorant creatures, who have little or no care taken with their principles; little or no notion of an all-seeing GOD, or a future judgment?" Slaves would be more reliable and better equipped for the tasks they were expected to discharge if planters would set "before them much greater rewards than our poor services, or even the whole world can afford; and awaken . . . their consciences by the dread of much greater punishments" than the fiercest slaveowner could mete out. Some slaveowners were persuaded by arguments like Bacon's: in 1762 Parson William Yates and the layman Robert Carter Nichols wrote that "by making them good Christians they would necessarily become better servants." On this view, slave baptism, far from being a threat, was a great utility to slaveowners.[21]

Of course, slaves were not passive screens on which conflicts between gentry and clergy were projected. Within the tightly circumscribed spaces of enslavement, Afro-Virginians made religious choices—and many of them chose not to embrace Anglicanism. Scholars often adduce three reasons that so few enslaved people converted to Anglican Christianity. First, slaves' attachment to the vital religious practices they brought to Virginia from Africa —be they indigenous African practices or Islamic—meant that they had little need for a new religious tradition. Second, especially through the early eighteenth century, a language barrier stymied meaningful exchange between Anglophone clerics and slaves who spoke Wolof, Manding, and other "Languages peculiar to themselves" (as the Rev. James Mayre, Jr., described indigenous African languages). Third, people whose "Rites [and] Ceremonies" engaged the heart and the body were unlikely to be interested in staid liturgical routines. (Of these three arguments, the third is the least persuasive. In an important article on slaves and religion in colonial South Carolina, Annette Laing has pointed out that West Central Africans did not perforce "reject a liturgically based Christianity"; the Kongolese, for example, were clearly attracted to many aspects of the Catholicism introduced to them by Portuguese Jesuits in 1485.)[22]

Still, some slaves chose to enter the Anglican Church. Emmanuel Jones, parson in Petsworth Parish, reported in 1724 that "masters very often bring [slaves] to read and send them to church or Minister to be further instructed that they be baptized and many are so." In one six-month period in the 1730s, the Rev. Mr. Anthony Gavin of St. James Parish in Goochland baptized 299 white people and 172 black people. Jonathan Boucher, the Anglican clergyman best remembered for his fervent Loyalism during the Revolution, recounted baptizing "313 Negroes" on Easter Monday in 1766.[23] These Afro-Virginians entered the Anglican Church for a variety of reasons. Some Afro-Virginians embraced Anglicanism because they found spiritual solace there. By the early eighteenth century, some slaves had begun to read their own lives in and through Scripture, connecting their situation and that of "the Chilldann of Issarall" who suffered under cruel Egyptian "task mastrs." At least one pastor, Adam Dickie of Drysdale Parish, wanted to "church" enslaved women after they gave birth; the ceremony may have provided succor for slave women in the midst of the terrifying and ambiguous experience of becoming a mother under conditions of slavery.[24]

Yet enslaved Virginians looked to Anglicanism for more than spiritual sustenance. Just as the gentry feared, slaves did expect baptism to lead to greater rights and privileges, including freedom. As James Blair noted, slave converts were "in hopes that they shall meet with so much the more respect, and that some time or other Christianity will help them get their freedom." In 1695 William Cattilah petitioned the York County Court for freedom based in part on his baptism. In 1723 an enslaved Virginian wrote the bishop of

London, pleading, on behalf of "people that is Calld molatters which are Baptised and brouat up in the way of the Chrisitan faith and follwws the wayes and Rulles of the Chrch of England," for the bishop to "Releese us out of the Cruell Bondegg and this wee beg for Jesus Christs his Sake who commaded us to seeke first the kingdom of god and all things shall be addid un to us." In the 1720s Mary Aggie, "a Christian slave," sued her owner for freedom, on grounds of her baptism. She lost, but the governor remembered her, and when in 1731 she was accused of a capital crime (stealing sheets), he helped her win the right to plead benefit of clergy. Rather than be killed, she was allowed to leave Virginia. The same year that Aggie won the right to plead benefit of clergy, white Virginians heard reports of a slave uprising. When they questioned the slaves who were thought to be involved, elites learned that slaves had heard a rumor that the king of England had ordered all Christian slaves freed. Believing that "his Majesty had sent Orders for setting of them free as soon as they were Christians, and that these orders were suppressed," the slaves began plotting rebellion. Although the planned revolt was quashed, Mary Aggie probably landed on a brutal sugar plantation in the West Indies, and the anonymous letter to the bishop did not translate into any great freedoms, all three episodes suggest how enslaved Afro-Virginians construed conversion: Anglican Christianity may have offered spiritual solace, but it was also a wedge for freedom.[25]

Christianity did sometimes translate into rights and privileges for enslaved men and women, although many of those rights dried up by the mid-eighteenth century (just when, not coincidentally, more and more Afro-Virginians seem to have been baptized in Anglican churches). As Rebecca Goetz's pathbreaking work in early Virginia court records has shown, throughout the seventeenth century, Christian slaves who were tried for crimes including fornication were often punished with the lighter ecclesiastical sentence (wearing a white sheet before the church congregation and repenting) rather than the whippings meted out to non-Christian slaves found guilty of the same crimes. Furthermore, until 1730 "negros, mulattos, and Indians" who "professed themselves to be Christians and been able to give some account of the principles of the Christian religion" could testify in court.[26]

Conversion also led to literacy. Many clergy believed that instruction in literacy went hand in hand with evangelism, and taught slaves reading alongside Christianity. Some Christian slavemistresses were willing, even eager, to teach slaves to read the Bible and other religious books: Elizabeth Foote Washington instructed two of her enslaved women, and Mrs. Willoughby taught her slave Mary (later, after a marriage, known as Mary Perth) to read

and gave her a Bible. Conversion brought some slaves into special relationships with clergy, relationships that carried dignity, authority, and occasionally perhaps remuneration. In 1764 Jonathan Boucher, then serving a church
in King George County, found that the most effective means of evangelizing
slaves was to employ other slaves as teachers: "I have employ'd a very sensible,
well-dispos'd Negro belonging to a Gentleman who lives about a Mile from
Me, to endeavour at instructing his poor fellow slaves in Reading & some of
the first Principles of Religion." Boucher gave the unnamed lay catechist
private lessons two or three times a week, and the catechist in turn instructed
between twenty and thirty other slaves on Saturdays and Sundays.[27]

When Afro-Virginians did join the church, their baptisms occurred in
very different circumstances than did the baptisms of elite babies. First, although both enslaved adults and enslaved children were baptized, slaves were
more likely than white free people to be baptized as adults. Second, it was
often not clear who would stand as slaves' godparents or sureties. As a letter
from Governor Spotswood to the bishop of London indicates, clergymen
preferred slaveowners to stand as godparents. The topic of Spotswood's letter
was the baptism not of Afro-Virginian slaves but of Indian children who,
educated at William and Mary, could "repeat the Church Catechism and
know how to make their Responses in the Church." These children and their
parents wanted the children to be baptized, but the clergy was divided, and
clergymen debated the matter at convention. The majority of the clergy felt
that since the children's parents were not Christians, the children could not be
baptized, unless they could give a completely compelling testimony of their
faith, because their parents, having received no Christian education, could
not plausibly promise to make sure they would receive a Christian upbring-
ing. Slaves presented a different case, explained Spotswood. "Negros who are
often baptized in their Infancy, tho not born of believing parents . . . [have]
Masters and Mistresses to stand Suretys for them who could with more
reason answer for their Christian education." The baptism of Indian children
was controversial because Indians had no lifelong masters to make a similar
pledge on their behalf. The letter implies that some masters did stand as
godparents for their slaves. But others refused: in Lawne's Creek Parish, some
slaveowners refused "to have their slaves baptised . . . by reason that they will
not be sureties for them in Baptism." Slaveowners' refusal to serve as godparents for slaves prompted Adam Dickie, the minister serving Drysdale
Parish, to ask the bishop whether slaves could serve as godparents for other
slaves. Unfortunately, the bishop's reply to Dickie's letter does not survive,
and evidence does not permit a confident claim about the frequency with

which slaves served as godparents. In at least one parish, Albemarle, it was common practice to baptize slaves without godparents.[28]

Afro-Virginians were baptized in different physical and liturgical settings than were elite Virginians. Afro-Virginians were more likely than elite children to be baptized in church, and the choreography of the church baptisms of Afro-Virginians was matter of some debate. James Marye, Jr., reported to an English correspondent that "great Quantities of Negroes in my Parish, who all bring their children to be baptised, & many Adults likewise are desirous of Baptism, which I perform after Divine Service." In other words, Marye officiated at the Sunday liturgy, dismissed the white members of the congregation, and then held a separate service for the baptism of Afro-Virginians. William Willie, a parson in Albemarle Parish, had the same practice: as he informed a correspondent, "As for the negro Children, them I baptize after the congregation is dissmiss'd (that I may give no offence)."[29]

A letter from another cleric, James Maury, fleshes out just how those baptisms were orchestrated, and illustrates the hostility that might lie behind Willie's statement that he wished to avoid giving "offence." Maury was holding Sunday services at the Fredericksville Parish church when some "white People presented their Children for Baptism at the Altar" and "some Negroes, as has constantly been the Custom I believe, all over the Colony, advanced at the same Time to present theirs also." Although the black families were "orderly, neither crowding nor jostling their Betters," the church-warden, Thomas Johnson, told the black families to sit down, and, "with some seeming Reluctance," the black families began to retreat. When the slaves were "half way down the Isle," Maury called out that they had misunderstood: the warden hadn't intended for the slaves to take their seats and forgo baptism, but rather to stand back so that they did not "intermingl[e] with" the white people. But Maury was wrong: warden Johnson clarified that "his Meaning was, they should entirely be gone, that, as Warden, it was his Duty to preserve good Order in that Place, & that he would not allow Whites & Blacks to be baptized together." After baptizing the white children, Maury asked the congregation whether there were more children to be baptized, but the only answer he got was silence: having been "intimidated . . . by the Warden's peremptory & repeated orders," the enslaved parents "adventured not to present any of their Children, &, at the Conclusion of the Office, carried them all away unbaptized." Maury was outraged.

Did Johnson object to the baptism of slaves *tout court* or did he simply want to keep quite separate the baptism of white children from the baptism of black children? Maury thought, but was not certain, that "it was not Mr Johnson's

Design entirely to exclude slaves from Baptism, but from being baptized with children of free Parents." Maury explained to his correspondent that he was familiar with two common strategies for segregating the ceremony of baptism. Some parsons baptized slaves on weekdays; other parsons, after baptizing free white children on Sundays, chose to "go over the whole Office of Baptism anew for Blacks in some other Part of the Church; in order, I suppose, that delicate Noses might be in no Danger of Offence by the unsavory Effluvia from those African Constitutions."[30] Maury liked neither of these solutions. The former was impractical; even the most indefatigable parson would find it a challenge to regularly travel to various plantations baptizing Afro-Virginians. Maury also found the idea of holding two separate baptisms in the middle of Sunday worship unacceptable, on both theological and liturgical grounds. Liturgically, such a practice would be a "manifest Breach upon the Order & Regularity of divine Service." Theologically, such a practice would reinforce in white parishioners the very "Pride & Arrogance" which Christianity aimed to "mortify & abate," and it would stage a division between "free & bond, black & white" that was contrary to the Gospel, "which no where, that I can recollect, warrants Such Distinctions."[31]

The debate in Fredericksville Parish points to the tension and drama surrounding the baptism of enslaved people—this was not just a debate at the level of theory (*should* enslaved Afro-Virginians be baptized?) but also at the level of practice (*how* should enslaved Afro-Virginians be baptized?). This debate about ritual practice suggests another reason that members of the gentry insisted that their babies be baptized at home. Simply put, household baptism allowed elite Virginians to ritually suspend the liturgical, theological, and political tensions provoked by the baptism of slaves. At home there was no danger of enslaved persons marching down the "Isle" wishing to be baptized, too; household baptisms bracketed the reality of enslaved persons becoming Christians and allowed members of the gentry to imagine that they alone were baptized members of the body of Christ. Segregated household baptisms not only guaranteed that the gentry's delicate noses would not be offended in the middle of a sacrament. They also allowed the gentry, at the moment of baptism, to ritually erase the theological and social tensions produced by the extension of the sacrament of baptism to slaves.[32] In this way, elite Virginians' practice of household baptism points willy-nilly to a tension that lurked in their households, a tension the gentry tried to ease with religious ritual; household baptism provided elite slaveowners a means of ritually evading the tensions that lay beneath the surface of households in which elite Christians held other Christians in bondage.

Competing Practices: Anglican, Quaker, and Baptist Rites of Initiation in Early Virginia

For enslaved men and women like Mary Aggie and the unnamed lay catechist who worked for Jonathan Boucher, Anglican baptism could represent a sharp break with their surrounding lives and circumstances. For the Virginia gentry, by contrast, baptism represented the incorporation of infants into a religious community that comfortably blended the prerequisites of faith with the social order in which they lived. The meaning of baptism for elite Anglicans can be illuminated by contrasting Anglican baptism with two competing models of baptism practiced in colonial Virginia: Quaker spiritual baptism and Baptist believers' baptism.

In eighteenth-century Virginia, two Protestant communities enacted baptismal rites that clashed, both discursively and in practice, with the baptismal rites of elite Anglicans like the Carters and the Masons. Simply put, Quaker and Baptist rites of initiation were more dramatic than Anglicans'. For elite Anglicans, baptismal candidates were required only to have been born to parents who lived in a parish and who wanted to have their children baptized. Baptists and Quakers, on the other hand, looked for initiates to have had a subjective crisis experience. The Anglican baptismal ritual was polite and decorous, and it bespoke a pious sensibility in which the demands of religion easily coexisted with the routines, rhythms, and refinements of the rest of life. For both Baptists and Quakers, the act of being called into the church perforce mandated being called out of and set at odds with the world, and the jarring ruptures of Baptist and Quaker conversion and baptism dramatically staged the jarring rupture that being called into the church represented for those communities.

The Anglican baptismal service was short and dignified. Following the rubrics of the prayer book, the clergyman gave a short introductory statement asking God to receive the child into the church. Then the minister led the gathered congregation in two short prayers. The first focused on the power and symbolism of water, recalling biblical stories from the flood to the Red Sea to Jesus' own baptism. The second prayer petitioned God to receive the infant and to grant him remission of sin. After these opening prayers, the cleric read a short passage of Scripture—Mark's description of the little children being brought to Jesus. After further exhortation and prayer, the minister addressed the godparents, asking them a series of questions on the child's behalf: "Dost thou, in the name of this child, renounce the devil? . . . Dost thou believe in God the Father Almighty?" Then the minister took the child and "*discreetly and warily*" dipped the baby in the water or poured or sprinkled water on him or her, saying, "I baptize thee in the Name of the Father, and of the Son, and of the Holy Ghost." Through this ritual, infant Virginians were, in the words of the prayer book, received "into the Congregation of Christ's Flock."[33]

Anglican Virginians, lay and ordained, wrote of the "advantages" of baptism. Some of these advantages were soteriological. Virginia clergy stressed that baptism was efficacious but did not, magically or automatically, get a person into heaven; rather, baptism set the practitioner on a path likely to culminate in salvation. "It is not enough that Men are made Christians by Baptism," wrote one minister. "They must understand the Nature of the solemn Vow that they made And as the Hope for the Blessed Fruits & Effects of Christ's death; so they must perform those *Conditions* upon which they are promised." "So by Bm we lay ourselves under a holy Obligation to practice the whole Rel. of X. & to wait for all its promised blessings," preached another minister. This dual emphasis—on the efficacy and the obligations of baptism—echoed the English writing about baptism with which Virginians would have been most familiar, the chapter on baptism in Richard Allestree's popular book *The Whole Duty of Man*. Allestree underscored that "Baptism entered us into a Covenant with God." But he also stressed the obligations entailed at baptism, warning that one who failed to embrace the baptismal covenant as an adult risked "forfeit[ing]" the "precious benefits and advantages" baptism conferred on one as a baby.[34]

Laity understood the soteriological advantages of baptism similarly, perhaps placing slightly more stress on the efficacy of baptism and slightly less on the obligations entailed therein. The Virginia layman John Page wrote that presenting one's child for baptism was a central parental duty, for by ensuring that his child would be baptized, a parent

> procure[s] it an early right in all those precious advantages which that sacrament conveys to it. This you ought not to delay, it being most reasonable that you who have instrumentally conveyed the stain and pollution of sin to the poor infant, should be very earnest to have it washed off, as soon as may be: besides, the life of so tender an infant is but a blast, and many times gone in a moment; and though we are not to despair of God's mercy to those poor children who die without Baptism, yet those parents commit a great fault by whose neglect it is that they want it.

Parents of babies who were "very ill and not expected to live" rushed to have them baptized as soon as possible. When a baby was in danger, parents may have been comforted by the idea that if their child died, he or she would go to heaven.[35]

As the historian Adrian Wilson has noted, baptism represented "the social birth of the child," and the "precious advantages" of baptism were not just soteriological but also social. When parents chose people to serve as the godparents of their child, they were cementing existing bonds between kin and friends. These connections were underscored by godparents' sometimes singling out gifts to their godchildren in their wills, and by Governor William Gooch's referring, in a letter to his brother, to political patrons as godfathers. There may even have been social benefit simply to attending a baptism: the occasions were seen as so important that the General Court could adjourn early when several of its members were scheduled to attend a christening.[36]

The social element of baptism may also be seen in the practice of announcing in the *Virginia Gazette* that one's child has just been baptized and named after a renowned Virginia figure. For example, William Rose announced that his son was "baptized after the name of our late good and amiable Speaker, the honourable Peyton Randolph, esq.," and Alexander Anderson announced that his twins had been "baptized, by the rev. mr. Treat, *George Washington,* and *Martha Dandridge,* which last was the maiden name of his excellency general Washington's lady."[37] These parents were naming, and broadcasting, an affiliation, a political persuasion, and a vicarious participation in a circle of fame or a circle of character. For Anglicans like Rose and Anderson, there was no tension between baptism's locating one's child both in an ecclesial order and in a social order (in these examples, specifically the order of the state). Publishing that information reified the enmeshment of ecclesial and social order and extended the identification of social hierarchy and religion through space and time.

In Anglican households, the actual "discreet and wary" washing of the baby was just one piece—the central piece—of a troika of rituals that constituted the larger celebration of baptism. The actual rite of baptism should be seen alongside the other two rites, feasting and "churching." Feasting and churching do not feature as prominently in the official interpretations of baptism, but they underscore the extent to which Anglican baptism may be read, in part, as a ritual of reintegration.

First, let us consider the rite known as "the Churching of Women." This ceremony, in which the community gave thanks for a safe delivery, was usually conducted about a month after birth. The rite consisted of the recitation of one or two psalms, and a prayer in which the minister implored the Lord to be for the new mother "a strong tower" and gave thanks that God "hast

1.6

In his multivolume work *Cérémonies et coutumes religieuses de tous les peuples du monde* (1723–1737), the French engraver Bernard Picart commented on the Church of England's allowing baptisms to take place in private houses. Picart understood that household baptism was to be performed only in an emergency, but household baptism was much more common than that among the gentry of Virginia. Special Collections, University of Virginia Library.

vouchesafed this woman thy servant from the great pain and peril of child-birth." (Puritans detected in the ritual shades of medieval beliefs about purity and impurity, and viewed the Anglican Book of Common Prayer's inclusion of a service for churching as just one more piece of evidence that the Church of England was hopelessly tainted with "popish" and even "Jewish" customs.)[38]

"The Churching of Women" was more than an opportunity to give thanks. It was also the ceremony in which a new mother was formally welcomed back into larger society from the cocoon of childbirth. Through this rite, the mother was being reintegrated into her social and familial world. She had withdrawn from her husband, sexually, near the end of pregnancy, and, once in labor, she had withdrawn from her normal domestic work. After churching she resumed her regular household duties, including her sexual duties—a point made explicit in Robert Herrick's seventeenth-century verse "Julia's Churching, or Purification":

All Rites well ended, with fair Auspice come
(As to the breaking of a Bride-cake) home:
Where ceremonious Hymen shall for thee
Provide a second Epithalamie.

The new mother had also withdrawn from her family and husband into the female world of birthing, where she was surrounded by the midwife and female relatives and friends who attended her during labor. Churching—a ceremony which wove religious ritual into biological and domestic realities—marked her return to ordinary sociability, in which a mother left the consoling company of female friends and helpers to resume her daily life in a world dominated by men and the hierarchies they implied.[39]

Churching persisted in Virginia until the time of the American Revolution, but it was clearly less common than baptism. There is no record, for example, of whether Ann Eilbeck Mason was churched after any of her eleven deliveries. Presumably, churching was most common among elite women, but, as we have already seen, a 1732 letter from the pastor of Drysdale Parish raises an intriguing possibility: the pastor wanted the bishop to tell him whether baptized slaves could be admitted to church rites, including, specifically, churching. This letter suggests not only that at least one parson churched enslaved women; it also testifies, tacitly, to the persistence of the practice among Anglo-Virginians. In England the churching of women was usually performed, unsurprisingly, in a church—as was fitting, since the ritual connected the women's world of birth to the public world of church, and was the channel through which a woman moved from the sequestered childbed to the busy and more public work of regular life. On October 16, 1774, the indentured servant John Harrower noted in his diary that "Mrs Daingerfield was Churched at Fredericksburg"—that is, at the local parish church. But earlier in the century, at a 1719 clergy convention, ministers complained about being expected to lead the service at people's homes.[40]

Evidence from England indicates that many early modern English women viewed the ceremony positively. Virginia women probably looked forward to and enjoyed the ceremony, too. Childbirth was a dangerous and frightening event that could culminate in a woman's death. Mothers probably welcomed a religious ritual that allowed them to give thanks for a safe delivery. New mothers also probably relished a few moments of ecclesial and social attention, and the formal recognition of their maternal role.[41]

The triptych of household baptism was completed by feasting. Philip Fithian noted in his diary that christening "is one of the chief times for a Diversion here." In 1709 William Byrd II recorded attending "the christening of Mr. Anderson's son, where we met abundance of company. There was a plentiful dinner . . . dancing and mirth. Mr. Anderson was beyond measure pleased with the blessing God had sent him." Such lavish parties were common in England, where the attendant feasting and exchange of gifts not only served as a general celebration but also cemented the relationships forged between the baptized child and his or her godparents. The food served at such fetes was often symbolic—sweets and spicy delicacies such as aniseed and caraway coated in sugar were popular—and were associated with good luck and bounty. The meal foreshadowed the heavenly banquet of feasting and fellowship, where all the baptized would gather together at the end of time. But the dining and dancing also had a straightforward enough social purpose: the great parties that accompanied baptism in the homes of Virginia gentry underscored the compatibility of Christian commitment and the obligations and pleasures of elite society. (At Gunston Hall, the silver christening bowl was perhaps pressed into service chilling wine glasses at this very postbaptismal fete.)[42]

The social meanings of the three rituals that constituted household baptism should not be read in a crassly functionalist way—that is, that the "real" meaning of baptism was found in its social, rather than its theological, register. Rather, the fact that baptism affirmed practitioners' place in society and the world suggests the easy integration of religion into the daily life of elite Anglican households. For families like the Masons, religious meanings and religious practices were integrated into everyday life, and religious commitments did not set one apart from the world. The extent to which, for Anglicans, belonging in the church was coterminous with belonging in the world is highlighted by considering the baptismal rituals of two other Protestant communities in early Virginia, Quakers and Baptists. For both Quakers and Baptists, baptism dramatized not a seamless integration of religiosity and polite sociability. Rather, Quaker and Baptist practice reminded practitioners that entering the church put one sharply at odds with the larger surrounding society.

The difference between Anglican practice and Quaker practice is captured in a conversation that Nicholas Moreau, parson in St. Peter's Parish in New Kent County, Virginia, had with a small child in 1697. That year, Moreau had become acquainted with two families who, though Anglican, had drifted over to the Society of Friends. They had been attending Quaker meetings for three years. Through Moreau's ministrations, these families eventually made their way back to the Anglican Church. The adults did not need to be rebaptized, but Moreau baptized one of their children, a three-year-old, who, according to Moreau's report, upon being christened, took the cleric's hand and said, "You are a naughty man, Mr. Minister, you hurt the child with cold water."[43] The cold water of which the newly baptized three-year-old spoke was baptism's most essential material component, and its most powerful symbol. Most churches, from at least the second century to the eighteenth, would have agreed that water, a metaphor for the ways baptism cleansed people of their sins, was the essential material of baptism.[44]

There are two ways of reading Moreau's record of the unnamed child's comment about temperature. Perhaps Moreau was simply recording the actual words of a precocious child. On that reading, we may surmise that the three-year-old not only was responding to the water's temperature but may also have already absorbed enough of Quaker practice to be startled by the very rite of water baptism, which the Society of Friends repudiated altogether. Alternatively, we may read Moreau's record more polemically: perhaps he was putting words in the mouth of the child, both to dress up his account and to highlight the crucial difference between Anglicans' faithful practice of water baptism and Quakers' heretical rejection of it.

Quakers spurned water baptism because they rejected the notion of Original Sin: since babies were without sin, they did not need to be cleansed with water. Furthermore, Quakers believed that water baptism was a mere external ritual and worried that people who practiced water baptism mistook it for something that actually had forgiving or even salvific power. They scoffed at the idea that one's spiritual identity could be forged in something external, like water, and insisted instead that men and women needed to rely only on the Inward Light of God's revelation and love. In the post-Pentecost age, when all could be baptized in the Holy Spirit, water baptism was not necessary.[45]

What was necessary was a sensible dramatic experience. Quaker conversion demanded that the convert experience intense emotion—occasionally joy, but, more normatively, great "trials and afflictions" and anguish.[46] This is captured well in an account by a seventeenth-century English Quaker minister named Alice Hayes, who, years after the fact, recalled a conversion to Quakerism that was at once gradual and dramatic. Hayes "found a very strange alteration and operation in me, the like I had never felt before; the foundation of the earth within me began to be shaken, and strange and wonderful it was to me." This subjective experience of "trouble and sorrow," of inner "wars and commotions"—not a mere dousing with water—was, in Hayes's view, "the baptism that doth people good."[47]

When they came to Virginia in the 1650s, Quakers brought with them their rejection of water baptism. Virginia Anglicans responded legislatively and homiletically. In 1663 the Virginia Assembly passed a law aimed at Quakers, "persons that refuse to have their Children Baptised":

WHEREAS many scismaticall persons out of their aversenesse to the orthodox established religion, or out of the new fangled conceits of their owne hereticall inventions, refuse to have their children baptised, *Be it therefore enacted by the authority aforesaid,* that all persons that, in contempt of the divine sacrament of baptisme, shall refuse when they may carry their child to a lawfull minister in that county to have them baptised shalbe amerced two thousand pounds of tobacco; halfe to the informer, halfe to the publique.

More than a century later, Anglicans were still defending water baptism against Quaker disdain. In a sermon on baptism, Charles Clay underscored that water was necessary to baptism in part because it carried theological and devotional meaning. Just as people relied on water for their physical sustenance, so water—"a necessary Elemt. The Natural Life of Man Can't Subsist without it"—was a cipher for people's spiritual reliance on baptism. As Anglican baptism was available to anyone born within the geographical parameters of a parish, water was "Cheap & easy to Come at without Cost." Most important, water conveyed the basic truth of the doctrine of Original Sin, insofar as it implied a "humble" recognition that the baptizand was, before baptism, defiled; "otherwise there wd be no need of washing." William Douglas, parson in St. James Northam Parish in Goochland County, also took aim at Quaker practice from the pulpit: "While there are oyrs, who fm mistaken principles, & an enthusiastick temper, are ready to throw off all ye external Ordinances of religion, & this of water baptism among ye rest, contending only for qt they call a baptism by ye spirit, wc we protestants allow as well as they, tho we maintain a baptism by water, & by ye spirit both." Lay people echoed the concern: Richard Bland—better known for taking up his pen against clerical salary increases during the Parson's Cause—wrote "a Treatise on Water Baptism Ag'st the Quakers."[48]

These legal and homiletical denunciations of Quaker practice indicate how much was at stake in Christian initiation rites. Theology was certainly at issue: just as Quaker rejection of water baptism was bound up with a critique of Original Sin, so Clay's defense of water was inseparable from his convictions about humanity's sinfulness. Beyond doctrinal disagreements, Anglicans knew that Quakers' rejection of water baptism could be read as a larger rejection of communal norms. Indeed, Quakers' unconventional conversions signaled their rejection of all sorts of conventions—their spurning of fine clothing and alcohol, their preference for plain speech, their refusal to take up arms, their resistance against certain taxes and tithes, their willingness to allow women to itinerate, teach, and preach. Their insistence on baptism by the Spirit, not by water, signaled their emphasis on people's unmediated relationship with God, and, with that, their social egalitarianism. The protracted and dramatic conversion experience privileged by Quakers significantly "changed the[ir] relationship between self and society," auguring not just their embrace of the Society of Friends but their rejection of Virginia society. They were refusing not just water but also the Masons' fine bowl, and the material refinements and social world it implied.[49]

By the time the Mason children were being baptized in the 1750s, another Protestant community in Virginia was enacting still a different baptism. Baptists had been present in the colony since the late seventeenth century, and had founded churches in Prince George County and Surry County in the first half of the eighteenth century. The Baptist faith began to flourish in the 1760s, when Regular Baptists and Separate Baptists came to the colony from Pennsylvania, New England, and North Carolina and started to attract converts all over the colony. The Baptist faithful brought with them to Virginia the practice of "believer's baptism," and they derided Anglican practices as formalistic and meaningless. The Baptist preacher John Leland's judgment is typical: "The manner of initiating members into the Church of England, is arbitrary and tyrannical." (These two adjectives carried all the more force because Leland's account was published in 1790, in the wake of a war fought to liberate Americans from the arbitrary and tyrannical rule of the British monarchy.) "The subject (for candidate I cannot call him) is taken by force, brought to the Priest, baptized and declared a member of the church. The little christian shews all the aversion he is capable of, by cries and struggles, but all to no purpose, ingrafted he is." Anglican clerics argued right back from the pulpit: "The Enimies of Infant ~~Salvation~~ Bm." were but "upstart reformers" whose assertion that babies are not fit to be part of the church was "Contrary so with the mild and merciful Jesus." (Parson Clay's orthographic error is itself revealing—his accidental writing of *Salvation* when he meant "baptism" suggests how closely joined salvation and proper Anglican baptism were in his mind.) As for Baptists' charge that the Bible didn't actually describe any babies' being baptized, "by the Same Reason ye Sacrament of the Lds Supper Shd be denied to women. For (to my Remembrance) it is not expressed in all the New Testament that any Woman did ever partake of it."[50]

If, on Leland's account, the baptized infant's cries revealed her hostility to the rite being thrust upon her, cries and struggles of a different sort attended Baptist believers' baptism. For Baptists the "most essential doctrine of revelation" was "the indispensable necessity of the new birth, or being born again." Those who became "convicted" during Baptist preaching would offer "earnest cries for mercy, with many tears and lamentations." Sometimes people would become "prostrate on the floor" and lose "the use of their limbs." "Screams, cries, groans, songs, shouts, and hozannas, notes of grief and notes of joy" accompanied new birth. Only after this dramatic experience would one be baptized. As David Thomas explained in *The Virginian Baptist,* "We baptize none but those whom we esteem as true believers before baptism." Baptists located the moment of Christian becoming in a subjective individual experience, a crisis of the self that, in the words of the historian Susan Juster, involved "an almost confrontational encounter with a very real savior," and that necessitated a "deep alienation from one's prior self."[51]

A Virginian seeking to be baptized by Baptists had first to give a persuasive account of "new birth," of "an internal change of heart . . . of the deepest sense of the corruption of his nature, the weighty burden of guilt pressing his soul down," and his recognition that "in the Lord alone he hath righteousness and strength." After testifying to that conversion experience, the candidate was interviewed about his or her morals. After satisfactory testimony to "manner of life," the candidate and minister "repair[ed] to the water, sometimes with singing an hymn or psalm." Then the minister said a few words, prayed, and took "the subject by the hand and walk[ed] down into the water, where the whole body of the person [was] immersed in the name of the Father, and of the Son, and of the Holy Ghost." This dramatic ritual invited unusual behavior, not just from the baptismal candidate but from the entire gathered community. As William Fristoe noted after one baptism, "In going away [from a baptismal service] I looked back and saw multitudes, some roaring on the ground, some wringing their hands, some in extacies . . . and other so outrageous cursing & swearing that it was thought they were really possessed of the devil. I saw strange things today."[52]

Just as Quaker spiritual baptism augured a rejection of social convention, Baptist conversion involved a rejection of the institutions and mores associated with one's earlier life. To become a Baptist was, in the words of the minister David Thomas, to become part of a "people separated from the world." Indeed, early Virginia Baptist ecclesiology could not be clearer: the church was, in the words of one Virginia Baptist, "a number of persons selected, and called out from an ungodly world, and subjected to the gospel by almighty, efficacious, and everlasting grace." Baptists in Virginia spurned the fripperies of genteel society and were known by elites for "quite destroying pleasure in the country." They called for "an entire Banishment of Gaming, Dancing, and Sabbath-Day Diversions" and in general cultivated bearings of "gravity." As with Quakers, one of the most visible indicators of Baptists' commitments was sartorial: those who practiced "genuine religion" could not be characterized by "a gaudy, superfluous appearance," so Baptists favored simple clothing and avoided anything that smacked of "the glittering world." Baptists regulated one another's flirtations with that glittering world carefully. Should a brother or sister in the faith show an interest in fine clothes or jewelry, fellow Baptists would accuse them of trading "humble religion" for "proud profanity." This rejection of worldly aspirations was part of what made it possible for some Virginia Baptists, between 1785 and 1797, to question the institution of slavery.[53]

When Baptists, Quakers, and Anglicans criticized one another's baptismal practices, the disagreement was about more than a single ceremony. It was a disagreement about the relationship of the Christian to the world, and a disagreement about the shape of Christian life. For all Christian communities, baptism (by water or the Spirit) was the channel through which practitioners entered the body of Christ. For Baptists and Quakers, entering that new body meant being called out of, and becoming a critic of, the world. For elite Anglicans like the Masons, baptism carried with it no such connotations of rupture: it did not require intense emotion, and it did not mandate a sharp break with the surrounding society. Rather, becoming a Christian occurred in the midst of a polite ceremony, and the religious life it inaugurated was one of polite coexistence with the world.

Christian Costumes

Two final texts—a satin gown and a newspaper article about silk and satin garments—will close our discussion of elite Anglicans' practice of baptism. First, a short article that ran in the *Virginia Gazette* in August 1739. It spoofed the dramatic sartorial and social changes that conversion effected in evangelicals, describing "Several fine Ladies" from London "who used to wear French Silks, French Hoops 4 yards wide, Tete de Mutton, Mouton Heads, (or Bob Wigs,) and white Sattin Smock Petticoats, are turned *Methodists,* and followers of Mr. Whitefield, whose doctrine of *the New Birth* has so prevail'd over them that they now wear plain Stuff gown, no Hoops, common Night Mobs, and plain Bays for *Jenny's.*" This mocking piece deserves a bit of exegesis. When the protagonists became enamored of the doctrine of "*the New Birth,*" they made four sartorial changes. First, the women traded "French Silks" for "plain Stuff gown." French and Italian silk were considered the finest in eighteenth-century England, and the "stuff" the new Methodists wore instead signaled a rejection of the refinement of elegant fabric. Linda

Baumgarten explains stuff's social meaning: "Stuff referred to a broad category of worsted textiles that were constructed from long fibers of fine combed wool, spun tightly, and woven firmly. . . . Worsted stuff was considered appropriate for poor workingwomen who owned few outfits. . . . In 1752, a convict servant woman who ran away in Lancaster County, Virginia, wore a motley assortment of clothing that included a stuff gown." Second, the women gave up French hoops. There is no particular style called the "French hoop"; the writer of the story was invoking the center of fashion. Hoops were their largest in the 1740s, right after the publication of this story. These hoops conveyed wealth and leisure, and they were also sexually suggestive; to spurn them was to embrace simplicity over elegance and modesty over seductiveness. Third, the women traded "Tete de Mutton, Mouton Heads, (or Bob Wigs,)" for "common Night Mobs." In other words, the women took off their false curls (tête de mouton literally means "sheep's head") and put on plain white caps that tied under the chin, and were typically worn in bed. Common night mobs made a pointed contrast with tête de mouton, and the switch was a significant one in a world where wigs were often considered more prestigious than one's real hair, and where the ability to wear a wig properly was one test of whether one belonged in the upper echelons of society. Finally, the Methodist women replaced their "white Sattin Smock Petticoats" with "Bays for Jenny's." The white satin smock petticoat is not a mystery, and bay was an English fabric used in "clothing by religious societies from the 16th to the 17th centuries and by peasants during the time of Queen Elizabeth I." But "Jenny" is the most elusive symbol in this article. Possibly it is a corruption of *Jean,* a type of fustian (linen-cotton twill) associated with working-class men. Alternatively, the newspaper account's *Jenny* might be shorthand for spinning jennies, wheels used for making filling yarn. A third possibility is that the *n* and the *m* were confused in type, and this refers to a "jimmy," or overcoat—the new Methodists traded their petticoats, which would not have been seen, for overcoats. "Jenny" may simply denote a woman—the protagonists traded their petticoats for rough fabric with which they would make something for themselves, "jennies." *Jenny* comes by the mid-nineteenth century to mean an effeminate man (as in Thomas Hughes's description in *Tom Brown's School Days* of an effeminate boy as "called Molly, or Jenny"). If this implication was in circulation as early as the 1730s, the article could be hinting at the gender bending involved in these sartorial changes; the women were desexing themselves by removing all the sartorial markers of femininity.[54]

    Clothing was the perfect vehicle for the author and readers of this article to cast their judgments about evangelical conversion. As Leigh Schmidt has noted, in early America, clothing carried messages about class, gender, age, and hierarchy. Yet "more than socially instrumental, dress was also highly expressive, for clothes were often invested with religious meanings and they carried significance for the spirituality of those who wore them." We have already seen that dissenting groups, like the women in the newspaper account, used clothing to mark themselves as a community set apart. Indeed, casting off one's fine clothing and putting on plain garb was rapidly becoming a set piece of evangelical conversion narratives. But here the clothing change is related not by an enthusiastic evangelical but by a coolly sardonic narrator who is mocking the new Methodists' sartorial cliché. It was not only dissenters who used clothing to define their boundaries and their mores.[55]

For elite Anglicans reading the *Virginia Gazette* article, clothing also created community, expressed religious sensibility, and featured in significant Christian rituals—as is evident in our last baptismal text: a baptismal gown made around 1754. The gown was cut and stitched by Mary Scott Randolph from several yards of cream-colored satin. Made in the sack style that was popular in the eighteenth century, it consists of four satin panels, each sixteen inches across. The opening at the front of the gown is pleated, and the pleats are topstitched. Randolph added a cape collar at the front, and she left the back plain, save for a hand-knotted fringe that follows the gown's square neck, waltzes down each side of the front opening, and finally encircles the bottom of the gown. A silk cord that is both practical and decorative draws the gown closed at the neck.[56]

The gown was a costume of sorts—intended to be worn, yes, but worn to be seen.[57] Like the Masons' bowl, the gown tells social, cultural, economic, familial, and theological stories. First, the gown bespoke luxury, displaying the Randolphs' wealth and taste. It connected colonial Virginia to England, where similar gowns were in fashion; Mary Scott Randolph's handiwork thus distinguished the Randolphs from colonial hicks and identified them as part of a transatlantic elite, in touch with the latest metropolitan styles.[58] The gown also spoke theologically. In the eighteenth century, most christening outfits were white; the white cloth symbolized the purity of the soul after being cleansed by the baptismal waters.[59] Richard Randolph, Mary's son and the first Randolph baby to wear the silk dress, was to be washed clean, made pure by water and certified as such by his white gown. The gown also told a mother's story. Sewing the gown marked Mary Randolph as an appropriately devout Anglican mother—although she had no formal role in the baptism ritual, she could make this offering of expensive cloth and hours of skilled

1.7
Mary Scott Randolph made this baptismal gown around 1754. Courtesy of
Wilton House Museum, Richmond. Gift of the Randolph-Turpin-Ayers
Family.

stitching. Mary probably sewed the gown before Richard was born. Making the dress was part of preparing for his arrival; the gown was a gift that would survive her in case she died in childbirth. She may also have been participating in the self-conscious creation of a family heirloom, making a gown that she intended to be worn not only by all of her children but by her grandchildren and subsequent generations as well. (Indeed, this gown was used by Randolph descendants until the end of the twentieth century.)[60] Thus, like the Masons' baptizing babies in a bowl emblazoned with their initials and family crest, Randolph was creating and imagining a family in the midst of a ritual that subtly challenged the order of the patriarchal family.

A satin baptismal gown and a sardonic article about enthusiasts who gave up their satin upon conversion: there, in the lingua franca of elegant and plain, Anglicans spelled out their understanding of conversion. For Mary Scott Randolph and her family, becoming a Christian did not mean casting aside satin gowns. To the contrary, becoming a Christian was the first occasion to put on satin. For Anglicans, the evangelical conversion was all histrionics. Where evangelicals saw a change of heart in their dramas, Anglicans saw merely a change of clothes. Turning dissenters' indictment of Anglican superficiality on its head, Anglicans stayed in their world of satin dresses and au courant coifs, of fine wine chilled in fine silver, comfortable in their politeness, certain that their surfaces gilded a respectable salvation.

CHAPTER TWO

Becoming a "Christian Woman"
Needlework and Girls' Religious Formation

Who can find a virtuous woman? for her price is far above rubies.
—Proverbs 31:10

In 1768 and 1769, sixteen-year-old Elizabeth Boush, the daughter of a prominent Norfolk, Virginia, family, stitched a remarkable pictorial embroidery. Nineteen and a half by 11½ inches, the silk-on-silk embroidery depicts the Sacrifice of Isaac (see fig. 1 in the Introduction). The needlework captures the moment at which the ram, which God has sent to be sacrificed in Isaac's stead, appears; Abraham and his son are about to be spared.

Producing this needlework was part of Boush's education in the arts of housewifery. The embroidery demonstrated that Boush was skilled with a needle, and that her parents could afford both education and embroidery floss. As I will argue in this chapter, embroidery was also part of Boush's religious education. As Boush stitched her scene from Genesis 22, she learned a host of related lessons: not only how to sew, but also how to comport herself with femininity, how to live in relationship to the God of Israel, and how to occupy her place in the hierarchy that God wove into the fabric of creation. Embroidery may be read as a map of the social and religious values parents sought to inculcate in their daughters, and girls' practice of making such needlework may be read as a religious act, a domestic, embodied catechesis.

Looking for Religious Education in Embroidery

Religious education and girls' education were both charged issues in eighteenth-century Virginia. Religious education was a topic of some concern because explicit in infant baptism was the promise that the child would be taught about the faith into which they had been inaugurated. Virginia law required ministers to catechize "youth and ignorant persons" of his parish. The men who crafted that law envisioned something particular when they prescribed clerical catechesis: not generic religious education, but the inculcation of specific religious knowledge as printed in the church-approved catechism, a scripted dialogue found in the Book of Common Prayer. In the prayer book's catechism, the student was asked, inter alia, to recite the Ten Commandments and explain his duty to God and neighbor, and to answer a series of questions about baptism and Holy Communion. Englishmen published hundreds of additional catechisms and catechetical materials, such as John Lewis's *The Church Catechism Explain'd by Way of Question and Answer, and Confirm'd by Scripture Proofs.* Some of these books were intended as supplemental texts. Others differed theologically from the Book of Common Prayer, or aimed to adapt the prayer book catechesis, which assumed an ecclesial context, for use in the home or school.[1]

The catechism was a means to an end—one applied one's self to the catechism not in order to become skilled at catechetical recitation but to master basic Christian doctrine. Mastery of this doctrine was linked to reception of communion. In theory, one could not receive communion until one had been confirmed—but confirmation required the hands of a bishop, and there was no bishop in the British colonies, so, in accordance with the prayer book's rubric that "none be admitted to the holy Communion, until such time as he be confirmed, or be ready and desirous to be confirmed," clerics could admit people to the communion table after they had mastered the catechism.[2]

Some clergy took seriously their obligation to catechize. They used the prayer book's catechism and books like Lewis's *Short Exposition* to instruct children on Sundays. Often, formal instruction from clergy happened during Lent, which, since the early church, had been designated as the season during which candidates for baptism were instructed in the faith: William LeNeve of James City Parish, Thomas Baylye of Newport, Isle of Wight, John Skaife of Stratton Major, John Brunskill of Wilmington Parish, and Daniel Claylor of Blissland Parish were among the rectors who regularly gave the youth "catechetical Lecturing" during Lent. Some ministers, like James Cox of Westminister Parish, reported to the bishop that they regularly instructed "Negroes" in the faith. Zachary Brooke said that he would not baptize slaves until they could recite the "Church Catechism." Some clergy also preached sermons aimed principally at youth.[3]

Yet as a cache of letters sent by Virginia clergy to the bishop of London in 1724 suggests, formal catechesis happened only sporadically in eighteenth-century Virginia. John Bell of Christ Church Parish wrote that he would catechize during Lent if only "Parents, Mr.s and Misstresses [could] be admonished to bring the Youth to Church." Lewis Latane complained that "The usual time [for catechizing] is the spring of the year, but the remoteness of the parishioners from Church prevents their sending their children to be Catechised." George Robertson of Bristol Parish lamented that although he had once offered catechetical instruction "in summer after the [Scripture reading] at morning prayer," he had fallen out of the habit, and had not offered catechesis for the last two years. He planned to resume his "former Custom of Catechising yearly" that very summer. Henry Collings of St. Peter's Parish also hoped to begin catechesis: "I have not as yet, the youth through long disuse and neglect of my predecessors, being incapable, &c., but shall, God willing, in Lent."[4]

If clergymen did not always fulfill their catechetical duties, teachers and parents sometimes did, as the rector of Henrico Parish suggested: "The distance of families from Church makes it so difficult to bring their Children when small that [catechising] is done by the Schoolmasters or parents and when they grow to any bigness they care not to abide the public Catechising of a Minister." Sometimes the teachers in question were private tutors who taught children at home: on Saturday, March 12, 1774, Philip Fithian "heard Harry, Miss Fanny & Be[t]sy repeat their catechism." Other Anglican children, like Jesse Lee, learned the catechism at the small, neighborhood schools they attended. Lee grew up in an Anglican household in Prince George County, Virginia. Though as an adult he became a Methodist revivalist and was generally censorious of Anglican practice, he recalled the catechism with esteem: at school,

> as soon as he was capable of reading tolerably well, his teacher directed him to procure a prayer book, with a strict injunction to carry it to church every Sabbath, and out of which he was taught the catechism. . . . We shall not doubt his testimony, when he assures us that he derived considerable benefit from this course of religious instruction. "In a thousand instances (says he,) when I felt an inclination to act or speak amiss, I have been stopped by the recollection of my catechism, some parts of which I did not understand; yet it was good upon the whole that I learned it."[5]

At the same time that clergy worried about religious education, people also debated girls' education, a topic that took on more and more urgency as the eighteenth century progressed. As many scholars have argued, pedagogy was explicitly gendered in the eighteenth century. Pedagogical strategy reflected widely held assumptions about boys' and girls' differences, and one of the aims of instruction was to mold girls and boys into exemplars of contemporary norms of masculinity and femininity. Boys' educations prepared them for active work in the world. Boys received formal schooling in reading and arithmetic (and their instruction in reading was often grounded in religious texts—for example, John Harrower, who served as tutor at Fairfax County's Belvedere plantation, used the psalter, specifically, and the Bible writ large, to teach his male charges to read). As Allan Kulikoff has noted, boys' educations regularly took them away from the household. Boys were sent to run errands, which taught them responsibility, introduced them to public spaces like local stores, and habituated them to the practice of moving easily between their household and the larger world. Fathers also took their sons hunting, schooling them in "the male ethic of aggressive behavior." Girls' educations were more likely to happen at home. As Kulikoff put it, "Daughters stayed closer to home and learned both housewifery and their inferior place in the family order." Girls were less likely than boys to study mathematics or classical languages. Even handwriting instruction reflected gendered assumptions about education. Boys were to learn "good" hands that would fit them for various business pursuits. Girls learned ornamental and delicate handwriting, which, in the words of the historian Tamara Plakins Thornton, "symbolized female physical delicacy, intellectual inferiority, and constitutional flightiness."[6]

As the example of Philip Fithian's listening to Frances and Betty Landon Carter recite the catechism shows, girls sometimes participated in formal, text-based, question-and-answer catechesis. But in a pedagogical context in which girls' education revolved not around printed books but around pursuits with overtly domestic utility, it is important to look for their religious education in places other than catechisms. For example, girls' jewelry, which was sometimes inscribed with religious messages such as "Fear God," may be seen as a tool of informal, embodied, religious instruction. Because needlework, as we shall see, was one of the few pedagogical activities that virtually everyone agreed was appropriate for refined girls, it makes sense to consider how embroidery complemented or replaced textbook catechesis in teaching elite girls religious lessons.[7]

Girls' needlework may be read as a religious undertaking on at least two levels. First, much of the content of needlework was explicitly religious: embroidery often featured pictures drawn from Scripture, and verses from biblical and extrabiblical sources heavy with moral instruction. To work a picture of a biblical scene was to put one's self literally in the posture of reflecting on Scripture. Surely girls daydreamed as they sewed, but they also probably thought about and absorbed that which they stitched. Second, working embroidery itself may be seen as a religious practice, a contemplative

2.1
Mary Broadnax, whose father was a goldsmith in Williamsburg, wore a ring engraved "Fear God Mary Broadnax." The ring suggests that to understand how girls were taught religious lessons, we must look beyond printed catechisms. Attributed to John Broadnax, gold ring ca. 1715. Colonial Williamsburg Foundation.

act: as the twenty-first-century embroidery artist Karin Birch has explained, the repetitive stitching required by fine needlework can help the needle-woman enter a meditative state.[8] To more fully explore the ways in which learning embroidery was part of girls' religious education, I offer in this chapter an overview of the history of needlework, focusing on the history of the craft's place in girls' educations. Then I will turn to a close reading of two surviving examples of girls' needlework from eighteenth-century Virginia.

Girls' Needlework:
Pedagogy and the Religious Lessons of Embroidery

Today we typically assume that needlework is women's work—that embroidery is a naturally female pursuit. But in fact, the coding of needlework as feminine is part of the history of embroidery. True enough, by the late nineteenth century, needlework was so uniformly understood as a female under-taking that in 1895 Freud could blame women's proclivity for hysteria on "women's handiwork," since sitting with a needle and thread "gives such ample opportunity" for the "daydreams" that were the basis for the hypnoid states that were themselves the "basis and condition of hysteria." But embroidery was not always the provenance of women and girls. In the Middle Ages, both men and women could aspire to be professional embroiderers, and in the fifteenth century needlework actually became more deeply associated with men, as guild regulations began to limit women's ability to achieve the status of master embroiderer. During the seventeenth and eighteenth centuries, embroidery became thoroughly marked as "feminine." In this period, the very act of making needlework became part and parcel of how girls learned to be girls.[9]

Typically, the first piece of needlework a girl made was a sampler. Now thought of as essentially domestic, samplers were originally artifacts of commerce. Boasting myriad types of stitches, samplers were used as early as the thirteenth century as tools with which Egyptian embroiderers showed off their handicraft to prospective clients. Traveling west across trade routes, samplers became popular in Europe by the Renaissance. Early evidence for European samplers comes from a fifteenth-century painting by Joos van Cleve: his *Holy Family* shows a spot sampler folded on a table in front of a Madonna and child.[10] By the sixteenth century, samplers were all the rage at the English court. Edward VI owned thirteen samplers, and in Shakespeare's *A Midsummer Night's Dream*, Helena describes her intimacy with Hermia by recalling how they had worked flowers in a sampler together. In act II of *Titus Andronicus*, when Marcus discovers that his niece Lavinia has been raped and had her tongue and hands cut off, he compares her plight to that of Ovid's Philomela—and transforms Philomela's weaving into a sampler: "Fair Philomela, why she but lost her tongue, / And in a tedious sampler sew'd her mind."[11]

Gradually, the function of samplers evolved; because paper was more expensive than cloth, samplers began to serve as record books of different stitches. Once samplers were no longer valued as merchants' advertisements, they became more clearly coded as feminine. Women kept samplers rolled up or stored together in a book, consulting them when, at work on a chair cushion or an embroidery for church, they needed inspiration or a reminder of how to make a particular stitch. John Palsgrave captured this function of a sampler in his 1530 dictionary: a sampler was an "exampler of a woman to work by." The function of samplers as sourcebooks for stitches persisted in Virginia until the late seventeenth century. A 1679/80 will probated in Accomack County notes that in the "Hall chamber" was "one basket with

Samplers et." The owner of that basket did not display her samplers but pulled them out of the basket when she needed to be reminded of a particular stitch.[12]

In the seventeenth century, parents and teachers began to appreciate the pedagogical potential of samplers; increasingly, sampler-making came to be seen as an economical and aesthetically pleasing way for girls to perfect their sewing skills. The hope was that making a sampler would teach a girl "a good vocabulary of stitches." (Indeed, samplers often included a dizzying array of stitches: herringbone, hem, flat, French knot, tent, eyelet, cross, and stem, among others.) This understanding of samplers is reflected in eighteenth-century dictionaries. A 1730 dictionary defined *samplar* as "a Pattern or Model; also a Piece of Canvas, on which Girls learn to mark, or work Letters and Figures, with a needle." Samuel Johnson's *Dictionary of the English Language* defined a sampler as "a pattern of work; a piece worked by young girl for improvement."[13]

Samplers came to the American colonies with the Puritan migration to New England. The oldest extant sampler made in New England was worked by Loara Standish, daughter of the Plymouth Colony leader Miles Standish, who made her sampler around 1633. Loara Standish was probably one of a very few girls in the seventeenth-century colonies with both the time and the materials to create a sampler. But by the 1720s supplies, leisure time, and aspirations to gentility had combined to encourage needlework, and sampler-making became widespread among elite and middling American girls, from New England to South Carolina. As the production of a sampler came to be seen as a standard girlhood activity, the decorative potential of samplers took on new importance. Square and rectangular samplers, broad rather than long, became more fashionable than the narrow strips on which samplers had been worked in the seventeenth century. In the eighteenth century a distinctly American sampler emerged, with technical variation from English samplers; girls began, for example, to stitch over two threads, rather than three. Colonial girls developed samplers that, in the words of Ethel Bolton and Eva Coe, "had form and coherence of design, which the English sampler lacks." Most finished samplers—typically silk thread on a rectangular piece of linen—included an alphabet, which demonstrated that the needleworker would be capable of marking household linens with her initials when she grew up. Samplers also often included a verse, a floral design or a scene with people, a row of numbers, or images drawn from nature—deer and birds, vines and fruit, moons, stars, and suns. Eighteenth-century samplers were not mere practical exercises. They were artistic and ornamental, and they were intended to be displayed, often in costly frames, and often in the most public rooms of the house.[14]

The display of needlework in early America, of course, was not an act of disinterested artistic production. As the historian Laurel Thatcher Ulrich has put it, "Bending over their embroidery frames, little girls added value to themselves as well as to the silk their parents purchased."[15] A finished and framed sampler testified to the social and economic standing of the embroiderer's parents. Artful and intricate, a sampler showed off a girl's skills to prospective suitors; it also assured young men that they were courting girls whose family could afford leisure, instruction, and silk. (This aspect of display was doubled when needlework was worked into portraits, which themselves testified to a family's status. The 1724 portrait of one of William Byrd's wives or daughters, depicted with needlework and a sewing basket, and, in the background, an enslaved boy, is a surviving example.)[16] Religiously influenced needlework testified that the girl would be not just an appropriately elite wife but also an appropriately Christian one—by making overtly religious needlework, girls demonstrated that they possessed both the right economic value and the right religious values.

For decades, scholars and antiquities dealers assumed that although girls in New England and the middle colonies were dab hands at the needle, Virginia girls had not produced much embroidery, and in particular had not made samplers. Why? Repeating the ubiquitous trope about the pernicious effects of slavery on white slaveowners, the standard explanation was that girls from Virginia were too lazy to sit with needle and thread. This view of Virginia girls as spoiled and indolent was given special force by a young Philadelphia woman named Sally Wister. In 1778 Wister described in her journal a visit her family had received from Alexander Spotswood, of Dandridge, Virginia. Spotswood, wrote Wister, "observ'd my sampler, which was in full view. Wish'd I would teach the Virginians some of my needle wisdom; they were the laziest girls in the world."[17]

In recent years, however, decorative arts scholars have determined that southern girls did indeed work samplers. Perhaps the oldest sampler to survive from the colonial Chesapeake was one made in Maryland in 1696. Inventories attest to needlework in Virginia, although some inventory makers accorded the form as little respect as some historians have: when Lemuell Newton's inventory was made in 1731, his household goods were said to include "some old useless Needlework Stuff." Newspaper advertisements make clear that needlework was part of the curricula at countless southern schools (though a "school" may have been nothing grander than three girls in the central room of

2.2

This 1724 portrait depicts one of William Byrd's wives or daughters with needlework and a sewing basket, and, in the background, an enslaved boy. Portrait of Wilhemina Byrd (unknown artist). Private Collection; photograph courtesy of the Museum of Early Southern Decorative Arts at Old Salem.

a teacher's house). As early as 1752 teachers of needlework were advertising for students in Virginia. John Walker offered to teach boys reading, arithmetic, classics, and geography, and his wife was available to teach "young Ladies all kinds of Needle Work." Virginia girls did not always like their teachers. Looking back on her Norfolk childhood, Helen Calvert Maxwell Read recalled "I was sent to a Mrs. Johnson—a very large fat woman, who died one day in her fat—and perhaps of it—for she was a monstrous woman, indeed. She taught me needle-work and marking on a sampler."[18]

In fact, by the mid-eighteenth century, parents and pedagogues came to see needlework as part of the answer to a pressing question: what educational pursuits were most likely to produce virtuous daughters? As the historian Martha Saxton has shown, during the eighteenth century Virginians channeled much of their anxiety about right living and moral behavior into girls' education. As the eighteenth century unfolded and tensions between the colony and the metropole intensified, safeguarding girls' virtue seemed ever more urgent. In Saxton's formulation, "feminine morality was an important subject in the complex relation between the colonies and the mother country," as colonists "associated femininity with the corruption of British society and its rulers." Girls increasingly represented the virtue of everyone in Virginia, allowing men to see themselves as better than the British without having to modify their own behavior. Men could keep drinking and betting on gamecock fights as long as they reared and married female models of elegant purity who would stand in for the virtue of the entire colonial society. In particular, Virginians worried about girls' sitting idle. They feared that, in the words of John Harrower, "idleness or play . . . [would offer an] inlet in any of the sex to laziness and vice."[19] To dam that inlet, Virginians filled elite girls' days with educational undertakings. A girl whose hands held violin bow or embroidery needle, and whose mind was taken up with conjugating French verbs, would be too occupied to go wandering down the primrose path to folly.

But exactly what educational activities should fill girls' days? Were reading, learning to dance, and playing instruments actually good for girls' moral formation? Would book learning defeminize girls and render them "insufferable" instances of "Female pedantry" that would frighten rather than attract men? Alternatively, would too much time devoted to ornamental "accomplishments" turn girls into coquettes? Should girls learn to dance (or would minuets and reels "allure their fond votaries from that purity and rectitude which are the chief embellishments of female character")? Should they study music (or would girls begin lusting after the praise they received after they took their turn at the piano)?[20]

Although they disagreed among themselves about the propriety of jigs and violins, moralists and pedagogues were in virtually unanimous agreement that needlework was a suitable and important component of girls' educations. When moralists enjoined girls and women to commit themselves to gainful employment and stand firm against a creeping idleness, they specifically encouraged needlework, which kept a girl both occupied and also still and out of public view. The first chapter of the popular moral guide *The Ladies Library*, for example, is devoted to the theme of "Employment." Its opening salvo warned against idleness, "which is not only the Road to all *Sin*, but is a *damnable Sin* itself, quite opposite to the great Ends of the *Creator*. . . . Can we imagine that *God*, who made nothing but for some excellent End, should make Man for no End at all, or for a very silly one?" After establishing that God frowns on idleness, the author took to task women who would think that "the Softness of their Sex excludes their idleness," and urged women to devote themselves to learning foreign languages and studying art. But most of all, the author advocated needlework: "Ladies would do well to remember that the Princesses in old Times did not disdain the *Distaff* and *Needle*." Needlework equipped girls with a useful skill, and unlike dancing and music, it kept them silent and immobile, in a chair, and not twirling about, on display.[21]

The enslaved child who stands in the shadows of Byrd's portrait points to one particular rationale for teaching elite girls embroidery: once grown up, they would need to evaluate their servants' sewing. At the end of the eighteenth century, Thomas Jefferson reminded his daughter Martha that she must master the needle because "In the country life of America there are many moments when a woman can have recourse to nothing but her needle for employment. In a dull company in dull weather for instance. . . . The needle is then a valuable resource. Besides without knowing how to use it herself, how can the mistress of a family direct the works of her servant?" John Gregory, the author of a popular moralistic work called *A Father's Legacy*, reminded his readers—both his literal and metaphorical daughters—that "the intention of your being taught needle-work, knitting and such like, is not on account of the intrinsic virtue of all you can do with your hands, which is trifling, but to enable you to judge more perfectly of that kind of work, and to direct the execution of it in others." Jefferson and Gregory thus inscribed class distinction within the feminine pursuit of needlework. In working a sampler, girls learned, first, a household skill with which they needed familiarity so that they could effectively instruct their slaves in sewing. At the same time, they learned something about their rank—they learned that they were growing up to be women who would supervise the labor of others.[22]

Beyond those lessons of class and housewifery, needlework schooled girls in a variety of literacies. Just as pedagogues juxtaposed book learning and needlework when they debated girls' education, typically we today tend to think of needlework as part of the "ornamental" component of girls' educations, but as Catherine Kelly and Bianca F.-C. Calabresi have recently argued, needlework ought be seen not as a "feminine accomplishment" that was wholly oppositional to other kinds of literacies. As map samplers and samplers featuring multiplication tables, calendars, family genealogies, and even complicated division problems suggest, some girls learned geography, arithmetic, family narratives, and timekeeping while also mastering the eyelet stitch.[23] The didactic potential of needlework went beyond multiplication tables. Needlework also schooled girls in social values. As Daniel Roche has shown for pre-Revolutionary France, "In teaching how to use needles and pins, mothers, older sisters, and schoolmistresses also taught the principles of good housekeeping, the elements of a female morality, in a word, its 'ways of speaking' and 'ways of doing,' that is, its culture."[24] Similarly, we can see in Virginia girls' needlework the social, cultural, and religious lessons their parents wanted daughters to learn.[25]

Many scholars have suggested that early American samplers reflected the religious sensibilities of the Christian girls who made them. But if religious imagery and verse pervaded needlework throughout early America, different themes emerge in different communities' needlework. Religious embroidery does not, in other words, merely attest to a generic pious sensibility. It may, upon close reading, suggest particular religious lessons that different religious communities valued. For example, one scholar of needlework from Plymouth Colony has found that Puritan needleworkers there most often chose to stitch "gloomy" sentiments, "sometimes bordering on the macabre"; the religious sentiments in early Puritan needlework often offered "a distinct parallel with what was carved on headstones." In other words, early Puritan needlework reflected—and taught—Calvinist soteriology. The Moravians of North Carolina also produced religiously distinctive needlework. Their embroidery featured oaks (interpreted as a symbol of Jesus' Cross, and more generally as strength to resist evil) and wreathes (symbolizing victory in Christ). An evangelistic theme also emerges in Moravian needlework, in quoting Mark 16:15 (Jesus' command to go into the world and make disciples) and in depictions of a well, which Moravians understood as a symbol of the woman at the well who left her water pot to follow Jesus and spread the Gospel.[26]

What religious lessons did Anglican girls in eighteenth-century Virginia encounter in their needlework? We will devote the rest of this chapter to a close examination of two pieces of eighteenth-century Virginia needlework, a sampler worked by Mary Johnson in 1742 and Boush's Sacrifice of Isaac. These two pieces of needlework bring together Scripture, fears about women's impact on the social order, and the moral and religious formation of genteel girls. They indicate the Virginia gentry's preoccupation with raising virtuous daughters, and they suggest that one particular virtue girls mastered as they sewed was obedience—the obedience girls owed their parents and would one day owe their husbands, and, reflexively, the obedience owed them by slaves.

Because no diaries, letters, or commonplace books by Johnson or Boush survive, we can't know exactly what the girls thought about the texts and images they embroidered. In the absence of diaries and correspondence, the devotional literature that Virginia Anglicans read can help interpret Virginia needlework.[27] Intended to form young women in the ways of deportment and etiquette, books like Richard Allestree's *The Ladies Calling* and James Fordyce's *Sermons to Young Women* were touchstones of the lived experience of Anglican religious practice, and they can help us see how Virginia Anglicans understood both the act of needlework and the particular verses and scriptural images that were stitched onto silk canvas. In fact, it is likely that girls would have read such texts in concert with their needlework educations: in a somewhat self-serving loop, authors of prescriptive texts that endorsed needlework as a suitable female pursuit often suggested that time passed sewing could be even more profitable if someone else in the room read aloud from an edifying text.[28] In the following sections, then, I will read Johnson and Boush's needlework alongside the prescriptive and devotional literature that illuminates how Virginia Anglicans would have understood the texts and images in the girls' embroidery.

Mary Johnson's Sampler: Becoming a "Christian Woman"

The oldest surviving Virginia sampler was made by twelve-year-old Mary Johnson in 1742. Little is known about Johnson. The girl who worked this sampler was probably the Mary Johnson whose birth was recorded in the St. Peter's Parish register, New Kent County, Virginia, in 1730. She was the daughter of James and Jane Johnson and the sister of a second Jane, born in 1737. Johnson's sampler is primarily textual—it is dominated by letters, numbers, and script, not pictures. Read top to bottom, the sampler presents three texts. First is an alphabet. Second is a short verse from Proverbs: "Favour is deceitful and beauty is vaine / But a woman that feareth the Lord she shall be praised. Give her of the fruit of her hands and let her own works praise her in the gates" (Prv 31:30–31). The bottom half of the sampler is dominated by a

2.3
Mary Johnson's 1742 sampler brings together two passages of Scripture: Revelation 14:13 and Proverbs 31:30–31. *Sampler* by Mary Johnson, New Kent County, Virginia, 1742. The Colonial Williamsburg Foundation.

verse from Revelation: "And I heard a voice from heaven saying unto me write, blessed are the dead which die in the Lord from henceforth: Yea saith the spirit that they may rest from their labours & their works do follow them" (Rv 14:13).[29]

In sewing the letters of the alphabet, Johnson was learning a skill she would need as a woman—the skill of marking bedspreads, tablecloths, and other household linens with her initials, to signal ownership. Johnson stitched this sampler mostly in the marking stitch, a reversible stitch which produces a neat back as well as a neat front; it can thus be read from either side and is an appropriate (and, of course, aptly named) stitch for marking household linens.[30] But the alphabet, set at the top, also establishes a framework for reading the sampler, and signals the sampler's instructive and didactic function. The alphabet's placement, directly above two passages from Scripture, reminded girls that alphabetic literacy made possible scriptural literacy. What girls who could read ought to be reading was the text underneath the alphabet: the Bible.

Let us turn now to the verses from Scripture in Johnson's sampler. Johnson may have chosen the verses herself, but it is more likely that her mother or a teacher told her which verses to sew. It is not surprising to find a verse from Proverbs 31 on a girl's sampler. Proverbs 31, one of the most extensive discussions of women in the Bible, figured prominently in eighteenth-century conversations about women's behavior. Virginia Anglicans read the text as a model for appropriate female behavior. Peter Fontaine, praising his recently deceased sister, recalled that "She had, after her duty to God, taken the excellent daughter, Proverbs 31st chapter, the 18th verse to the end, for her pattern." William Byrd praised a Mrs. Allen of Surry County by likening her to the Proverbs 31 woman: Allen "seem'd to pattern Solomon's Housewife if one may judge by the neatness of her House, & the good Order of her Family." Eighteenth-century prescriptive writers often based their codes of feminine comportment on Proverbs 31. In commentaries on the biblical passage, writers urged young girls and women to "copy" the "modest but exalted original" portrayed in Proverbs 31. The virtues in the Proverbs text apply most obviously to mothers and wives, but young girls were instructed to apply themselves to these ideals from an early age: "Would the Virtuous woman . . . so particularly marked by the characters of married and maternal excellence, have been what she was, if in her single state she had not studied the necessary principles?"[31]

One of the most extended engagements with Proverbs 31 is found in James Fordyce's 1766 *Sermons to Young Women.*[32] Fordyce devoted the sixth of his sermons to a lengthy exegesis (or, perhaps more accurately, isigesis) of Proverbs 31:10–31. This sermon, written over two decades after Johnson

2.4

Proverbs 31, quoted here on the title page of the popular prescriptive guide *The Ladies Calling*, was a central text in eighteenth-century conversations about female behavior. The Proverbs 31 woman was considered an ideal. Rare Book, Manuscript, and Special Collections Library, Duke University.

stitched her sampler, recapitulates a half-century's worth of rumination about the appropriate behavior of Christian women.[33] Fordyce was concerned about how girls passed the time, and he praised Proverbs 31 for providing a comprehensive picture of the "Domestic, Elegant, and Mental" aspirations suitable for the "Christian Woman." Women were to avoid inappropriate activities, such as "gaming," which "transgress[es]" the "laws of humanity and friendship," and "tends to harden and contract the heart." Instead, girls and women should devote themselves to those "elegant Accomplishments" that are "consistent with" and "conducive" to "Christian Sobriety." Fordyce approved of dancing, so long as it was "moderate" and "discrete," and he countenanced singing, too, especially when it "lift[s] your hearts to heaven, prove[s] a kind of prelude to the airs of paradise, and prepare[s] you for joining the choir of angels."[34]

Fordyce was especially enthusiastic about needlework, which had the explicit imprimatur of Proverbs 31. "We find it spoken of in Scripture with commendation," Fordyce wrote. Fordyce found in Proverbs 31:19—"she layeth her hands to the spindle, and her hands hold the distaff"—a suggestion that the virtuous woman's fingers "show a dexterity that is alike pleasing in the performance, and beneficial in the effects." To further induce girls to take up the needle, Fordyce praised a lady he once knew—"noble by her birth, but more noble by her virtues"—who was "a perfect mistress of her needle." Whenever she was in company, sat with her thread, "working something useful, or something beautiful." This hardly distracted her from making charming conversation; to the contrary, in several years of "intimate acquaintance," Fordyce never once saw this noble lady fail to "assist . . . in supporting the conversation, with an attention and capacity which I have never seen exceeded."[35]

In Fordyce's treatment of Proverbs 31, we see both the domestic formation of girls like Mary Johnson, and the domestication of a text. In its original historical context, the Proverbs 31 woman was a forceful, even ambitious woman: she oversaw crop production, preserved grain, fed and milked animals, made cloth, and bought and sold real estate.[36] In Fordyce's hands, the Proverbs 31 woman was not decisive, or even especially active. Rather, she was one who sang with angels, made decorative needlework, and assisted in supporting good conversation. Fordyce's reading of Proverbs 31 appears to be, on its face, a strange one, but it was a reading that was plausible in Anglican Virginia. A submissive station that is to some extent alien to the text has become engrafted into both Proverbs 31 and the eighteenth-century "Christian Woman."

Girls and women were to pattern themselves after the Proverbs 31 woman because she was the anti-Eve. As one homilist explained, though Eve sinned, she was created to be a helpmeet to her husband, "ordained from the beginning, to comfort and assist him in all the Necessaries and Uses. . . . The very reason for her formation . . . was the Benefit of Man, that she might be helpful and profitable to him." Eve's prelapsarian qualities were the very characteristics that "Solomon takes notice of in his large description of a Good wife" in Proverbs 31. In other words, the Proverbs 31 woman—the woman girls were to become through their careful stitching—was Eve as Eve was meant to be.[37] Women in early Virginia labored under the shadow of Eve, but through their scriptural stitching, girls inverted and righted Eve's story. Eve looked for pleasure; Mary Johnson, needle in hand, was working. Eve led her husband astray; through her needlework, Johnson was becoming the kind of woman who could build her husband up. Above all, Eve shrugged off the words of God; scriptural samplers ensured that girls repeated the words of God precisely. Through needlework, girls like Mary Johnson became the Proverbs 31 woman, the anti-Eve, the mischievous woman made right through virtuous practice.

After Proverbs 31, which spoke specifically to what it meant to be a good Christian woman, Johnson's sampler moved to a second text about patterning one's self after virtuous models. Revelation 14:13, which points to the dead saints as a model for the living to emulate, was an apt passage for a young girl's needlework. A surviving sermon indicates how the verse was read in colonial Virginia. Parson William Douglas took the verse, understandably, as an opportunity to preach about death. He explained that death was a blessing for the decedent because he was no longer able to sin. The death of a loved one could also be a blessing for survivors because it would help them realize the foolish "vanity of this world" and could inspire the living to rededicate themselves to righteous living. Indeed, survivors should reflect on the character of their recently deceased friend, and "coppie after their virtuous example." Seen through Douglas's sermon, Revelation 14:13—with its reminders to spurn frivolous vanities and emulate virtuous forebears—was a fitting choice for a girl's sampler.[38]

Finally, after the two biblical passages, the sampler gives a fourth text: immediately after the verses from Revelation is Mary's name. The message is clear: it is Mary who will conform herself to the patterns offered by these texts—and maybe one day she will be a worthy Christian woman whom others will "coppie."

Johnson's sampler was, at two levels, about conformity. As William Hunting Howell has argued, girls' needlework was an exercise in replication; needlework derived its meaning from "a calculus of emulation and imitation: a well-formed stitch indicates a well-wrought mind and proper femininity because it shows how well a girl can conform to a given model." In general, girls were not praised for making original or inventive needlework; they were praised for learning how to make exact stitches, and for executing embroidery that conformed to the pattern from which they were sewing.[39] Women were also praised for how well they conformed their lives to a pattern, the pattern of upright people who had gone before ("coppie after their virtuous example") and the pattern of Proverbs 31: Fontaine's sister had "taken the excellent daughter, Proverbs 31st chapter, the 18th verse to the end, for her pattern," and Mrs. Allen "seem'd to pattern Solomon's Housewife." There was resonance between girls' and women's conforming to a pattern in their needlework and conforming to the patterns of biblical virtue in their lives. Through their needlework, girls like Mary Johnson conformed to an ideal type of Christian femininity.

Mary Johnson's needlework was more than just an exercise in mastering the cross-stitch. It was part of a larger cultural conversation about needlework and appropriate behavior for the Christian woman. Johnson's sampler suggested eighteenth-century Virginians' urgent fears about safeguarding female virtue, and it supplied two aids to virtue—meditation on Scripture and needlework itself, a virtuous practice endorsed by the writer of Proverbs (and by Proverbs' eighteenth-century interpreters). A generation after Mary Johnson worked her sampler, Elizabeth Boush sewed the Sacrifice of Isaac with which this chapter opened. Boush's pictorial needlework spoke to the same concerns that animated Johnson's sampler; indeed, Boush's Sacrifice of Isaac supplies an additional piece of Virginia Anglicans' thinking about virtue and feminine behavior. Boush's needlework was preoccupied not with girls' virtue broadly but with the particular virtue of obedience.

Elizabeth Boush's Sacrifice of Isaac: The Virtue of Obedience

We know a bit more about Elizabeth Boush than we do about Johnson. Boush, fondly known as Betsey, was the daughter of Samuel Boush and Catherine Ballard Boush. She grew up in Norfolk, Virginia, a relatively cosmopolitan port city that attracted the political and economic elites of colonial Virginia. Her great-grandfather, Samuel Boush, was a leader in Norfolk. Born in nearby Lynnhaven Parish, Boush had purchased a lot in Norfolk by 1696. An Elizabeth River merchant and successful land speculator, he served his community as sheriff, justice of the peace and county lieutenant. He was also a leader in the church (to which he donated a handsome silver chalice engraved with his coat of arms). Boush owned the land on which Norfolk's first ducking stool, used to punish disobedient wives, dishonest merchants, and other criminals, was erected in 1716, "at the upper end of the town, at the end of Major Samuel Boush's wharf, good and substantial." Boush ran both of Norfolk's ferries, a job that netted him an annual salary of about three thousand pounds of tobacco. When Norfolk was officially chartered as a town in 1736, Governor Gooch appointed Boush to be the town's first mayor, but he died before he could take office.[40]

Betsey's grandfather, Samuel Boush II, followed in his father's footsteps. He served as school trustee, alderman, justice of the peace, and county clerk, and he appears to have donated the bricks with which St. Paul's church was built. Savvy about real estate, he laid out lots on Church Street, inaugurating what Thomas Jefferson Wertenbaker has termed "Norfolk's first suburban development." Betsey's father, Samuel Boush III, was a local hero long remembered for saving Norfolk's records from destruction during the Revolution. Betsey's mother, Catherine, was the daughter of merchant Thomas Ballard, who died when she was young.[41]

Not surprisingly, Elizabeth Boush leaves a scarcer documentary trail than her male antecedents. Her embroidery, in fact, is one of the best sources we have for her life. At the bottom of her Sacrifice of Isaac she embroidered a sort of needlework footnote, "Elizth Boush Workd this Piece at E. Gardners 1768 9." That is, Boush studied at the Norfolk school of Elizabeth Gardner. This elder Elizabeth advertised her Norfolk school as early as 1766. At her school, Gardner taught "young Ladies" not only embroidery but also "Dresden lace work, catgut, &c. Shell work, wan work, and artificial flowers." Gardner married Freer Armston on November 25, 1769, and, as best we know, she continued to teach until Loyalist sentiments prompted her return to England during the Revolution.[42]

Additional sources yield a bit more information about Boush. John Durand's portrait of her, painted in 1769, shows her to be fair-skinned, with chocolate-colored hair and a high forehead. In the portrait she holds a garland of flowers that, as Betty Ring has suggested, she may have learned to make at Gardner's school. The *Virginia Gazette* reported her marriage to Champion Travis in 1772; he was a student at the College of William and Mary in 1768, and the Travises lived in Williamsburg after their marriage. Champion Travis had a distinguished record of public service: he served as a justice and a sheriff in James City County and as burgess and member of the Revolutionary conventions in the 1770s. He was one of five naval commissioners appointed by the Virginia Convention in 1776 to build a navy. Champion and Betsey had seven

2.5

In John Durand's portrait (1769), Elizabeth Boush holds a garland of artificial flowers that she may have learned to make at Elizabeth Gardner's school. Attributed to John Durand, portrait of Elizabeth Boush. Private Collection; photograph courtesy of the Museum of Early Southern Decorative Arts at Old Salem.

children. John and Edward are mentioned in their grandfather Boush's will, but then they fall out of the historical record (they do not, for example, appear in their father's will), so they may have died young. Marriage records—which testify not only to people's matrimony but also, simply, to their having survived to adulthood—exist for the other children, Catherine, Betsy, Robert, Samuel, and Susan, the last of whom grew up to marry the Confederate firebrand Edmund Ruffin.[43]

Boush's Sacrifice of Isaac, a silk thread tent stitch on a silk canvas, is an example of the pictorial embroidery some girls made after working a sampler. In the early nineteenth century, when silk pictorial embroideries were more common, taught at girls' schools across the country, they were often regarded as "the crowning achievement" of a girl's education.[44] A piece like the Sacrifice of Isaac required more skill than even elaborate samplers; this was not practice but art, a painting made with a needle and thread.

Boush did not design the needlework herself—she worked it from a pattern.[45] A 1777 book, *The Young Ladies School of Arts* by Hannah Robertson, describes the process of transferring a pattern onto cloth:

> Ladies who have not a genius for drawing or painting, may procure good patterns, and clap them on a pane of glass in the window, placing a sheet of fine paper above it, and with a black lead pencil trace all the outlines which done prick it with a fine needle, then place it on the silk or cloth you intend to draw; powder a little coal, or wood burnt to coal, very fine, put it in a piece of thin cloth, and pounce it thro' the holes of your pattern, and you will have the figure compleat; draw it with gunpowder beat fine and mixed with milk; as blue, &c. is difficult to wash out.[46]

Given the extent to which the patterns girls traced and then sewed onto cloth were the very patterns after which girls were to fashion their lives, the elegant violence of pricking and pouncing is suggestive and unsettling.

Eighteenth-century colonists had relatively easy access to needlework patterns: although patterns did not become readily available in American printer shops and milliners until after the Revolution, earlier in the century colonists could select patterns from the pages of periodicals, they could order them individually from England, or they could purchase needlework pattern books, which had been available in England and on the Continent since 1523. Catalogues of engravings and prints—such as Sayer and Bennett's, which provided Revolutionary-era Virginia with many decorative prints—included patterns that could be used for needlework. According to the *Lady's Magazine*, these patterns enabled a young lady to "display the art with which she

2.6
The needlework scholar Kathleen Staples has recently determined that Egbert van Panderen's engraving, ca. 1600, may have been the source for Elizabeth Boush's needlework of
the sacrifice of Isaac. Collection Rijksmuseum, Amsterdam.

can manage her needle." Elizabeth Gardner, Betsey's teacher, did not, like the Charleston schoolmistress Jane Voyer, advertise that she herself hand-drew patterns and would teach her students to do so as well. Nor is there any clear evidence that Norfolk was home to anyone selling patterns before the 1790s, when Eliza Wallace advertised "All kinds of Lady's Fancy Patterns drawn fit for Working." So when she was teaching Betsey Boush in the 1760s, Gardner almost certainly procured her patterns from England—though it is possible that Betsey selected the Isaac scene from a pattern book owned by her mother. In either case, young Betsey surely had some control over which image she would devote so many months to reproducing. Boush may have been inspired by Samuel Richardson's *Clarissa* to work an embroidery about Abraham and Isaac. One of Virginia girls' favorite novels, *Clarissa* mentions needlework based on the Isaac story: "'Tis true, this pretty little Miss, being a *very* pretty little Miss . . . who always minded her book, and had passed through her sampler-doctrine with high applause; had even stitched out, in gaudy propriety of colours, an Abraham offering up Isaac."[47]

Considered as part of a centuries-long tradition of English girls' and women's embroidery, Genesis 22 seems at first blush an odd subject for Boush to stitch. In the Renaissance era, English girls often stitched biblical scenes featuring women, and strong, heroic women at that: Queen Esther was perhaps the most popular subject, and Judith and Jael, wielding their weapons, appeared frequently as well. But considered in the context of the eighteenth-century South, Boush's choice is not so surprising. The image was not unusual among the visual arts that adorned elite houses in early Virginia. Thomas Jefferson included a painting of the Sacrifice of Isaac among the twenty-six biblical paintings he acquired in France (only three of which depicted Old Testament scenes). Illustrated Bibles included a picture of the same scene: Abraham, ready to sacrifice Isaac, his hand being stayed or his vision arrested by the angel. Mary Byrd owned an engraving of the scene. Nor was Boush the only needleworker to stitch Genesis 22: the South Carolina girl Dorothy Jans worked the scene into her 1752 sampler.[48]

But what did the image of Abraham and Isaac mean to Betsey, and to the many friends and relatives who would have gazed upon her handiwork? Scholars of needlework have read her subject as a political statement: Abraham's sacrifice signaled the political sacrifice made by the Boush family, patriots all.[49] Indeed, that is a fairly standard reading of the image of the Sacrifice of Isaac in pre-Revolutionary and Revolutionary Virginia: Susan R. Stein, the Gilder Curator at Monticello, has suggested that Thomas Jefferson may have found in the painting a symbol of his "political experiences and

2.7
The Tunstall family owned an illustrated Bible; one of the engravings depicted the binding of Isaac. Special Collections, University of Virginia Library.

those of his country. . . . Jefferson and his compatriots, like Abraham, were called upon to test their beliefs and principles, and prevailed."[50]

This political reading is certainly plausible.[51] Yet however politically suggestive the story might have been, revolutionary sacrifice was not, in fact, the dominant theme pre-Revolutionary Virginians found in the story of the binding of Isaac. The story occupied a specific and central place in the early modern Anglican imagination, freighted with meanings that resonated not with the revolutionary political aspirations of colonists determined to break free from England but rather with the psychological and social imperatives of elite slaveowners. To understand the place that Abraham and Isaac occupied in the Anglican Virginians' imagination, we can turn again to the devotional and prescriptive literature that white Anglicans in eighteenth-century Virginia read. The binding of Isaac figures in this prescriptive literature, whose authors read the story as an object lesson in obedience.

Obedience was the moral backbone of the slave system; it was socially, economically, and psychologically imperative for elite white Virginians to understand themselves both as people who owed a debt of obedience and as people to whom a debt of obedience was owed. In Virginia, each person was yoked to others through clear-cut, reciprocal chains of obedience; the obedience owed white gentry by their slaves was inseparable from the obedience white women owed white men, and the obedience that white children owed white parents. Virginia girls occupied their own place in the hierarchy; they learned obedience to parents, and when they graduated from being daughters to being wives, they transferred that obedience to their husbands.[52] This elaborate chain of human obedience was set inside the frame of creaturely obedience—everyone owed obedience to God, and the obedience that low-ranking Virginians owed their social betters was often described or understood as expressing that obedience owed to their Creator.

These bonds of obedience were explicit in Virginia households, which, in the eighteenth century, were characterized by what Allan Kulikoff has termed "domestic patriarchalism." As Kulikoff has argued, demographics made "the practice of domestic patriarchalism difficult" for most of the seventeenth century, but as life expectancy lengthened and the slave trade flourished in the late seventeenth and early eighteenth centuries, families increasingly "took on patriarchal characteristics."[53] In these patriarchal households, obedience and duty were gendered. Virginia was a society in which everyone was subject to hierarchy, in which duty defined the lives of both master and servant, parent and child, man and woman; as scholars such as Kathleen Brown have argued, women's obedience was the ideological and domestic linchpin of the entire domestic and social hierarchy.[54] Many elite white women seemed not to question contemporary teachings about the necessity of their obedience, to wit, the Fairfax County mistress Elizabeth Foote Washington, who wrote in her diary that she owed her marital happiness to her willingness to defer to "Mr. W." on all matters. When faced with a difference of opinion, thought Washington, too many wives insisted on being right: "our mother eve when she transgress'd was told her husband should rule over her,—then how dare any of her daughters to dispute the point." (As we will see in Chapter 3, Washington was also quite clear about the obedience the Washingtons' twelve slaves owed her.)[55] It is in the context not of proto-Revolutionary sacrificial zeal but of a social world in which obedience was a virtue of signal importance and in which girls' obedience had special valence that Boush's Sacrifice of Isaac may best be read.

Children learned their most formative lessons about social and domestic hierarchy at home. Parents and teachers aimed to habituate children to their particular place in social, political, and domestic hierarchy. As Kulikoff has explained, "Parents instructed their children to take their proper place in white society by training them to perform tasks appropriate to their sex. . . . White children in the Chesapeake were trained to take their place in society through repeated instruction by adults. Parents taught their children patriarchal principles at home and sent them to school and church to reinforce the lesson."[56] In teaching their children these "patriarchal principles," parents often invoked Scripture. Contemporary devotional and prescriptive literature used the Sacrifice of Isaac to teach children the importance of obedience. The popular *Plain and Easy Catechism for Children* by Isaac Watts, for example, draws on the story of Abraham and Isaac to explain faithful obedience in simple terms:

> Q 51. How did Abraham further, and most eminently show his obe-
> dience to God?
> A. In readiness to offer up his son Isaac in sacrifice to God's command.

Allestree's *The Ladies Calling* also points to Abraham as a model of obedience to God: "It is not only the interest, but the duty of all that have Families, to keep up the esteem and practice of Religion in them. 'Twas one of the greatest endearments of *Abraham* to God, That he would command his household to keep the way of the Lord." This theme was echoed in Anglican homiletical literature. John Tillotson dramatically imagined the difficult sacrifice God asked of Abraham: "What conflict this good Man had within himself, during those three daies that he was travelling to the Mountain in Moriah; and how his heart was ready to be rent in pieces, betwixt his duty to God, and his affection to his Child; so that every step of this unwelcome and wearisome journey, he did as it were lay violent hands upon himself." All the more reason, concluded Tillotson, that Abraham is to be praised for his "remarkable," deliberate, and "glorious" obedience.[57] In hindsight, the story of the binding of Isaac—with its seamless yoking together of social, familial, and divine order, and its clearly articulated connections between obedience within families and obedience to God—seems almost as though it were written for the slaveowning patriarchs of the early South.

Of course, one wishes for some direct evidence about what Betsey Boush thought about as she stitched her embroidery. Did she identify with Isaac? Or, as a slavemistress in training, did she identify with Abraham, with the one who owed obedience and to whom obedience was owed? Certainly there are biblical examples of daughterly duty, not least the frankly terrifying tale of Jephthah's daughter (Jgs 11:34–40), whose father sacrificed her in fulfillment of a rash vow. (One of Jefferson's three Old Testament paintings depicted this scene, which was also not uncommon in English needlework in the eighteenth century.)[58] Did Boush take a secret delight in seeing that boys, too, were subject to filial and divine duty? Did she ponder God's intervening on Isaac's behalf, but not on behalf of Jephthah's daughter? Did she even think of Jephthah's daughter? There is no evidence to answer these questions, but it is not unreasonable to suppose that Boush was familiar with the story of Jephthah's daughter, and it is intriguing to speculate that she may have drawn a connection between the two stories.[59]

We can speculate further about one meaning that Boush may have found, years after she stitched it, in her needlework of Genesis 22. Hester Chapone, in her popular *Letters on the improvement of the mind addressed to a young lady,* offered a reading of Genesis 22 that surely would have resonated with and offered solace to Virginia gentlewomen. Like other writers, Chapone offered Abraham as an example of the virtue of obedience. It was, Chapone wrote, Abraham's "unshaken faith and obedience, under the severest trial human nature could sustain, [that] obtained such favour in the sight of God, that he . . . promised to make of his posterity a great nation." Using the language of pattern and imitation, Chapone explained that the tale of Abraham's climb up Mount Moriah "is affecting in the highest degree, and sets forth a pattern of unlimited resignation, that every one ought to imitate, in those trials of obedience under temptation, or of acquiescence under afflicting dispensations, which fall to their lot." This was no abstraction for the women of colonial Virginia, but a palpable encouragement, for every Virginia mother knew that she might watch one or more of her children die. "If the almighty arm should be lifted up against" one's child, wrote Chapone, a mother should conform to Abraham's pattern; she must, like Abraham, "be ready to resign [her child], and all that we hold dear, to the divine will."[60] Perhaps, as I suggested earlier, one of Elizabeth's sons died before reaching marriageable age. And perhaps the story that she had stitched into art comforted her.

Conclusions: Girls' Needlework as Religious Practice

In interpreting Anglican girls' religious embroidery, the literary scholars Ann Rosalind Jones and Peter Stallybrass's reading of Renaissance needlework is helpful. Jones and Stallybrass argue that although girls' needlework is, at first blush, all about conformity, it in fact may contain the seeds of resistance to the larger social mores that kept girls docile and still, placed squarely in domestic space, obediently sewing. In their reckoning, embroidery and other work produced by "needlewomen . . . challenge any simple opposition between public and private, the domestic and the political." In the increasing frequency with which Renaissance needlewomen stitched their names into their pieces, Jones and Stallybrass see girls and women asserting their identity. In pieces of needlework that announce both the name of the maker and the name of the girl for whom the embroidery was intended as a gift, Jones and Stallybrass find testimony to connections between women. In the purchase of needlework pattern books, Jones and Stallybrass see that domestic work involved women in the world of commerce. In adapting the patterns they used, girls and women were being creative rather than passive. In stitching scenes with both explicit and implicit political meaning, Renaissance needlewomen were, with their threads, involving themselves in the world of politics. In stitching objects intended for display (and, in the case of cushions and fire screens, use), women at the needle were not indulging "a private habit" but were creating objects that were appreciated by a larger community of friends and relatives. Renaissance needlewomen turned "domestic stitchery into a public practice, recording their engagement with one another and communicating their responses to the larger world of culture, commodities, and politics."[61]

Jones and Stallybrass's focus on the public meanings of women's needlework is a helpful framework for considering the religious work of Virginia girls' needlework, and many of their observations apply to eighteenth-century Virginia. For example, Betsey Boush's declaration that "Elizth Boush Workd this Piece at E. Gardners 1768 9" suggests that she took real pride in her work, and testifies to the relationship between teacher and student. More broadly, Jones and Stallybrass's framing of needlework as public and even political illuminates one important aspect of Virginia girls' embroidery: the production of religiously inflected needlework intended for display transformed girls from students into religious teachers; when their needlework was framed and hung, girls became, tacitly, instructors, having created pictures that taught religious lessons to those who would gaze upon them.

Yet Stallybrass and Jones's focus on the political and emancipatory meanings of early modern needlework should not obscure the extent to which, at least in Anglican Virginia, needlework disciplined girls. The very act of stitching kept girls not just busy but immobile. The religious content of girls' needlework stressed virtue and obedience. Making the needlework was an act of obedience to parents and teachers; the words and images girls sewed conveyed lessons about obedience; and the practice of engaging Scripture through needlework, which had itself become enmeshed with the ideological project of making feminine and docile girls, may have subtly taught Anglican girls to have an obedient relationship, rather than a relationship of contest, with Scripture itself.[62]

The production of religious needlework in eighteenth-century Virginia was synthetically social and religious: in embroidery, ordinary household work, femininity, and Christian practice were literally intertwined. Sewing decorative needlework was one way girls learned how to be Christians—in particular, how to be Christian women in a hierarchical slave society, a society in which white girls' virtue stood for all social order, and in which elite girls both owed and were owed obedience. They were, at once, mastering the skill of sewing, learning how to read the Bible, and beginning to occupy their God-given station. Through religiously inflected needlework, girls stitched themselves both into Scripture's story and into their own particular place in eighteenth-century Virginia society. To stitch scriptural stories about virtue and obedience was to participate in a religious *discipline* in both senses of the term.

CHAPTER THREE

People of the Book
Liturgical Culture and the
Domestic Uses of Prayer Books

Your son William and daughter give their duty to you, & desire when you come
home that you would bring each of them a Prayer Book.
—Elizabeth Cabell to William Cabell, 1739

In May 1739 Elizabeth Burks Cabell wrote a letter to her husband, William, who had been in England for almost four years. The letter was long and chatty: Elizabeth reported that on the Wednesday before Easter, she had developed a serious fever; the children had been sick, too, but none of their slaves; some of the goods William had sent from England were "received safe at home," but the "fine linen, the quilts & the bed ticks are very much damnified," and most of the "china ware" and glass had been broken. She reported on some business, the children's schooling, and some marriages of friends and family. She also included a shopping list—clothing and furniture she wanted for herself and her sister, and a few things she wanted for the children. She asked him to send his daughter Mary "one red silk petticoat, a very good broad silver-laced hat and hat band, one pair of stays, bigness 17 inches around the waist and the hind part of the stays must be 14 in oblong—2 Pr fine shoes—2 Pr fine stocking—one hoop petticoat—1 Pr Bobbs—one pair of clasps,—1 pair of silver buttons set—a very handsome knot & girdle, and a fine cloak & short apron." Just before that long shopping list was another sort of request: "Your son William and daughter give their duty to you, & desire when you come home that you would bring each of them a Prayer Book."[1]

Or was the request for prayer books so different? Were the prayer books Elizabeth Cabell asked her husband to procure simply one more ornament in a long list of accessories? Indeed, Elizabeth Cabell's prose suggests that prayer books were in some ways like silk and silver (they were among the refinements she wanted for her family; they were easily purchased abroad),[2] but, by asking about the prayer books first, followed by, but not precisely part of, the long list of clothing and bibelots, she was also subtly noting their difference. The prayer book cannot be fully assimilated into the other accessories. To be sure, the gentry's prayer books, with their leather bindings and gilt-edged pages, were objects of display and refinement. Yet they were more than that. Prayer books represented a particular theology and practice of prayer; they were a crucial part of the material and devotional culture of Anglicanism. Just as fine stockings and silk petticoats helped define young Mary Cabell as a genteel girl, so owning a prayer book would have helped defined the Cabell children as devout Anglicans. Taking as a jumping off point Edward L. Bond's observation that "the *Book of Common Prayer* was the greatest single influence shaping Virginians' devotional lives,"[3] I shall in this chapter explore the many ways that people like the Cabells used their prayer books: yes, as objects of social differentiation, but also in polemical debate and in pious practice, at church and at home, in ecclesially sanctioned prayers and in extraecclesial courtship rituals, as a text for navigating their relationship with God and as a text for navigating their relationship with their slaves. I will also suggest a shift that occurred over the eighteenth century in Virginia Anglicans' sensibility about prayer. By the last decade of the century, Anglicans' sturdy defenses of liturgical prayer, and their concomitant critiques of more self-reflexive prayers, had softened, and their prayerful sensibilities had begun to encompass both traditional liturgy and the more subjective prayer associated with evangelicalism.

A Brief Word about Books in Eighteenth-Century Virginia

Anglicans in colonial Virginia were people of the book—people of religious books. As David Hall has noted, secular books came in "a very distant second to religious books" in Virginians' purchases. In the libraries of elite gentlemen, religious titles typically outnumbered tomes of classical learning, scientific experimentation, and philosophical musing. When families of humbler means scraped together the money for a book purchase, they almost always chose a Bible or a Book of Common Prayer. The books were treasured, often listed specifically in people's wills, passed down from parent to child at the time of death. William Teague of Accomack County, for example, left the "Common prayerbook," bequeathed to him by his "own revered father," to his elder son; his neighbor George Morris left the "familys bible" to his wife, who in turn passed it on to her grandson. In 1701 Sarah Fitzhugh chose seven of her recently deceased husband's books to keep; the Bible, Allestree's *The*

The BOOK of

COMMON PRAYER,

And ADMINISTRATION of the

SACRAMENTS,

AND OTHER

Rites and Ceremonies of the Church,

According to the USE of

The Church of England :

Together with the

PSALTER or PSALMS

OF

D A V I D,

Pointed as they are to be sung or said in Churches;

And the FORM or MANNER

Of Making, Ordaining, and Confecrating

OF

BISHOPS, PRIESTS, and DEACONS.

O X F O R D,

Printed by *T. Wright* and *W. Gill*, Printers to the UNIVERSITY:
And fold by *R. Baldwin, S. Crowder*, and *J. Coote*, in Paternofter Row, London;
and by *W. Jackfon*, in Oxford. 1769. [Price Five Shillings, *unbound.*]

CUM PRIVILEGIO.

3.1
The Book of Common Prayer was central to Virginia Anglicans' devotional lives. It shaped how they interacted with God, and with one another. The Colonial Williamsburg Foundation.

Whole Duty of Man, a Book of Common Prayer, and four other works of divinity. As Elizabeth Cabell's letter to her husband suggests, parents sometimes gave children a prayer book. Not quite two years after marrying Martha Custis, George Washington bought Bibles and Books of Common Prayer for his six- and eight-year-old stepchildren; the books, bound in Turkey, were to have Patsy's and Jack's names "wrote in gilt Letters on the Inside of the cover." Perhaps receiving one's first Bible or Book of Common Prayer was a rite of passage of sorts, as one graduated from leaning over a parent's shoulder or being dandled on a parent's knee at church to having one's very own prayer book.[4]

The centrality of religious books to Anglican Virginia may be seen in the efforts of one unnamed cleric to procure religious books for the poor of his parish. He took up a collection from wealthy families and ordered Bibles, prayer books, "Treatises on [the] Sacrament, & other Religious Tracts" from England. Such books had great potential to transform people's lives, even to save their souls, said the minister. "Pious Books" could "furnish their Minds with all necessary knowledge, which must be laid as a Foundation for their Practice. By this means they are instructed in the great Points of Christian Belief & acquainted with the several branches of their Duty, which relate to God, their Neighbour, and themselves." Distributing such books to "Families which live without any Sense of Religion, and consequently are running headlong to Hell, may by the Blessing of God, recover them from the Misery that threaten them & make them serious & devout." Indeed, books were crucial to people's religious formation and even salvation, more important than holy conversation or preaching, for "good Tracts . . . mak[e] a much deeper Impression [on] the Mind than either general Admonitions from the Pulpit, or particular Admonitions by Word of Mouth." Contributing funds to this effort, said the cleric, was perhaps the most important form of charity the gentry could offer, and buying religious titles for poor parishioners could turn the gentry metaphorically into both clergy and authors: "This method will make them Preachers of Righteousness, & give them a Share with the Authors of such good Books, in the Reward of such Performances."[5]

But the books could not finally speak for themselves—they could substitute only so far for "particular Admonitions by Word of Mouth." When the books finally arrived from England, the clergyman announced that he would be willing to distribute the books himself, or, if they wished, patrons could collect the books and disburse them to "their Servants & poor Neighbours." Whoever actually handed out the books needed to take care to explain the books to their recipients: "Whosoever distributes this Excellent Charity, this must be insisted upon, that some suitable & good Advice be given at the same tim[e] for it will always be as Bp. Wilson observes 'that the Best of Books, when lightly given, will be lightly valued, & as lightly made use of.'"[6] Books required interpretation by those with education or social power. Those learned elites who distributed the books needed to mitigate the possibility that an unlearned man or woman might heretically misconstrue the books' teachings, or perhaps perceive in those books something that might be unsettling to the social order.

Some of the "poor Neighbours" or "servants" receiving the books would have been illiterate: only about half of white women could read, as could barely two-thirds of white men.[7] This illiteracy rate, coupled with the concern to get religious books into the hands of poor people, suggests that book ownership had a range of meanings, beyond individual pious reading. Most obviously, devotional books may have been read aloud, communally; indeed, as we saw in Chapter 2, devotional writers themselves encouraged this practice. Second, religious books may have functioned as talismans; the sanctity or power of a religious book was so great that simply owning one had value, even if the owner could not read it. Third, book ownership had value as a social signal.

Yet even if religious books had value when they were not read, the authors of such books, and many of their owners, understood that they were intended to be read—indeed, read in a particular way. When discussing religious books with their families, Virginia fathers told their children not merely to read but to internalize the text as though the words were food. In a 1762 letter to his son, the Rev. Mr. Maury expressed pleasure that James Jr. had requested a new shipment of books, and he urged his son to "reflect, & remark on, & digest what you read." He cautioned James Jr. against devoting so much time to reading the *Iliad* that he neglected Scripture: "Dear James among other books make it a rule each day of your life . . . to read, mark & digest some portion of those inspired volumes the contents of which are able to make men wise unto salvation; which is the most useful, important and desirable wisdom."[8] In *A Deed of Gift to My Dear Son*, the Virginia layman John Page urged his son to "diligently read, steadfastly believe, and obediently conform" to the writings of Scripture: "Eat, and eat daily of this heavenly manna," he instructed, "that your hunger may be satisfied, and your soul nourished to eternal life."[9] When fathers like Maury and Page urged their sons to digest Scripture, they hoped that the boys would be filled with and formed by, not merely informed by, the Bible. Maury and Page were advocating what the scholar Paul J. Griffiths has termed, simply, "religious reading"—that is, reading that is undertaken "with the goal of incorporating what I read, of writing it upon the pages of my memory," not just cognitively remembering the words one reads but taking them into one's person, so that the reader is reshaped and reformed by reading.[10] Religious books, then, were not only those that contained religious content; they were those books whose content practitioners aimed to absorb and internalize through devotional practices like study, prayer and transcription. Evidence suggests that men and women in Virginia did indeed actively engage with their religious books. One woman, for example, found her books too large to "carry about me," so she transcribed excerpts into "some small manuscripts that I can conveniently carry in my pocket to peruse occasionally,—which I have receiv'd great comfort from."[11]

Virginia Anglicans were not unique in their dedication to religious books and the devotions of the word those books made possible. Anglican practice bore the marks of Europe's sixteenth- and seventeenth-century devotional revival. Both Catholic and Protestant reformers emphasized personal piety, and laity increasingly sought experiences of God that were less directly mediated by clergy and the church. Catholics published countless devotional manuals and encouraged congregants to commit themselves to a regimen of private prayer and veneration of saints. In the 1600s Puritans and Anglicans strove both to catch up with the Catholics and to distinguish their communities' devotional practices from those of Rome and each other.[12] The most distinctive feature of Anglican devotions of the word was the centrality of the Book of Common Prayer, a book that figured significantly in both Virginians' actual practice of prayer and in their polemics about prayer.[13]

Prayer Books in Polemics

Liturgical prayer had been central to corporate Christian worship since at least the fifth century, and English people's prayers had long been shaped by prayer books.[14] Even before the Reformation—before the Book of Common Prayer was written—many English laypeople turned to books, specifically books of hours, to structure their prayer lives.[15] Books of hours were modified versions of the prayer books monks used, and as the Book of Common Prayer would later connect to the church's liturgy people who lived far from churches (and Virginians to England), medieval books of hours connected laity to the important work of monastic praying. But during the English Reformation, liturgical prayer came under assault by dissenters, who thought prayer should be spontaneous and heartfelt. In the seventeenth century, a crucial flash point between Anglicans and nonconformists in England was the appropriate mode of praying: liturgical or free-form?

Puritan advocates of extemporaneous prayer argued that to read a set liturgy was not to pray but to perform hypocritically; the practice of liturgical prayer, in the Puritan view, was an invitation not to genuine piety but to the alarming and duplicitous separation of one's words from one's affections. As Lori Branch has argued, these nonconformists were articulating a crisis of representation: their defense of free prayer was forged in the moment when words like *ceremony* and *ritual* took on, for the first time, the connotation of hollowness and artifice. Increasingly, Puritans, Quakers, and other dissenting Protestants dismissed liturgical prayer as "merely" performative, artificial, boring, and repetitious, whereas free-form prayer was authentic and bespoke the heart's true desire. Indeed, free-form prayer was understood both to foster and to represent an undivided subject: the person at prayer who spoke only those words that he meant, who could never say something that contradicted his feelings.[16]

At stake here was a new conception of self-knowledge and self-fashioning. Advocates of extemporaneous prayer privileged an interiority that was inseparable from a Puritan theology that demanded self-scrutiny for marks of sin and grace. Their spontaneous prayer articulated a kind of inwardness, a transparency of subject, and an emerging subjectivity that have come to be seen as hallmarks of the modern self. In this free-form praying, emotion took on a new importance, since it was sensible emotion that authenticated the praying heart, and with that the very self. In what we might call a sacramentality of spontaneity, emotion became the outward sign of the inward grace of which the words of prayer partook.[17]

In the face of this critique, Anglican churchmen in England vigorously defended liturgical prayer. Four arguments dominated their defense of liturgy. First, they noted that Jews, including Jesus himself, had prayed with set forms. Second, they argued that liturgical prayer helped unify the church. Third, they worried that extemporaneous prayer, in which unlettered men and women simply spoke whatever came into their minds at the moment, opened the way to heresy. Far better for ordinary people to pray those prayers, crafted by people with more theological learning, that were sure to express orthodox views about God and man. These churchmen, in other words, were not foremost interested in whether prayer truthfully articulated what was in the heart of the person praying; they were more concerned that prayer articulate the truth about the nature of God, and man's relationship to him. Anglican divines were also concerned about the congruence between people's prayers and their actions— in other words, Anglicans wanted prayer to be a truthful indicator of how people lived. Prayer was judged hypocritical not if it failed to reflect the feelings of the person praying but if it failed to be reflected in the actions of the person who prayed. Finally, defenders of liturgy, most notably the Anglican theologian Richard Hooker, understood that there was indeed some sense of interiority in liturgical prayer. The liturgy of the prayer book guided the pious man or woman in approaching God, day in and day out, without treading on the terrain of emotional subjectivity; nonetheless, on Hooker's account, the true self was realized through corporate, liturgical prayer. The prayer book ordered and encouraged the performance of prayer, and in so doing it slowly transformed the person who prayed.[18]

Although debates about liturgy and spontaneous prayer arose first in England, where the Book of Common Prayer was written and where Puritan objections to it were first and most fiercely articulated, the debate continued in Virginia.[19] By midcentury, Presbyterians, Baptists, and Methodists were beginning to reshape Virginia's religious landscape. They brought with them ejaculatory prayer, self-styled as spontaneous, and they attacked Anglican liturgical prayer in terms similar to those articulated by English dissenters a century before. Dissenting preachers like Samuel Davies warned against prayer that proceeded merely from "your tongue," and not from "the bottom of your hearts." This "thoughtless, unmeaning prayer" was akin to blasphemy, and would bring down punishment, not blessing, on those who uttered it.[20]

Virginia Anglicans, in turn, lambasted evangelicals' decidedly public, passionately embodied, and apparently impulsive bursts of praise and supplication: these were not prayers, but rather "Tumults and Distractions . . . Discords & Confusions." The unseemly, unruly ejaculations by "a newfangled set of Methodist Enthusiasts" and other evangelical dissenters were sharply at odds with the restrained, "private Way of praying in our Closets" commanded by Jesus. Commissary James Blair devoted several sermons to the explication and defense of liturgical prayer. In these sermons, he both defended liturgy and criticized the prayers of nonconformists. He aimed to establish "the Lawfulness and Usefulness of Set Forms of Prayer." Jesus gave a set prayer—the Lord's Prayer—to "his weak Disciples, to assist them, till the Descent of the Holy Ghost, when it is to be supposed they would learn to walk alone, without Leading-strings, and to frame Prayers of their own, fitted for all Occasions." Despite the Holy Spirit's guidance, "Set Forms" remained appropriate for "Devotion at this Day," because "the Generality of Christians [today] . . . want as much Assistance in their Devotions now, as our Saviour's Disciples did then."[21]

Blair echoed some of the English churchmen's specific defenses of "set forms." First, given the "difficulty of forming and framing our Devotions aright . . . well composed Forms of Devotion are useful." Because people were "ignorant of . . . the Nature of God," it was better to pray "well composed Forms of Devotion" than to make up your own. Second, there was a long precedent of liturgical praying: "the Jewish Church, in our Saviour's Days, used several Set Forms of Devotion," and, indeed, Scripture was shot through with examples of people making "Repetition of the same Words and petitions in Prayer." Furthermore, for centuries, most churches had followed Scripture's precedent: "not only the Romish, but the Greek and the Reformed churches too, every one of them have their set forms."[22]

While Blair saw praying "set forms" as something that Anglicans had in common with those other churches, he also understood that liturgy distinguished Anglican devotional life from newfangled sects, sects whose leaders attacked Anglican liturgical prayer as formulaic and mindless. Though dissenters charged that liturgical praying affected a hypocritical separation of words and affections, it was, Blair argued, the dissenters who were hypocrites. Puritans, for example, railed against liturgical prayer, but it was they who were puffed up pridefully—to disastrous political consequence: "Time has been, and that in the Memory of some yet living, when a Sett of Hypocrites by their long Prayers and other acted Devotions, came not only to impose upon Widows and the more simple Sort, but upon a whole Nation, till they destroyed the King and Country by a Civil War; and seated themselves in the chief Seats of Government, and glutted their Pride, Ambition, Covetousness and Cruelty to the uttermost." Blair also attacked the dissenters more nearly in his midst, especially Quakers. The centuries-long precedent of liturgical prayer "makes it so much the stranger, that the Presbyterians, Independents, Anabaptists, and Quakers, those late sects among us, should muster up This as an Objection against the Church of *England,* that she has prescribed a Form of Common Prayer." Quakers and others who prayed with "unusual affected Gestures, Faces and Grimaces; as Pretences to a more sublime and elevated Sort of Devotion," were clearly contravening Christ's injunctions to pray and fast in private, not advertising their piety abroad. Whether undertaken at home or in church, decorous Anglican prayer stood in marked contrast to the "undiscreet Acts of publick Devotion, in which Men affect a Singularity and draw the Eyes of Spectators upon them. Such as . . . the enthusiastical extemporary Prayers and Sermons of Monks and Quakers in the Streets or other publick Places, where Men are met about their lawful Business or Recreations."[23]

Nor did Blair accept dissenters' charges that Anglicans were uninterested in the relationship between a person's words and his affections. Blair insisted that "Prayer is not a drawing near to God with the Lips, but with the Heart." When Jesus, in Matthew 6:7, cautioned his followers against making "vain repetitions" in prayer, he was not condemning praying with set forms. Rather, he was condemning praying with a stony heart. It is not "unlawful to make a Repetition of the same Words and Petitions in Prayer, so it be done from a Spirit of Devotion." Thus Anglicans were to take "great Care" that prayer, "the Language of the Heart to God," not be "turned to *A drawing near to God with the Lips, while the Heart is far from him;* that is, to an outward Formality, instead of an inward Devotion." If Blair was concerned with the alignment between words and feelings, he also wanted people's prayers to be aligned with their actions. Christians must avoid "pronounc[ing] the Prayers with our Mouths," without "trouble[ing] ourselves to make good the meaning of them" in their lives.[24]

In the Anglican frame, having prayers by habit or rote was not something to be avoided; it was something to be aspired to, for it indicated not that the person praying was bored or simply engaging in formulaic recitation but that he had come to own and absorb the prayers. When a Mr. Cole, who served as a clerk or lay liturgist of St. Mark's parish in Culpeper County, died, the clergyman who preached his funeral sermon approvingly noted Cole's command of the psalter. Leading the congregational recitation of Psalms was one of the clerk's duties, and in describing Cole's piety and service, Parson John Thompson recalled, "As for ye Book of Psalms he had it mostly by Rote, it was his great Delight to meditate therein Day & Night."[25] Here, Thompson's declaration that Cole prayed by "Rote" was high praise—it suggested not that Cole was merely reciting out of meaningless habit but that he had ingested and internalized the Psalter.

The propriety of prayer-book prayer was, then, central to Virginians' apologetics of prayer. Whether they knew it or not, Anglicans in England and Virginia were entering contested terrain every time they opened a prayer book. The prayer book distinguished Anglican churchmen from dissenters, and the books themselves symbolized the whole debate between Anglicans and dissenters about how best to pray. Yet as we will see later in this chapter, when we consider a prayer that Maria Carter copied into her commonplace book and the practices of prayer that Elizabeth Foote Washington described in her diary, Anglican practitioners did not always hew to Anglican apologetics of liturgical prayer. In the end, the dichotomy between "ritualistic" Anglican and "spontaneous" evangelical prayer would become far less clear as individual people's performance of prayer began to mix the two.

Prayer Books in Practice

How, when, and where did people actually use their prayer books? Perhaps most obviously, people used prayer books in corporate worship on Sundays. Occasionally, because parishes were so large, Sunday corporate worship happened in people's houses. The Rev. Alexander Forbes described "Preach[ing] at a private house on Sunday" in 1724. The vestry of Fredericksville parish paid Robert Barrett to preach eight sermons a year in private homes. The vestry of Augusta parish insisted that the rector would have to preach in the Court House or "in People's Houses of the Same Persuasion in different Quarters of the Parrish as shall be most Convenient."[26] More often, Sabbath worship happened in church buildings. Wherever the location, individuals who owned prayer books brought them to corporate worship. There a parson or clerk led the congregation in the recitation of the liturgy, and men, women, and children would follow the liturgy in their prayer books. Jesse Lee, the Anglican-turned-Methodist who nonetheless fondly recalled his childhood catechetical training, "when summoned to church on Sunday, . . . would seat himself in his pew, with his prayer book in his hand, and repeat the service in a manner which did credit to one of his age."[27] Because prayer books were used in corporate worship, people sometimes purchased them bound with the Tate and Brady metrical psalter, which was used in church: when William Dawson ordered Bibles "for the use of my Parishioners" from England, he specified "the New Version of the Psalms by Brady and Tate bound up with the Common Prayer Books," and the "red Morocco" prayer book George Washington purchased in 1771 was bound with the same.[28] That all church-goers did not use their prayer books as their parsons hoped is evident from homiletical complaint: in a sermon preached in 1769 and 1770, Parson Charles Clay lambasted those members of his congregation who daydreamed during church, would not "be Caught with a prayer Book in their Hands there," "And while the Psalms for ye Day are Reading, instead of having a book & answering in turn; are playing with their Snuff Box; dancing their foot with one leg across the other for amusement; or twirling their Hat about."[29]

If people did not always apply themselves to their prayer books in church, the books had another function: display. The gentry's prayer books were lovely, and not inexpensive; they were "bound in the most elegant manner," "in *Turkey* and gilt."[30] The historian Albert Zambone has noted that the leather-bound prayer books that gentry owned were trim enough to carry, and ornate enough to merit display. Thus, in Zambone's apt observation, Rhys Isaac's influential description of gentry trooping en masse up the aisle for Sunday services "should be amended to include gilt-edged prayer books held by the side or tucked under a gentlemanly arm. In this way the liturgy of the [Book of Common Prayer] was not merely something that fused a congregation together; in its printed and visible form, it led to social and economic distinction and differentiation. Like so many things in Virginia Anglicanism, it was double-edged, capable of cutting in two directions."[31] In this way, the prayer books that Elizabeth Cabell wanted for her children were not wholly different from the ear bobs and hatbands she also hoped to procure. Though prayer books could not be reduced to accessories, when carried into church, books with lovely leather bindings did bespeak wealth, and they cast an aura of devoted religiosity.

Laypeople opened their Books of Common Prayer in church once a week. They opened them at home more often. At least they were supposed to. As the historian Edward L. Bond has noted, "Unlike English divines who treated private devotions as a form of preparation for the church's public worship, ministers in Virginia reverse this sequence, placing greater emphasis on private devotions than on public and communal prayer."[32] And those ministers were, predictably, unsatisfied with the frequency with which parishioners prayed at home. Clergy complained that "this Duty . . . is very much neglected."[33]

We don't know exactly how widespread household prayer was, but enough shreds of evidence exist to indicate that some gentry took private and family prayer seriously. In the devotional manual he wrote for his son, the layman John Page encouraged prayer in church and at home, and he hoped his son would pray at home at least twice a day, in the morning and the evening. Page distinguished between—and commended—two types of household prayer. First, he noted that it was the "duty" of "the master of the family" to make sure that his wife, children, and "servants" prayed. These family prayers should follow the Book of Common Prayer, for the paterfamilias "cannot make a better choice than of the church prayers." In addition to praying with his family, Page wanted his son to engage in "private prayer," "that which is used by a man apart from all others."[34]

Testimonies to women's prayerful practices dot the reminiscences of their children and grandchildren. Ann Mason led her children in bedtime prayer: "one or two at a time," recalled her son John; the children would "kneel down before her sitting, put our hands on her lap, and say our prayers every night before we went to bed." Eleanor Parke Custis Lewis recalled that her grandmother, Martha Custis Washington, "never omitted her private devotions." In 1810 Edmund Randolph recalled the piety of his dead wife, Elizabeth Nicholas

3.2
This Book of Common Prayer, in an eighteenth-century Williamsburg binding, was owned by Catherine Blaikley. Colonial Williamsburg Foundation.

Randolph, noting specifically that "in her closet prayer was uni[formly?] addressed to the throne of mercy."[35] That some of these recollections were set down on paper long after the women's deaths does not invalidate them, but John Mason, Eleanor Lewis, and Edmund Randolph were writing in the early and mid-nineteenth century, and their recollections may have been colored by nineteenth-century assumptions about the normativity of feminine piety.

The most detailed and intriguing record of the actual devotional practices of a Virginia Anglican is found in the early diary of the wealthy and politically prominent William Byrd. Byrd's devotions of the word included morning reading and study of Scripture (March 19, 1710: "I rose at 6 o'clock and read the Psalms and four chapters in the Greek Testament"). What did Byrd's engagement with Scripture entail? What were the specific practices through which Scripture came to engage Byrd's imagination? One, no doubt, was regularly hearing Scripture read aloud in church. During an ordinary Sunday morning church service, Byrd would have heard readings from the Old Testament and the New Testament, and he would have prayed the day's appointed psalms. Furthermore, vast quantities of Scripture were interwoven into the liturgy itself—passages from the Gospel of Luke were recited as prayers during the morning and evening offices, for example. Beyond encountering the Bible through the liturgy, Byrd adopted additional devotional practices that helped him apprehend Scripture. For example, he rewrote biblical scenes. Extant is his retelling of the end of Deuteronomy and the beginning of Joshua, recounting Moses' death and Joshua's triumphal entry into the Promised Land. On December 23, 1711, Byrd also copied "a chronology of the Bible which the Governor lent me." In August 1710 his devotional exercises included translating "Solomon's Song" from Hebrew.[36]

Byrd, the proud owner of a massive library, read devotional texts as well. For example, he read his "black morocco, gilt and blind tooled" copy of Allestree's *The Whole Duty of Man* in its entirety at least twice. Few of his books survive, but those that do reveal Byrd's active engagement with his devotional reading. In his copy of Jeremy Taylor's *The Worthy Communicant,* Byrd inscribed a nineteen-line prayer, a modified version of Psalm 51. That psalm figured in the Ash Wednesday liturgy, and we can surmise that Byrd may have read *The Worthy Communicant* during Lent, as part of penitential preparation for receiving communion in church on Easter. One of Byrd's favorite authors was John Tillotson. Byrd often read Tillotson's sermons, and sometimes his wife read one of Tillotson's sermons to him. (Perhaps the most remarkable instance occurred on July 30, 1710: "I read a sermon in Dr. Tillotson and then took a little [nap]. I ate fish for dinner. In the afternoon my wife and I had a little quarrel which I reconciled with a flourish. Then she read a sermon in Dr. Tillotson to me. It is to be observed that the flourish was performed on the billiard table.") Tillotson's rational and moralistic Latitudinarianism did not mean his work was unmoving. Byrd seems to have been emotionally affected by his reading of Tillotson, and occasionally, reading Tillotson moved Byrd to a place of reverence, repentance, or worship. On May 7, 1710, for example, Byrd rose at 6, read two chapters in the Old

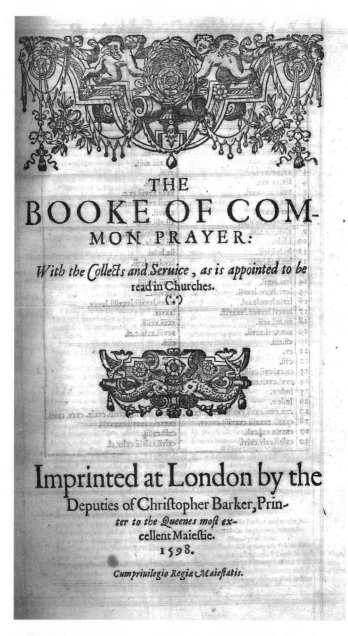

THE
BOOKE OF COM-
MON PRAYER:

*With the Colle*ɛ̃*ts and Seruice , as is appointed to be*
read in Churches.
(.·.)

Imprinted at London by the
Deputies of Chriſtopher Barker, Prin-
ter to the Queenes moſt ex-
cellent Maieſtie.
1598.

Cumpriuilegio Regiæ Maieſtatis.

3·3
This leather-bound, 1598 folio was one of four Books of Common Prayer
that William Byrd owned. Special Collections Research Center, Earl
Gregg Swem Library, College of William and Mary.

Testament and two in the New Testament, prayed, breakfasted on milk, exercised, and then "read a sermon of Dr. Tillotson's which affected me very much and made me shed tears of repentance."[37]

These varied devotions of the word, from translating Scripture to reading sermons, hung on the skeleton of morning and evening prayer. Byrd strove to pray each morning, sometimes noting in his diary that he had prayed "devoutly," "with devotion," or "shortly," and also recording when guests or ill health prevented his praying.[38] In the evening he prayed too, and in the early years of his diary, he typically concluded his diary entries with a short mantra: "I said my prayers. I had good thoughts, good health, and good humor, thanks be to God Almighty." Byrd's morning and evening prayers undoubtedly followed the orders for morning and evening prayer in the Book of Common Prayer. The liturgies for morning and evening prayer included a confession, psalms, the Lord's Prayer, the Creed, and various canticles and prayers of praise and intercession. Morning Prayer and Evening Prayer were quite similar to each other, although some of the prayers culled from Scripture varied; Morning Prayer included the Benedictus ("Blessed be the Lord God of Israel: for he hath visited and redeemed his people," from Luke 1), whereas Evening Prayer included the Magnificat ("My soul doth magnify the Lord," also from Luke 1) and the Nunc Dimitis ("Lord, now lettest thou thy servant depart in peace," from Luke 2). These services took Byrd and other practitioners through a variety of prayerful postures, as summarized by Pastor James Maury, who once preached that prayer "comprehend[s] several Particulars . . . acknowledging our Sins & Unworthiness to God, is called Confession; requesting of him such Things, as are requisite for our Bodies or Souls, is called Petition or Supplication; beseeching him to remove an Evils, under which we labour, or to avert those we apprehend, is Deprecation; soliciting Blessings for others is Intercession; admiring and extolling his glorious Perfections, is Praise; & gratefully declaring our Sense of his Goodness & Love towards ourselves or others is Thanksgiving."[39]

Getting beyond the words of the prayer book to the subjective experience of Byrd and other practitioners is difficult. It is difficult in part because the dissenters' critiques largely won the day, so twenty-first-century scholars often approach historical inquiry into prayer with assumptions that reflect the dissenters' view of what constitutes authenticity and, more specifically, authentic prayer: that truth comes from within, that it moves from the heart to the mouth. Thus it is hard for us to understand liturgical prayer—the apprehension of someone else's words, which somehow permeate our consciousness and become the truest expression of our beliefs and sentiments. Furthermore, it is hard to get inside eighteenth-century liturgical prayer because although the books that shaped Virginians' devotions provide good evidence of the words Virginians said to their maker, they do not reveal much about the experiences people had while praying. We can read the words that people like Byrd uttered, but we have little access to what he thought and felt about those words. As Eamon Duffy has written, "Where everyone who prayed at all used the same words, it is hard to isolate what was particular in any individual's appropriation of them."[40]

One way to dig more deeply into the liturgical prayer of Anglican Virginia is to examine contemporary apologies for liturgical prayer, which make clear what liturgical prayer was supposed to accomplish. In his study of the Anglican Church in seventeenth-century Virginia, Edward Bond helpfully recovers what Anglicans thought liturgy was supposed to do:

> The set liturgies of the *Book of Common Prayer were intended* to work a gradual transformation in the lives of individuals. . . . Divine worship following the rites of the prayer book *was intended* to grasp an individual's affections, thereby swaying the person toward living a holy life. . . . *In theory,* the set liturgies in the *Book of Common Prayer* were to help form the souls of Anglican Virginians. . . . These rites *attempted* to transform people. . . . Over time, active participation in the prayer life of the established church *might* lead people to practice self-discipline for the sake of salvation, thus providing evidence of the internal reorientation of the heart which had occurred as a result of repentance.[41]

Liturgical prayer was intended to do all this—can we say anything about what it actually did?

I think we can suggest at least three things. First of all, we can identify liturgical prayer's socially and ecclesially disciplinary quality. In praying from the prayer book, people like Byrd, though praying alone, were not practicing a private faith; rather, their household devotions partook of the corporate practices of the church. As Anthony Sparrow, a seventeenth-century bishop of Norwich, wrote: "Let every man say the Office in private by himself. Let every Layman say this Morn and Even office . . . and let him know that when he prays this alone he prays with company, because he prays in the church's communion, the Common prayer."[42] Liturgical prayer, in other words, worked at the level of social replication. Byrd was praying the same liturgy as other prayerful Anglicans in Virginia, in England, and elsewhere. This common praying knitted people into an imagined community of sorts. Liturgical prayer at home helped people over far-flung spaces know that they belonged to the same church.

Second, praying the liturgy fostered a sense of the rightness of order. Liturgy, after all, is about order—as Timothy Rosendale has observed, "liturgical form itself is an order-based discursive mode, restricting improvisation and randomness by imposing a set formulae of religious expression on those under its aegis." In this way, liturgy spoke to the imaginations of people like Byrd, who were economically, socially, and theologically invested in maintaining a fairly rigid hierarchical social order. Byrd's praying from the Book of Common Prayer bound him to specific orders, such as (in praying prayers for the Crown and authorized by the Crown) the state. Furthermore, the prayer book—which, not incidentally, named its daily liturgies "The Order for Morning Prayer" and "The Order for Evening Prayer"—also asserted the rightness of order generally. As Rosendale has argued, the Book of Common Prayer "established hierarchical order as the proper and definitive context for individual identity and conduct." At the same time, built into the logic of this liturgy, and thrown into especially stark relief in the case of individual prayer at home, was the principle that the individual, through proper application to the liturgical orders, could have direct contact with the divine without clerical mediation. Thus Rosendale finds in the Book of Common Prayer a "perpetual negotiation" between external, hierarchical order, and interiority.[43]

As is well known, Byrd was a man who very much liked routine and order. In the view of Kenneth Lockridge, Byrd's biographer, Byrd inhabited his daily routine—waking early, studying Hebrew and Greek texts, praying, eating breakfast, exercising, writing letters or working on his accounts, studying Latin, taking midday dinner, tending to business affairs, overseeing his plantations, walking with his wife, praying again—"with appalling regularity." Byrd's diary was "obsessive in the set pattern of each day, which disturbed him when it was disturbed and was disturbed usually only when he was most disturbed."[44] Whether or not Byrd's penchant for order and repetition is appalling, it should not be a surprise that a man who so liked order and routine would make a habit of liturgical prayer. Indeed, his recourse to liturgical order was part of his larger program of self-discipline. To pray regularly and routinely was to embark on an act of self-discipline in which the dangerous, even sinful self was mastered and controlled; at the same time, the liturgy gave Byrd a mechanism for dealing with that sinful self's periodic interruptions of his efforts at self-regulation, as when Byrd prayed for forgiveness after masturbating or committing adultery.[45] The "appallingly" and "obsessively" ordered Byrd who emerges from the pages of his diary is inseparable from these liturgical practices.

Third, we can see glimpses of practitioners' subjective engagement with and appropriation of liturgical prayer. For example, although Byrd does not write in much detail about his own experience of prayer, he does, as observed above, occasionally note that he prayed "devoutly" or "shortly." This suggests at minimum that Byrd was self-consciously engaged with the liturgy. He had some model in his mind for what appropriately pious prayer looked like, and he measured himself against that model. Additionally, although at times the liturgies that Byrd and others prayed surely bore no direct relationship to their affections or emotions, at other times the words of the liturgy expressed prayerful people's deepest thoughts, values, and sentiments. For example, when Byrd's son Parke died on June 3, 1710, and Byrd was "Very sensible of the loss," he responded with words from Job: "God gives and God takes away; blessed be the name of God." The same verse opens the Anglican funeral liturgy (although Byrd modified them slightly: he would have usually heard, at funerals, "The Lord gave and the Lord hath taken away.")[46] At a time of great anxiety and stress, Byrd turned to a liturgical formulation. Here Byrd illustrates James Blair's argument that liturgy could be "the Language of the Heart to God." But this did not happen on the dissenters' terms—terms in which a person's affections preceded prayer. Rather liturgical prayer ordered Byrd's religious affections according to the prescribed sensibilities of Anglican devotion. Liturgical prayer provided a language that shaped his grief, and made it speakable.

Byrd's response with the words of Job provides one example of liturgical appropriation. Another intriguing example comes from the commonplace book that the young lady Maria Carter of Cleve kept in 1763. On the last page of her commonplace book, she copied the following:

A PRAYER.
Almighty God, the Fountain of all wisdom, who knowest my Necessities before I ask, and my Ignorance in asking; I beseech thee to have Compassion upon my Infirmities, and those things which for my Unworthiness I dare not, and for my Blindness I cannot ask, vouchsafe to give Me for the Worthiness of thy Son Jesus Christ, my Lord & Saviour. amen.[47]

This prayer comes from the Book of Common Prayer; it is one of the collects from the Order for Holy Communion. But Carter did not simply transcribe the prayer. She modified it. In the prayer book, the prayer, which is meant to be uttered by the entire congregation just before they come together to receive communion, is quite sensibly cast in the first-person plural. Carter recast the prayer in the singular, absorbing the liturgical *we* into her personal *I* (in so doing, she personalized not only the prayer, but also the prayer's narrative about personal unworthiness). She made the prayer book's public, performative language her own.

The Book of Common Prayer beyond the Bounds of Ecclesial Practice

John Page's turning to the Book of Common Prayer to guide his family devotions, William Byrd's praying Morning Prayer, and Maria Carter's transcribing a prayer into her commonplace book—these all represent ordinary, ecclesially sanctioned household uses of the prayer book. In early Virginia, prayer books could also be drawn into rituals that historians sometimes categorize as "magical" or "superstitious"—those extraecclesial rites that coexisted with the Christian practices the church smiled upon.[48] The use of the prayer book in extraecclesial rites provides another sort of evidence of the importance of the prayer book in the religious culture of Anglican Virginia, for the books people use in "superstitious" practices like biblomancy and divination are only those books that overflow with meaning and cultural power—books that, in David Cressy's formulation, have "totemic" significance.[49]

Byrd himself supplies an example of this extraliturgical use of a prayer book. On September 28, 1720, Byrd, recently back from several years of living in London, went to visit his friends the Carters at Corotoman on the Rappahannock River. There he saw Anne Carter, "a very agreeable girl." Byrd was searching for a wife (his first wife, Lucy Parke Byrd, had died in 1716), and Anne quickly became the object of Byrd's affection. A few weeks later, after chatting with Anne at a ball, Byrd returned home and "committed uncleanness." The next day, at another fete, Byrd asked Anne to dance, and she spurned him. Carter and Byrd's circle, of course, knew of Byrd's pursuit, and one night, after supper, Byrd's cousin Hannah Ludwell and another girl indulged a bit of enchantment meant to bring Byrd luck in his wooing: they "put a drawn sword and common prayer book open at the matrimony on [Byrd's] head." Byrd hoped the ritual would help him win Anne. Instead, it just prompted him to dream of her that night. She married Byrd's neighbor Benjamin Harrison in 1722.[50]

What exactly was going on in this parlor game? Love magic was commonplace in early modern England and Europe. Although I have found no precise precedent for Hannah Ludwell's ritual, each of four components of the ritual—the women who worked the ritual, the head, the sword, and the book—has an antecedent. First, it is noteworthy that the ritual was performed —and presumably suggested—by a woman. In medieval and early modern

Europe, people believed that women were more likely to practice love magic than men. This association of women with love magic might have reflected misogynistic fears of the ways women could control men by withholding or dispensing sex and love. Alternatively, the association of women and love magic may stem from women's relative powerlessness; spells and charms were indeed often the only tools available to women who wanted to shape their own nuptial fates.[51]

The head was central in a variety of English love charms, which involved placing something (daisy root, yarrow) under one's pillow and sleeping on it— the assumption being that the spell would work only if the magical object was placed close to the participant's head.[52] The head also figured significantly in many African rituals, and it is intriguing to speculate about whether Hannah Ludwell's ritual resonated with or was influenced by surviving African rituals that she may have observed among enslaved Virginians. African practitioners of ritual magic saw the head as a major power center; thus it was often the site of magical and superstitious acts, especially love spells. For example, a man might wear a lock of his intended's hair in his hat, linking the two individuals' power centers. Ethnographers have noted the persistence of this practice among black Southerners through the early twentieth century.[53]

The meaning of the sword is somewhat opaque. Swords figure as powerful objects in various rituals; for example, soldiers who used swords in battle sometimes attributed magical power to them. Occasionally, the sword appears in love divination. In some English villages, a man seeking to know the identity of his future wife could go to a churchyard at midnight and walk three or nine times around the church while holding a drawn sword. Then he would "thrust [the] sword into a keyhole," and say "Here is the sword, but where is the sheath?" The woman he would one day marry would then appear. Women could practice a similar ritual, instead saying, in biologically appropriate idiom, "Here is the sheath, but where is the sword?"[54] Heads and swords also came together in the English marriage custom of making the first incision into one's wedding cake with a sword, and, in some cases, cutting the cake over the head of the bride as she knelt down.[55] All in all, aside from the obvious phallic symbolism, it is difficult to determine the precise meaning of the sword in Hannah Ludwell and William Byrd's ritual. Perhaps it is enough to say that Byrd hoped to cut through or pierce Anne Carter's resistance to him.

What is clearer than the meaning of the sword in Hannah Ludwell's ritual is the freestanding power of the prayer book. From one vantage point, the use of the prayer book as an object of enchantment is not surprising. As Robert Scribner has argued, after the Protestant Reformation eliminated many "superstitious" rituals, Protestants, determined to find enchantment somewhere, attributed magical power to the holy word and any books containing it. Indeed, in the wake of Reformation—which did away with saints' relics, described the consecrated host in decidedly unmagical terms, and generally purged religious objects imbued with special power—books were the only especially powerful objects to which the laity had access. In Scribner's phrase, these books became "a potent form of the word of God materialized in the secular world." In New England and Europe, books—specifically, Bibles—figured in countless rituals of enchantment. Bibles placed on heads were thought to help children sleep. Fanning a sick person's face with the pages of a Bible was believed to restore health. Bibles (and sharp metal objects with points—pins, silver knives) also figured in romantic divination. Young men or women eager to learn the identity of a future spouse could jab a specific place in the Bible: "Read the third verse, 17th chapter of the book of Job after supper, and on going to bed, put the Bible under your pillow with the verse you have read thrust through with a pin, and you will call up the image of your future mate." From Reformation Germany to Anglican England to Puritan New England, it was precisely the esteem and reverence people felt for Scripture that prompted them to use the Bible in these "irregular" ways.[56]

In light of all this biblical divination, what is striking about the ritual in Hannah Ludwell's great room is not that she used a book but that the book she used was a Book of Common Prayer, not a Bible. There is occasional precedent for using prayer books in love charms; specifically, in some English villages and towns, a young woman could open her book to the ceremony of matrimony, place in it a bit of myrtle or rosemary, close it, and sleep with it under her pillow to dream of the man she would marry.[57] Virtually all other surviving evidence in England and New England points to Bibles, not prayer books, being used in courtship rituals. In Hannah Ludwell's great room, then, the "common prayerbook" assumed a status typically reserved for Scripture in Europe and New England, the status of a totemic object, overflowing with meaning and powers that went beyond those that clerics would have prescribed.

Prayer and Slavery: Prayer as Ideology at Elizabeth and Lund Washington's Hayfield

The prayer book, then, was central to Anglican religious life in at least two senses. It was at the heart of polemical debates between liturgically minded Anglican churchmen and dissenters who favored spontaneous prayer, and it was central to a range of household practices, from daily prayer to courtship ritual. By the end of the century those two loci—polemical debates about appropriate prayer, and the actual practice of household praying—came together at Hayfield, the Fairfax County estate of Lund and Elizabeth Washington. At Hayfield, Elizabeth Foote Washington came into repeated conflict with her slaves about how best to pray, and, over time, Washington's own prayer practices were reconfigured. Washington and the enslaved men and women of her household enacted, in a somewhat different frame, the disagreements that clerics and moralists had been having since the sixteenth century about the advisability of liturgical prayer.

Elizabeth Foote Washington began writing in a "little Book" in November 1779, right around the time that she married Lund Washington, first cousin of George and caretaker for Mount Vernon during the Revolutionary War. (The couple lived at Mount Vernon for the duration of the war.) Washington's "little Book" is not a diary in today's sense of the term. Washington wrote in the book only sporadically, making eleven entries over a period of seventeen years. Her stated purpose was to create a record for her daughters. Washington worried that she would die before her daughters grew up (in fact, neither of her children lived beyond early childhood), and she wanted to leave instructions about how to run a household—in particular, how to manage slaves. Shot through this ostensible treatise on home economics are Washington's considerations of prayer. It turns out that her practice of prayer and her attempts to control her slaves were intricately linked.

The Washingtons owned twelve slaves, including a man named Daniel and a woman named Felicia.[58] Two aims—one conscious, one less so—animated Washington's interactions with Daniel, Felicia, and the other enslaved men and women of her household. She wanted them to be obedient, and she wanted to conceive of herself as a benevolent slaveowner. To those ends, Washington pledged, four years into her marriage and her life at Mount Vernon, to treat her "family" with "friendly kindness." She pledged not to chastise her slaves in front of Lund Washington, guests, children, or other slaves. She vowed to restrain herself from addressing them "with harsh expressions, because they are in my power,—such as fool—Blockhead—vile wretches."[59] Here, Washington tacitly defined herself against other slaveowners. Although she did not single out and name those slaveowners who did deride their slaves with epithets like "blockhead" and "vile wretch," it is reasonable to suppose that Washington may have been thinking about the mistress she would have seen up close during the five years of marriage she lived at Mount Vernon: Martha Custis Washington.[60]

Shortly after she recorded those rules, Washington set up housekeeping at Hayfield. Five years later, she reported that "no one could have put the forgoeing resolutions more in practice than I have." Yet the enslaved men and women in her household disappointed her. Washington's refusal to criticize her servants in front of anyone or complain about "the fatigue & trouble of a family" and tell "Every fault they commit" had misled Washington's friends into thinking that her slaves were terrifically hardworking and docile. But if anyone truly knew "how little my servants did they would not think them good." Indeed few people "would put up with their servants doing so little as mine." Why did Washington tolerate this (perceived) shiftlessness? Her self-image required that she conceive of herself as benevolent; the only way to get good work from slaves was to scold them and whip them, wrote Washington, and as a good Christian mistress, she refused to do either. Still, at times Washington was perplexed that her slaves, whom she thought were exceedingly well treated, did not respond to her kindness with dutiful hard work: "I think there is Servants,—that was they to meet with the same treatment from their Superiors that mine does from me,—they would be better Servants then any I have,—for to consider how mine has ever been treated they are not such Servants as a person would expect—for surely they ought to be the best of Servants—which is not the case,—but I believe thy might be made much worse by frequently being scolded at."[61]

Rather than exercising the naked power of the whip, Washington aimed to exercise the subtler power of religious instruction. She took "pains . . . to perswaid my servants to do their business through a principal of religion" and repeatedly told her slaves that "I do not wish they should behave well for my sake, but because it will be pleasing in the eyes of the almighty—& that if they will do their business for his sake I shall be well serv'd if they never think of me."[62] Washington may have believed that her use of religion rather than physical violence was proof of her benevolence. But to control people with ideological tools could be more powerful than controlling them with weapons. Had the whip been her chosen means of authority, Washington would have needed to be ever present, whip in hand to ensure that her labor force worked; but if she could "perswaid" them to worship a God who wanted them to obey her, she would guarantee their work even when her back was turned. Thus creating a "truly religious family" and an obedient labor force were aims that went hand in hand.

Washington sought not merely to foster a generically Christian commitment among her slaves but also to combat the form of Christianity to which her slaves were attracted. By 1784 she worried that her "family" was being "led away with Baptistical notions."[63] Baptists had been present in Virginia since the beginning of the eighteenth century, and by the 1780s both Regular and Separate Baptists had been active in Virginia for more than twenty years. Regular Baptists had established a particularly strong foothold in northern Virginia, including Fairfax County. The enslaved men and women of Hayfield likely encountered the Baptist faith through the ministry of David Thomas, a Regular Baptist minister active in northern Virginia after 1760. They probably attended either Back Lick Church (called Accotink until 1792) in Fairfax County or Occoquon Church, which, although in Prince William County, was close to Hayfield.[64]

Washington worried about her slaves' getting "Baptistical" because she disapproved of Baptist prayer and other worship practices: she judged Baptist worship to be too performative, and she thought Baptist piety was all "outside show," mere religious display that was reflected neither in practitioners' hearts nor in their lives.[65] But her disdain for Baptists' performances of prayer was only one reason she wanted to turn her slaves away from the Baptist faith. She was also doubtless worried about the political impact of her slaves' getting "Baptistical." The biracial fellowship practiced in Baptist churches was demarcated by racism, to be sure—but as Donald Mathews has noted, it was nonetheless quite "revolutionary within a hierarchical society." In Baptist churches, enslaved men and women worshiped, sang, and prayed with white people. Church leaders claimed the right to adjudicate disputes between slaves and their owners—sometimes they sided with an owner who had punished his slave for disobedience or disrespect, and sometimes they censured owners for "misconduct." Some biracial Baptist churches sent black men as their delegates at association meetings. Furthermore, during the 1780s and 1790s, some Baptists in Virginia publicly questioned the legitimacy of slavery. In 1785 the Baptist General Committee of Virginia stated that "hereditary slavery [was] contrary to the word of God." Five years later, the General Committee issued another statement, written by the minister John Leland, resolving that slavery violated natural rights and was "inconsistent with a republican government" and recommending that Baptists "make use of every legal measure, to extirpate the horrid evil from the land, and pray Almighty God, that our Honourable Legislature may have it in their power, to proclaim the general Jubilee, consistent with the principles of good policy."[66]

This general willingness of Virginia Baptists to question slavery took particular form around Hayfield. In 1774 a visiting Baptist minister preached a sermon against the slave trade in Fairfax County. Calling slavery a "capital crime," Elnathan Winchester came quite close to insisting that slaveowners free their slaves. He hedged, because he knew his auditors "cannot set them free by the law," but he bade them to repent, and he sketched a picture that surely terrified and angered elite men and women: slavery was "a national sin, and will bring down national punishment, unless it be repented of." Eventually, God's justice would prevail, "the slaves will at length be free . . . you will be enslaved, or devoured by the sword." In 1787, thirteen years after Winchester preached this alarming sermon in Fairfax County, the Ketocton Association (of which Occoquon and Back Lick churches were a part) turned its attention to slavery. Back Lick Church was one of the congregations most forcefully pushing for the Association to take an antislavery stand. The Association decided that "hereditary slavery was a breach of the divine law," and even went so far as to appoint a committee "to bring in a plan of gradual emancipation." The Association quietly dropped the plan, which had "excited considerable tumult." It was in the context of that tumult that Washington was discomforted by her slaves "getting Baptistical."[67]

Washington tried to shape the religious sensibilities of her slaves through reading, conversation, and prayer. First, Washington was, like her coreligionists, convinced that edifying reading was crucial to right religious living. She owned "religious Books of every description," and she taught at least two enslaved women to read and "put good Books into their hands." Second, she conducted one-on-one conversations about religious matters with the enslaved members of her household. Finally, and most important to Washington, she attempted to lead her slaves in regular "family" devotions, morning and night.[68]

Many sources may have taught Washington that she had the authority—and a duty—to lead family prayer. In devotional works like her prayer book, Elizabeth Foote Washington would have found this language: "*The Master or Mistress having called together as many of the Family as can conveniently be present, let one of them, or an other whom they shall think proper, say as follows, all kneeling . . .*"[69] As Joan Gundersen has noted, these words "empowered women explicitly to lead family worship, and gave them the actual words to say."[70] In the pulpit, ministers argued that praying with one's dependents was key to running a well-ordered household. As William Douglas of St. James Northam Parish in Goochland County explained, family prayer was tied to the authority that "Superiors" had over children and "servants." "Family religion" included both prayer and governance; devotions went hand in hand with reprimand: "The whole of family religion is not t[o] be placed in acts of worship properly so called; It includes family government & discipline; ye daily reading of y Scriptures to ym, and sometimes, especially on ye Lords day, oyr practical books on religion, numbers of [which], thank God, they may be furnished [with]: Watching over ye ways of your household; catechizing children, instructing servant(s) Reproving, admonishing, & correcting for irregularities of temper & conduct; & more especially for sins agst God." After listing the many ways religious discipline and household management were imbricated, Douglas concluded that "family worship is ye most important part; & will have great influence to promote ye regular & useful discharge of ye rest." Douglas explained that those in authority should use their authority for the good of those in their care: "You have 1st authority over . . . your children by nature; & your servants by yr consent: & yr authority was given you by ye Supreme Lord, & is to be used for him. . . . Why was ye authority given? Not merely [so that] they may be serviceable to ye temporal, worldly interest at ye family; & be compelled to do qt may promote it; but yt they might be made wise & good." Making one's servants good was not purely altruistic: "If you expect your servants should (u)se yr reason & understanding in serving you, & not do things mechanically as ye brutes, it is your duty, not to treat ym like brutes, by only providing ym food & hatiations, but to take care of yr minds, & by reason & admonition, to form ym to habits of sobriety, diligence, & good behavior." Finally, Douglas explained that praying with one's family would give a "Superior" greater authority in matters not related to prayer: "Family worship will give weight to all your admonitions." These ideas were in widespread circulation. For example, *A Present for Servants from their Ministers, Masters, or Other Friends*, an English volume that was published throughout the century and that clergy, including Commissary William Dawson, circulated in Virginia, yoked prayer and household government. Though principally aimed, as the title suggests, at servants, the book's preface is addressed to masters themselves. The preface explains why masters should pray with their servants: "*Family-Duties, Prayer, Reading, Singing Psalms, Repetition of Sermons, Catechizing of Servants, &c. are like so many Fences, or* Battlements *on one side; Commands Reproofs, Corrections, and Restraints from Sin, are Rails, or* Battlements *on the other.*" Elizabeth Foote Washington, then, had good reason—both spiritual and temporal—to prioritize leading her "family" in prayer.[71]

Yet Washington's efforts to lead her slaves in prayer did not go as smoothly as she wished. Three years into her regimen of daily prayer with her "domesticks," Washington noted with discontent that "they do not seem fond of it." Washington was perplexed—she couldn't fathom why her slaves did not like attending her prayer sessions, and she attributed their diffidence to fallen human nature, which is always inclined away from the good. Three years later, the slaves of Hayfield had only grown more resentful of Washington's prayer gatherings. "I am griev'd greatly to have this to set down," Washington wrote, "that my family is got so Baptistical in their notions, as to think they commit a crime to join with me in Prayer morning & evening." When she would try to have family prayer, her "Servants will go out of the way at the time they are going to be call'd to Prayer—it is impossible for them to have it,—& if they are made to come—they appear quite angry."[72]

The religious experiences of the enslaved men and women of Hayfield are known to us only through the mediations of Elizabeth Foote Washington's diary. Yet Washington has given us a rare glimpse of slaves' engagement with Anglican piety. According to Washington, the slaves resisted praying with her for at least two reasons. First, "the creatures has taken it into their heads, that the Prayers I used was too good for them to use." In other words, Washington's slaves disliked liturgical prayer, and preferred Baptists' more spontaneous praying. Second, Washington's slaves resisted praying with her because they realized that their "family prayer" would have no material impact on their lives at Hayfield: "One thing my poor creatures expected was to be the consequence of my having prayers in my family, that I should never find fault of them, nor even reprimand them for anything at all, but when they found that I continued to do it in my way . . . they thought my religion was all pretence." Just as Washington judged Baptist piety to be merely "outside show," so did the enslaved men and women of Hayfield assess Washington's religious performances—they found her prayers wanting because they did not change her behavior, and they rejected her prayers when they realized that praying with her would not concretely improve their lot.[73]

Washington did not try to meet the slaves' second objection, but she did try to accommodate their dislike of liturgy, and in so doing, her own prayer practices changed. In order to "keep up the attention" of her "family", she departed from the practice of reciting morning and evening prayer solely from the prayer book, and "wrote nine morning Prayers and the same number of evening ones for to use in my family."[74] Here we see played out in a household the arguments that Anglicans and dissenters had been having at the level of propaganda for two centuries. Elizabeth Foote Washington had criticized Baptist piety, but she allowed her own prayerful sensibilities and practices to be reshaped by her encounters with her "Baptistical" slaves. That Washington's understanding and practice of prayer was changed by this encounter may be seen not only in her using the eighteen prayers that she had written but in her diction when discussing these prayers. "It may perhaps be wondered of," she wrote, "why I wrote so many morning Prayers & evening ones, when it is customary to use only one morning and evening prayer through the course of the lives of those who prays in their familys—my reason for it is this, when a person is accustomed to say only one particular prayer of a morning & one of night for a length of time, those who join with them will be apt to repeat them & not think of them at the same time, having got them by rote, so that instead of praying it is but mere babbling." At the level of idiom, Washington has absorbed dissenters' critiques of Anglican prayers. To have prayer by rote was no longer, as it was in John Thompson's funeral sermon for Cole, something to which devout people aspired; to the contrary, "rote" praying was to be avoided. For people like Commissary Blair, the dissenters' ejaculatory prayer was meaningless chatter and babbling; in Washington's view it was the recitation of liturgy that threatened to degenerate into babbling.[75]

Despite Washington's attempt to accommodate her slaves' religious sensibilities, they still refused, ultimately, to pray with her. Finally, Washington admitted defeat: she was "oblig'd to give out having Prayers" with her slaves. In her final entry, Washington remained worried about her inability to control her slaves. Specifically, she feared that after her death, her "Female servants" would take her "little Book," and every other "manuscript they can lay their hands on, & many of my other religious Books. . . . I am certain they will think they have a greater right then any one else." Washington hoped that on her deathbed, she would have her wits about her, and that she would be attended by a friend whom she could "warn . . . of my servants."[76] She concluded her "little Book" with a prayer: "Do thou O lord in mercy look on my state, & influence the hearts of my servants & cause them to treat me with respect."[77] If Washington's own efforts to pray with her slaves couldn't control them, perhaps her direct petitions could.

CHAPTER FOUR

Sarah Foote Stuart's Fish Sauce
The Liturgical Year around the Table

Take a little thyme, horse-radish, a bit of onion, lemon-peel, and whole pepper; boil them in a little fair water; then put in two anchovies, and four spoonfuls of white-wine; then strain them out, and put the liquor into the same pan again, with a pound of fresh butter; and when 'tis melted take it off the fire, and stir in the yolks of two eggs well beaten, with three spoonfuls of white-wine; set it on the fire again, and keep it stirring till 'tis the thickness of cream, and pour it hot over your Fish. Garnish with lemon and horse-radish.

—"Sauce for Fish in Lent, or at any Time," E. Smith, *The Compleat Housewife*

For elites in eighteenth-century Virginia, the table provided a stage for numerous religious performances. For example, meals provided an occasion for prayer. When John Mason, eldest son of George Mason, recalled his childhood, he noted that his father "was always sent for when meals were served and nobody sat down until he came in. He always had grace said; most generally he performed that office himself, but sometimes [he] desired one [of] his elder sons to do so. That grace was uniformly delivered in the following words: 'God bless us and what we are going to receive.'"[1] Another religious valence of the table may be found in elite Anglicans' vaunted hospitality. Virginia gentry prided themselves on being generous hosts, and, as Cynthia Kierner has argued, in an environment inflected with the imperatives of Christian piety, hospitality may have been understood in part as a religious virtue, connected to the many instances of Scripture's urging God's people to open their tables and homes to friends and strangers alike.[2] Eating could also occasion religious danger. Clergy worried about fashionable cuisine. Culinary fads could breed envy and discontent, with diners becoming dissatisfied with their perfectly fine meats once they "have seen . . . a newer cookery at anothers Table."[3] But the most overt nexus of religious practice and culinary practice in Anglican Virginia was the preparation and consumption of holiday food. The major festivals of the church year called for eating special foods, and refraining from other food, at ecclesially appointed times. During the Christmas season people ate extravagant cakes; during Lent people abstemiously modified their usual diet. This cycle of feasting and fasting gave a liturgical flavor to the social lives and seasonal lives of elite Virginians.

As is evident from even the cursory foregoing survey of the many ways the gentry's table practices were religiously inflected, religious engagement with food was never *only* about connecting church and household. Alimentary religiosity was always bound up with power and authority. John Mason notes not only that his father said grace but that the entire household waited on his presence before being seated (which communicated the household's respect for, acquiescence in, and submission to Mason's God-given patriarchal authority). Elites' lavish hospitality was in part about display. So, too, festival meals tied eating to the church and made the church's calendar manifest around the table; at the same time, the preparation and consumption of such meals involved several negotiations of power. Elite laity, deciding to conform to or ignore subtle clerical attempts to direct household holiday celebrations, negotiated the boundaries between clerical authority and lay authority. The preparation and consumption of holiday meals also involved negotiations among members of the household. Elite men tried to check their wives' and daughters' authority over food preparation, and elite women, in turn, exercised authority over the enslaved men and women whose labor made the gentry's alimentary religiosity possible.[4]

Of Keys and Cookbooks: White Women and Authority in Gentry Kitchens

As we saw in the previous chapter, Books of Common Prayer were important props in the performance of Anglican domestic religiosity. Alongside those overtly religious prayer books, another manual shaped religious practice in elite Anglican households: cookery texts that guided women in the preparation of meals for two major festival seasons, Christmas and Twelfth Night, and Shrove Tuesday and Lent. Like prayer books, cookery texts made it possible for elite men and especially women to connect their households to the church, specifically to the rhythms of the Anglican year.[5]

Elite women in Virginia kept two kinds of cookbooks. First, they bought published cookbooks printed in England and, by the mid-eighteenth century, Virginia. One especially popular published cookbook was Mrs. Glasse's *The Art of Cookery Made Plain and Easy*, which appears in the inventories of great estates such as Mount Vernon and Monticello.[6] E. Smith's *The Compleat*

Housewife, originally published in London in 1727, was another cookery text that was popular in Virginia. It became the first cookbook published in the American colonies when Williamsburg's William Parks printed it in 1742.[7] A copy of *The Compleat Housewife* that is now housed at the Library of Virginia gives us a glimpse of how much women valued such books. Inside the front cover of the Library of Virginia's 1752 Parks edition is a note, written in a sure, elegant hand: "This book was my sister Stuart's her daughters gave it to my sister Washington and she left to her Niece Mrs Ann Thompson and I had it new bound because it is an old family book." The note is signed "Eliza Washington Hayfield July 1810."[8]

This note tells us two things: first, the book was well used—otherwise it would not have needed rebinding. Second, the book was transmitted among female relatives through the generations. In the 1750s the book was first purchased by or given to Sarah Foote Stuart. When she died, the book passed to Stuart's sister, Katherine Foote Washington. When Katherine—who had no daughters—died in 1799, she left the book to her niece Ann Thompson, who, around 1810, gave the book to her aunt, Elizabeth Foote Washington, whom we met in the previous chapter. Elizabeth was related to the book's previous owners twice over: she was the sister of Sarah and Katherine, and she was the widow of Lund Washington, whose brothers included both Katherine's husband and Ann's father.[9] Through use and through inheritance and gifting, the book had, like the Masons' baptismal monteith, acquired status as a treasured family object—it was a beloved "old family book."

In addition to purchasing books like Glasse's and Smith's, elite women in Virginia wrote down recipes themselves. Several manuscript "receipt" books survive from eighteenth-century Virginia. Recipes in these manuscript cookery books range from beer to cake to "Sirrup of Marsh Mallows." They include instructions for getting spots out of silk, and recipes for cures for pleurisy and "ye Green Sickness" (an "anemic disease" that afflicted pubescent girls and sometimes gave their skin a greenish cast). Some of these recipes were copied from cookery texts published in England, but Virginia women's recipe files also testify to Virginians' culinary innovation; they include recipes for food and drink unknown to British palates, like persimmon beer, a drink Anglo-Virginians adapted from their Native American neighbors.[10]

As women's ownership, bequeathing and inheritance, and compiling of cookery books suggests, cooking was associated with women. Cookery texts could be passed down through "umbilical" lines of sisters, nieces, and aunts. Furthermore, exchanging recipes was a form of social intercourse among women—Jane Bolling Randolph's manuscript cookbook, for example, in-

4.1

Around 1810, a 1752 Parks edition of *The Compleat Housewife* came to Elizabeth Foote Washington. In the book, she wrote, "This book was my sister Stuart's—her daughters gave it to my sister Washington and she left to her Niece Mrs. Ann Thompson—and I had it new bound because it is an old family book." Special Collections, Library of Virginia.

cludes recipes friends gave her, including "Mrs Byrds' Jumbals" (presumably Maria Taylor Byrd, William Byrd's second wife) and "Mrs. Chiswel's Receipt for a Cake, very good" (Elizabeth Randolph Chiswell).[11] Cookery texts were currencies in women's social networks, and they suggest that eighteenth-century Virginia gentry understood the kitchen as an arena in which elite women could make judgments, claim ownership, and exercise expertise and authority. This association of women with cooking was bolstered by the convention of women's owning items related to the preparation of food; Jane Jefferson, for example, owned tea and tea implements, a corkscrew, sugar, and coffee, whereas her husband's inventory did not include foodstuffs.[12] But, as we shall see, women's authority over culinary matters was ambiguous.

Gentry women in Virginia had *relative* authority over the preparation of food, but that authority was always checked by their husbands and fathers. Often, husbands and fathers interfered with women's food management. For example, Landon Carter clashed with his daughter-in-law, Winifred Beale Carter, who lived, with her husband and son, on Landon's sufferance at Sabine Hall. Landon hated Winifred, and Winifred's control of the kitchen was one of the many topics over which they rowed. Landon accused Winifred of slovenly housekeeping. According to Landon's account of the exchange in his diary, Winifred in turn "broke out that until I sent Mrs. Woods to take the keys from her every drop of Milk, Spoonful of butter, of fat, every ounce of sugar plumbs, etc., passed regularly though her hands. I laughed at the care we then experienced in Milk, butter, fat, sugar plumbs, soap, Candles, etc. Not one of these innumerations lasted my family half the year. New soap was obliged to be made in June. Fat gone by July. Sugar continually brought in. . . . All gone. No body knows how. Butter merely vanishing." Landon Carter insisted that Winifred—whom he referred to in his journal as "Lady Fat"—had grown too insolent and "heavy to do anything but trust to thievish servants," so he told Mrs. Woods to take the keys to the kitchen from her.[13]

Kitchen keys symbolized household authority. There was more at stake here than vanishing butter; "carrying the keys" was a synecdoche for the domestic responsibilities of plantation mistresses, a shorthand among Virginia mistresses for all "the hardships of keeping house."[14] Landon blamed Winifred for the diffidence, disrespect, and dissolute habits of his son, her husband, Robert Carter. By taking the kitchen keys away from Winifred, Landon was symbolically stripping her of her identity as an integral member of their family; he was demoting her from her presumptive place as plantation mistress with charge over preparation and service of food. Reading between the lines of Landon Carter's journal, it is clear that Winifred was outraged and embarrassed by Landon's usurpation of her authority, with its unavoid

4.2
Alimentary items from Monticello. The manuscript cookery book belonged to Thomas Jefferson's granddaughter Septimia Randolph. The larger key, ca. 1800, opened the Monticello wine cellar. Kitchen keys constituted a material symbol of household authority. Thomas Jefferson Foundation. Photo by Edward Owen.

able reminder that she was not the mistress of her own house but only the unwelcome daughter-in-law waiting for the master of Sabine Hall to die.

If white women struggled to maintain culinary authority vis-à-vis husbands and fathers-in-law, they exercised tremendous authority in the kitchen over their slaves. Indeed, we can imagine that, given the fights white women had with their husbands and fathers over control of the kitchen, when gentry women were in the kitchen, keys literally and metaphorically in hand, they may have been all the more ruthless in their exercise of power over their slaves. Elite women did not do much actual cooking. Rather, they directed other people in the preparation of food. At Shadwell, for example, where enslaved cooks worked in a building about one hundred feet east of the main house, Jane Randolph Jefferson's role in getting dinner served was not to wash potatoes or stir a great pot of soup but to oversee "the movement of food from storage to kitchen and from kitchen to table." As Kirsten Wood has argued, overseeing culinary preparation without actually dirtying one's hands was part of what defined elite women: having black slaves to cook for them was a singular indicator of privilege, and well into the nineteenth century, white women who found themselves on hard times often clung to kitchen help as proof that, although they might face economic straits, they remained elite.[15]

In the kitchens of the great Virginia estates, both enslaved men and enslaved women served as cooks. Ads placed in the *Virginia Gazette* by slave-owners hoping to sell slaves might describe either a man or a woman as a skilled baker or "a very good Cook." At Nomini Hall, cooks included Sam Jones and Daniel in 1775; at Sabine Hall, Peg the "cook wench" prepared food for the Carters; in 1760 one of Martha Custis Washington's dower slaves, Doll, was the cook at Mount Vernon; twenty-six years later, two male cooks, Hercules and Nathan, had replaced Doll. Thus elite women's ownership and circulation of cookery texts does not mean that cooking was "women's work." The actual labor of cooking was tied not to sex but to enslavement.[16]

The enslaved men and women who were doing the cooking were thus the unfree shadow audience of books like *The Compleat Housewife*.[17] The recollections of Isaac Jefferson, whose mother was the pastry cook at Monticello, give us a hint about how cookery books were used in a context in which the people doing the cooking were likely to be illiterate: "Mrs. Jefferson would come out there with a cookery book in her hand & read out of it to Isaac's mother how to make cakes tarts & so on." Of course, we have no way of knowing the extent to which enslaved cooks followed the directions their owners called out to them. It is easy to imagine that cooks, who probably knew more about what went into preparing a decent-tasting meal than their owners, would have acted obedient while ignoring half of what the cookbooks and their owners said. An 1823 letter from Virginia Jefferson Randolph (Thomas Jefferson's granddaughter) to her future husband, Nicholas P. Trist, provides a second picture of a cookery text's being used in kitchens staffed by enslaved cooks. Apologizing to her beau for failing to answer his letter sooner, Randolph notes, "I received it, seated upon my throne in the kitchen, with a cookery book in my hand." That designation of a "throne" in the kitchen of Monticello was doubtless ironic, but nonetheless revealing. White women remained the queens of the kitchen.[18]

The Anglican Calendar: Christological Time

The religious calendar that women like Sarah Foote found in their cookbooks was spelled out most fully in the Book of Common Prayer. There the Table

4.3
A freestanding kitchen at Oakley, in Lancaster County. Many southern elites' kitchens were freestanding outbuildings; part of what distinguished a gentry estate from a lesser household was the presence of freestanding outhouses. Virginia Department of Historic Resources.

and Rules for the Feasts and Fasts and the Rules for Special Days named the holy days that shaped the Anglican year: Christmas and Easter, Whitsunday and Ascension Day, the feasts of Saints Mark and Luke, the Purification of the Blessed Virgin Mary, Rogation Days, and so on. This calendar was, essentially, the Roman Catholic calendar, less many Marian festivals and saints' days.[19] These days structured the seasons and invited practitioners into rhythms of feasting and fasting, celebration and penance, contemplation of the infant Jesus and encounter with the fiery Holy Spirit.

But Anglicans in Virginia did not conform to the many intricacies of the prayer book's calendar, in part because the church's calendar conflicted with the dictates of the agricultural calendar. The rhythms of planting ordered Virginians' lives. Slaves could find themselves sowing tobacco in January, or as late as June; their owners worried over frost and pests. April, May, and June were "spent in planting the Corn and making the tobacco hills," and in spreading dung; May might also call for harvesting fruit like cherries. During the spring and summer, Mount Vernon's slaves "seined for fish . . . cradled and bound the grain harvest, shocked wheat and oats," and more. Fall meant harvesting corn and peas, and cutting, hanging, and drying tobacco leaves; packing tobacco could occupy people through December, just when new beds had to be prepared and sown. During winter, slaves also "dug ditches; cut rails, posts, and firewood; slaughtered hogs; filled the icehouse; built new roads; framed . . . barn[s]; made baskets and horse collars; tanned leather; and tended the stable." And then the cycle began again. This repeating pattern of planting and harvesting marked the seasons and gave shape to time.[20]

The ecclesiastical calendar and the agricultural calendar sometimes complemented each other. For example, during the Christmas season there was a break between harvesting and planting, and slaves were not required to work on Christmas Day. Virginians also continued the English practice of paying salaries on feast days—the governor's quarterly salary was paid on the feast of St. John the Baptist, Michaelmas, Christmas, and the Annunciation of Mary —and terms of land grants were also demarcated in ecclesial time: "For the term of ten years next ensuing after the feast of St. Thomas the Apostle last past." The two calendars occasionally came together in common parlance, as when merchant William Tatham observed that the tobacco seedbeds were sown "as early after Christmas as the weather will permit." But, as Edward L. Bond has demonstrated, the agricultural calendar sometimes fought with Anglican liturgical time, and when the imperatives of the prayer book conflicted with the imperatives of a developing tobacco economy, tobacco won. As early as the 1620s, the Assembly began to modify, and indeed restrict, ecclesial time, perhaps, Bond says, because "too many people took off feast days to attend religious observances" or because holiday merriment left people too hungover to work the next day. "Whatever the reason," argues Bond, "the abundance of religious festivals in the spring, summer, and early fall threatened tobacco cultivation and made an accommodation necessary."[21]

Eighteenth-century Virginia Anglicans did not keep many of the minor festivals spelled out in the prayer book. The holidays most robustly observed in Virginia included Christmas and Twelfth Night, and the season of Lent. Easter—which did not occasion elaborate celebrations anywhere in America until the Victorian era—was largely unremarked, celebrated, if at all, through a visit to church, where, if a parson was present, some parishioners took communion. Ascension Day was celebrated in some parish churches with a liturgy and sermon; even in wartime, parishes that had lost their parsons to military service held Ascension Day services. Other holidays persisted in certain families and were often overlaid with meanings both religious and familial. In 1728, for example, Mary Lee wrote her son to express the glee she felt about a rumor she had heard from a friend: "that you, have made your addresses, to Miss Benson, & that you intend to have an entertainment at our house on candlemus day." The celebration of Candlemas, the feast that marked Christ's presentation at the Temple, might have seemed to Lee an auspicious day for her son to present his intended to his friends and family.[22]

Although Virginians practiced a pared-down liturgical calendar, the practice of liturgical time was part of what defined them as Anglicans and set them apart from other Protestants in both England and the colonies. Since the seventeenth century, the Book of Common Prayer's calendar of days (which was itself a modified version of the calendar of the Church of Rome) was a flash point between Anglicans and Puritans. The latter saw feast days as a papal imposition of which the church had to be purged. In the words of Horton Davies, Puritans "rejected the Christian year and substituted the Sabbath as its sole regularly recurring festival." Most famously, finding no explicit biblical imprimatur for a celebration of Christ's birth, Puritans banned Christmas. In the English colonies, disagreements about the calendar continued. In 1659 the Massachusetts Bay General Court was shocked to discover that some in the colony were "still observing [Christmas] Festiualls," and specifically forbade, on penalty of fine, "forbearing of labour, feasting, or any other . . . [observance of] any such day as Xmas or the like." The Puritan calendar, in which the only necessary and legitimate Christian feast was the weekly observance of the Lord's Day, was a bold theological statement: God's people need not reprise Christ's incarnation (via Christmas) or his struggle in the desert (via Lent), for all of that was trumped by his resurrection. Puritan faithfulness required simply standing at the empty tomb.[23]

The Anglican annual cycle of feast days, fast days, and ferial (ordinary) days differed not only from the calendar of Puritan New England. It also differed from the calendar practiced by the evangelicals who increasingly challenged Virginia's Anglican establishment in the second half of the eighteenth century. One way of marking yourself as an evangelical dissenter in Virginia was to ignore Christmas. In 1758 Samuel Davies, the great "New Light" Presbyterian preacher who served in Hanover County, Virginia, preached a sermon denouncing the Anglican holy calendar. Faithful Christians, proclaimed Davies, should not

> religiously observe days of human appointment in commemoration of Christ or the saints. What I have to say shall be particularly pointed at what is called *Christmas-day;* but may easily be applied to all other holy-

days instituted by men. . . . I would take my religion just as I find it in my Bible, without any imaginary improvements or supplements of human invention . . . [for I] content myself with the old, plain, simple religion of the Bible. Now that there is not the least appearance in all the Bible of the divine appointment of Christmas, to celebrate the birth of Christ, is granted by all parties.

Thus, says Davies, "a Bible-christian" ought not celebrate it.[24]

Anglican clerics argued back from the pulpit. In a Christmas sermon, Charles Clay obliquely criticized evangelicals who did not celebrate Christmas. The holiday was a valuable opportunity to recognize the "great instance of God's love & goodness to take any notice at all of the lost state of Mankind . . . [and] to Seek after them when they were not capable of seeking after him. . . . This love & goodness of God will appear still more illustrious, if we consider the astonishing means & method of Our Redemption"—that is, that God sent Jesus "into the world, that we might live [with] him." As for those Christians, like Davies, who scorned Christmas, Clay noted that the holiday had "from early times been celebrated by the Ch with all the solemnities of Devotion Joy & Thanksgiving." On "this Joyful Day of Our blessed lords Nativity which was at first ushered in by the Songs of Angels, & which they are now perhaps Solemnizing with us, in the Court of Heaven," Christians should "endeavour to affect Our hearts with a lively Sense of that unspeakable mercy & blessing, which we now commemorate."[25]

Although Virginia Anglicans modified the official church calendar, the practice of liturgical seasons defined community and demarcated the boundaries between Anglicans and dissenters. The Anglican liturgical calendar also conveyed a certain theological emphasis—in the modified religious calendar that Virginia Anglicans observed, the important festivals all turned practitioners' attention to the life of Christ. Christmas was, as Landon Carter summarized in his diary in 1774, "set apart to remember the Nativity of our Lord & Saviour Jesus Christ."[26] Twelfth Night inaugurated Epiphany, the season in which the church bade practitioners to reflect on the events in Jesus' life—such as his visit from the three kings, his baptism, and the miracles he worked—that revealed him as the Christ. During Lent, practitioners not only recalled, but through fasting reenacted, Christ's struggles and temptations in the desert. In contrast to Puritans' emphasis on the empty tomb, an emphasis that focused the practitioner's gaze on Christ's resurrection, the Anglican calendar shepherded practitioners through a reprise of Christ's life.

How did Anglicans actually observe these holidays? In Virginia that calendar was evidenced, most straightforwardly, on Sunday mornings in church. There the appointed Scripture readings and collects (special short prayers that "collect," and focus participants' attention on, the themes of the day) were keyed to the seasons. Some church vestries were procuring linens for the altar in green and purple, "perhaps," surmises Edward L. Bond, "to indicate the seasons of the church's liturgical year." The celebration of the Eucharist was tied to feast days: most Virginia parsons celebrated the sacrament only on Christmas, Easter, Michaelmas, and Whitsunday.[27]

Holidays were also celebrated in the household, around the table, where special meals located practitioners in the Anglican liturgical cycle and gave concrete, embodied, even sensory shape to the otherwise potentially abstract church calendar. The two major festival seasons that elite Virginians observed around the table were Christmas and Twelfth Night, and Shrove Tuesday and Lent.

Twelfth Night Cake and Fish Sauce for Lent: Holiday Observance around the Table

The Christmas season, which extended from mid-December through the first week of January, was much commented upon by visitors to Virginia. On December 18 the tutor Philip Fithian wrote, "Nothing is now to be heard of in conversation, but the *Balls*, the *Fox-hunts*, the fine *entertainments*, and the *good fellowship*, which are to be exhibited at the approaching *Christmas*." The balls and foxhunts accompanied gastronomic feasts. Theophilus Bradbury described one late-eighteenth-century Christmas meal at Mount Vernon:

> In the middle of the table was placed a piece of table furniture about six feet long and two feet wide, rounded at the ends. It was either of wood gilded, or polished metal, raised about an inch with a silver rim round it like a round tea board. . . . The dishes were placed all around, and there was an elegant variety of roast beef, veal, turkey, ducks, fowls, hams &c.; puddings, jellies, oranges, apples, nuts, almonds, figs, raisins, & a variety of wines & punch . . .

In 1771 the Fairfax family hosted fifteen guests at a Christmas ball. Other relations came and went throughout the Christmas holidays. Their holiday menu included "six mince pies, seven custards, twelve tarts, one chicken pie, and four puddings."[28]

These domestic feasts coexisted with Christmas church services, although laypeople were somewhat lackadaisical about church attendance on the holy day. When they did attend, they heard a special Christmas sermon.

When the Carter family went to church on Sunday, December 26, 1773, the minister preached on Isaiah 9:6, "For unto us a child is Born." One of Charles Clay's Christmas sermons took 1 John 4:9–10 as its text: "In this was manifested the love of God toward us, because that God sent his only begotten Son into the world, that we might live through him. Herein is love, not that we loved God, but that he loved us, and sent his Son to be the propitiation for our sins." Clay's Christmas sermon was no anodyne, babe-in-a-manger message: it was a lesson about sin. Clay found in 1 John 4 "the most agreeable & most important Doc. of the Gospel, the gracious Method & design of Redeeming love the glad tidings of Salvation to sinful creatures." Clay hoped his sermon would "warm & affect your hearts with a lively sense of the Divine Mercy in Our Redemption, quicken Our Faith Enliven Our Hope & Excite us to a Ready & Cheerful Obedience," for "this holy Season, devoted to the Memory of Our blessed Saviours Mysterious Incarnation & Birth" was an especially appropriate time to reflect on one's redemption from sin.[29]

Christmas was one of four festival days on which clergy typically celebrated Holy Communion. Those parishioners who chose to take communion were likely to receive the bread and wine from their church's silver chalice and paten, which, as Dell Upton has noted, resembled the silver that graced the tables found in elite dining rooms. After this celebration of Holy Communion, elite families would have returned to their dining rooms. There was a close but fraught relationship between the Eucharist that laypeople observed or participated in at church and their domestic feasting. As Daniel Sack has argued, for many American Protestants, communion sets the framework in which other meals are understood. The religious meaning of dinner at home derives at least in part from reference to the Lord's Supper. Christmas feasts like the Fairfaxes' were times of gastronomic indulgence and social display, but, as the stylistic similarity between Eucharistic silver and the gentry's tableware indicates, they can also be read as domestic Eucharists. Anglicans were prepared by the Eucharist to experience food as a site of religious meaning.[30]

But the "domestic Eucharist" of Christmas feasting did not simply quote or restate the Eucharist celebrated in church. The folklorist Charles Camp once noted that it is significant when a meal's cooks are "excluded from its proceedings"—that is, when they are barred from participating in the meal whose food they prepared. This observation suggests that we read the gastronomic feasts gentry celebrated at home as undoing the social meanings inscribed at the church altar rail. Anglican gentry were notably uncomfortable receiving communion with black slaves. They understood that to kneel humbly at all, let alone next to your slave, was to suggest a social leveling that was fundamentally at odds with the hierarchies of slave society. Domestic feasting inverted—or, from the gentry's perspective, righted—the Eucharist's implied erasure of the differences between freepeople and bondspeople. The proper hierarchy was reinscribed in domestic feasting, where enslaved men and women provided all the labor and were excluded from partaking in the meal.[31]

The culminating bash of the Christmas season came less than two weeks after Christmas proper, on the festival of Twelfth Night, the moment when Christmas shaded into Epiphany, the liturgical season in which the church invited Christians to focus on recalling, and making manifest, the identity of Jesus in the world. Since the late fourth century, clerics in the western church focused during Epiphany on the three kings who brought Jesus gifts. Those gifts, church fathers knew, told readers of Scripture something about who Jesus was: the gold, a present befitting royalty, announced he was a king; the frankincense, a special incense burned by ancient Israelites before the Tent of Meeting, announced that Jesus was the true place to meet God; and the myrrh, used for embalming, announced that the infant Jesus was born to die. These three kings and their gifts became the center of much Epiphany preaching.[32] By the early years of the English Reformation, the focus on biblical kings had expanded to include earthly royalty. On Twelfth Night, kings, queens, and their courtiers participated in ever more elaborate masqued balls, in which their subjects paid them homage and indulged in sumptuous feasts. Here Christianity glossed ancient pagan midwinter solstice practice, and the state in turn glossed Christianity, as the homage owed King Jesus blurred into homage owed earthly kings. These practices, unsurprisingly, were interrupted by the English Civil War. Twelfth Night was one of the "papal inventions" the Puritans denounced, and even after the Restoration, Twelfth Night never quite regained its role in public, political life. Instead, the festival retreated to individual households, where it flourished in the form of parties marked by revelry and inversion.[33]

There were two alternative ways of celebrating Twelfth Night in one's home. One celebration gave pride of place to the Twelfth Night cake. Bakers slipped a bean into the cake batter just before baking. Whoever ended up eating the slice that contained the bean became king for a day; sometimes the king was even given a crown to wear. It was the king's job to offer toasts and encourage everyone at the table to keep drinking. The king also had to pay— either for that evening's entertainments or for next year's party. By the late seventeenth century, a new ritual had begun to replace or augment the eating of Twelfth Night cake. In the new ritual, the search for the bean was replaced with a ritualistic drawing of lots. Samuel Pepys describes the ritual in his diary: "In the evening I did bring out my cake—a noble cake, and there cut it into pieces, with wine and good drink; and after a new fashion, to prevent spoiling the cake, did pour so many titles into a hat, and so drew cuts; and I was the Queene; and Th[eophilia] Turner, King—Creed, Sir Martin Marrall; and Betty, Mrs. Millicent: and so we were mighty merry till it was night; and then, being moonshine and fine frost, they went home."[34]

Virginians adopted elements of both forms of Twelfth Night celebration. Recipes testify to the persistence of the Twelfth Night cake. One extremely lavish recipe for Twelfth Night cake is attributed to Martha Custis Washington, who married George on Twelfth Night; it was taken down by her granddaughter:

> Take 40 eggs & divide the whites from the yolks & beat them to a froth then work 4 pounds of butter to a cream & put the whites of eggs to it a spoon full at a time till it is well work'd then put 4 pounds of sugar finely powdered to it in the same manner then put in the Youlks of eggs & 5 pounds of flour & 5 pounds of fruit. 2 hrs will bake it add to it a half an ounce of mace & nutmeg half a pint of wine & some frensh brandy.[35]

Beyond recipes, diary evidence and travel accounts attest to the practice of Twelfth Night in Virginia. William Byrd's diaries tell us that he celebrated the holiday. He may have been introduced to it while living in England: in 1719 he went to Lord Percival's for a Twelfth Night celebration. "I found an abundance of company met together to be merry," he recorded in his diary. "We drew king and queen. Then came three women in masks and stayed about half an hour. Then we played at [little plays] and were merry. We had some punch. . . . About 11 o'clock we took leave and went to Court where was abundance of company, where the King played at dice and several danced. I stayed till 1 o'clock."[36] Byrd brought the celebration home with him. He was ambivalent about returning to Virginia; perhaps the festival helped him feel tied to England. In 1721 he had at least nine guests to a Twelfth Night party; after dinner, everyone danced and played games.[37] Years later, an older Byrd was still celebrating the holiday, though more modestly: on Twelfth Night in 1739, Byrd "talked with my people, drew twelfth cake, gave the people cake and cider, and prayed."[38] A second, less taciturn description of a Virginia Twelfth Night celebration comes from Nicholas Cresswell, visiting Alexandria from England in 1775:

> It seems this is one of their annual Balls supported in the following manner: A large rich cake is provided and cut into small pieces and handed

round to the company, who at the same time draws a ticket out of a Hat with something merry wrote on it. He that draws the king has the Honor of treating the company with a Ball the next year, which generally costs him Six or Seven Pounds. The Lady that draws the Queen has the trouble of making the Cake. Here was about 37 ladies dressed and powdered to the life, some of them very handsome and as much vanity as is necessary. All of them fond of dancing, but I do not think they perform it with the greatest elegance. Betwixt the Country dances they have what I call everlasting jigs. A couple gets up and begins to dance a jig (to some Negro tune) others comes and cuts them out, and these dances always last as long as the Fiddler can play. This is sociable, but I think it looks more like a Baccanalian dance than one in a polite assembly. Ole Women, Young Wives with young children in the lap, widows, maids, and girls come promiscuously to these assemblies which generally continue till morning. A cold supper, Punch, Wines, Coffee and chocolate, but no Tea. This is a forebidden herb. The men chiefly Scottish and Irish. I went home about two o'clock, but part of the company stayed, got drunk and had a fight.[39]

One need not overread Twelfth Night as a carnivalesque social "safety valve" to note the suggestiveness of Byrd's celebrating the holiday of inversion with his slaves, and to sense the tensions, promiscuity, and blurring of the hierarchies that emerge in Cresswell's account.

The extravagant, tipsy, sometimes violent celebrations that unfolded in gentry households in December and January made some ministers nervous. In their Christmas sermons, clergy tried to circumscribe Anglican laity's domestic celebrations. Pace the evangelicals and Puritans, Anglican clerics wanted Christmas to be celebrated joyfully. As William Dawson preached to a congregation in Williamsburg in 1732: "Joy is a Passion w[h]ich God himself hath implanted in our Natures: and it cannot be thought therefore that the Design of Religion is entirely to root it out." But that joy should not "degenerate into Sin and Sensuality." Practitioners should not "express it by Luxury and Intemperance, to the great Scandal of our Saviour." Christmas joy "is not only lawful, but commendable," but only when it is "founded upon a right Principle, directed to its proper Object, kept within its due Compass, and not suffer'd to exceed either in its Measure, or Duration." Another parson told parishioners that they should certainly celebrate Christmas, but censoriously instructed laypeople to "let your Joy be such as becomes Xns; is the way to praise God . . . to game, to get Drunk"? In particular, this parson chastised those who began their Christmas "Feast in the morning, & are early enflamed with strong Drink, & never once lift up your hearts to God in Prayer."[40] Clergy sensed in the gentry's domestic celebrations a displacement of their own ecclesial authority, and they worried about the excesses of household holidays. As we shall see presently, wintertime revelry was not the only domestic holiday celebration that clergy tried to shape.

Seasons of gastronomic feasting like Christmas and Twelfth Night were complemented by—and, arguably, derived part of their meaning from—periodic fasts. In Virginia fasts were sometimes called for by the governor and observed for political reasons. In 1729, for example, the colony was afflicted with caterpillars and Governor Gooch called a fast; this action partook of the biblical paradigm of communities or political bodies fasting when they were under siege. Sometimes political and religious imperatives intertwined more overtly in state-appointed fasts. For example, after "a wicked and horrid Rebellion ha[d] been raised against our Sovereign Lord King GEORGE," Gooch called a fast for February 26, 1746, instructing Virginia to pray for pardon and divine blessing; less than a decade later, because the colony had "but too much reason to fear that our Sins have justly provoked the Almighty to send down upon us his heavy Judgments of War and Famine; and as a national Repentance is the only Remedy for national Guilt," Governor Dinwiddie declared a fast on Wednesday, September 24, 1755. These fasts were prompted by the Jacobite Rebellion and Braddock's Defeat, respectively. Both fasts were obviously political—but there was an ecclesial aspect as well, since victory by Bonnie Prince Charlie would have meant Catholic rule, and defeat at Fort Duquesne left the North American English empire open to French Catholicism. Thus even "political" fasting was bound up with the production of specifically Anglican identity.[41]

The major ecclesial fast in Virginia was the season of Lent. During Lent, Christians reprised the forty-day fast of Jesus in the desert. Anglican clerics taught that penitential Lenten fasting could prompt a turning away from sin, obstinacy, and disobedience and a return to God. Jeremy Taylor, for example, described fasting as an "instrument" that serves as "the nourishment of prayer, the restraint of lust, the wings of the soul, the diet of Angels, the instrument of humility, and self-denial, the purification of the Spirit."[42]

Because Christians ostensibly refrained from eating dairy products, sweets, and meat during Lent, special dinners, designed to use up those ingredients and get them out of the kitchen, were held on Shrove Tuesday, the day before Lent began. Some Virginians followed the practice of eating pancakes on Shrove Tuesday.[43] Sometimes that custom occasioned reflection and introspection appropriate to the Lenten season. The most intriguing instance comes from the diary of Landon Carter. It appears that it was William Beale's custom to invite his extended family over for pancakes on Shrove

Tuesday. Beale was closely related to the Carter family—his sister, Elizabeth, was the third wife of Landon Carter, and Beale's daughter Winifred was the daughter-in-law with whom the contentious Landon Carter tangled over the cupboard keys. Around 1772 Judith Carter, Landon's youngest, took a shine to Winifred's brother, Reuben. Landon Carter tried to stifle their courtship, but the young couple was determined. Defying her father, Judith left Sabine Hall and took up residence at the home of William Beale, her uncle and Reuben's father. Carter refused to be reconciled to the situation, but Judith nevertheless married Reuben (his moniker in Landon's diary was "the monster") in 1773. In 1774 father and daughter undertook a gradual rapprochement, but it was bumpy—Landon began to suspect that the Beales were after his property, and although he visited with Judith, he refused, until close to the end of his life, to recognize her husband.

Throughout this drama, Beale invited Carter to his annual Shrove Tuesday party, and Carter continually refused to attend. In 1774 that refusal occasioned a troubled rumination in his diary. His entire family headed to the Beales' for Shrove Tuesday pancakes, and Carter "was left alone without one Soul but my Servants. . . . Appetite I had none, and the Cholic upon me." Still, he forced himself to eat a little something, and there, alone at his table, his obdurate pride keeping him from celebrating with his family, Carter was moved to reflect on his own miserable state and his Lord's mercy. "It proved a Melancholly day indeed; Yet I had a God to hope in and adore. . . . I called on my God, wished for a more placid moment, though with grateful acknowledgements I remembered his past Mercies, and was thankful. If I have not deserved such mercy, I trust it can only be imputed to those frailties which are incident to human nature, and in no instance the effect of ingratitude or disinclination to adore All goodness and Mercy."[44] Alone and despondent, the irascible lord of the manor turned to God, and for a moment, he allowed his Shrove Tuesday meal—which, because of his own stubbornness, was no Shrove Tuesday meal at all—to puncture his own swagger. At the same time, his lonely meal did not prompt Carter to repent or extend himself to the Beales. The Beales' pancake supper served its purpose of building the community (that is, the Beales), and teasing (but only teasing) the conscience of one who placed himself outside that community.

After Shrove Tuesday pancakes came the Lenten fast. The practice of fasting during Lent dates to the Patristic Era, and the nature of the fast became an issue of serious debate during the Reformation. Before the Reformation, the church calendar was punctuated by many fast days, including the days of Lent, Fridays, and some saints' days. "Fasting" did not mean wholesale avoidance of all food, but, for most Christians, limiting one's self to one meal a day, a simple meal, generally consisting of fish and vegetables. Reformers attacked the stringent fasts required of the laity—Luther famously asserted that Rome forbade butter on fast days because Italians wanted to sell more "inferior Italian oil." Still, most Protestant churches maintained the practice of abstemious eating on Fridays and during Lent. In England, both James I and Charles II attempted to enforce meatless fasts during Lent. "The talk of the town," wrote Samuel Pepys in his diary on February 14, 1661, "is whether Lent shall be kept with the strictnesse of the King's proclamation, which is thought cannot be, because of the poor, who cannot buy fish."[45]

Two surviving sets of texts tell us about Lenten fasting in eighteenth-century Virginia. The first comprises the many recipes in both printed and manuscript cookery texts for Lenten food. These recipes suggest how the ecclesial imperative to fast was translated, interpreted, and put into practice in people's daily lives. More than any other ecclesial season, authors of cookery texts were interested in Lent. Recipes for pea soup were the most common Lenten recipes. An anonymous Virginia cookbook from 1700 offers several recipes for pea soup, including "Pease-Soup for Lent or any Fasting day." The published English cookbooks Virginians used also recommended "Pease Soup for Lent": in lieu of the bacon and beef bones that Elizabeth Raffald called for in her "Common Pease Soup" recipe, anchovies and red herring featured in her Lenten pea soup. Cooks were encouraged to garnish the soup with "a little dried Mint if you wish it." Elizabeth Moxon's recipe for "Peas Soop in Lent" also substituted anchovies for the beef, bacon, and mutton called for in her "Peas Soop in Winter" recipe. Virginians' cookery texts also encouraged eating fish during Lent. In *The Experienced English House-keeper,* Elizabeth Raffald recommends dressing cod rounds "as little turkeys" by stuffing them with a mixture of oysters, butter, nutmeg, pepper, salt, and egg yolk. After roasting the cod, dress it in oyster sauce, and garnish with barn-berries: "It is a pretty Side Dish for a large Table, for a Dinner in Lent." E. Smith's "Sauce for Fish in Lent, or at any Time" was a horseradish-lemon concoction.[46]

The Lenten cook did have options beyond pea soup and fish. Mrs. Glasse offered a "Variety of Dishes for Lent"—eel soup, rice soup, barley soup, "Rice-Milk" (a sort of rice pudding), stewed spinach and eggs. Glasse also included a few modest Lenten desserts, including apple fritters, stewed pears, a tansey (made with cream and orange-flour water, dyed green with spinach juice), hasty pudding, and a creamy orange fool. Other cookery books popular in Virginia suggested that "Herb Pye" (made from lettuce, leeks, "spinage," beets, and parsley) and potato pie were suitable Lenten dishes. Martha Bradley's manual *The British Housewife* told cooks how to transform endive, parsley, chervil, onion, butter, and egg into "White Soup for Lent." E. Smith instructed cooks to fry up "balls for Lent" made from white bread, egg, and some spices, and she included recipes for Lenten spinach soup, and a currant-and-raisin-filled "Bread and Butter Pudding for Fasting-Days." Cookery texts also included suggestions for adapting standard recipes for the penitential season: when making oyster soup, the cook "may add strong broth or fried gravy if not in Lent." The Virginia cookbook from 1700 and E. Smith's *Compleat Housewife* both include recipes for wigs, wedge-shaped buns that people often ate during Lent. All of these recipes were meatless—yet the authors did not explain why one might avoid meat during Lent. The silence is suggestive: unlike the proper way to set a table, something many of the books explained, cookery authors assumed that readers would already know the reasons behind Lenten culinary practices.[47]

These recipes are usefully read alongside Parson Robert Paxton's sermon "On Repentance," which gives some sense of what Anglican laypeople heard from their clerics about the meaning and practices of Lent. On the first Sunday of Lent, a "season of devotion & humiliation so solemnly observed in the former & purer ages of the Christian Church," Paxton took Joel 2:12–13 as his text: "Turn ye even to me saith the Lord to all your heart & to fasting & to weeping & to mourning. And rent your heart & not your garments, & turn unto the Lord your God for he is gracious & merciful, slow to anger & of great kindness, & repenteth him of the evil." Lent, Paxton explained, was "a season of recollectn & repentance to all" who "by examining the state of yr own Souls, would find occasion more than enough" for penance. Paxton believed that the practice of private penance was more important than ever, since "the decay of publick & judicial chastismt hath left us more in our own hands." The central "help to & instrumt of repentance" was fasting, a practice, Paxton underscored, that had the imprimatur of both Jews and Christians—indeed it may even be found in "natural religion" for "it is a very natural expressn of sorrow . . . for persons in grief to neglect ymselves, to find no relish in, & lose all appetite to the usual refreshmts & Comforts of life." The end of fasting was inward change—God desires not wailing, said Paxton, but "the grief of our hearts"—and to fast was no small undertaking. "Now by this is not meant meerly a change in the kind of our meals, or in the usual time of taking ym," exhorted Paxton. Rather, Lent required "a denying our selves in the quantity & quality of our refreshmts in such manner as may be a real punishmt & humiliation to the body & its appetites."[48]

Paxton's sermon echoes the Christmas sermons we have already considered. At both Christmas and Lent, clergy tried to shape domestic religious practice. Christmas preachers tried to rein in what they perceived to be the excesses of domestic Christmas celebrations. During Lent, Paxton tried to inspire practitioners to a more vigorous domestic engagement with the penitential season. Paxton's sermon, with its nostalgia for some bygone era in which people took Lenten fasting and repentance more seriously, was labored. He strained to convince his congregants to fast because, quite simply, most elite Virginians were not inclined to observe a fast with a rigor sufficient to please Paxton.

There seems to be a gap between the sermon and the recipes, and it is a gap our imaginations must fill in. Mrs. Glasse's Lenten apple fritters do not betoken a severe fast in which practitioners "subdue the flesh & its appetites." Women like Sarah Foote Stuart, Katherine Foote Washington, and Elizabeth Foote Washington did not defer to clerics' authority and accept a rigorous regime of fasting, but, using cookbooks tied to the church calendar, they did oversee the preparation of a modified Lenten diet. In serving foods like Elizabeth Smith's balls for Lent or Elizabeth Moxon's Lenten pea soup, elite Anglican women in Virginia were able to maintain the rhetoric of Lenten fasting even as they have freed themselves from the homiletical imperative of a difficult and transforming fast. Of course, this is an old story in the church—clerical elites articulating a high standard, and laity modifying clerical instruction, cobbling together a practice that seems manageable, but nonetheless suffices to keep the laity bounded in the church community. Overseeing the preparation and consumption of modified Lenten dishes allowed elite women to imagine that they had performed their Christian—indeed, specifically Anglican—duties, without engaging a painful or rigorous "real punishmt & humiliation to the body & its appetites."

Perhaps the clergy's discomfort with domestic holiday celebrations was, in part, discomfort with women's roles in domestic feasting and fasting. Women's authority in food preparation was contested, but at the same time, women were associated (in part through ownership of cookery texts, cooking implements, and foodstuffs) with cooking, and women had a more prominent role in gentry's liturgical foodways than they did in many other religious activities. (To put it another way: if household feasts may be read as "righting" the egalitarianism implied in the ecclesial Eucharist, they may also be seen as reversing Eucharistic gender roles. Elite white women's presiding over the preparation of domestic feasts ritually displaced the male clerics who presided over the ecclesial Eucharist.) Clergy, who in general wanted to delimit elite laity's domestic religion, may have tried especially keenly to reshape laity's holiday table celebrations because in the elite's alimentary religiosity, *women's* challenge to clerical authority was particularly on display.

The Foote sisters' cookery book, and those cookery texts owned by other gentry women in Virginia, may be read not only as manuals for cooking but also as manuals for the religious ordering of a household. Such books were used by the women who owned them and by their enslaved cooks in the preparation of such dishes as Twelfth Night cake and spinach soup for Lent. Women like Sarah Foote, as they oversaw the preparation of mince pies and "Bread and Butter Pudding for Fasting-Days," were at once tying their households to the order of the church and subtly flouting clerical instruction to produce merely moderate Christmas feasts and to embrace punishing Lenten discipline. Through overseeing the production of liturgically timed feasting and fasting, women framed settings in which members of their families could forge an embodied connection to Anglican time and the events of Christ's life. At the same time, women were also framing social dramas, depending on slave labor to stage domestic Eucharists that inverted the implied egalitarianism of the church Eucharist. When Elizabeth Foote Washington noted that her copy of *The Compleat Housewife* was a beloved "old family book," one she had rebound so that it might survive another generation, she was naming its meaning and its emotional and familial value. That value came not only from use, gifting, and inheritance but also from its place in the production and consumption of meals through which the Foote sisters linked their families to the church while simultaneously asserting their prerogative to orchestrate celebrations in the household, where, from their "throne," they could preside.

CHAPTER FIVE

"To Comfort the Living"
The Household Choreography
of Death and Mourning

The end of funeral duties is . . . to testify the care which the church hath to comfort the living, and the hope which we all have concerning the resurrection of the dead.

—Richard Hooker, *Of the Laws of Ecclesiastical Polity*, book 5

We began this book with George Mason, writing his will shortly after the death of his wife, Ann Eilbeck Mason.

Let us go now to Gunston Hall, a few months before Ann died. Ann lay languishing in bed. Her tenth pregnancy had been difficult, and the twins she had delivered in December 1772, Richard and James, had died within a day of their premature birth. Ann suffered in bed for weeks after the delivery, perhaps unable to shake her sorrow, certainly unable to overcome the "slow fever" that drained her of strength. By early March, Ann realized that she was dying. A few days before her death, she called her son John Mason to her "sick bed." She took him in her arms, and, as John recalled years later, "told me she was soon going to leave us all, kissed me and gave me her blessing, and charged [me] to be a good boy, to love and obey my father, to love and never quarrel with my brothers & sisters, to be kind to the servants, and if God spared me, when I grew up, to be an honest and useful man."[1] On March 9, Ann died. She left nine sons and daughters, ranging in age from three to twenty, and a grief-stricken husband. Ann was thirty-nine years old.

Deaths like Ann Eilbeck Mason's, and those of her twins, were facts of life in eighteenth-century Virginia.[2] Virginia gentry, like most early modern people, encountered death regularly, as part of their everyday lives. People died at home. They were buried there, so the living regularly encountered tombstones, visual markers of death. The bereaved announced their grief sartorially, wearing black garments and mourning jewelry. Men and women

5.1
Ann Eilbeck Mason died in 1773 at age thirty-nine. She left behind nine
sons and daughters and a deeply bereaved husband. Virginia Museum of
Fine Arts, Richmond. Gift of David K. E. Bruce.

transcribed reflections on mortality into their commonplace books.[3] Over
dinner in the dining rooms of great estates, husbands and wives discussed
where they would be buried, and whether or not they would have elaborate
grave markers.[4]

    An astute anthropological literature on death has helped historians un-
derstand that the ways people dispose of their dead reveals a great deal of
what they think about life. Many of the great twentieth-century anthropologists, from Durkheim and Hertz to van Gennep and Turner to Malinowski
and Geertz, have made significant contributions to historians' understandings of death. This anthropological literature has suggested that many societies enact "elaborate rituals of death that stretch out the death from a

physical moment to a drawn out series of rituals of separation." Anthropologists have helped historians see that death may generally be read as a rupture —a rupture to individual lives, to families, to communities, to the social order—and that the practices that are enacted around death are *attempts:* attempts to suture the rupture that death created, attempts to restore order to a social body disordered by death, attempts to create lasting memories of parents, children, and spouses, attempts to make meaning and find comfort in the face of calamity.[5]

In recent decades a small but quite sophisticated literature on dying in early Virginia has emerged. Scholars have drawn connections between white Virginians' "deathways" and those of men and women in the regions of England to which Virginians traced their roots.[6] At the same time, white Virginians' death practices were gradually if subtly reshaped by contact with the mortuary practices of Afro-Virginians.[7] In this chapter, I will explore the ways that death and mourning, like much else in gentry religious life, was situated in the household, and I will suggest that in gentry practices of death and bereavement we see further the blurring of the ecclesiastical and the domestic. In his 1976 study *The Religions of the People in Sixteenth Century Champagne,* A. N. Galpern described the Christianity of medieval Europe as "a cult of the living in the service of the dead."[8] In the deathways of Virginia gentry, we glimpse this formulation's reversal; Anglican mortuary practices represent a cult of the dead in the service of the living. Unlike medieval mortuary practice, in which the bereaved used funerary rituals in part to placate the souls of the dead and affect the decedent's eternal fate, eighteenth-century gentry's deathways preeminently and deliberately worked for the living. Mourning rites comforted the living and kept the memory of the dead both contained and yet ever-present. Furthermore, the death practices considered in this chapter helped elite Virginians maintain and intensify familial identities, and to perpetuate those identities through time. In rites that directed practitioners to attend both to their progeny and to their ancestors, Virginia gentry actively concocted their lineage—their physical lineage and their spiritual lineage.

In his magnum opus, *Of the Lawes of Ecclesiastical Polity,* the Anglican theologian Richard Hooker offered a theological apology for Anglican funeral practices. His defense is apposite to our investigation of eighteenth-century Virginia Anglican practices because the practices Hooker defended against Puritan criticism were those practices still undertaken by elite Anglicans in colonial Virginia: wearing mourning attire, using a set funeral liturgy, preaching funeral sermons, serving a "funeral banquet." In arguing for these practices, Hooker marshaled examples of mourning from Scripture: because David "being in heaviness went up to the mount with his head covered," people could wear mourning clothing; because Proverbs instructed readers to "give wine . . . unto them that have grief of heart," funerary repasts were appropriate. Hooker read in these practices an explicit theological meaning: they showed "that love towards the party deceased which nature requireth"; they "do him that honour which is fit both generally for man and particularly for the quality of his person"; and they "testify the care which the Church hath to comfort the living, and the hope which we all have concerning the resurrection for the dead." It was this final meaning that was the most important to Hooker: "The greatest thing of all other about this duty of Christian burial is an outward testification of the hope which we have touching the resurrection of the dead. . . . Take away this which was ordained to show at burials the peculiar hope of the church of god concerning the dead, and in the manner of those dumb funerals what one thing is there whereby the world may perceive we are Christian men?"[9] In an early modern Christian vocabulary, *hope* often meant not a wishful desire that might or might not come to pass, but a confident anticipation. As noted in John Brown's *A Dictionary of the Holy Bible*—a book owned by Landon Carter and perhaps other Virginia gentry—hope means "EXPECTATION," "a confident persuasion of obtaining some future good."[10] This confident hope about the resurrection was characteristic of Virginia gentry deathways. Hooker's assertion that one "end of funeral duties is . . . to testify the care which the church hath to comfort the living" is also germane to colonial Virginia. When faced with death, Anglican gentry turned to practices of dying and mourning that were, in the earlier sense of the term, "comfortable": they comforted the dying and the bereaved with the hope of resurrection, and they solaced those who anticipated their own death with the thought that just as they actively mourned and perpetuated the memories of their dead friends and relatives, so too their own memories would be perpetuated after their deaths.

Before we consider the specific practices of death and mourning found in elite Anglican households, one overarching observation is in order. The material objects that were produced in and made possible household religious practice—embroidery, prayer books, pancakes and pea soup, baptismal bowls and christening gowns—have figured prominently throughout the present study. But the sheer number and diversity of material objects related to death is striking: tombstones, funeral food, mourning jewelry, family Bibles in which the names of the dead were inscribed. Material objects played a significant part in the process of social reintegration that must happen after death.

Most of the items that figure in Virginians' rites signify permanence—perhaps a comforting reassertion of survival in the face of death's reminders of impermanence. (This is not true of all objects that attend death rituals. The flowers that are ubiquitous in present-day American funerals, for example, reiterate rather than contradict the evanescence and brevity of life.) Furthermore, these objects effect a kind of substitution—the hair in the mourning ring worn by Ann Mason's husband became an embodied synecdoche of Ann; the terse lists inscribed in treasured family Bibles in a sense replace the children whose short lives were narrated there.[11]

The material culture of mourning was not unnoticed by practitioners, who commented on it in their writings and even in their dreams. In her commonplace book, Maria Carter inscribed a verse from Pope about the impropriety of desiring to have one's body dressed for burial in clothes too fine: "Let a charming Chintz, and Brussels lace, / Wrap these cold Limbs, and shade this lifeless face." William Byrd's dreams incorporated material markers of death and burial—suggesting that the external features of mortality and mourning did not just express the fact of death but shaped Byrd's interior and imaginative understandings of it. Specially, Byrd dreamed of coffins ("I dreamed a coffin was brought into my house and thrown into the hall"), mourning coaches ("I dreamed a mourning coach drove into my garden and stopped at the house door"), and mourning biscuits ("I dreamt last night that I received letters from England with a paper of funeral biscuits, by which I expect letters from thence to tell me of the death of Colonel Parke very soon"). The memories of deceased people were sustained through the circulation of objects like mourning rings. As Edmund Randolph noted in the recollection he wrote of his dead wife, Elizabeth Nichols Randolph, seeing "objects with which she was associated" called her to his mind. Mourning objects were commonplace, and they made memory and mourning part of everyday experience. Randolph and Byrd didn't have to go to a churchyard to encounter death—reminders of death stole into their bedrooms at night and were wrapped around their fingers.[12]

Dying in Virginia

Both dying and mourning were finely choreographed in the gentry households of eighteenth-century Virginia. The first step in the choreography of dying was *preparing* to die. A small library of English manuals on the "art of dying" stressed that all of life should be viewed as preparation for death. At the same time, they also urged dying people to acknowledge the imminence of death, and get ready for it, materially and spiritually.[13] Virginians themselves took up the same themes. Virginia parsons taught that preparation for death was a lifelong process—as James Maury noted, "The grand business of life is to prepare for death." Virginia clergymen took deaths in their communities as opportunities to remind other parishioners to prepare for their own deaths. When Lewis Burwell died, for example, Stephen Fouace wrote to a mutual friend, "I Pray God makes us all mindful; of the place [Burwell has] gone to yt we may be well-fitted and ppared wn our turn comes." Virginians nursing ill relatives also tried to help the critically ill see that their end was near, as when Mary Anne Fontaine Maury's sister "acquainted her she was dying." It was hoped that critically ill people would recognize the severity of their condition and prepare for immediate death.[14]

For elites, especially elite men, preparing for death often involved making a will. Virginians who left wills (wealthy, white men were the most likely to do so) typically wrote them quite close to their own deaths, after the onset of illnesses judged potentially fatal.[15] Recognizing the imminence of death also prompted some people to plan their funerals. Parson John Thompson praised clerk Cole, who lost three children to the same distemper that then killed him, for becoming "Some Days be fore his Death . . . sensible of his approaching Dissolution." Cole "took all possible care, to make due Preparation for it." For example, before Cole died, he chose the biblical text on which he wanted his funeral sermon to be preached (Ps 90:6). Because Cole responsibly attended to matters like his funeral, and perhaps his will, he was, Parson Thompson noted, freed to reflect on eternal matters, to "looke up wth a cheerful Assurance to ye great Supporter of his Being, & enabl'd . . . to see through ye darkest clouds of Sorrow & Affliction, to beyond wth an Eye of Faith ye Heavenly Country whither he was travelling, a where he hop'd shortly to arrive; being confident, I say, a willing rather to be absent from ye Body, & to be present with ye Lord."[16]

As John Mason's recollections of his mother's last days suggest, the death-bed was often the site of important encounters—rituals of reconciliation, comfort, and leave-taking. The deathbed was a place of memory making, a space where, in anticipation of death, religious ritual was enacted, dying parents gave speeches to children, and people tried to reconcile with those with whom they had quarreled.[17] Deathbeds were not spaces dominated only by close kin, and deathbed scenes were not necessarily intimate. Rather, the deathbed was a more broadly social scene, in which clergy and neighbors participated. Clergymen regularly visited the sick, sometimes leaving home in the middle of the night to celebrate Holy Communion at a parishioner's bedside. Dying people sometimes spoke to friends and family of reconciliation. For example, during one sickbed visit, William Byrd's friend Major Burwell begged Byrd to pray for him and to "make up any disagreement" with his children.[18]

Slaves were also present at gentry deathbeds, doing the work of caring for the seriously ill: fluffing pillows, cleansing fevered bodies, changing soiled linens.[19] At a symbolic level, slaves' presence at deathbeds contributed to the pageantry of mourning and allowed dying members of the gentry to see their whole world—their wealth and their accomplishments and those persons over whom they had mastery—arrayed before them at death. But slaves may have had their own reasons for devotedly attending their masters' deathbeds. The death of an owner could spell disaster for enslaved men and women, as the terms of their owner's will could order them sold away from family. By the same token, deathbed devotion sometimes resulted in manumission, as when Charles Smith of Norfolk County freed Mary, pending her serving his grand-daughter for one year, because of Mary's "assiduous and painful Attendance on her said Master during a long lingering Illness."[20]

The choreography of the deathbed scene often provided dying women a powerful opportunity to speak—to have their words listened to attentively, and recorded. Although Ann Mason herself left no known writings, her words have made it into the historical record because her son John listened carefully to the blessing his mother gave him on her deathbed and immortal-ized her deathbed speech in his memoirs. Martha Jefferson's dying words were remembered and recorded years later by her daughter, Martha Jefferson Randolph, and were also circulated in secondhand tales, as when Edmund Bacon, Monticello's overseer, years later recalled that "Mr. Jefferson sat by her, and she gave him directions about a good many things that she wanted done. When she came to the children, she wept and could not speak for some time. Finally she held up her hand, and spreading out her four fingers, she told him she could not die happy if she thought her four children were ever to have a stepmother brought in over them. Holding her other hand in his, Mr. Jefferson promised her solemnly that he would never marry again." Similarly, William Fitzhugh's sister Dorothy Fitzhugh Luke left behind a scant trail. Yet her final wishes are known to us because her brother listened carefully as on her deathbed, Dorothy "by her last dying words entreated & desired" her husband to send her mother, who still lived in England, money and "her cloaths linen & silks." When Mary Anne Fontaine Maury died, her sons recorded, and then told other relatives in letters, how "she spent her last moments in wholesome admonitions to all about her, and in blessing us her children."[21]

We do not know much about the moment of death itself—Virginians seem not often to have reflected in writing about the moment when a mother or husband or child died, the moment when dying body became a corpse. But once a person did die, family and friends moved from preparing for death to preparing for burial. The body was typically wrapped in a shroud, which could be made from almost anything—a sheet, a piece of flannel, a curtain. The winding sheets were left loose at the corpse's hands and feet so that, at the resurrection, the person would have an easier time getting up. When Priscilla Dawson died at Belvedere plantation, John Harrower wrote that "the corps was dressed in a Calico gown and a white apron was put in a black walnut coffin lined with flannel and pinchback handles. The corps had also a sheet round them." Harrower's passive voice—"the corps was dressed . . ."—is maddening, because one of the great mysteries of gentry Virginia deathways is *who* prepared the corpse for burial. English precedent would suggest that Virginians assigned this task to women, but were gentry women lovingly preparing the bodies of their husbands and children for the grave, a last act of attentive, embodied devotion? Or did gentry delegate the preparation of the corpse to slaves? The evidence is too sketchy to permit a confident answer.[22]

Some families followed the custom of refusing to allow the body to be left alone between the time of death and the time of burial. John Harrower described keeping watch with Dawson's corpse until Dawson could be buried: on Saturday, he "sat up all night with the Corps in Company with Miss Lucy Gaines, Miss Molly White and Mr. Frazer our overseer," and Sunday night, Harrower again "sat up this night also in company with the former young ladies and Mr. Heeley Schoolmaster at Mr. Spotswoods." The custom of keeping vigil has roots in antiquity; those keeping vigil were keeping the potentially restless dead person company until his or her body could be laid safely in the ground. Vigil keeping also helped certify that the person presumed dead really was dead, and would not be mistakenly buried alive.[23]

After being prepared for burial, the body was absorbed into the ecclesial rituals of funeral and burial. Historians of England have identified this as the moment when the body left domestic space and entered public space, when English corpses ceased being the object of customs that were "home-based and largely female in character" and became the object of rituals that are more public and overseen by men.[24] For Virginia gentry, that dichotomy did not hold as neatly. To be sure, the funeral service itself was the moment in the rituals of death that was most public and most likely to happen in a church building, and the one where a clergyman was most central. But Virginia's deathbed rituals, as we have seen, had both a public and a clerical dimension, and the rituals of burial and funeral had "home-based" components, too.

The funeral rituals had four central elements: a burial, a meal, a liturgy, and a sermon. The order of these events varied—sometimes, for example, the sermon and the interment were held on the same day, but at other times the burial and sermon occurred days apart.[25] The most obvious "home-based" element of gentry deathways is Virginia gentry's preference to be buried at home. As Hugh Jones explained in 1724:

> The parishes being of great extent (some sixty miles long and upwards) many dead corpses cannot be conveyed to the church to be buried: So that it is customary to bury in gardens or orchards, where whole families lye interred together, in a spot generally handsomely enclosed, planted with evergreens, and the graves kept decently. Hence likewise arises the occasion of preaching funeral sermons in houses, where at funerals are assembled a great congregation of neighbors and friends; and if you insist upon having the sermon and ceremony at church, they say they'll be without it, unless performed after their usual custom.

Throughout the century, travelers commented on the custom: an English woman who visited Virginia in the 1750s noted, "It is the Custom of this Place to bury their Relations in their Gardens." A visiting Frenchman noted that the stepdaughter of a man he met in Gosport, "lies in the garden, where a tablet gives the details of her life and death." Just as the elite practice of domestic baptism annoyed clergy, clerics complained about backyard burials. But the practice continued nonetheless.[26]

As there were practical reasons for household baptism, there was also practical utility in household burial. Given the distance between the church and the house, families wanted beloved decedents to be interred near the home so that mourners could visit graves easily. Home burials also allowed survivors to look after the cemetery and ensure that animals did not root up and feed on the graves of the dead or break down the gravestone. Robert Carter "observed that he much dislikes the common method of making burying yards round the churches and having them open to every beast."[27] But Hugh Jones's testy comments suggest that the gentry's desire for household burial was about more than just convenience, since, as Jones noted, when clergymen "insist[ed] upon having the sermon and ceremony at church, they say they'll be without it, unless performed after their usual custom." Household burial was also a marker of status. As Philip Fithian observed pointedly, "only the lower sort of people are buried at the Church; for the Gentlemen have private burying yards."[28] The historian Patrick Butler has found that "by the eighteenth century, with the exception of Williamsburg, those buried at churches were usually landless and had no permanent identity within the context of Virginia culture."[29] Of course, churchyard burial potentially bespoke status, too: ornate and imposing headstones in the Bruton Parish churchyard in Williamsburg broadcast decedents' wealth and prominence to the entire church community. Household burial was a marker of status because household burial made clear that the decedent was a property owner (or identified with the family of a property owner). Furthermore, household burial precluded the tacit social leveling suggested by burial in the churchyard, where a certain "everyone" had the same resting place. Choosing to be buried in one's garden, instead of in church, also had implications for what one thought about one's estate: church was "holy ground," sanctified, and Anglican theologians such as Jeremy Taylor underscored that it was important to be buried there because the churchyard was "the field of God . . . sowen with the seeds of the resurrection."[30] To insist on household burial was to suggest that one's estate was holy ground, too, and that one wanted to be resurrected with one's kin. The gentry's home burials thus tacitly endorsed the existing social order, and the gentry's chosen burial location suggests the triumph of household identity over ecclesial. Gentry people's final identification was not with the church but with their own property; perhaps in this burial pattern we see the seeds of the storied southern attachment to the land, and the imbrication of familial identity and identity with the land.

The ongoing connections between the dead, the living, and the family estate were further reified by the iconography and writing on tombstones. The words on Virginia tombstones were patently didactic, instructing the viewer to follow the deceased's "pattern": "In the several Regards of Private Life a Pattern Worthy of Imitation," "a pattern of piety and virtue," "a pattern of true piety," "an Illustrious Pattern of Living Well." A recurring "pattern of piety" was family. Epitaphs praised women for faithfully "discharge[ing] the Several Duties of Wife, Mother, Daughter, Neighbor," and they noted when someone had been "A careful Mother teaching Vertuous Life / Happy and making happy when a wife." Epitaphs observed tenderly that "Susanna . . . and her infant son lie here," or noted just as bluntly when a woman was "Issueless." Fatherhood was lauded, too, as was being a "Compassionate Master."[31]

If words tied the deceased to their families (and the living to their ancestors), the iconography on Virginia tombstones tied graves to houses. The predominant images were not death's heads or otherworldly angels (though both can be found). Instead, as Patrick Butler has observed, Virginia tombstones often featured architectural elements—the baroque and classical curves, swirls, flourishes, and geometric patterns that decorated Virginians' homes were quoted in their tombstones. Even when members of the gentry chose to be buried in churchyards, not in their own gardens, as was the case with the Ball family, their tombstones featured architectural imagery that visually and imaginatively tied the tombs back to the deceased's estate. These architectural elements can be read in two ways. First, architectural images would have directed the viewer's attention not heavenward with the angels but back to the decedent's estate, suggesting the continued links between the dead and those who still lived there, and tying the decedent's identity not to church but to the household. At the same time, the architectural designs did not unambiguously connote, as one might expect, the seeming permanence of imposing manors. Anglican devotional writers read architecture as a symbol of decline—the inevitable decline and decay of even the grandest buildings. Man-made buildings in earthly cities, wrote Richard Allestree, are "but of Clay and Stuble, the Work of Mens Hands, and those that make 'em are like unto 'em, of a Frail dissolution: but this Coelestial City is made by him who made the Hands, whose Architecture is the Almighty, these Buildings therefore are, *John* 14.2. the abiding Mansions, whereas those Earthly ones: 2 *Cor.* 5.1. are but Gourds, but Fleeting Tabernacles." The architectural images found on gentry tombstones, then, both connected mourners and the decedent to the household and the family that lived within, and subtly communicated the fragility of those very institutions.[32]

Another "home-based" element of Virginians' funerary rites was the postmortem meal, which the family of the deceased served the day of the funeral. These meals served the purpose of postmortem social reintegration and reminded the living that they were indeed alive, that life went on. The meals could be rather involved—when Peter Jefferson died, the funerary feast included between thirty-five and one hundred gallons of punch made from £2 6s worth of sugar. The funeral fetes were so elaborate that sometimes the women overseeing them were unable to participate in other social activities. When William Leigh's father died in 1779, he wrote to accept an invitation to visit with a friend. His wife had been invited, too, but "My better Half is so engaged in preparing for my Father's Funeral, that she cannot possibly do as her Inclination would prompt her to do, and therefore I trust you will excuse her." The standard funerary meal consisted of "funeral biscuits" or "mourning biscuits" and wine. Three days after William Byrd's son Parke died, Byrd and his wife gathered friends and family for a special meal of claret and cake. After the funeral of a Captain Llewellyn, friends and family "had wine and biscuits according to custom." "Wine and cake were served very plentifully" at Benjamin Harrison's funeral. Mourning biscuits had a long pedigree in England —predictably, the Puritans tried to stamp out the practice of serving such

5.2
Virginia gentry's tombstones typically featured not angels or death's heads but, like these tombs of the Ball family, architectural elements, which tied the tombs, and the deceased, to the deceased's estate. Photograph by Charles Lawson, Courtesy of St. Mary's Whitechapel, Lancaster, VA.

5.3
This funeral mold, from Virginia's Eastern Shore, would have been used to make "mourning biscuits," which were molasses cookies seasoned with caraway and ginger and eucharistically dipped in wine before being eaten. Courtesy Roughwood Collection. Photo by Rob Cardillo.

biscuits and wine at funerals, to no avail. The biscuits were probably molasses cookies, seasoned with caraway and ginger. They were made with special molds; a heart was the most popular design; cherubim were also popular. The funeral biscuits were typically dipped in alcohol before being consumed. This memorial meal had obvious resonance with the bread and wine of Holy Communion and connected the death of the person just buried to the death—and resurrection—of Jesus Christ. Postmortem meals thus not only signaled that terrestrial life continued for the mourners; they also reminded the bereaved of the resurrected life that followed death.[33]

The third component of the funeral rituals was the "ORDER for the BURIAL of the DEAD." Participants noted that they found this liturgy "affect[ing]." This burial liturgy was so prevalent that neighbors thought it odd when James Gordon decided not to use the Book of Common Prayer for his daughter's funeral, even though everyone knew that Gordon was a Presbyterian sympathizer. Though little is known about the death and burial practices of eighteenth-century Afro-Virginians, one detailed account of a slave's funeral tells us that when an enslaved girl on Robert and Ann Carter's plantation died, the tutor Philip Fithian read the prayer book's liturgy at her burial. Like the Eucharistic mourning biscuit and wine, the liturgy sounded notes of resurrection. The funeral liturgy consisted almost entirely of Scripture, beginning with "I am the Resurrection and the Life" and "I know that my Redeemer liveth. . . . And though after my skin worms destroy this body; yet in my flesh shall I see God." The officiant then read either or both Psalm 39 or 90, each of which chronicles the temporal nature of man and observes that people can accomplish little during life. A reading from 1 Corinthians 15 followed, reminding auditors that "Christ risen from the dead, and become the firstfruits of them that slept." The service ended with a collect that asked God that all present would be included in the "general Resurrection in the last day."[34]

Anglican funerals in Virginia sometimes, but not always, included a sermon. The heart of the sermon was not a eulogy but a meditation on a passage from Scripture. As the aforementioned example of clerk Cole suggests, some dying people selected the text on which they wanted their funeral sermon preached. Mary Bland Lee chose as the text for her funeral sermon "A Favourite text in the bible Psalms . . . wch is marked down in the old Family Bible." Choosing the verse on which one's own funeral sermon was preached showed the decedent's concern for the auditors and what they would learn from the sermon. For example, in his 1749 will, Thomas Lee directed that after he died, "a Funeral sermon for Instruction to the Living be preached." Similarly, William Churchill of Christ Church parish in Middlesex County wanted his funeral sermon to "admonish the living upon the words, 'Set thine house in order, for thou shalt dye and not live,' in the 2d Kings, 20 chapter, and the latter part of the first verse." By choosing this text, Churchill was, in a sense, instructing the living from beyond the grave.[35]

Sermons also included recollections of the decedent and his or her virtues. These biographical reflections were secondary to scriptural reflection, and they were typically brief and not very specific. Pastors preached the same funeral sermon over and over, only modifying slightly the encomia they pronounced about the dead. Charles Clay, for example, preached a funeral sermon on John 16:33b—"In the world ye Shall have good cheer"—at least eight times between 1774 and 1788. The opening varied depending on whether Clay knew the decedent. If he did, Clay pronounced that the gathered mourners had come "together to perform the last sad obsequies to the deceased, on whose Character & in whose praise I might much enlarge." If he did not know the deceased, Clay announced that the congregation had come "together to perform the last sad obsequies to the deceased to whom as I was almost a Stranger; it Cant be supposed that I shd enlarge upon his Character." Other preachers were more inclined to fulsome praise of the decedent—a habit that irked auditors. When the parson who preached Benjamin Harrison's funeral went on at great length offering "an extravagant panegyric," Harrison's neighbor and good friend William Byrd was put out. "At every turn he called him 'this great man,' and not only covered his faults but gave him virtues which he never possessed as well as magnified those which he had."[36]

Preachers thought that funeral sermons were "Chiefly designed to Convey instruction to the living, who alone can be benefited by them." Several of Clay's funeral sermons survive, and it is clear that he thought the sermon was an opportunity to offer congregations important theological instruction, not to carry on lauding the dead: "I might Say much in praise of the deceased," he said at the outset of one sermon, "but instead of Spending Our time in fruitless praises of the Dead who Cannot be benefited by them, I shall take an Opportunity from this Solemn Occasion to press you to preparation for the like Awful Change which ~~they have~~ she has lately experienced." Here was the chance for pastors to tell the congregation what they needed to do to assure eternal life: the "useful lesson" Charles Clay hoped "Discourses of this kind" would convey was "that all flesh is frail, the time of Our Continuance here uncertain, that Eternity depends upon Our present determinations." Insofar as sermons did include discussions "in praise of the deceased," those praises highlighted qualities and behaviors that clergy hoped auditors would copy. One parson praised a Mrs. Jones as a "good Christian who made a constant Profession of all ye Articles of ye Christian Faith; & as often as her health wou'd permit, duely attended ye Publick Worship of God, & constantly communicated at ye Table of Ye Lord; all wh Duties she performed wth great seriousness & Devotion." Another lauded a deceased invalid's "Cheerful Resignation to the will of Heaven and patient endurance of an incurable malady for near 20 years of the better part of her life, which by depriving her of the use of her limbs confined her as a prisoner to her Chambers, which She bore with Xn Patience & Cheerfulness" thus becoming "a worthy example of Piety & Religious Deprtmt." When Thomas Davis preached a funeral sermon for

Peyton Randolph, he both "honour[ed] . . . the deceased," and "recom-mend[ed]" that his auditors imitate Randolph's "virtues."[37]

Critics of Anglicanism dismissed Anglican funeral sermons—to borrow James Gordon's judgment of David Currie's funeral sermon for Mrs. Tayloe—as "superficial discourse." Currie "don't touch upon real religion," thought Gordon.[38] But parsons' desire to inspire people to imitate the virtues of the deceased was closely tied to the theology of salvation that emerged in their sermons. Virginia clergymen's funeral sermons made three main points about death and salvation from the pulpit. First, salvation was not absolutely as-sured. Second, salvation came from God but was related to living a good and holy life (whether the parsons were suggesting that a good and holy life testified to or earned salvation is not entirely clear). Third, parishioners should not postpone repentance until just before death.

In making the first point—that salvation was not a given—Anglican par-sons were not afraid to invoke hellfire. Charles Clay, for example, told his auditors that a man who lived a dissolute life and failed to repent might, at death, face "punishment, and the torments of Hell," doomed. Parsons were not trying to instill in their parishioners the kind of terror and anxiety about salvation that we associate with seventeenth-century New England. They were trying to inspire parishioners to lead good and holy lives. John Thomp-son warned that "A Man, by a long course of wickedness, may arrive at such a hardened state . . . his Soul may be sear'd, as it were, with a hot Iron, & be fallen into such a deep and fatal Letharge, [such that] nothing perhaps shall be able to awaken it, 'till it comes to feel ye very Torments of ye damn'd." To avert such a fate, "The best Preparation for Death & Judgment, is ye consis-tent exercising of Piety & Virtue, in ye whole Course of our Lives." Charles Clay sounded a similar note: in order to avoid a harsh judgment from God, one should live "a good & Virtuous li[f]e . . . before we Come to Die." On a deathbed, "Reflections on a well spent life will comfort us in our Weakness."[39]

This encouragement of virtuous living was related to the third theme in Virginia funeral sermons: cautions against deathbed repentance. Because par-sons wanted to inspire their auditors to live lives wholly devoted to holiness, they warned auditors not to imagine that they could carouse and blaspheme for decades, then blithely repent on their deathbeds. As Parson John Thomp-son asked rhetorically, "How little is it, yt a sick & dying Man can do . . . [in] ye midst of so much Pain & Weakness of Body, & of such Confusion & Amazement of Mind. With what Heart, can he set a 'bout so great a Work, for wch there is so little Time. . . . I will not pronounce any thing concerning ye Impossibility of a Death-bed Repentance: But I am sure yt it is very difficult, & I believe very rare." Charles Clay offered a similar caution: fatal illnesses "may be such as will give us no time to *repent* in." Illness may "utterly hinder . . . composed thinking; we may Die in [con]vulsions, in a stupid Lethargy, or in [the] ravings of a fever, or under such [ripped] & racking pains as shall . . . effectually hinder us from doing any thing towards a happy Departure." Virginia parsons used their criticisms of deathbed repentance to draw a distinction between Anglicans and Catholics, who practiced the "pretended Sacramt" of "extream unction," that is, "the anointing the head of a dying Person." The "Papists" were "infatuated" with this practice, charged Anglican parsons, believing that "if a person is thus anointed before he dies, he is Certainly happy."[40]

Despite parsons' gestures toward hellfire, laypeople seemed to approach death (their own and those of their friends and relatives) with comparative optimism about their eternal prospects.[41] Virginia laypeople were not overly concerned about "the torments of Hell" in part because their theological imaginations had been shaped by the funeral liturgy from the Book of Common Prayer, especially by the prayer for the committal of the body:

> Forasmuch as it hath pleased Almighty God of his great mercy to take unto himself the soul of our dear brother here departed, we therefore commit his body to the ground; earth to earth, ashes to ashes, dust to dust; in sure and certain hope of the Resurrection to eternal life, through our Lord Jesus Christ, who shall change our vile body, that it may be like unto his glorious body, according to the might working, whereby he is able to subdue all things to himself.[42]

This prayer captures the difference between Puritan and Anglican soteriology: as late as 1661, Calvinists were trying to get the phrase "sure and certain" omitted from the prayer book.[43] The phrase was significant to Virginia Anglicans. In another example of the liturgical appropriation we saw in Chapter 3, Virginia Anglicans picked up the liturgy's language of a "sure and certain hope" and used it in their wills and tombstones to speak of their own eternal hope. Some wills, such as Benjamin Harrison's and Mary Ligon's, drew precisely on the language of the prayer for committal, expressing "sure and certain hope of a Joyfull resurrection thro' the death and Passion of my blessed Saviour Jesus Christ" and "sure and certain hope of a joyful resurrection at ye last day." Tombstone inscriptions also echoed the prayer. For example, a tombstone at Teddington tells passersby that Philip Steptoe's body "reposes . . . in the sure and certain hope of a joyful resurrection." Philip Lightfood reposed in Charles City County "In sure and certain Hopes of a joyfull resurrection." Other tombstones included variations on the theme, such as Alice Page's "firm & certain Hopes of a joyfull Reserrection." The 1746 tombstone of twenty-year-old Elizabeth Washington (not Elizabeth Foote Washington, whom we have met before) asserted:

> In a Well grounded Certainty of an
> Immortal Resurrection
> Here lyes the Remains of Elizabeth
> the Daughter of
> John and Catherine Washington.

A striking example from another colony illustrates just how powerfully this liturgical phrase had impressed itself upon colonial Anglicans' imaginations: people in Savannah, Georgia, observed news of the Declaration of Independence by burning an effigy of King George, and enacting a mock version of the Anglican "Service of the Burial of the Dead." They interred "George III" before the courthouse, proclaiming "we therefore commit his political existence to the ground, corruption to corruption, tyranny to the grave, and oppression to eternal infamy; in sure and certain hope that he will never obtain a resurrection to rule again over these United States of America." Prayer-book language had pervaded the culture to the point that it could be used to make a political protest; this was language people used commonly—in at least two senses of the term.[44]

Although preachers warned their auditors that they needed to live virtuous lives in order to avoid eternal perdition, preachers did not explicitly cast doubt on the decedent's eternal prospects. Indeed, parsons told auditors that they could be confident about their deceased friend's eternal state, and because of that confidence they should not mourn too intensely. John Camm made the point in his funeral sermon for William Nelson—a sermon that, tellingly, takes as its text 1 Thessalonians 4:13, "But I would not have you be ignorant, brethren, concerning them which are asleep, that ye sorrow not, even as others which have no hope." When one's spouse or child is "snatched away," it is "a pardonable weakness to be for some time inconsolable." And yet even as one expressed "allowable" grief, Christians were not to "*be sorry as men without hope,*" for they could rest assured that they and their dead beloved would "in a little, perhaps a very little time . . . rejoice [together] in the mansions of the blessed for ever and ever." Mourners' grief should not be excessive because "they who sleep in Christ are secure in peace." Writing about his own mother's death, the Virginia parson James Maury averred that "the decease of a person of her character, if we listen to divine revelation and unbiased reason, cannot be lamented on the person's own account, except we think it acting a rational and Christian part to grieve that the deceased has exchanged mortality and corruption for immortality and incorruption, and removed from the busy, perplexing and toilsome scenes of life to a permanent and immutable state of rest, and peace, and bliss." He admitted that bereaved people do feel grief, "prompted . . . partly by the tender affections of humanity, and partly by a very singular regard for ourselves, which makes us reluctant to part from the comfort and pleasure we used to enjoy in the conversation and society of the departed." But because of "the precious promises of the Gospel," sons of Christian mothers, like Maury, grieved a grief tempered by hope. His grief was not "quite void of comfort, because thence we have hope, that she now rests in a much happier place than a changeable and fleeting world." Anglican mourning was meant to be moderate, because Anglican mourners were to be confident about the eternal prospects of their dead friends.[45]

Laypeople made the same point when they tried to comfort one another after a death. After he learned that his sister had died, for example, John Parke Custis wrote to comfort his mother, Martha Custis Washington. Though himself "sunk under" with grief, Custis implored his mother, "Comfort yourself with reflecting that she now enjoys in substance what we in this world enjoy in imagination." Some Virginia mourners did seem to find some comfort in the promises of postmortem resurrection. Robert Spotswood was deeply grieved by his wife's sudden death, but "[I] thank god the assurance I have of a future with ye conduct of a religious life." That thought "support[ed]" him in his "unhappy circumstances." Elizabeth Foote Washington outlived both of her children, and when her second daughter died, Washington recorded that "surely no woman could have felt more then I have for three months past." Yet Washington took "comfort in thinking that their Redeemer should think them worthy to enjoy heaven, without experiencing any of the troubles that attends mankind in passing through this vale of misery."[46]

Virginia historians have argued that the conventions of grief changed during the eighteenth century. Early-eighteenth-century members of the gentry both enacted a more moderate, restrained bereavement and felt less intense grief than mourners later in the century. In the late eighteenth and early nineteenth centuries, members of the Virginia gentry began to experience more intense sorrow when close relatives, especially children, died. Daniel Blake Smith has connected this change to demography. As life expectancy lengthened, parents felt emotionally free to develop closer ties to their children, and spouses articulated a more affectionate attachment to one another;

thus when death occurred, the pitch of grief was higher. By the end of the eighteenth century people wept more freely, mourned longer and more loudly, than they had at the beginning of the century. Jan Lewis has augmented this analysis with her nuanced consideration of the more emotive grief that emerged among Virginia gentry in the early nineteenth century; Lewis ties this more affective and emotional grief to the rise of "sentimental" religion and to the increased sense among gentry that the world was a place of woe.[47]

To be sure, the conventions of mourning changed between 1710 and 1810. Still, we ought not caricature the earlier style of grief as stoic or overly austere. There are hints that members of the pre-Revolutionary gentry, even as they tried to perform a moderate and restrained mourning, responded to the death of relatives with emotion. Edward Hill was reported, for example, "very disconsolate for the loss of his wife." Robert Spotswood wrote to his mother that he now labored "under the greatest affliction at the loss of my dear wife." Her death was "the most shocking catastrophe." Friends commented on the ways grief was not merely emotional, but also embodied: Mrs. Harrison "trembled" at her husband's funeral.[48]

Throughout the eighteenth century, Virginians typed women as more likely to grieve extravagantly. William Byrd prided himself on holding up well when his ten-month-old son died; his wife, by contrast, succumbed to grief. Lucy Parke Byrd "was much afflicted," wrote her husband, "but I submitted to His judgment better, notwithstanding I was very sensible of my loss, but God's will be done." Byrd was somewhat ambivalent about Lucy's emotion. He wanted her to keep her mourning within "the bounds of sub-mission," but her continued grief—her "several fits of tears for our dear son"— did vicarious work for him, expressing the family's loss without requiring an emotional display from William Byrd himself. Virginians' association of women with intense grief is not unique; in many societies it is women who are expected to weep, women who wear mourning garb, and women who are cas-tigated for their emotion. The anthropologist Maurice Bloch has suggested that this stems from a deep identification grouping death, disorder, and fe-maleness: death signals disorder, so "women are *given* death while the social order is reaffirmed elsewhere"—elsewhere, that is, in a male preserve. In this casting of mourning as feminine, men are identified with order, and women with disorder.[49]

People's emotional experience of grief was shaped by practices of mourn-ing—performances (including the performance of emotion itself) based on convention. Practices of mourning gave practitioners concrete actions that helped them remember the deceased; concomitantly, mourning rites suggested to mourners that their own memory would be hallowed by their survivors. Practices of mourning extended the experience of death beyond the hour, day, or week of the death itself; concomitantly, mourning rites delimited grief and did not let it go on too long.[50] In the remainder of this chapter I will consider two practices—wearing mourning garb, and writing in family Bibles—through which elite Anglicans perpetuated their memories of the dead in their households. These practices both styled bereaved people as such, and contained and calibrated their grief.

"Indicating Outwardly One's Grief": Wearing Mourning Garb

Observing a late-eighteenth-century Virginia gentleman wearing mourning for his stepdaughter, a visiting Frenchman reflected, "The custom of indicating outwardly one's grief at the cruel loss of those to whom one has given life seems to me natural and praiseworthy."[51] Elite Virginians did indeed display and cultivate their grief outwardly, through the wearing of mourning garb. Mourning garb helped people remember their dead and imagine that they too would be remembered; mourning garb communicated grief, both to the mourner herself and to others; and mourning garb drew lines around and between different communities of mourners.

Mourning attire took two forms: textiles (or mourning clothing) and jewelry (principally, but not exclusively, rings). Mourning clothing of the sort worn in colonial Virginia had antecedents in the Middle Ages, when elite mourners wore black clothes (although other colors, including brown and red, were also considered proper for mourning). The tradition moved into the emerging middle classes of Europe in the seventeenth and eighteenth centuries, and it took root in the British Atlantic colonies.[52] As early as 1737 "All Sorts of Goods for Mourning, both for Men and Women" were for sale in Williamsburg. Among the mourning accoutrements that gentry purchased were coats and suits "prop'r for Second Mourning," and mourning gloves and fans; some of this paraphernalia echoed the "mourning banners" that mourners sometimes carried in procession as the coffin was being carried to its interment. Consistent with the tendency to delegate mourning to women, men tended toward simpler mourning garb. Robert Rose illustrated the typical male garb when he wore a mourning armband for five days after the death of his daughter; so did John Blair's friend, Mr. Skelton, who "got a black coat" before the burial of his wife. Women's mourning garb tended to be more elaborate. The gendering of mourning clothing is evident from advertisements—for example, in 1738, Sarah Green Packe in Williamsburg advertised

"Bombazeens, Crapes, and other Sorts of Mourning, for Ladies; also Hat-bands, and Gloves, for Gentlemen." Women more often observed the stages of first (or deep) and second mourning. First mourning or deep mourning typically lasted for three months, during which time more severe sartorial restrictions were in place; women typically wore plain black fabric, such as bombazine. During second mourning, which also lasted for three months, women could wear gray, and their outfits could be accessorized a bit more freely.[53] In establishing a calendar of mourning, with movement from "deep mourning" to "second mourning," mourning clothes thus answered an important question: when does mourning end? Taking off one's mourning clothes was an embodied way that people could conform to the clerical prescriptions not to let their mourning go on too long.

More widespread than the practice of wearing mourning clothing was the practice of wearing mourning jewelry, especially mourning rings. Like black mourning clothing, the custom of presenting rings to the friends and relatives of a recently dead person dates at least to the Middle Ages and became increasingly popular in the American colonies by the middle of the eighteenth century. In Virginia, some mourning rings quoted the color of mourning clothes. For example, in 1741, a black enamel ring with an amethyst was made to commemorate the death of Sarah Berkeley Wormeley of Middlesex County; the black enamel signified the mourner's bereavement. Mourning rings sometimes held hair, as did the ring that George Mason wore, a gold ring with a glass oval top, under which was sealed one of Ann's locks. Perhaps even more than other mourning jewelry, rings with hair allowed for continued intimacy between the deceased and the one who wore it. While New England mourning rings frequently featured "death's heads, skeletons, coffins, and other reminders of the frailty of life," only occasionally does one find a Virginia ring with a standard memento mori image or phrase, such as "prepared be to follow me." Virginians' rings tended more often to be engraved with phrases like "When you see this remember me," or simply the name and death date of the decedent. These engravings, by which rings stressed remembering the decedent more than anticipating one's own death, underscore that, in Virginia, this mourning jewelry functioned principally as a *memento mei* rather than a memento mori. Indeed, people nearing death used mourning rings to actively perpetuate their own memories. Men and women often spelled out in their wills who was to receive mourning rings. For example, Ann Fox wrote in her will that each of two cousins was to inherit a "mourning ring." John Stott designated that his grandsons receive mourning rings and stated that one should read "When this you see Remember me. J.S."

5.4
This ring was worn in memory of Sarah Berkeley Wormeley. The engraving on the outside of the ring band—SW / OB 3 / DEC / 1741 / AE 27—suggests the ring's memento function. Courtesy of the Virginia Historical Society, Richmond.

5.5
This mourning ring was probably worn by George Mason's daughter, Mary Thomson Mason. It is engraved GEORGE MASON: OB: 7: OCT: 1792 and may have contained a lock of his hair. Courtesy of the Board of Regents of Gunston Hall.

This allowed Fox and Stott to direct, before they died, the ways they would be remembered after their deaths.[54]

The rings were distributed either at the funeral or later. Mourning rings, in other words, were gifts from the dead. In understanding how mourning rings subtly functioned as part of a gift economy, it is worth considering the ways that their roles changed as the Reformation inaugurated new soteriologies, in which praying for the dead was no longer seen as an act that would help them achieve salvation. In the medieval English church, a person who received a mourning ring was implicated in a frank, reciprocal economy of gift exchange: the recipient accepted the ring and in exchange prayed for the soul of the dead person. Changing doctrines of salvation eliminated the urgent need to pray for the souls of the dead, but the gift of postmortem jewelry nonetheless implied reciprocity and continuity. The reciprocity tacit in the giving of mourning rings may have been especially poignant when mourning rings were given to children: as Clare Gittings has suggested, a young child given a ring in memory of a father or mother incurred the obligation "to grow up into a new generation of adults, thus preventing death from totally destroying human life."[55]

Mourning garb was communicative. It communicated bereavement, first, to the mourner herself. To wear mourning clothing is to tell one's self that one is bereaved; it is to shape oneself into one who mourns—*fashion* is, after all, a verb as well as a noun. Mourning clothing also externalized mourning and communicated a mourner's bereavement to other people. The Virginia girl Lucinda Orr noted that she saw "Mrs. Brook, Mrs. Selden, and Nancy" wearing "deep mourning" in church. There in the social-cum-spiritual theater of church, the three mourners' clothing wordlessly informed everyone they saw that they were bereaved; the clothing requested, even required, that members of their community respond to them as mourners. Orr was doing her part, too —she noticed what the three women were wearing, and what stage of mourning they were in, and she found this detail significant enough to record.[56]

Mourning garb created boundaries among and between different groups of mourners, drawing borders between and among those closely affected by a death and other more distant kin, neighbors, and associates. Two groups of people wore mourning clothes: men participating in burial rites (as suggested by Elizabeth Stith's will which stated that "the Parson and Clark with the four Men that beir me to the Grave shall have Hat bands and Gloves"),[57] and relatives (of course, the men participating in the funeral were often related to the deceased). Mourning clothing thus instantiated familial identity: it marked the family as such. But it is worth noting that the relatives who wore mourning were not necessarily only the closest relatives. This can be seen by an exegesis of Lucinda Orr's succinct observation that she saw "Mrs. Brook, Mrs. Selden, and Nancy" in deep mourning. The deceased was probably Mary Mason Selden Page, who had died September 17, 1787. The three people in mourning were Sarah Ann Mason Mercer Selden, the second wife of Samuel Selden, and the deceased's stepmother; Maria Mercer Brooke, Mrs. Selden's sister, thus Mary's step-aunt; and Ann Mason Mercer Selden, Mary's half-sister.[58] Thus mourning clothing might extend (as in the case of Brooke) beyond the deceased's direct line. Ties of familial association and affection may have been as important in determining which relatives wore mourning as any abstract etiquette that dictated that certain relations merited mourning clothes and others did not.

Members of the Anglican gentry also used mourning garb to draw and redraw lines of belonging within households, as they negotiated the question of whether to clothe domestic slaves in mourning clothes after the deaths of their owners. Some Virginians, perhaps following the English custom of requiring household servants to wear mourning, did so: Martha Custis ordered mourning clothes, for example, for some of her household slaves after the death of her husband, Daniel Parke Custis. Other Virginians specifically eschewed this custom in their wills. Charles Carter of Cleve wrote in his will, "I do positively forbid the putting of any of my servants in mourning, having always determined within myself as much as in my power lay, by setting a proper example, to put a stop to the ridiculous custom of involving familys by pompous funerals and mourning which serve only to enrich men who watch for these occasions to impoverish their neighbours." When Virginia gentry put their slaves in mourning clothes, they were giving material expression to a kind of paternalism—this was the sartorial equivalent of referring to one's slaves as "family."[59]

At the same time that some members of the gentry physically drew their slaves into the process of mourning them, white Virginians tried to curtail Afro-Virginians' ability to mourn one another. Since the late seventeenth century, the council had banned public slave funerals because "makeing and holding Funeralls for Dead Negroes gives them the opportunityes under protection of such publique meetings to Consult and advise for the Carrying on their Evill & wicked purposes & Contrivances." Masters were to prohibit slaves from holding "any solemnity or Funeralls for dec[ase]d Negroes." In some slave societies, such as South Carolina and Antigua, slaves were forbidden from wearing and exchanging mourning garb in honor of one another.[60] More than simply reflecting slaveowners' concerns about what would happen when slaves gathered together, there is significance in the specific regulation of *funerary* gatherings. Prohibiting slaves from mourning rites was a particularly forceful way of dehumanizing them, and of drawing boundaries between (free) people who were permitted to mourn their dead, and (enslaved) people who were prohibited from mourning their own dead and whose bodies were conscripted into their owners' mourning pageantry when gentry died. Here members of the gentry used the rituals of mourning to differentiate themselves from their slaves, to simultaneously incorporate them into the planter household "family" while denying their full belonging and denying them the means to fashion a separate, communal identity.

Rings also demarcated a community of mourners, but in a way different from clothing. Sometimes, Virginians gave rings only to their nearest and dearest—Sarah Henry left mourning rings to her three sons. But often, a broader range of friends and associates received mourning rings: in his will, Robert "King" Carter instructed that rings be given to thirty people. Yet even as mourning rings often demarcated a larger circle of friends and associates, they cultivated a certain kind of intimacy. As Rachel Monfredo has observed, unlike black clothing, rings' public meaning was limited. In public, especially if one was wearing gloves, passersby could not see that one was wearing a ring at all, let alone the words engraved on it or the hair clasped within it. While a mourning ring communicated little or nothing to a passerby, it could convey a great deal to an intimate friend or relative. The practice of wearing mourning rings also created a new bond of intimacy between sometimes far-flung mourners who wore rings in mourning of the same person. In the colonial context, mourning jewelry could connect people even across oceans, as when Thomas Ludwell wrote from England to Philip Ludwell "I have put on a mourning ring in Memory of yr good Father."[61] If Thomas and Philip both wore a ring in memory of the same person, they were participating in a shared act of memory; wearing mourning jewelry could compensate for their inability to be physically present with each other in their grief.

Mourning rings and mourning clothing thus not only allowed elite Virginians an embodied expression of grief. Mourning garb also allowed them to draw lines of intimacy among family and friends and to create communities of mourners. Mourning garb allowed them to negotiate the publicity and privacy of mourning, and it allowed them to actively perpetuate their own memories before they died. Some of these same themes—the instantiation of family identity through mourning, the need for both publicly communicative and more private mourning practices, and people's active construction of the means by which they would be mourned and remembered—were also at play in the final mourning practice we will consider, writing in family Bibles.

"This Old Book . . . Shows . . . Love": Genealogical Record Keeping as Memorial Practice

In 1870 P. R. Carrington took two halves of an old family Bible to a Richmond bookbinder for repair. The halves of this oft-opened Bible had, for a time, resided in different states—half with P.R. and his wife Sarah in Virginia, and half with Sarah's brother Eugene Carrington in Maryland. On a recent visit, P.R. had persuaded Eugene to part with his half, and then P.R. engaged a bookbinder, who fit the halves together and bound the volume in "handsome Red Russia leather." P.R. took the opportunity of the book's restoration to record what he knew of its history. Published in 1718 and bound with a prayer book, "in heavy boards covered with calf, with brass hinges," the book had been in the Carrington family for almost 150 years. It had originally been given to Sarah Carrington's great-grandfather, George Carrington, "the founder of his name in Virginia," as a "parting gift of his mother" when, in 1723, young George left his home in Barbados. In the years to come, Carrington "recorded the dates, of birth, of his Eleven children, in this book, and with many of them, the very hour, they were born, he also recorded, the deaths of his three sons, George, & the two Williams, and likely, the marriage of his daughter Henningham, & Mary." George Carrington's son, Major Mayo Carrington, inherited the Bible in 1785 and made still more genealogical entries from the Carrington manse, Boston Hill, in Cumberland County. After his death, the Bible was passed among several other relatives; somewhere along the way, it fell apart. P. R. Carrington was exultant that the book was finally restored, and in his and Sarah's possession. "The history of this old book, in its transmission to its present owner," P. R. Carrington opined, "shows the love, that each generation, had for it."[62] What gave the Bible so much meaning, of course, was not the printed biblical text; the Carringtons could easily have purchased another Bible. This Bible gained meaning from the Carringtons' hands. In passing the book from relative to relative and inscribing its pages with family tales, those hands imbued the book with significance. By 1870, a moment at which Christians were increasingly anxious about and implicated in commodification, this family Bible was an anticommodity: worth so much it could not be exchanged, replaced, or re-created.

Carrington's sentimental reflections are revealing, of course, about the era in which he wrote them. In the late nineteenth century, middle-class Americans' devotion to the Bible was rivaled only by their obsession with memory and family. (As Michael Kammen has put it, the late nineteenth century was an era of "memory and ancestor worship by design and by desire.") Nineteenth-century men and women were preoccupied with polishing up their pedigrees, and family Bibles were big business. America's emerging middle class eagerly embraced the practice of recording family genealogies—not just in Bibles, but in family trees, memorial artwork, and embroidered, watercolored, and painted family registers. Bible publishers began to include specially decorated pages, designated for family records (the first of these seems to have appeared in a Bible published in Worcester, Massachusetts, in 1791 by Isaac Thomas). The explosion of designated family Bibles reflected nineteenth-century shifts in printing technology, consumer culture, and missionary efforts, and was part and parcel of the rise of an affectionate and emotional religious sensibility. In the Victorian context, these family registers conferred the respectability of "lineage" on upstart middle-class families, and they served to establish the priority of the family as the central institution in which morality, virtue, sentiment, piety, and emotion thrived.[63]

But the practice of recording genealogical information in Bibles was not new in the nineteenth century; when publishers began printing Bibles with special "family register" pages, they were, to be sure, creating a market, but they were also catching up to an already established practice. Beneath P. R. Carrington's nineteenth-century patina, we may discern a story about eighteenth-century Virginians' recording familial genealogies in their Bibles.[64] Few such Bibles survive today in Virginia archives. The relative scarcity of such Bibles may at once suggest that the practice was not ubiquitous in elite families; that families who did keep such records were loath to give them to archival depositories; that archives are principally interested in collecting the genealogical information in Bibles, not the objects themselves; and that Bibles that were written in and read since the early 1700s fell apart from overuse, as the Carrington Bible did.

The "family Bible" is a familiar yet surprisingly neglected object of study.[65] Yet far from being of interest solely for the rich genealogical information they contain, family Bibles are interesting in their own right. They may be read as props in a number of different social activities. As the historian Karin Wulf has shown, family Bibles may be implicated in property law and inheritance; they may testify to people's hailing from "respectable" families; in a colonial context, they may reflect people's desires to affirm or fabricate a connection to their country of origin.[66] Family Bibles may also be seen as another way in which ecclesial tasks were brought inside the house—the records of births and deaths recorded therein may be seen as a domestic iteration of parish records.[67] Here, I will consider the act of writing records in a family Bible as an act both genealogical and religious, an act of mourning and memory making. Although the practice of keeping a family Bible ought not be reduced to a practice of mourning, mourning is one register on which family Bibles operated.

No one is certain exactly when or where the tradition of writing family records in Bibles began. In the Middle Ages, some people recorded the death dates of family members in books of hours. After the Protestant Reformation created an imperative for people to read and own Bibles, and the print revolution made that ownership possible for an ever expanding number of people, laypeople increasingly began to use their Bibles as repositories for family records. The choice to keep family records in a Bible was doubtless driven by practicality: paper was not readily available, so it made sense to record one's records in the white spaces of a book one already owned.[68] The Bible may also have seemed a logical place for recording family genealogies because Bibles were already full of genealogies—in the Old Testament and the New Testament, in Genesis, in Chronicles, in the prophetic writings of Ezra and Nehemiah, and in the Gospels of Matthew and Luke.[69] (It is also worth noting that in colonial Virginia, some families kept their records in a Book of Common

Prayer—this both echoes the medieval practice of keeping family data in books of hours and underscores my point in Chapter 3 about the centrality of and multiplicity of uses for the prayer book in Anglican Virginia households. Just as, in Virginia Anglican households, the prayer book could be used in the kind of "superstitious" extraecclesial activities in which Englanders and New Englanders would have used the Bible, so too some Virginia Anglicans turned their prayer book, rather than their Bible, into a family register.)[70] Whatever the initial reason people chose to keep these records in Bibles, doing so created a new document—a family narrative, which included memorials to the dead, bound in the book that gave hope, through Christ's death, of eternal life. Transformed by genealogical embellishments, Bibles became not just props in a generic Protestant piety but instantiations of family identity and sites of mourning and memory.

One surviving example of this practice comes from Gunston Hall. Sometime in the 1770s, probably in one or two sittings, George Mason opened his Bible and recorded the creation of his family, beginning with his 1750 marriage to Ann Eilbeck. He recorded the births and baptisms of their children, the deaths of three of those children, Ann's death, and his second marriage. When Mason's twin sons, Richard and James, died the morning after being baptized, Mason noted that they "were buried in the new Burying Ground at Gunston-Hall; being the first of the Family who are buryed in that Place."[71] Unlike more taciturn contemporary genealogical records, which simply noted deaths, Mason glossed the record of the twins' death dates, recording the location of their burial and noting the inauguration of the family cemetery. Putting the children's names in the Bible inscribed their death in a familial-cum-ecclesial object even as their interment in a family burial ground removed them from the church. Mason's gloss shows the multiple ways the twins were included in the family lineage: they were included in the family burial plot, they were included in the family Bible, and their deaths became an especially noteworthy episode in the family narrative because they inaugurated the family burial ground.

But the most striking section of the records in Mason's Bible is the discussion of his wife, Ann. By all accounts, theirs was a love match, and after her death, Mason grieved with an intensity atypical for genteel eighteenth-century men. He said that her death plunged him into a "settled melancholy . . . from which I never expect, or desire to recover," and he performed that melancholy in a number of spaces. For example, he grieved at home: John Mason remembered that after Ann Mason's funeral, his father, George, "for some days paced the rooms, or from the house to the grave (it was not far)

(2)

John Mason was born on Thursday the 4:th of April 1766. about ten o'clock in the Morning at Mrs Eilbeck's in Charles County Maryland, and was privately baptized by the rev.d Mr James Scott.

Elizabeth Mason was born on Tuesday the 19.th of April 1768, about two O'Clock in the Morning, at Gunston-Hall, & was privately baptized by the rev.d Mr Lee Massey, Rector of Truro parish. Mr Martin Cockburn standing God-father & Mrs Ann Cockburn & Miss Elizabeth Bronaugh God-Mother.

Thomas Mason was born on Tuesday the 1:st Day of May 1770. about two O'Clock in the Afternoon at Gunston-Hall & was baptized by the rev.d Mr Lee Massey; Mr Martin Cockburn & Cap.t John Lee standing God-fathers, and Mrs Mary Massey and Mrs Ann Cockburn God-mothers.

Richard Mason and James Mason, Twins, were born on Friday the 5:th Day of December 1772, about eleven o'Clock in the fore-noon at Gunston-Hall, & baptized the same Day by the rev.d Mr Lee Massey; but being born about two Months before their due time (occasioned by a long Illness of their Mother) they both died the next Morning, and were buried in the new Burying-Ground at Gunston-Hall; being the first of the Family who are buried in that Place.

On Tuesday the 9:th of March 1773. about three o'Clock in the Morning, died at Gunston-Hall, of a slow fever, Mrs Ann Mason, in the thirty-nin_____ her Age; after a painful & tedious Illness of more than t__ one with truly Christian Patience & Resignation, in ___ of eternal Happiness in the World to come. ___ the blamelyss & exemplary Life. She retain___ the last, & expending her later 1720 m____ ___d to is me without the usual

5.6
George Mason recorded the deaths of his newborn twin sons in this Bible, noting that Richard and James "were buried in the new Burying Ground at Gunston-Hall; being the first of the Family who are buryed in that Place." Courtesy of the Board of Regents of Gunston Hall.

alone." There are hints that Mason took Ann's funeral as an opportunity to mourn, as well. The funeral itself was simple, "(at her own Request) without the common Parade & Ceremo[ny] of a Grand Funeral." (By recording that detail in the family Bible, Mason both captured a picture of the funeral and cast Ann as a modest woman who spurned vulgar pomp.) Yet the text on which the funeral sermon was based—a text George Mason may have chosen —was intimate, emotional, and sad: "Nevertheless I am continually with thee: thou hast holden me by my right hand. Thou shalt guide me with thy counsel, and afterward receive me to glory. Whom have I in heaven but thee? and there is none upon earth that I desire beside thee" (Ps 73:23–25). In the context of the Psalm, the "thou" of these verses is God. In the context of a funeral, the pronouns take on additional resonance: the speaker became the grieving widower, and the "thou" his absent, dead wife.[72]

One space in which Mason enacted his "settled melancholy" was the family Bible, which became a container for his grief and his memories of Ann. Mason's long ode recalls Ann as self-sacrificial, gentle, kind, devout. During her long illness, "she was never heard to utter one peevish or fretful Complaint." Throughout her life "Her modest Virtues shun'd the public-Eye, Superior to the turbulent Passions of Pride & Envy, a Stranger to Altercation of every Kind, & content with the Blessings of a private Station, she placed all her Happiness here, where only it is to be found, in her own Family." She was, indeed, an ideal eighteenth-century Proverbs 31 woman: "an easy & agreeable Companion; a kind Neighbour; a steadfast Friend; an humane Mistress; a prudent & a tender Mother; a faithful, affectionate, & most obliging Wife; charitable to the Poor, and pious to her Maker; her Virtue & Religion were unmixed with hypocrisy or Ostentation." Mason also memorialized Ann's comely appearance:

> In the Beauty of her Person, & the Sweetness of her Disposition, she was equalled by few, & excelled by none of her Sex. She was something taller than the Middle-size, & elegantly shaped. Her Eyes were black, tender & lively; her Features regular & delicate; her Complexion remarkably fair & fresh—Lilies and Roses (almost without a Metaphor) were blended there —and a certain inexpressible A[ir of] Chearfulness, Health, Innocence & Sensibility diffused over her Coun[tenance] form'd a Face the very Reverse of what is generally called masculi[ne.]

Ann Eilbeck Mason, it turns out, was not just the Proverbs 31 woman but the Song of Songs woman, too: the "lilies" and the "roses" that Mason found in Ann Mason's complexion are found first in Song of Songs 2:1–2: "I am the rose of Sharon, and the lily of the valleys. As the lily among thorns, so is my love among the daughters."[73]

The end of the Mason Bible records testifies both to the conclusion and the persistence of Mason's grief: "[Her] irreparable Loss I do, & ever shall deplore; and tho' Time I hope will [soften my sad im]pressions, & restore me greater Serenity of Mind than I have lately enjoy[ed, I shall ever retain the most tender and melancholy] Remembrance of One so justly dear." That cri de coeur was Mason's penultimate entry. Later, he recorded his second marriage, with no trace of emotion: "George Mason of Gunston Hall in Fairfax County Virginia, aged abt. fifty four Years, and his second Wife, Sarah Brent (D[aughter] of George Brent Esqr. Of Woodstock in the County of Stafford) aged abou[t fifty] Years, were married on Teusday the 11th. Day of April in the Year 1780. [by] the revd. Mr. James Scott, Rector of Dettingen Parish in the County of Prince William in Virginia." In marrying again, and recording that marriage in his family Bible, Mason was perhaps signaling a return to life. But the flat notation of his second marriage, far from pointing beyond his grief, redirects attention to it. The family Bible both contained and kept alive Mason's mourning.[74]

A more typical surviving example of the practice of writing genealogical lists in Bibles is found in one now held at the University of Virginia Library.[75] While it lacks the descriptive detail of Mason's family memorials, it sheds light on the ways women also used family Bibles in the practices of memory making and mourning. Ann Hill Tunstall began the process of transforming this book into a site of family memory one day in the mid-1740s, when she opened her Bible to the blank page before the Apocrypha and recorded the births and deaths of her children:

> Ann Tunstall the daughter of Richard & Ann Tunstall was born the 19th day of October 1728.
> Elizabeth Tunstall was born the 18th Day of Aug 1730 & departed this Life the 23rd day of June 1743.
> Katherine Tunstall Daughter of Richard & Ann Tunstall was Born 1732 & died in 1733
> John Tunstall was born the 8th day of July 1733. . . .
> Katherine Tunstall was born the 19th day of August 1734. dyed the 23d of June 1743.
> Frankey Tunstall was born the 29th. Day of December 1736. & dyed the [blank] day of [blank]
> Richard Tunstall was born the 22d day of July 1738.
> Thomas Tunstall was born the 16th. Day of November 1739 & dy'd the [blank] day of Decembr. 1769.

Leonard Tunstall was born the 4th day of March 1741.
William Tunstall was born the 25th. Day of May 1743.

On the blank page after the Apocrypha, in another hand, are more births
and deaths, beginning with a notation about James Maury's birth, to Matthew and Mary Anne Maury, April 8, 1718, and ending with the 1817 marriage
of Matilda Hill Maury and Richard Eggleston. The birth entries, at least, in
this later list appear to have been made by Mary Walker Murray. Turning
forward a few more pages, we find, on the leaf before the Gospel of Matthew,
still more births, deaths, and marriages, beginning with "William Tunstall
the Son of Rich. & Esther Tunstall was born the 2nd day of June 1766." Taken
together, these family notations suggest that Ann Hill Walker Tunstall
owned the Bible and recorded the Tunstall births; then she passed it to her
daughter, Mary Walker Maury, who in turn passed the Bible to Matilda Hill
Maury Eggleston. Matilda, who was forty-eight when she married, had no
children, yet someone recorded her death after she died.[76] Lists like those
Ann Hill Tunstall and her descendants wrote in their Bible created a kind of
domestic or familial immortality. In recording their children's births and
deaths, women like Ann Tunstall kept alive the memories of others. They
also established a pattern by which their own memory could be perpetuated
by their descendants. A woman recorded the deaths of her children and knew
that in the same book, one of her own surviving descendants would one day
record her death. The practice of writing such records was thus part of how
men and women responded to the deaths of loved ones, and how they prepared for their own deaths.

The genealogies that Virginians like Tunstall inscribed in their Bibles
were, in some ways, quite similar to the genealogies they found printed in the
Bible's pages. Like the Bible's genealogies, Virginia records name family
relationships, connecting parents to children. Through selective inclusion
and exclusion, these genealogies focus the reader's attention on the relationships deemed most crucial. Yet in at least two ways, the genealogies Virginians drafted differ from those found in the Bible. First, most biblical genealogies focus on "begetting" rather than deaths, whereas the genealogies in
Virginia Bibles note both birth and death.[77] Second, biblical genealogies tend
to follow the male line closely, and only rarely include women. Virginians'
genealogies reinscribe patrilineal assumptions at the same time that they
include both men and women.[78] The presence of women and the presence of
death in Virginians' genealogical lists are not unrelated: bereaved mothers
were moved by the imperative of grief to pick up the pen, and their lists,

Ann Tunstall the Daughter of Richard &
Ann Tunstall was born the 19th day of
October 1728.

Elizabeth Tunstall was born the 18. day of Aug.t 1730
& departed this life the 23.d day of June 1743. &
Katherine Tunstall Daughter of Richard & Ann Tunstall was
John Tunstall was born the 8th day of July 1733.
born 1732 & died in 1733

Katherine Tunstall was born the 19th day of
August 1734. & dyed the 23.d of June 1743.

Frankey Tunstall was born the 29th. day of
December 1736. & dyed the   day of

Richard Tunstall was born the 22.d day of
July 1738.

Thomas Tunstall was born the 16. day of
November 1739. & dyd the   day of Decemb.r 1769.

Leonard Tunstall was born the 4. day of March 1741.

William Tunstall was born the 25th. day of
May 1743.

5·7
Ann Hill Tunstall transformed this Bible into a site of mourning and family memory. The
practice of writing death records was part of how men and women responded to the deaths
of loved ones, and how they prepared for their own deaths. Special Collections, University
of Virginia Library.

studded with the names and dates of dead children, enunciate women's suffering. Especially when women wrote these lists, we can see here an insistence
that women's generations mattered, too, that women had stories to tell.[79]

Creating these lists in family Bibles was not only about mourning the
dead but also about creating a particular kind of family identity. By keeping
her list in a Bible, Tunstall identified her family with certain virtues—piety,
literacy, and the financial means to own an elegant Bible. She was also creating a family identity in which new generations were connected to their dead
ancestors. Which relatives merit inclusion is significant. When Tunstall
wrote the lists of births and deaths in her family Bible, she was drawing a
sharp line around who was part of her family and who was not—for all their
paternalistic language about slaves as their "families," slaveowning elites did
not typically record the births of slaves in their family Bibles. As Karin Wulf
has noted, "Thomas Jefferson wrote a more complete family history into the
pages of a 1752 edition of the *The Book of Common Prayer,* with separate pages
for his parents' histories, marriage and children, his own marriage and the
birth of his children by Martha Wayles Jefferson, and those children's marriages and children. . . . His children by Sally Hemings are conspicuously
absent from this Jefferson account, their illegitimacy under the law and in
Jefferson's own mind consigning them, instead, to his Farm Book account."[80]
What a genealogist omits is as crucial as what she records.

Finally, Tunstall and other men and women who wrote family records in
Bibles were connecting their families to the family of God. Keeping family
records in a Bible opened up new devotional possibilities. A mother might be
moved to pray for the children listed in her Bible when she opened it for
devotional reading (all the more likely when, as was the case with the Carrington Family Bible, it was bound with a Book of Common Prayer). Of
particular significance are the pages on which men and women like Ann Hill
Tunstall wrote their records. Unsurprisingly, people wrote on the blank pages:
on the blank leaf that follows the publisher's page; on the leaves just before
and after the Apocrypha; and, perhaps most commonly, on the leaf between
the New Testament title page and the Gospel of Matthew. For example, Jane
Jefferson recorded "The births & deaths of the Son and daughters of Peter
Jefferson by Jane his wife" before the preface of her Bible, and "The Births &
Deaths of the Sons and Daughters of Isham Randolph by Jane his Wife with
whom he intermarried in Byshopsgate" before the Gospel of Matthew.[81] To
write on the blank page before the Gospel of Matthew was doubtless a choice
driven by practicality, but whatever the intention (or lack thereof) behind
keeping family records in that space, to do so created a new text that allowed

for a particular kind of reading experience: when men and women recorded their own genealogies immediately before the genealogy of Jesus, they were then able to literally read their own family stories into the story of the family of God. When Ann Hill Tunstall wrote her own offspring into this genealogy, she was suggesting that she and her children were characters, too: *Here is Jesus, and here is my child, who died (and by extension, here am I, another Mary, another bereaved mother)*. In writing themselves into the Bible, they were literally inscribing themselves into the Christian story. At the same time, they were establishing familial precedents, beginning narrations that they could assume their children would continue when they died; thus they both grieved their dead and established modes of mourning that assured them that their own memories would one day likewise be preserved.

Now we turn our attention to a different kind of death: the death of the Anglican establishment.

Lucy Smith Digges's "Little Old Fashioned Oblong Black Walnut" Table

Household Religious Practice in Episcopalian Virginia

In the 1850s, in the middle of his tenure as the third bishop of the Diocese of Virginia of the Protestant Episcopal Church, William Meade wrote down all he knew of the history of the *Old Churches, Ministers, and Families of Virginia.*[1] Parish by parish, county by county, drawing on his own recollections and on the memories of others, Meade assembled information on countless topics: vestry resolutions, genealogy, funerals, the religious character of George Washington, daring Revolutionary War exploits, ill-advised elopements. He moved from the droll (what happened when Parson Latane offered some of his parishioners a drink) to the political (the colonization movement). A major theme in the two-volume work, which was published in 1857, was decline—the decline of the churches, and the great families, after the Revolution.

Take Middlesex County. The old order had collapsed in Middlesex. "What has become of the old Episcopal families, the Skipwiths, Wormeleys, Grymses, Churchills, Robinsons, Berkeleys, and others? What has become of, or who owns, those mansions where were the voluptuous feasts, the sparkling wine, the flowing bowl, the viol and the dance and the card-table, and the dogs for the chase, and the horses for the turf?" Those families had lost everything, that's what. "The whole of the county was at one time in possession of some few of these old families, and . . . now not a rood of it is owned by one of their name, and scarcely by one in whom is a remnant of their blood." Even Meade's antecedents were not exempt: "Old Brandon, the seat of my maternal ancestors, the Grymses, is gone, except a small part of it." Some of the sites of the great houses could no longer even be located. "The ploughshare has been over them, as it has been over the ruins of many an old church in Virginia." Ah yes, the churches—which had literally collapsed. The church that once stood "midway between Rosegill and Brandon," for example, had been deserted over fifty years before. "Its roof decayed and fell in. Everything returned to its native dust."[2]

Meade was, on one level, distraught at the collapse of those two great institutions, the aristocratic oligarchy and their church. But, truth be told, he also thought those families and churches had gotten what they deserved. The colonial Skipwiths and Wormeleys were, in Meade's view, largely dissolute and impious, and what could follow a trail of impiety but decline? Quaffing sparkling wine at the card table—that kind of behavior sowed the seeds of collapse. So Meade was not entirely distressed to report the broken down church buildings and bankrupt families. In fact, at times, he seemed to be enjoying it.[3]

The wine and fine clothes did, indeed, have something to do with the spectacular decline of the Virginia oligarchy. Many gentry families had entered the Revolution heavily in debt, paid little attention to their business matters during the war, and came out of the war in a still more precarious financial situation—yet they couldn't seem to rein in their spending. The tobacco boom was over, land and slaves were worth less than they had been, the soil was depleted. The Panic of 1819 and its attendant depression and other scares punctuated a long economic slide. As the historian Jan Lewis reads the situation, the Virginia planter class, with its lavish and indolent ways, was ill-equipped to cope with the new economic realities. Changing inheritance laws were also partly responsible for the disappearance of the Grymeses and the Robinsons from their seats. Fathers now divided their property among their many sons, which often meant that none of them could sustain the lifestyles Meade simultaneously castigated and yearned for.[4]

The decline of the church had multiple causes. The Revolution sparked a clergy shortage—at the end of the war, roughly half of Virginia's Anglican pulpits were empty. The Methodist Episcopal Church, which was formally organized in 1784, drained Anglican churches of some of their energetic clergy and laypeople. And then there was Disestablishment. Beginning in the mid-1770s, the Virginia legislature passed a series of laws that, over the course of the next twenty-five years, would vitiate the Anglican establishment: ministerial salaries could no longer be paid with tax money, for example, and a limited number of non-Anglican ministers in each county were newly licensed to perform marriages. More significant was the 1786 bill "for establishing religious freedom," which did just that, and the 1802 "Act Concerning the Glebe Lands and Churches Within this Commonwealth," which allowed the state to claim churches' glebes. The land was given to the newly created

6.1

In *Old Churches, Ministers, and Families of Virginia,* William Meade chronicled the decline of the church after the American Revolution. He included this illustration of "Ruins of the Churchyard, Jamestown." Rare Book, Manuscript, and Special Collections Library, Duke University.

county officers known as the "Overseers of the Poor"—so the bill stripped the church both of its property and of its civil responsibility for poor relief.[5]

All this spelled disaster for the Anglican—now Episcopal—Church. In 1784 Virginia boasted 107 Episcopal parishes. Between 1802 and 1811, only 40 of those could pay for ministers. After the Glebe Act, some vestries simply folded. Congregations abandoned their church buildings. Like the church in Middlesex County, many churches fell into disrepair or worse. "The destruction" of both churches in South Farnham Parish, Essex County, "has been complete," wrote Meade. One church was pulled down, the other burned. "The flagstones . . . from the aisles, may be seen in walks and in hearths; but not a whole brick, much less one upon another, nor a piece of timber, is to be seen where the temples of the living God stood." In Washington Parish, a brick church was first used as a tavern, then as a stable, and in Manchester Parish, Falling Creek Church "was taken possession of by those who did not feel it was holy ground. . . . Its walls were desecrated with scribbling" and a local drunk was once found dead, "much defaced by the rats," in front of the pulpit. At Hungar's Church in Northampton County, the organ was melted down for fishermen's sinkers. At Yeocomico Church, the canvas renderings of the Ten Commandments, the Lord's Prayer, and the Creed that had once decorated the chancel lay in shreds on the pews. In an inversion of the Masons' using their monteith as a baptismal bowl, church baptismal fonts were put to "convivial purposes": one was turned into a flower bowl, another "used as a vessel in which to prepare the excitements to ungodly mirth." One church's paten was used as a cheese tray.[6]

By 1811 Virginia's Episcopal Church was, in the estimation of one historian, "almost dead."[7] And then, over the next two to three decades, the church was resurrected.[8] Many personalities, strategies, and practices helped bring about the revival of the Episcopal Church in Virginia. Regarding finance, Virginia's Episcopalians began to develop voluntary fund-raising strategies. Regarding polity, they learned to embrace a resident bishop. Devotionally, theologically, and spiritually, the revitalization of the church is often chalked up to the evangelical revival that swept the South during the early nineteenth century. Episcopal clergymen's sermons in the nineteenth century called for "the renewing of the Holy Ghost" and for "conversion." Sounding like the very Baptists they'd vilified not a century before, both laity and clergy (including Meade, who had adopted an evangelical theological orientation when studying for ordination) urged strict Sabbath practice and denounced gambling. Clergymen held long prayer meetings on weeknights, which they hoped would help stir people's hearts with an awareness of their own sinfulness, and their absolute need of Christ's atoning work on the cross.[9] By 1839 Virginia could be termed, in the estimation of the historian Edward L. Bond, "one of the most vigorously evangelical of all dioceses in the Episcopal Church in the United States."[10]

Evangelicalism was certainly key to the resurrection of Virginia's Episcopal Church. But the explanatory dazzle of "evangelical revival" can mask the ways that Anglican and Episcopal religious practice endured during those years when the churches were being used as taverns. Anglican religious practice survived where it had always flourished—inside people's houses. The historical record is replete with examples of people whose religious lives— and, specifically, their connections to Anglicanism—were sustained by lay-led household religious practice during the decades of post-Revolutionary ecclesial decline. For example, before Thomas Lewis of Augusta County, Virginia, died, he "requested that his friend and brother-in-law, old Peachy Gilmer should read the burial service of the Prayer-Book over his remains, there being no minister in the parish at that time." Judith Lomax lived in Caroline County, Virginia, where, in her view, the Episcopal Church was spiritually dead. She often worshiped with other denominations but remained an Episcopalian and led a Sabbath service at home with a congregation of six free

African-American women. She used "the Liturgy of my Church." Meade himself recalled how central domestic devotional practice was to his childhood. He only dimly remembered rituals that happened in church buildings: "I have but an indistinct recollection of [Bishop Madison's] having heard some of us the Catechism at church, and, as I suppose, laying his hands upon us in conformation afterward." What Meade remembered more vividly was his father's reading "the service and a sermon" at home "when there was no service at chapel or we were prevented from going." And he remembered his mother's guiding the children in morning and evening prayer from the Book of Common Prayer. The formative church experiences of this influential evangelical church leader happened not at church but at home.[11]

The vital eighteenth-century tradition of household religious practice stood Virginia Episcopalians in good stead after the post-Revolutionary decline of the church. As one final narrative from early-nineteenth-century Virginia will suggest, habits of household religious practice ensured that when church buildings were turned into taverns or barns, Episcopalians did not have to join another denomination or stop practicing Christianity altogether. They could remain practicing Episcopalians, in their homes.[12]

Not too many years before Meade began writing everything he knew about Virginia's churches, ministers, and families, a Yorktown, Virginia, woman named Lucy Calthorpe Smith Digges came across a copy of the Church of England clergyman John William Cunningham's novel *The Velvet Cushion*. The pillow of the title, a highly opinionated pulpit cushion at a small church in Westmoreland, narrates its centuries of adventures in English parishes.[13] *The Velvet Cushion* was not the first novel to be narrated by an inanimate object—there was also *The History and Adventures of a Lady's Slippers and Shoes Written by Themselves*, for example, and *The Genuine and Most Surprizing Adventures of a Very Unfortunate Goose-Quill*—but *The Velvet Cushion* captured Lucy Digges's imagination. Ever since encountering the talkative pillow, she found herself looking "with longing eyes, (whether bodily or mentally it signifies but little) at a certain little old fashioned oblong black walnut table, with nearly the same feeling of the devoted Poet, when he wrote 'Oh that those lips had language!'" One night, she lay awake thinking about the table and "the events connected with it." She wished the table "could tell me all it had been witness to, of the good, and evil, of this transitory scene." Then, suddenly, "some one seemed to whisper in my ear, as if speaking for the table." The table began to reminisce, and with the table's help, Lucy began to recall her family's story.[14]

First, the table told its own history: it was owned by Lucy's paternal grandmother, Mary Calthorpe, who often sat "at work"—needlework, that is—with the table beside her. When Mary died, the table was sold, "for little or nothing," to a family that did appreciate the fine piece of furniture. Many years later, Lucy's father, Augustine Smith, came across the table, recognized it as something his mother had owned, and purchased it. For many years, the table was "kindly taken care of" by Lucy's mother, Alice Grymes Page Smith, who kept the table in her bedroom.[15]

After that supellectile introduction, Lucy and the table began to talk of Lucy's childhood. The table helped her "remember all I can, of my early, happy days." Lucy fondly recalled passing many hours in the bedroom of her mother, Alice. The table held "the Candle, tea things, work or Book, which-ever she required." It was "a treat" for Lucy and her brothers to have tea on the table on evenings their mother was out. The table reminded Lucy that it held more than tea pots and needlework. "You also remember that I held the large Bible, and Prayer book, out of which your Brothers, and yourself, read the Psalms and Lessons for the day, every morning before your Mamma was dressed." Alice Smith's bedroom was a place of sociability and prayer, and the little table aided in both. The bedroom devotions Lucy Digges remembered would have happened between 1793 and 1812, when Alice, Lucy, and their family lived in Yorktown. Those were shaky years for Yorktown's Anglican church, which had been damaged when Lord Cornwallis used it as a maga-zine: "The pews & windows of the Church [were] all broke & destroyed." Alice's bedroom prayers helped sustain her family's religious practice and Anglican identity during a period when their local church was failing.[16]

After the widowed Alice Smith moved to Louisa to marry Dudley Digges, the table was passed on to Lucy Grymes Nelson (who was the first cousin twice removed of Lucy Smith Digges). Lucy Grymes was born in Middlesex County in 1743. At eighteen or nineteen, she married Thomas Nelson, of York County. Thomas and Lucy Nelson had eleven children who lived to adult-hood. As an adult, Lucy lived in Yorktown, and then, after 1820, in Hanover County, in a house called Springfield (to which Lucy Nelson moved after the death of her husband and the sale of his house to cover his war debt).[17]

The Episcopal churches in both Yorktown and Hanover were floundering. We have already seen that the church in Yorktown had been damaged in the Revolutionary War. In the years after Alice Smith left Yorktown, transferring her table to Lucy Nelson, the Yorktown church suffered another blow: the church building burned down in 1814, not to be restored for decades. Richard Channing Moore, second bishop of Virginia, visited at least once "in the

Ruins at Yorktown.

6.2
Henry Howe sketched the Yorktown church ruins. "Silence reigns within its walls," wrote
Howe, "and the ashes of the illustrious dead repose at its base." Rare Book, Manuscript,
and Special Collections Library, Duke University.

years after the fire"—he officiated at the courthouse and "at the house of Mr.
Nelson" (that is, Lucy Nelson's son). When Lucy Nelson moved to St. Martin's Parish, Hanover County, the church she found was also struggling. In
the years after the Revolution, a clergyman from a neighboring town occasionally officiated at services, but, reported Bishop Meade later, "so low was
the condition of the church, and so few disposed to respond, that he used to
read only such parts as needed no response, and not all of them." The church
began to revive in the second decade of the nineteenth century. With the
arrival of John Philips in 1815 or 1816, St. Martin's Parish received a permanent
minister. Philips served St. Martin's Parish until 1820, when he died while
riding in "a plain conveyance" with his wife, who didn't notice he had died
until she stopped at a tavern to get her horse some water. Three more clergymen would come to St. Martin's parish before Lucy Nelson's 1830 death.[18]

Her local churches may have been shaky, but Lucy Nelson's faith was not.
During these decades, she maintained robust religious practices in her household. To be sure, her household religiosity was not identical to that which her
ancestors might have practiced a century before. Her devotional life bore the
marks of the early-nineteenth-century evangelical revival; indeed, Lucy Nelson was creating a hybrid domestic religiosity that was identifiably both "Epis-

copal" and "evangelical." Nelson adopted many of the practices that evangelicals like Meade called for. For example, she kept the Sabbath, permitting no work and only spiritual reading on Sundays. The religious idiom Lucy favored reflected an evangelical theological sensibility: she knew she had a "sinful nature," and her daughters and granddaughters spoke of having "converted." Lucy's favorite song was "Jesus, Thou Art the Sinner's Friend," by the English Baptist minister Richard Burnham. It emphasized human sinfulness, the individual's relationship with Jesus, and the atoning work of the Cross:

> Jesus, Thou art the sinner's Friend;
> As such I look to Thee;
> Now, in the fullness of Thy love,
> O Lord, remember me!
>
> Remember Thy pure Word of grace,
> Remember Calvary;
> Remember all Thy dying groans,
> And then, remember me.
>
> Thou wondrous advocate with God,
> I yield my soul to Thee;
> While Thou art pleading on the throne,
> O Lord, remember me.
>
> I own I'm guilty, own I'm vile,
> But Thy salvation's free;
> Then, in thine all-abounding grace,
> O Lord remember me![19]

Yet although flavored by evangelicalism, Lucy Nelson's household piety remained recognizably Anglican, connected to the practices of her eighteenth-century forebears. Lucy brought up her children "in the nurture and admonition of the Lord," recalled her daughter (echoing both Ephesians and the marriage ceremony in the 1662 Book of Common Prayer),[20] and just like Alice Grymes Page Smith, Lucy Nelson conducted devotions guided by the Book of Common Prayer and the church's lectionary with her children in her bedroom. Every morning, Lucy's children "were brought"—presumably by one of the thirty-seven slaves who lived at Springfield[21]—to her room, where they then "said their prayers and a short catechism, such as who made you? Who Redeemed you? &c. and then read the Psalms and lessons for the day, with the collect Gospel and Epistle, for the preceding Sunday." Also in the mornings, female relatives and one "young servant" gathered either in her room or the dining room to "read the Family prayers." Lucy also devoted nearly an hour

6.3
Lucy Grymes Nelson lived the last years of her life at Springfield, in Hanover County.
Library of Virginia.

each morning "'Locked up,' as was the term throughout the house, for her being at prayers" by herself.[22] Lucy's prayers were guided not only by the Book of Common Prayer but by at least one other Anglican devotional: *A New Manual of Devotions in Three Parts,* which included several sets of prayers for morning and evening, and an office for sick people. It was first printed in England sometime before 1713, was available in a twenty-first edition in 1797, and was used by Episcopalians in America, including the bishop of Maryland, as late as the 1880s.[23] Lucy's reliance on prayer books distinguished her religious practice from that of many of Hanover County's evangelicals. (For Methodists, for example, "Prayerbooks functioned as a stopgap only until an individual could pray" extemporaneously.)[24]

Lucy Nelson's bedroom was also the site of sacramental celebration. Some of her household encounters with the sacraments were quite extraordinary. Once, one of Lucy's grandsons visited from Kentucky, where there was no Episcopal bishop. When the grandson told the bishop of Virginia that he wished to be confirmed, the bishop said that he would happily confirm the boy in "Grandmama's chambers" at Springfield. Lucy also frequently received communion in her room. The parson regularly came to "'give her a prayer,' as she used to say," and to celebrate "the Sacrament of the Lord's Supper" with Lucy and any of the friends and relatives gathered in her room. During those visits with the pastor, the small walnut table sat covered with "the purest white damask," and it held the bread and wine for communion. Lucy received communion regularly because she wanted to be "always ready, shod, and girded, for the last long journey."[25]

For well over a decade, the "Little Old Fashioned Oblong Black Walnut" table found it "a blessed holy service," an "honour" to "serve [Lucy Nelson] until she was removed to a better world."[26] Thereafter, the table continued its service to Nelson's cousin, Lucy Smith Digges. The table's role in Lucy Digges's life was not only to hold prayer books and teapots but also to spur memories. The table had witnessed difficult events—deaths, family property sold to pay off debt. And the table held memories of family, sociability, and piety. It remembered decline—the decline of an oligarchy and its church. And it remembered how one family's quotidian, domestic religious practice had survived.

Notes

Introduction

For the epigraph see *William and Mary Quarterly* 7 (1898): 93–98, 95–96.

1. Stitt, *Museum of Early Southern Decorative Arts,* 19, 45; Brown, "Such Luxuries as a Sofa," 1–50.

2. Smith, *Inside the Great House,* 82.

3. Cranmer, "On the Sacrament of Baptism," 48.

4. *Oxford English Dictionary,* 2nd ed., 1989; Oxford English Dictionary Online, Oxford University Press, http://dictionary.oed.com/cgi/entry/50044726. See also the usage of *comfortable* in John Brown's *Dictionary:* e.g., "the comfortable doctrines of the gospel" (508), "the poor Heathens lived . . . without the comfortable presence of God" (372). Landon Carter's copy of Brown's *Dictionary* is preserved in Special Collections, University of Virginia Library, F 229.C28 Z9.D53 1759. On eighteenth-century Anglo-Americans' increasing use of *comfort* to "express their satisfaction and enjoyment with immediate physical circumstances" and to denote "a middle ground between necessity and luxury," see Crowley, "The Sensibility of Comfort," 749–782.

5. For "the Amiableness of Religion" see George Shaw to Edward Ambler, January 5, 1767, folder 3, Papers of the Ambler Family, ms. 1921, box 1, Special Collections, University of Virginia Library.

6. In this depiction of Virginia gentry's Anglican religiosity as "comfortable" in both senses of the term, I am influenced by, but also hope to add nuance to, the work of Jan Lewis and Philip Greven. Greven argued for a tripartite division of early American Protestant temperaments—the "evangelical," the "moderate," and the "genteel." He found that practitioners of genteel religion were not animated by guilt, were comfortable in the world to the point of complacency, and were not inclined to brooding introspection, or even minimal self-reflection: "In their piety as in their temperaments, the genteel were remarkably comfortable and contented." Like Greven, Lewis found a decided lack of "self-examination" among elite Anglicans of the pre-Revolutionary years, and in her insightful but brief consideration of elite religion before Disestablishment she concluded that An-

glicanism as practiced by the elites was a religion "well suited to the gentry," who were "comfortable in this world and sanguine about the next." Greven, *The Protestant Tempera-ment,* 14, 298–299, and passim. See also Lewis, *Pursuit of Happiness,* 45, 46; Sobel, *World They Made Together,* 177. On my reading, the register of gentry religion (as the foregoing discussion of *comfort* suggests) encompassed both the notes of complacency on which Greven and Lewis focused, and (softer) notes of reflective wrestling and active attempts to use religion to make comfort in troublesome situations. The Anglican gentry of Virginia were, indeed, not given to deep introspection, but they were not devoid of self-reflection or, especially in the face of death or trauma, wrestling and struggle.

7. Isaac, *Transformation of Virginia,* esp. 58–65, 164–166, 172–173. Isaac was reiterat-ing a description of Anglicanism that, mutatis mutandis, was circulated a century earlier by William Meade, who became the Episcopal bishop of Virginia in 1841. Meade himself was an evangelical, and in his *Old Churches, Ministers, and Families of Virginia,* he caricatured his Virginia forebears as faithless: their liturgical piety was staid and habitual, their church a mere shell. Meade was reiterating an old, old story that evangelical revivalists in the eighteenth century loved to tell. This view came to modern historiography in the works of scholars like Carl Bridenbaugh—who wrote that "it was as a social rather than a religious institution that the church served the Chesapeake Society of these years"—and then, most powerfully and insightfully, Isaac, and also in Dell Upton, *Holy Things and Profane;* Bridenbaugh, *Myths and Realities,* 30. See also Morgan, *Virginians at Home,* 181–182. For a consideration of the shadow Meade's evangelical biases cast on twentieth-century histories see the Nichols and Gundersen review of Upton, *Holy Things and Profane,* 380.

8. Smith, "'Autonomy and Affection,'" 50. See Butler, "Transatlantic Pieties," 417.

9. McDougall, *Freedom,* 125.

10. Lewis, *Pursuit of Happiness,* 43; Heyrman, *Southern Cross,* 11–15; Nelson, *Blessed Company;* Bond, *Damned Souls;* Butler, "Knowing the Uncertainties." This revisionist literature was aptly summarized and commented upon in Tarter, "Reflections on the Church," 338–371. Albert Zambone's Oxford dissertation, "Anglican Enlightenment," is forthcoming. All of these scholars have benefited from the work of Joan Gundersen, who, in numerous studies for more than two decades, has painted a picture of a vital Anglicanism. See especially her articles "The Double Bonds" and "The Non-Institutional Church." For South Carolina and the West Indies, see Nelson, *Beauty of Holiness,* and Beasley, *Christian Ritual.* Bond and Nelson have had an enormous impact on the historiography of Virginia; numerous scholars of early Virginia whose central interest is not Anglicanism have drawn on their studies in characterizing Anglicanism; thus we see this revisionist narrative about Virginia Anglicanism becoming mainstreamed. See, e.g., Kerrison, *Claiming the Pen,* 38–42; Spangler, *Virginians Reborn,* 33–41; Evans, *A "Topping People,"* 164–168.

11. Isaac, *Transformation of Virginia,* 65.

12. On Hunt's preaching, see Bond, "Colonial Origins and Growth," 165. Hening, *Statutes at Large,* 1: 58, 149, 155–158, 183, 241; MacDonald, *Documentary Source,* 14, 2; Stith, *Discovery and Settlement of Virginia,* 36–37. See also Brydon, *Virginia's Mother Church,* 1: 426–449; Cobb, *Rise of Religious Liberty,* 74–93. On the charters of Virginia, see Seiler, "Church of England in Virginia," 480–481; Weir, *Early New England,* 27–30; and Finkle-man, "Colonial Charters and Codes," 326–328. Painter, "Anglican Vestry," 39. For more on this 1619 meeting of the General Assembly, see Bond, *Damned Souls,* 108–109; Seiler, "Church of England in Virginia," 482. For more on this 1632 law, see Hening, *Statutes at Large,* 1: 123. There was a clear colonial utility to the establishment of the church in

England's first colony in the Atlantic world. A central concern in any colonial enterprise is maintaining links between the colony and the metropole, and familiar church routines helped connect colonials to England. In the broadest sense, the intersection of Englishness and Christianity meant that colonials' practice of Anglicanism solidified and demonstrated publicly their allegiance to and status as loyal subjects of the realm. At subtler levels, too, practicing familiar English church rites connected colonials' imaginations to England, and made the unfamiliar landscape of the New World a bit less alien. Carving the countryside into parishes was part of transforming an edenic but scary wilderness into a familiar quasi-English landscape. Opening the Book of Common Prayer forged a connection not only with God but with the king. If the natural seasons in Virginia were strange, practicing liturgical seasons made the passage of time feel familiar. Virginia's church was the Church of England, and it imaginatively and institutionally connected colonials to the mother country. On the imbrication of Anglicanism and England's colonial impulses, see Miller, "Religion and Society," 99–140; Strong, *Anglicanism and Empire*, 1–15 and passim; Beasley, *Christian Ritual*, esp. 21–53.

13. See, especially, Bond, *Damned Souls*, 181–182, 185, 215, 239.

14. In England, selection was typically made by whoever owned the advowson, and confirmed by the bishop, though over the course of the eighteenth century, vestries in England began to play a larger part in the process. See Seiler, "Anglican Parish Vestry," 320; Jacob, *Lay People and Religion*, 29–30. On lay strength in the face of a weak clergy, see Bond, *Damned Souls*, esp. 203–208, 218–219.

15. Seiler, "Anglican Parish Vestry," 314; Bond, *Damned Souls*, 205.

16. This summary compresses a complicated history. For a more detailed account, see Bond, *Damned Souls*, 215–238. On Compton, see also Cross, *Anglican Episcopate*, 25–51; Seiler, "Anglican Parish Vestry," 310; Bennett, "English Bishops," 175–188. See also Rutman, *Small Worlds*, 153–154; Seiler, "Church of England in Virginia," 499–502.

17. This account relies chiefly on Nelson, *Blessed Company*, 122–127, 30, 32, 294, and passim. On Blair, see also Bond, *Damned Souls*, 225–235 and passim; Bond, "Prologue," 12–28; Tate, "James Blair," 539–543. On clergy scandal, Nelson notes, the ten percent "figure is about on par with clergy scandal in South Carolina, and lower than clergy scandal in New England"; *Blessed Company*, 145–162. On clergy, see also Gundersen, *The Anglican Ministry in Virginia*, and on clergy recruitment, Gundersen "Good Men." On the College of William and Mary, see also Tate, "The Colonial College, 1693–1782." For an example of a previous generation of scholarship's claiming that Virginia clergy were dissolute, see Bridenbaugh, *Myths and Realities*, 30–31. For an illuminating discussion of South Carolina laity's "redesigning Anglicanism in the absence of any meaningful church authority," see Laing, "'Heathens and Infidels,'" 198. On the relations between laity—specifically vestries —and clergy see Gundersen, "Myth."

18. Nelson, *Blessed Company*, esp. 13–16, 70–84; Hallman, "The Vestry," 120–130, 137; Seiler, "Land Processioning." On poor relief, see also Rutman and Rutman, *Place in Time*, 195–200; Cassel, "An Analysis of the Poor Relief System."

19. Jones, "Anglican Church," 31. Perry, *Papers*, 1: 234; Bonomi and Eisenstadt, "Church Adherence," 256–259; Blosser, "Irreverent Empire," 601–602. For the size of Virginia parishes at this time, see Upton, *Holy Things and Profane*, 8. On chapels of ease, see Nelson, *Blessed Company*, 28–29; on terminology for churches, see Rutman and Rutman, *Place in Time*, 122–123. On the legal requirements for church attendance, see Bond, *Spreading the Gospel*, 12, 52n45; Hening, *Statutes at Large*, 3: 360–361. On skipping lay-led

services, see Dent, "God and Gentry," 89–94, 124n50; also, e.g., Fithian, *Journal and Letters*, 114, 122, 126, 169, 189. On skipping church because of bad weather, see Bonomi and Eisenstadt, "Church Adherence," 258. For numerical estimations of church attendance, see ibid., 253–261, esp. 256; Kulikoff, *Tobacco and Slaves*, 234. For the quotations about full churches, see Jones, "Anglican Church," 31; Perry, *Papers*, 1: 301.

20. Maria Taylor Byrd to William Byrd III, September 23, 1759, Tinling, *Correspondence*, 2: 679.

21. Maria Taylor Byrd to William Byrd III, May 26, 1760, Tinling, *Correspondence*, 2: 688–689.

22. On church as an important place for socializing, see Rutman and Rutman, *Place in Time*, 125; Nelson, *Blessed Company*, 187. On the Grymeses' coach, see Digges, "My Table and Its History," 4, Smith-Digges Papers, Colonial Williamsburg. I am grateful to Al Zambone for introducing me to this source. Churches were not the only nondomestic space in which women socialized. On stores as another space where women could socialize, see Sturtz, *Within Her Power*, 121–125. On church's staging social hierarchy, see Nelson, *Blessed Company*, 64; Frey and Wood, *Come Shouting to Zion*, 76–77; Isaac, *Transformation of Virginia*, 58–65; Goodwin, *Colonial Church in Virginia*, 89; Holmes, "Anglican Tradition in Colonial Virginia," 74–75. For Fithian's observation, see Fithian, *Journal and Letters*, 29. For Isaac's reading of that passage, see Isaac, *Transformation of Virginia*, 61. For information on Wayles, see Gordon-Reed, *Hemingses of Monticello*, 57–76.

23. The analysis of this paragraph and the next paragraph follows Nelson, *Beauty of Holiness*, 141–174. On angels in Virginia churches, see Upton, *Holy Things and Profane*, 119. On Mattapony Church, see Mason, "King and Queen and King William," 451. On the Mattapony mural, see Mason, "Westmoreland and King George," 2: 292; on the Poplar Springs mural, see Mason, "Gloucester," 331–332; "Westmoreland and King George," 2: 292; Upton, *Holy Things and Profane*, 119. On Lamb's Creek Church, see Mason, "Westmoreland and King George," 2: 292. On Yeocomico's tablets, see Mason, "Westmoreland and King George," 1: 168. On St. Mary's White Chapel, see Mason, "Northumberland and Lancaster," 239; Upton, *Holy Things and Profane*, 120–121. See also Mason, "Warwick and Elizabeth City," 391. On Churchill, see Mason, "Middlesex," 18. On Southwark Parish, see Mason, "Sussex and Surrey," 296. Colors in churches also directed people's attentions heavenward. As Dell Upton has noted, the white interior finish common to churches (white ceilings and walls, often white pews) signaled purity: one Anglican clergyman noted that white "aptly represents the innocence and righteousness wherewith God's ministers ought to be cloath'd." Purple altar cloths were used in St. Paul's Parish, Bristol Parish, and Nottoway Parish, and green cloths in Petsworth Parish, perhaps to mark the liturgical seasons of Lent and Pentecost. On white, see Upton, *Holy Things and Profane*, 108. For the purchase of purple cloth, see *The Vestry Book of St. Paul's Parish, Hanover County*, 26. See also Chamberlayne, *Bristol Vestry Book*, 132. For speculation about the possible use of colored cloth to mark liturgical time, see Bond, *Damned Souls*, 218.

24. Mason, "Gloucester," 334; Bond, *Damned Souls*, 218n87; Chamberlayne, *Kingston Vestry Book*, 11–12; Mason, "Westmoreland and King George," 1: 159–160; *Virginia Gazette* (hereafter *VG*), July 3, 1746, p. 4, col. 2; Chamberlayne, *Petsworth Vestry Book*; Upton, *Holy Things and Profane*, 120–121.

25. Lay readers or clerks were nonordained men who led their fellow parishioners in "prayers & a Homily every Sunday the Minister is not there." These lay clerks were, in the observation of Hugh Jones, a "kind of curate." Some of these lay clerks decided to sail to

England and present themselves to the bishop for ordination. Painter, "Anglican Vestry," 47, 57–58. See Nelson, *Blessed Company*, 191, for the service as led by lay readers, and 193 for the limited number of organs. For a detailed discussion of the length of sermons, see ibid., 420n48; and Blosser, "Irreverent Empire," 625–626. For boredom and disrespect at church, see Blosser, "Irreverent Empire."

26. My identification of "Parson Fenney" differs from that of the editor Marion Tinling, who identifies the Fenney in the letter as William Finnie—but he was dead by 1727. Alexander Finnie is the more likely candidate. On Alexander Finnie and William Finnie, see Nelson, *Blessed Company*, 309.

27. For the Byrds' discussion of parish matters, see also Byrd, *Secret Diary*, 272. On desks, see Dierks, *In My Power*, 93–95.

28. On the layout of the main house, outbuildings, and improvements to the land, see Wells, "Planter's Prospect," 15–21, 23. On the meaning and motivations of gardening, see Martin, *Pleasure Gardens of Virginia*, xix and passim; Mooney, *Prodigy Houses*, 269. On the planter's view see Wells, "Dower Play/Power Play," 3–5, 16n3.

29. Mooney, *Prodigy Houses*, 16–29. For William Jordan's Richmond County house, see Wells, "Planter's Prospect," 14; for the wainscoting and wallpaper, see ibid., 5.

30. Upton, "Vernacular Domestic Architecture." For more discussion of the central passage, see Wenger, "Central Passage," 137–139. My rather oversimplified schematic of the evolution of the gentry's houses is usefully fleshed out, especially, by Mooney, *Prodigy Houses of Virginia*, 9–78. See also Gilliam, "Evolution," 181–188. For changes in the use of the dining room, see Wenger, "Dining Room," 155. The differentiation of public and private space within the household also changed how people thought of and used bedchambers. At the beginning of the century, bedchambers were public spaces. People entertained and did the work of household management there. By the middle of the century, central passage-ways pushed bedchambers into the more private half of the house, and bedchambers lost their social utility. See Chew, "Inhabiting the Great Man's House," 234.

31. On Delft tiles, see Austin, *British Delft at Williamsburg*, 28–29; Jonge, *Dutch Tiles*, 46–49. On images, see "Report on Scripture Prints," Margaret Pritchard research card file, Colonial Williamsburg; 1757 Sarah Green Will, York County Wills and Inventories 20 (1745–1759), 512–513. On the formation resulting from seeing such images, see "The Use and Design of Scriptural Prints." For messages on spoon handles, see Pennell, "'Pots and Pans,'" 201–216; see also Morall, "Protestant Pots," 263–273.

32. On Rebecca Burwell's quiet spot, see Dent, *God and Gentry*, 225; Kerrison, *Claiming the Pen*, 74. On gender and access to space see Chew, "Inhabiting the Great Man's House"; Kross, "Mansions," 399; Mooney, *Prodigy Houses*.

33. On the public dimensions of seemingly private household practices in the colonial South, see especially Kierner, *Beyond the Household*, esp. 1–4, 37–39, 47–59; Brown, *Good Wives*, 249–287. On the gendered nature of public and private spaces within mansions, see Kross, "Mansions," esp. 388–403. On the ideological construction of the categories "public" and "private" during the eighteenth century, see especially McKeon, *Secret History of Domesticity*, xix–48; Spacks, *Privacy*, 1–5, 25, 224.

34. My investigation of religious practice takes as its methodological starting point David Hall's observation that "the religious lies in what we do—in practices and in the meanings that energize such practices"; Hall, "From 'Religion and Society' to Practices," 159. I take as a given that religious identity and belonging inhere in practice, not just in belief or creedal commitments; at the same time, I also assume that the dichotomy be-tween belief and practice may itself reflect Protestant convictions about the centrality of

belief in Christian identity. Insofar as the dichotomy between belief and practice is helpful, it is imperative to recall that practices and beliefs are mutually reinforcing; that "believing" is itself a "practice"; and that, as Leigh Schmidt has noted, "practices should not be separated from the ideas that inform them"; Schmidt, "Practices of Exchange," in Hall, *Lived Religion*, 73. (Parsing the relationship between belief and practice is, of course, not a new undertaking; eighteenth-century Anglicans in Virginia did it too, as when the parishioners who ordered a tombstone for their parson, Bartholemew Yates, declared "He explained the doctrine by his practice." See Meade, *Old Churches*, 1: 360.) My consideration of the category of practice is indebted to Maffly-Kipp, Schmidt, and Valeri, *Practicing Protestants*, and David Hall, "From 'Religion and Society' to Practices."

35. Lived religion scholarship has reflected scholars' general interest in marginalized people and their religious practices. In addition to directing our attention to women, people of color, and practitioners who left behind few written sources, scholars in pursuit of "lived religion" have specifically tried to focus on the experience of laypeople, as opposed to the ideas of clergy and theologians. Scholars examining lived religion have tried to heed David Hall's observation that "while we know a great deal about the history of theology and (say) church and state, we know next-to-nothing about religion as practiced and precious little about the everyday thinking and doing of lay men and women"; *Lived Religion*, vii. Lived religion scholarship often uses the term *elite* to denote clergy and the term *ordinary people* to denote laity. See, for example, David Hall's observation that to explore the workings of popular religion is also to assume that ordinary people—or, in churches, the laity—were actors in their own right; "From 'Religion and Society' to Practices," 149. This conflation of *laity* with *ordinary*, the opposition of *laity* to *elite*, may mask the tendency of lived religion scholarship to ignore the experiences of wealthy laypeople, who are social and economic elites, but in the clerical-lay divide, religious nonelites. On lived religion, and especially the focus of lived religion on elite or marginalized people, see Hall, *Lived Religion*, especially Hall, Introduction, vii–ix; Orsi, "Everyday Miracles," 3–21, esp. 19n10; and Schmidt, "Practices of Exchange," 73. My effort to move away from a functionalist focus on social control is also indebted to Thomas Tweed's discussion of practices, e.g., that "the meaning of practices can never be reduced to their cognitive content or social function"; *Our Lady of the Exile*, 188n2.

36. On gender and church attendance, see Bonomi, *Under the Cope of Heaven*, 113. For Gundersen's description of household religiosity, see "The Non-Institutional Church," 347–356. On Puritanism's provision of space for women to act as moral agents, see Saxton, *Being Good*, 137 and passim. On evangelicalism and women's individuation, see Kerrison, *Claiming the Pen*, 34–69.

37. For Gundersen's argument that Virginia households were "gender-integrated spaces" and that "Virginia women did not have . . . female religious spaces," see "Kith and Kin," 91, 108n37. One of the most forceful presentations of the significant presence of men in elite households—and of the heterosocial and the all-male sociability and public performances within those households—is Kross, "Mansions," esp. 390–398. See also Mooney's discussion of "the mansion . . . as the stage for both male and female identity formation and performance," *Prodigy Houses*, 259 and passim.

38. See Terri L. Snyder's argument that in colonial Virginia, "ideas of white masculinity came increasingly to depend on mastery, sexual prowess, and genteel patriarchy . . . while white womanhood increasingly depended on domesticity, the private power of gossip, and displays of fashion, learning, and material culture"; *Brabbling Women*, 5.

39. Kulikoff, *Tobacco and Slaves*, 240–260; Tate, "The Colonial College, 1693–1782," 6. See also Walsh, "Community Networks," 229; Greene, *Pursuits of Happiness*, 94.

40. For meals with clergy, see, e.g., Byrd, *Secret Diary*, 20, 35, 67, and passim; also, Kierner, "Hospitality," 455–456; Gundersen, *The Anglican Ministry in Virginia*, 81–103, and passim. On "sharp conflict between the clerical view of the ministerial position . . . and a lay view," see Rutman, "Magic and Christianity," 153. Perhaps the most famously tense relationships between grandee and clergyman were between Landon Carter and Isaac Giberne and William Kay. See Greene, *Landon Carter*, 36. Tension between clergy and elite laity may have been related to elites' general feelings about professions. Gentlemen were, above all, tobacco farmers, but gentry men tried their hand at virtually all the professions—they doctored their dependents, they dabbled in law. But they could not play at being clergy. On gentry's involvement in a variety of professional endeavors, see Evans, *"A Topping People,"* 12; Roeber, *Faithful Magistrates*, 53 and passim; Isaac, *Landon Carter's Uneasy Kingdom*, 105–120; and Byrd, *Commonplace Book*, 39–40, 48–57, 210–211. The tensions between clergy and elite laity were also related to land: clergymen needed land if they were to aspire to genteel status. The vestries provided them land—in the form of a glebe. But the glebe came with obligations. Unless a clergyman married someone who brought a great deal of land to the marriage—John Thompson of Salubria did just that—he was indebted to gentry who had provided the economically necessary and deeply symbolic "gift" of land. On the vestries' keeping clergy "in more Subjection and Dependence," see Hartwell, Blair, and Chilton, *Present State of Virginia;* Fithian, *Journal and Letters*, 169. On John Thompson's marriage: Mooney, *Prodigy Houses*, 111. On clergy's social station more broadly: Nelson, *Blessed Company*, 134–144.

41. On Puritan diary keeping, see Brekus, "Writing as a Protestant Practice," 21–26; Webster, "Writing to Redundancy," esp. 40, 50.

42. In a hugely important corrective, Louis Nelson notes that "when material religion does surface, scholars usually embrace a functionalist view, discussing religion in terms of social structure, elite hegemony, or, more generally, as evidence of cultural identity. Our ignorance of Protestant material religion is perpetuated by our incorrect assumption that early Protestantism was a religion of 'The Word,' largely devoid of material dimensions." Scholars too often assume that materiality profanes religion; Nelson, "Sensing the Sacred," 203–204.

43. Ochs, *Inventing Jewish Ritual*, 94. On the relationship between material objects and religious practice see also Glassie, *Art and Life in Bangladesh*, 144 and passim; McDannell, *Material Christianity*, 1–2 and passim. McDannell eloquently captures the ways that "people learn the discourse and habits of their religious community through the material dimension of Christianity." On material objects as "essential for establishing a religious identity or cultivating religious sentiments," see Kieschnick, "Material Culture," 223–237.

Chapter One. With Cold Water and Silver Bowls

1. George Mason, Last Will and Testament, March 20 1773, Rutland, *Papers of George Mason*, 1: 151.

2. Green, *Christian's ABC*, 513.

3. "Mason Possessions Return," Gunston Hall. On monteiths' going out of fashion in the 1730s, see Lomax, *British Silver*, 60–61.

4. Bushman, "Complexity of Silver," 1–15, esp. 1–5, 10. Silver was the commodity

most likely to be purchased by Virginia elites: see Martin, *Buying into the World of Goods*, 40. On the refined and divine meanings of silver, see also Peterson, "Significance of Silver," 728–736, esp. 729–732; Peterson, "Puritanism and Refinement," 307–346.

5. Upton, *Holy Things and Profane*, 143–145. Peter Marshall gives a characteristically nuanced account of the role of angels in post-Reformation English deathways, concluding that to some extent "the ministry of angels became a less prominent theme of English mortuary culture after the Reformation," but that they nonetheless remained present at English deathbeds, and in fact "Protestant writers concerning themselves with death self-consciously reinvented the role of angels in order to help underwrite a crucial socio-religious change—from a pattern of dying inviting human effort and invocation, to one totally dependent on divine initiative." Marshall, "Angels around the Deathbed," 102–103. On cherubim in English grave iconography: Deetz and Dethlefsen, "Death's Head," 29–37; Gorman and DiBlasi, "Gravestone Iconography," 86. Scott is quoted in Thornton, *English Spirituality*, 267. On childhood mortality, see Kulikoff, *Tobacco and Slaves*, 61–62; Fischer, *Albion's Seed*, 311, 326; Smith, *Inside the Great House*, 26–27, 261–262, 265–266; Mason Family Bible Records, Rutland, *Papers of George Mason*, 481.

6. Kulikoff, *Tobacco and Slaves*, 240–255 (quotation on 255), 263–286.

7. See Smith, *Inside the Great House*, 40–44.

8. The phrase "domestic patriarchalism" is drawn from Kulikoff, *Tobacco and Slaves*, 166; for his discussion of the difficulties of establishing patriarchal order within the household during the seventeenth century, and the relative achievement of that order in the eighteenth century, see 167–199.

9. For a discussion of the crest, which is no longer visible, see the appraisal of David Allen, Fine Arts, October 9, 2004, in the monteith file at Gunston Hall. I am grateful to curator Caroline M. Riley for sharing this file with me.

10. Oxford wags probably invented Monsieur Monteigh, whom no one has ever identified. Nonetheless, the eponymous form was in general enough usage that in 1707 William King honored it with a scrap of poetry: "New things produce new words and thus Monteith / Has by one vessel saved himself from Death"; Cornelius, "An Important Loan of American Silver," 152. See also McNab, "Legacy of a Fantastical Scot," 173–174; Gardner, "Silver Plate," 125. On other monteiths in Virginia, see Davis, "Historical Silver," 112–114; Davis, *English Silver at Williamsburg*, 44; McNab, "Legacy of a Fantastical Scot," 180.

11. The Masons were not the only family to use in baptism bowls designed for other functions. The Dandridge family, for example, used two porcelain punch bowls for baptism. See Thompson, *"In the Hands,"* 36; on punch bowls in Virginia, see Beaudry, "Or What Else You Please," 72–74.

12. On "scrambling the sacred and the profane," see McDannell, *Material Christianity*, 4–8.

13. On the inscription on the chalice and paten and Upton's description of the social order, see Upton, *Holy Things and Profane*, 161–162.

14. *Statutes at Large*, 1: 183; Blair, "April 10, 1719 Proceedings," in Perry, *Papers*, 225. See also Carter, *Diary*, 249, 811. Until recently, there was consensus among students of colonial Virginia that most Anglican baptisms happened at home. However, in his 2001 study *A Blessed Company*, John Nelson questioned whether domestic baptism really was "the prevalent practice." He suggests that the evidence for domestic baptism comes from "the most illustrious of gentry families" and wonders whether "families of lesser gentry, ordinary farmers, merchants, shopkeepers, and artisans, much less servants and slaves" can

also be assumed to have been baptized at home (214). For further discussion of domestic baptism in Virginia, see Gundersen, "The Non-Institutional Church," 350; Washington, *Diaries,* 2: 154 (May 31, 1769); Holmes, "William Meade," 52. On clerical-lay tensions over household baptism, see Gundersen, *To Be Useful,* 129. On the relative rareness of domestic baptisms in Puritan New England, see Brown, "'Bound Up in a Bundle,'" 1. Domestic baptisms were certainly not unheard of in early modern England (see Wilson, "Ceremony of Childbirth," 80), and were commonplace in the British West Indies (see Beasley, *Christian Ritual,* 64–83).

15. Carter, *Diary,* 376–377.

16. Fithian, *Journal and Letters,* 138, 141–142, 195. On tobacco inspection, see Kulikoff, *Tobacco and Slaves,* 109–116; Evans, *A "Topping People,"* 48–49, 82–83.

17. Thomas Dell to Bishop Gibson, June 1, 1724, Fulham Papers, vol. 12, no. 13, Lambeth Palace Library; William Robinson to the Bishop of London, August 17, 1764, in Perry, *Papers,* 493. There had been controversy since at least the sixteenth century in the English church about whether parents could even be present at their children's baptism; see Coster, *Baptism and Spiritual Kinship,* 67; Cressy, *Birth,* 149–151; Bailey, *Sponsors at Baptism,* 92–93. There was no express permission for parents to serve as godparents until the 1789 Book of Common Prayer. See Hatchett, *Commentary,* 265, and Marshall, *Prayer Book Parallels,* 1: 234.

18. Morgan, *American Slavery,* 331–332.

19. Hening, *Statutes at Large,* 2: 260; Frey and Wood, *Come Shouting to Zion,* 69–70; Olwell, *Masters, Slaves, and Subjects,* 123; Raboteau, *Slave Religion,* 103.

20. Perry, *Papers,* 315, 263; Frey and Wood, *Come Shouting to Zion,* 64, 75; Van Horne, *Religious Philanthropy,* 289.

21. Bacon, "Second Sermon on Colossians 4:1, 1750," 441; Van Horne, *Religious Philanthropy,* 186.

22. Frey and Wood, *Come Shouting to Zion,* 47–51, 64; Gomez, *Exchanging Our Country Marks,* 59–87; Raboteau, *Slave Religion,* 115–133; Morgan, *Slave Counterpoint,* 561–564; Laing, "Heathens or Infidels," esp. 199, 206–210; Perry, *Papers,* 283. Laing makes another extremely important suggestion in her study of Anglicanism in the South Carolina Low Country. Clerics' records, which provide the bulk of the evidence for slaves' embrace of Anglicanism, turn on the question of baptism: clerics recorded their efforts, and failures and successes, at baptizing slaves. But there may have been many slaves who— either because they chose not to be baptized or because they were not offered access to baptism—were not baptized but nonetheless drew selectively from Anglican practice and teaching, incorporating into their lives select practices, such as church attendance, as they found those practices meaningful. See ibid., 211. As Laing has found fault with the argument that people of African descent were perforce uninterested in liturgical Christianity, Charles Irons has insightfully criticized the argument about the language barrier, noting that evangelists in many other settings overcame language barriers, as when John Eliot translated the Bible into Massachusett. Irons, *Origins,* 25–26. In addition to the three specific arguments regularly adduced to explain Anglican clergymen's limited success converting slaves, it should be noted, simply, that some slaves rejected Christianity because of its associations with their captors. Enslaved men and women who connected the spiritual liberation of the Gospel with physical liberation from the chains of bondage could not have missed the fact that many of the clergymen who attempted to teach them about Christianity were themselves slaveowners. This doubtless made the clerics' gospel less

compelling. On Virginia clergy owning slaves, see, e.g., Middleton, "Colonial Virginia Parson," 429; Nelson, *Blessed Company*, 262. Rebecca Goetz has suggested that James Blair may have been indifferent to, ambivalent about, or even hostile to the project of evangelizing slaves. Goetz, "Potential Christians," 243–244. The Anglicanism practiced by people like George and Ann Mason largely presumed the goodness of life as it was. The piety represented by their monteith—a piety in which the promises and claims of Christianity coexisted cozily with worldly pleasures like cool wine—made good sense to people who were at home in the world. But slaves surely wondered what the religion of their tormentors had to say to people living lives of bondage, toil, and suffering. The successes, in the later decades of the eighteenth century, of evangelicals who sought to convert slaves may be explained in part by the fact that, in contrast to an Anglicanism that was at ease in the world, the gospel evangelicals preached traded on rupture rather than continuity. Is it any wonder that the evangelicals' message, which promised new life, calling people out of the world, resonated more deeply than did genteel Anglicanism's cheer and comfort with people for whom daily life was a constant struggle?

23. On masters sending slaves to church, see Emanuel Jones, Petsworth Parish response to "Queries to be answered by every minister," in Perry, *Papers*, 287. For Gavin's baptisms, see Anthony Gavin to the Bishop of London, August 5, 1738, ibid., 360. For Jonathan Boucher's baptisms, see Middleton, "Colonial Virginia Parson," 433–434.

24. On the slaves' interpretation of Scripture, see Ingersoll, "'Cruell Bondegg,'" 782. On the churching of slave women after childbirth, see letter dated June 27, 1732, Fulham Papers, vol. 12, nos. 182, 183, Lambeth Palace Library.

25. On the motives for slave conversions, see Blair letter to Bishop Gibson, June 18, 1729, Fulham Papers, vol. 12, no. 134, Lambeth Palace Library. See also Nelson, *Blessed Company*, 263; Olwell, *Masters, Slaves, and Subjects*, 128; Raboteau, *Slave Religion*, 123. On Cattilah's petition for freedom, see Parent, *Foul Means*, 244. On the 1723 letter to the bishop of London, see Ingersoll, "'Cruell Bondegg,'" 781; Goetz, "Potential Christians," 249–251. For Mary Aggie's case, see Jones, "Anglican Church," 200; *Executive Journals of the Council of Colonial Virginia*, 243; Goetz, "Potential Christians," 247–249. On the rumor concerning emancipation, see Van Horne, *Religious Philanthropy*, 32; Frey and Wood, *Come Shouting to Zion*, 70; Parent, *Foul Means*, 260–261.

26. On the lighter ecclesiastical sentences for Christian slaves, see Goetz, "Potential Christians," 155. On the permissibility of slave testimony, see Nelson, *Blessed Company*, 260–261.

27. Cornelius, *When I Can Read*, 13–14; Mungo Marshall to John Waring, October 1756, in Van Horne, *Religious Philanthropy*, 120–121; Irons, *Origins*, 41; Clifford, *From Slavery to Freetown*, 9; Van Horne, *Religious Philanthropy*, 205; Journal of Elizabeth Foote Washington, Manuscript Division, Library of Congress LC-MS-56408-3 (hereafter EFW), spring 1789. (The journal is also available as photostat, RM-573/PS-4259, Mount Vernon Ladies' Association; typescript, Mount Vernon Ladies' Association; and as the appendix to Parris, "'Dutiful Obedient Wife.'" Since pagination of these versions differs, I will throughout cite Washington's journal by date, not page number.)

28. Governor Spotswood to Bishop Robinson, January 27, 1714, Fulham Papers, vol. 11, no. 224; Perry, *Papers*, 289, 299; Adam Dickie to Newman, June 27, 1732, Fulham Papers, vol. 12, nos. 182, 183, Lambeth Palace Library. On the evidence from Albemarle Parish, and for an insightful analysis of slaveowners' refusal to serve as godparents for slaves, see Goetz, "Potential Christians," 255–257.

29. On Marye's baptismal service, see Van Horne, *Religious Philanthropy,* 149. Willie quoted in Walsh, *From Calabar to Carter's Grove,* 158.

30. For an extended discussion on the place of smell in the construction of race and slavery, see Smith, *How Race is Made,* 13–18 and passim.

31. James Maury, Fredericksville Parish, to unnamed recipient, October 10, 1759, photostat at Special Collections, University of Virginia Library. See also Frey and Wood, *Come Shouting to Zion,* 77–78. Thomas Johnson (who also appears as Thomas Johnson, Sr., and Major Thomas Johnson) was appointed to the Fredericksville Parish vestry on January 24, 1758, and became warden on October 25, 1758. He was a man of some means. In 1767 he was taxed on 6,432 acres of land and twenty-five tithables, including sons Thomas Jr. and Richard, two overseers and twenty-one tithable slaves. Rosalie Edith Davis, *Louisa County Tithables and Census, 1743–1785,* 12. Documents of a lawsuit in which Thomas Johnson, Sr., was involved suggest that he had a certain fractious personality. Abercrombie, *Louisa County, Virginia Judgments 1766–1790,* 21–25. This conflict in Maury and Johnson's church over the baptism of black parishioners may have contributed to the emotional pitch and intensity of the Parson's Cause. (It appears that the Johnson directly involved in the Cause was Warden Johnson's son, Thomas Johnson, Jr., who was one of the collectors for the vestry. One of Patrick Henry's ledgers contains a charge dated 1763 to Thomas Johnson, formerly Subsheriff of Louisa County, for fees in a suit against Maury. An entry in what appears to be a minute book for Louisa County notes that Thomas Johnson, Jr., was sworn undersheriff on August 25, 1761. Davis, *Fredericksville Parish Vestry Books, 1742–1787,* 1: 63, 67; Patrick Henry Ledger, 29, Accession no. 20473, Business Records Collection, Library of Virginia, Richmond; Bell, *Louisa County Records You Probably Never Saw,* 110.)

32. For a discussion of rituals' creating an idealized world that participants know to be at odds with reality, see Smith, *Imagining Religion,* 53–65.

33. Marshall, *Prayerbook Parallels,* 1: 232–280. A surviving baptismal sermon from a Virginia parson can help us envision what clergy actually did in response to the prayer book's instructions "discreetly and warily" to "dip" the infant. Some clergy no doubt did dip infants, especially if they were baptizing in deep church fonts. Others, though, sprinkled rather than dipped. Charles Clay spoke as one "who practice the Bm of Infants by pouring or Sprinkling water on them" and who "Suppose a little [water] is Sufficient, & yt he who has the Face or head washed in this Solemnity; has as true a Significancy of Gos. Benefits, & Obligations as he who has his whole Body put under Water." See Charles Clay Papers, Sec. 2, Mss1 C5795 a 20–21, Virginia Historical Society (hereafter VHS).

34. See the untitled anonymous document about the distribution of religious books, Library of Virginia (Richmond), Virginia microfilm, Virginia Miscellany, miscellaneous reel 19, n.p.; Charles Clay, sermon on Matthew 28:19, Charles Clay Papers, Sec. 2, Mss1 C5795 a 20–21, VHS; Allestree, *Whole Duty of Man,* 53, 60; Blosser, "Irreverent Empire," 597n5. On the popularity of Allestree's *Whole Duty of Man* in Virginia, see Davis, *Intellectual Life,* 499, 505, 540, 580; Kulikoff, *Tobacco and Slaves,* 198; Spruill, *Women's Life and Work,* 208; Hall, *Cultures of Print,* 129–130; Wright, "Pious Reading," 384; Smart, "Private Libraries," 44–45; Butler, "Thomas Teackle's 333 Books," 457; Butler, "Knowing the Uncertainties," 68; Kerrison, *Claiming the Pen,* 42–46 and passim; and James, "Libraries in Colonial Virginia," 94–95. See also Hardwick, "Mirrors for Their Sons," 242, 244. Virginians' understanding of baptism had long roots in Anglican thought. See the writings of Thomas Cranmer, who explained that "by baptism we enter into the kingdom of God, and shall be saved forever, if we continue to our lives' end in the death of

Christ. . . . Express baptism in your life, and baptism shall be the greatest comfort to you, both in your lifetime, and also in your deathbed." Cranmer, "On the Sacrament of Baptism," 46.

35. Page, *Deed of Gift*, 190; Harrower, *Journal*, 52. See also Thompson, *"In the Hands,"* 35–36. Because midwives might need to perform emergency baptisms immediately upon birth, they were licensed by the church in Anglican colonies of Virginia and New York; see Wertz and Wertz, *Lying-in*, 7.

36. Wilson, "Ceremony of Childbirth," 80; Byrd, *Secret Diary*, 249; Goetz, "Potential Christians," 170.

37. *VG*, November 16, 1775, p. 3, col. 3; *VG*, May 17, 1776, p. 2, col. 3. On spiritual kinship in England, see Cressy, *Birth*, 156–161, and Coster, *Baptism and Spiritual Kinship*, passim.

38. Indeed, the Book of Common Prayer dropped the traditional language of "purification" and renamed the rite "the thanksgiving of women after childbirth, commonly called churching"; Marshall, *Prayerbook Parallels*, 1: 462. On the shifting emphasis from purification to thanksgiving, see Cressy, *Birth*, 205–210, 228–229; Wilson, "Ceremony of Childbirth," 78. On churching more broadly, see ibid., esp. 71–92; Karant-Nunn, *The Reformation of Ritual*, 72–90; Muir, *Ritual in Early Modern Europe*, 24; Cressy, *Birth*, 197–229.

39. Cressy, *Birth*, 223. On churching as a rite of passage that accomplished social reintegration, see Rieder, *On the Purification of Women*, 135. On childbirth as a withdrawal into an all-female world, see Gundersen, "Kith and Kin," 93–94.

40. For the 1732 letter from the pastor of Drysdale Parish, see letter dated June 27, 1732, Fulham Papers, vol. 12, nos. 182, 183, Lambeth Palace Library. For references to the churching of women in Virginia, see James Blair, April 10, 1719, proceedings of the Convention of the Clergy at Williamsburgh, in Perry, *Papers*, 225; Hening, *Statutes at Large*, 1: 160. See also Harrower, *Journal*, 66; Nelson, *Blessed Company*, 258.

41. On women's positive feelings about churching, see Cressy, "Purification," 110, 141, 144; Wilson, "Ceremony of Childbirth," esp. 89–93; see also Rieder, *On the Purification of Women*, 134.

42. Fithian, *Journal and Letters*, 35; Byrd, *Secret Diary*, 2. On feasting as a means to deepen the relationship between the baptized child and godparents, see Bossy, *Christianity in the West*, 15. On the food at these gatherings, see Swinburne and Mason, "'She Came from a Groaning,'" 73–74.

43. Nicholas Moreau to the Right Honorable the Lord Bishop of Lichfield and Coventry, His Majesty's High Almoner, Virginia, April 12, 1697, in Perry, *Papers*, 30–31.

44. See, e.g., Jensen, "Living Water," 191–220, passim; Spinks, *Early and Medieval Rituals*, passim.

45. Hewlett, *A Refined Quaker's Remarks*, 3–20; Davies, *The Quakers in English Society*, 37; Braithwaite, *The Beginnings of Quakerism*, 137; Barbour, *The Quakers*, 115.

46. Hamm, *Transformation of American Quakerism*, 4.

47. Evans, "A Short Account of Alice Hayes," 68–83.

48. Hening, *Statutes at Large*, 2: 165–166. See also Charles Clay, sermon on Matthew 28:19, Charles Clay Papers, Sec. 2, Mss1, C5795 a 20–21, VHS; Charles Clay, sermon on John 3:5, Charles Clay Papers, Sec. 2, Mss1, C5795 a 24–25, VHS; William Douglas Sermon Collection, 1: 295, Virginia Theological Seminary Archives. On Bland, see "Letters of Roger Atkinson," 356. For another kind of denunciation—a caustic satire—see Hardwick's discussion of "How to Make a Perfect Quaker," Hardwick, 379–380.

49. Davies, *The Quakers in English Society,* 37–38; Beeth, "Outside Agitators," 63, 96, 116–120; Frost, "From Plainness to Simplicity," 23–29; Tarter, "'Varied Trials,'" 82–83; see also Hatfield, *Atlantic Virginia,* chapter 5, esp. 129–130; Worrall, *Friendly Virginians,* 108–112; Bond, *Spreading the Gospel,* 57n100, 58n108.

50. Lindman, "World of Baptists," 55–58; Lindman, *Bodies of Belief,* 33; Worrall, *Friendly Virginians,* 107; Leland, "Virginia Chronicle," 456; Charles Clay, sermon on Matthew 28:19, Charles Clay Papers, Sec. 2, Mss1 C5795 a 20–21, VHS. See also William Douglas Sermon Collection, 1: 295.

51. Semple, *History of Baptists,* 10, 22, 37; Thomas, *The Virginian Baptist,* 45; Juster, *Disorderly Women,* 47–50; Juster, "'In a Different Voice,'" 37, 56; Spangler, *Virginians Reborn,* 167–184.

52. Fristoe, *Ketocton Baptist Association,* 26–29; Kidd, *The Great Awakening,* 251–252; Beliles, "Christian Communities," 7–8; Scully, *Nat Turner,* 66–67. In 1768 Ambrose Coleman wrote his pastor a letter inquiring about the meaning of "new birth." Coleman, who lived in Albemarle County, had probably heard the phrase from the lips of neighboring Baptists. (Baptists would not establish a church in Albemarle for another five years, but many of the forty-eight men and women who founded Albemarle's first Baptist church in 1773 had been part of a Baptist church in nearby Orange since it was organized in 1768. See Turpin, *Albemarle Baptist Association,* 11; Moore, *Albemarle,* 79; Cosby, "Survey of the Rural Baptist Churches," 72.) In response, Coleman's pastor, James Maury, struck quite a different note from the Baptist discourse of "new birth." Maury emphasized a tripartite understanding of new birth—it involved water (with reference to water, Maury underscored that "by *Baptism*" one "admitted into a *new State,* & so become a Member of [the] visible Church by that baptismal Washing, by which you say your Proselytes become as Infants *newly born,*"), the Spirit, and a change of life that the Christian experiences in part by sincerely seeking a change in affections and sympathies. See James Maury to Mr. Ambrose Coleman, 1768, in Bond, *Spreading the Gospel,* 271.

53. Fristoe, quoted in Kroll-Smith, "Transmitting a Revival Culture," 558; Essig, "A Very Wintry Season," 170–171, 177, 179, and passim; Lindman, "World of Baptists," 187–203; Lindman, *Bodies of Belief,* 142–146; Sobel, *Trabelin' On,* 85–86. Jewel L. Spangler has recently offered a nuanced analysis of Virginia Baptists' relationship with their surrounding society. She persuasively argues that Baptist success in Virginia was due in part to the creative ways that Baptists upheld and drew on established communal rituals and norms. Although Baptists "tended to describe themselves as a people apart from the dominant order," Baptist practice "fit with and supported the fundamental social mores of the colony and codes of proper public conduct, as well as reinforcing the hierarchies of gender and race that ordered Virginians." For example, Baptists' "attempts to restrict the sexual activity of church members" dovetailed with "the code of sexual conduct that civil officials sought to enforce in Virginia." Baptists' concerns about fancy dress "engaged Virginians at precisely the moment when a sexual interest in purging excessive luxury from daily life was on the rise across the colony." It is thus "possible to overemphasize Baptist uniqueness and separateness." Nonetheless, Spangler maintains that Baptist practice "had some distinctive features" and that there is still some truth in the "long historiographical tradition that places evangelical southerners in cultural opposition to the dominant order in the Revolutionary period." For example, in spurning racing and dancing, "Baptists distinguished themselves from 'the world' to a significant degree." Furthermore, "Baptist community departed from the norms of the secular community when it came to some points of class

relations, departures that marked an important social adjustment for free male congregants." Spangler, *Virginians Reborn,* 119–166, 184–193.

54. *VG,* August 24, 1739, pp. 1–2; Baumgarten, *What Clothes Reveal,* 64, 82–84, 114; Buck, *Dress in Eighteenth-Century England,* 189; Cunnington and Cunnington, *Handbook;* Calvert, "Function of Fashion," 265–270; Montgomery, *Textiles in America,* 271; Sykas, "Fustians in Englishmen's Dress," 6; Wingate, *Fairchild's Dictionary of Textiles;* Martin, "'Boys Who Will Be Men,'" 490, 501n8. I am grateful to Jeff Stout for calling this passage in *Tom Brown's School Days* to my attention.

55. Schmidt, "Church-Going People," 38. In a world where women were increasingly associated with fashion, it is not surprising that the protagonists of this story are women; indeed, the author of the piece at once notices, sneers at, and constructs the association of women with fashion. (On women's association with fashion in Virginia, see Sturtz, *Within Her Power,* 165.) See also Calvert's persuasive argument that in the eighteenth century the ability to read sumptuary codes and the cues of costumes, the ability to read clothes for social meaning, was a marker of class, gentility, and education; Calvert, "Function of Fashion," 252–253. On the trope of casting off fine garments in evangelical conversion narratives, see Bushman, *Refinement,* 314–319.

56. The Randolphs were one of the most prominent families in colonial Virginia. During his travels in America in the 1780s, the marquis de Chastellux observed that in Virginia "you must be prepared to hear the name of Randolph frequently mentioned. This is one of the first families in the country. . . . It is also one of the most numerous and wealthiest." Thomas Jefferson was descended, on his father's side, from the Randolphs, and the colonial Virginia politician and pamphleteer Richard Bland's mother was a Randolph. Most famous, today, is the Tuckahoe branch of the family, which was at the center of the great scandal of Jefferson's Virginia: Nancy Randolph was accused of sleeping with her sister's husband, then aborting or murdering the child that was conceived during the tryst. The Randolph family's presence in Virginia dates to around 1670, when William Randolph I (he would be known in Virginia as William Randolph of Turkey Island) arrived from England. (William's uncle Henry Randolph had been in Virginia for more than twenty-five years, and may have had a hand in bringing his nephew to the colony.) William Randolph held many public offices, including clerk of Henrico County court and representative to the House of Burgesses. He and his wife, Mary Isham Randolph, had ten children and forty-three grandchildren. These three generations of Turkey Island Randolphs claimed three speakers of the House, three attorneys general, one president of the College of William and Mary, and two delegates (and one president) of the Continental Congress. The eighth of Mary and William Randolph's children was Richard Randolph of Curles. He grew up on the plantation at Turkey Island, was educated at William and Mary, and grew into a prominent planter. Around 1724, Randolph, then thirty-three, married twenty-one-year-old Jane Bolling. The fourth of their seven children was Brett Randolph, born around 1732. When he turned twenty-one, he received an inheritance of twenty-one thousand acres from his father. In 1753, while in London, he married Mary Scott. The two set up housekeeping in Chesterfield County shortly thereafter. The best source for information on the Randolphs is Cowden, "Randolphs of Turkey Island."

57. On Virginia's colonial gentry as people interested in—indeed, people who derived their principal sense of self from—how others saw them, see Breen, *Puritans and Adventurers,* 153–154.

58. On English and American christening gowns, see Baumgarten, *What Clothes Reveal,* 160–162.

59. Jensen, "Living Water," 256.

60. Abatt, "Restored Heirlooms"; Turpin Ayers, "Randolph Christening Dress—110 years old," both in Wilton House Randolph christening gown file. On people's emotional attachment to and the multigenerational nature of christening gowns, see Taylor, *Study of Dress History,* 5.

Chapter Two. Becoming a "Christian Woman"

1. For the legalities of catechizing, see Hening, *Statutes at Large,* 1: 155–157. On the use of Lewis's catechism in Virginia, see John Thompson to Samuel Smith, August 25, 1743, in Van Horne, *Religious Philanthropy,* 96. See also Monaghan, *Learning to Read and Write,* 95–97. For adaptations of the prayer book catechism in the home, see Green, *The Christian's ABC,* esp. 62–92.

2. On confirmation and the relationship between confirmation and communion, see Bond, *Spreading the Gospel,* 490–491; Nelson, *Blessed Company,* 218–221; Spangler, *Virginians Reborn,* 31.

3. On the use of Lewis's text, see Lawrence DeButte to the Rev. Mr. Berryman, July 14, 1722, Fulham Papers, vol. 10, no. 285, Lambeth Palace Library. On ministers catechizing during Lent, see responses to "Questions to be Answered by Every Minister," in Perry, *Papers,* 261–318. On sermons aimed at youth, see William Douglas's two sermons on Proverbs 8:17, Sermon Book 2, William Douglas Sermon Collection. See also Dawson, "A Confirmation Sermon," 490–495.

4. Perry, *Papers,* 284, 286, 267, 269.

5. Henrico Parish in the Upper District James River response to "Questions to be Answered by Every Minister," in Perry, *Papers,* 304–305; Fithian, *Journal and Letters,* 76; Thrift, "Memoir of the Rev Jesse Lee," 3–4. Heyrman first made the point that "ironically, the most reliable testimony to Anglican rigor issues from those men who became the South's leading evangelicals during the latter half of the eighteenth century." Their sweeping criticisms of Anglicanism were, Heyrman astutely notes, "undercut by their recollections of the devotional regimen of Anglican mothers, the stern rectitude of Anglican fathers, and the common parental practices of teaching young Anglican children to read the Bible as their primer, drilling them in the catechism, and stocking their households with books of sermons and other religious treatises." Heyrman, *Southern Cross,* 14–15.

6. On Harrower, see Harrower, *Journal,* 73, 150. See also Monaghan, *Learning to Read and Write,* 13, 150–152, and passim; Kulikoff, *Tobacco and Slaves,* 195. On learning handwriting, see Thornton, *Handwriting in America,* 37–39; Monaghan, *Learning to Read and Write,* 343–344.

7. On one inscribed ring, see Higgins and Muraca, "Archaeological Data," Shields Tavern Archaeological Report, block 9, building 26B, Williamsburg, VA, 1990, Colonial Williamsburg's Digital History Center Archive. On needlework as a historical source for early American women, see Ulrich, "Of Pens and Needles," 204–209.

8. McFadden, *Pricked,* 66.

9. Breuer and Freud, *Studies in Hysteria,* 15. See also Parker, *Subversive Stitch,* 11, 67.

10. Parmal, *Samplers from A to Z,* 7.

11. Ring, *Girlhood Embroidery,* 6–8; Sebba, *Samplers,* 23.

12. Parker, *Subversive Stitch,* 85; Will of "Coll. Southey Littleton," Accomack County, Virginia, Wills and Deeds, 1676–1690, 295, MESDA Research File.

13. Howell, "'A More Perfect Copy,'" 167; Parmal, *Samplers from A to Z,* 7–8; Garrett,

"American Samplers and Needlework," 94–95; Ring, *Girlhood Embroidery,* 11; Goggin, "'An *Essamplaire Essai,*'" 317.

14. On Standish's sampler, see Bolton and Coe, *American Samplers,* 5; Smith, "'First Effort,'" 35; Sebba, *Samplers,* 50. On sampler making as girlhood activity, see Ring, *Girlhood Embroidery,* 12. On variations from the English style, see Ivey, *Neatest Manner,* 31, 38. It is worth noting that the English style persisted longer in Virginia than in other colonies, with a distinctive Virginian or American style of needlework emerging only in the 1790s. See Ivey, *Neatest Manner,* 53, 62; Bolton and Coe, *American Samplers,* 10–11. On samplers and marking later linens, see Swan, *A Winterthur Guide to American Needlework,* 13; Bolton and Coe, *American Samplers,* 12, 16–17; Ivey, *Neatest Manner,* 19. On frames, see Deutsch, "The Polite Lady," 751; Kelly, "Reading," 135. One nonagenarian, reflecting on the ubiquity of decorative samplers in the early nineteenth century, recalled that "large and elaborate specimens of handiwork . . . often formed the chief ornament of the sitting room or best parlor." Swan, *A Winterthur Guide to American Needlework,* 13. Early-nineteenth-century wills locating framed embroidery in the "front room" also tell us that embroidery was given pride of place in public domestic space. See, for example, the November 18, 1828, will of James Crocker, Isle of Wight County, Virginia, Wills and Accounts, vol. 18, 1828–1831, MESDA research file.

15. Ulrich, *Age of Homespun,* 147.

16. Deutsch, "The Polite Lady," 744. No one is sure which Byrd woman is depicted: either Wilhelmina Byrd, her sister Evelyn Byrd, or their mother Lucy Park Byrd. See ibid., 751n4.

17. Smith, "'First Effort,'" 31.

18. Newton inventory, March 13 1721, Norfolk Co., Virginia, MESDA research file. On needlework as part of curricula, see Staples, "Tangible Displays," 199. *VG,* November 17, 1752, p. 2, col. 2. See also Ring, *Girlhood Embroidery,* 12; Bolton and Coe, *American Samplers,* 18–19; Spruill, *Women's Life and Work,* 196, 199. For descriptions of girls' schools run in houses, see *VG,* March 21, 1766, p. 3, col. 3; *VG,* February 20, 1772, p. 3, col. 2; Read, *Memoirs,* 39. Museums boast large collections of samplers from New England and the middle colonies and relatively few examples of Virginia needlework, but, as Kimberly Smith Ivey has persuasively argued, this is a problem of preservation, not production. Some Virginia samplers deteriorated due to humidity. (In an August 1769 letter about her niece Betsey Braxton, Anne Blair described the problem: "She has finish'd her work'd Tucker, but the weather is so warm, that with all the pain's I can take with clean hands, and so forth she cannot help dirtying it a little.") Others were carried off by marauding Yankee soldiers during the Civil War. (Martha Carter Fitzhugh's sampler, worked in 1793 in Stafford County, Virginia, eventually came to be owned by Martha's niece, Mrs. Robert E. Lee. Union soldiers looting Arlington House in 1861 made off with the sampler, which then found its way to the Essex Institute in Salem, Massachusetts. In 1897 the Essex Institute included the sampler in a display at the world's fair. Douglas H. Thomas, editor of the *Virginia Historical Magazine,* was one viewer who recognized the sampler as a piece of Virginia handiwork. "This sampler was no doubt 'obtained' during the war by some of the 'visitors' to Virginia," he wrote. In 1979 the Essex Institute returned the sampler to Arlington House.) Ivey, *Neatest Manner,* 49; Smith, 32.

19. Harrower, *Journal,* 76; Saxton, *Being Good,* 103.

20. See Fordyce, *Sermons to Young Women,* 33; Kelly, "Reading," 127.

21. On the suitability of needlework for girls' education, see Kelly, "Reading," esp.

125–127, 137. See also Kierner, *Beyond the Household,* 48. On advocating needlework, see Steele, *Ladies Library,* 1–34; Parker, *Subversive Stitch,* 62, 74.

22. Smith, "'First Effort,'" 39; Gregory, *A Father's Legacy,* 86. These are useful reminders that it was not only elite girls who knew how to do needlework. For evidence of slaveowners' valuing needle skills in female slaves, see, e.g., *VG,* January 1, 1775, p. 3, col. 1. On slaves' needlework in South Carolina, see Staples, "Girlhood Embroidery," 16–19.

23. Calabresi, "'You sow, Ile read,'" 79–104; Kelly, "Reading," 131–135, and passim; Goggin, "'An *Essamplaire Essai,*'" 323.

24. Roche, *Culture of Clothing,* 266. See Ulrich, "Creating Lineages," 9–10, and van Keuren's discussion of sampler-making as "values education for young girls," "American Girl," 86–87.

25. Of course, sewing was not the only exercise through which girls learned social and religious lessons. Despite pedagogues' ambivalence about girls' reading, books were also used to teach religious and social norms, and elite girls read actively, transcribing bits of their reading into commonplace books. Perhaps unsurprisingly, similar verses and themes run throughout both needlework and commonplace books. As Catherine E. Kelly has recently shown, needlework and commonplace books are usefully seen in tandem. Not only do the same verses sometimes crop up in needlework and commonplace books; the pictures and phrases that appear in needlework were often drawn from books—thus needlework itself testifies to girls' participation in print culture and the seemingly "masculine" arena of literacy. This paradigm suggests that we ought not too sharply juxtapose religious education grounded in the textbooks of catechesis with the religious education of needlework. Kelly, "Reading," 131. On Virginia commonplace books, see Chapter 3, note 46; Miller, *Assuming the Positions.*

26. Davidson, *Plimoth Colony Samplers,* 10; Locklair, "'The Beautiful Embroidery,'" 14–20; Kathleen Staples, "Advantages of Religious Instruction"; Johanna Brown, Director of Collections, Museum of Early Southern Decorative Arts (MESDA), untitled lecture on Moravians in North Carolina and girls' work, copy in author's possession.

27. To rely on prescriptive literature as an interpretive grid is to come up against the gap between text and reader. Prescriptive books that people like Boush read brim with conventional, conservative pieties about God-ordained hierarchy and women's submissive role. Did girls internalize these lessons, or did they read against them? Because girls and women in early Virginia left few discussions of their reading, it is hard to know, but the historian Catherine Kerrison has imaginatively drawn on commonplace books and diaries to argue that Anglican women in the early South did, indeed, absorb many of the lessons they found in their devotional reading. In a brilliant analysis of Mary Ambler's short journal, Kerrison suggests the ways in which prescriptive literature's gendered lessons about hierarchy could serve the interests of genteel women in the early South. Ambler, a widowed mother of four, traveled from Virginia to Baltimore to have her children inoculated against smallpox in 1770. Her journal describes a trip fraught with peril and marked by many small annoyances. At the end of her travelogue, Ambler transcribed a paragraph from James Fordyce's *Sermons to Young Women,* which she had read during her trip: "If to Your natural softness You join that christian meekness, which I now preach; both together will not fail, with the assistance of proper reflection and friendly advice, to accomplish you in the best and truest kind of breeding. You will not be in danger of putting your-selves forward in company, of contradicting bluntly, of asserting positively, of debating obstinately, of affecting a superiority to any present . . . or of neglecting what is advanced by

others, or of interrupting them without necessity." In her journal, Ambler "beg[ged] her Daug[hte]r to observe" Fordyce's words "well all her Life." Kerrison argues that although Ambler asserted her prerogative to have her children inoculated, she ultimately found in Fordyce's conservative conventions and his vision of her own subordinate status a useful map for successfully navigating both a perilous trip, and, indeed, a life. As Kerrison puts it, "Ambler . . . recognized her vulnerability and dependence, was grateful for the many kindnesses she received, and never 'affect[ed] a superiority to any present.'" While girls and women were not blank slates on which the lessons of prescriptive literature were written, on Kerrison's quite persuasive reading, they did internalize much of the prescriptive literature they read. Kerrison, *Claiming the Pen,* 34–69. See also Kierner, *Beyond the Household,* 29.

28. Fordyce, *Sermons to Young Women,* 213. On reading aloud, see Kelly, "Reading," 126.

29. Smith, "First Effort," 100n23. On Mary Johnson's parents, see Chamberlayne, *St. Peter's Vestry Book,* 470, 540. On the sampler, see Smith, "First Effort," 48–50, 89, 94; Ivey, *Neatest Manner,* 7, 53, 55, 106n27. Although Johnson's is the earliest sampler to survive, samplers that did not survive may have been worked as early as the 1730s. There is documentary evidence, for example, of a Virginia sampler made in York County in 1734.

30. On the reversible marking cross-stitch, see Ivey, *Neatest Manner,* 28–29, 53, 55. On alphabets in samplers, see Parmal, *Samplers from A to Z,* 12.

31. Peter Fontaine to "Dear Brothers," March 2, 1756, in Fontaine, *Memoirs of a Huguenot Family* [hereafter Maury/Fontaine memoirs], 346; *William Byrd's Histories of the Dividing Line,* 33. See also Fordyce, *Sermons to Young Women,* 184–190. See also title page of *The Ladies Calling,* which quotes Proverbs 31:30; the passage thus sets the tone for, and provides a hermeneutical key for reading the rest of the work. Allestree, *Ladies Calling,* n.p. See also Dodd, *Common-place-book,* 175; Kennett, *The Excellent Daughter,* 23; Gregory, *Father's Legacy,* 59; Allestree, *Government of the Tongue,* 394.

32. On the popularity of Fordyce, see Kerrison, *Claiming the Pen,* 18–19, 34–35; Kross, "Mansions," 397; Kierner, "Hospitality," 455, 460; Saxton, *Being Good,* 103–104.

33. During the eighteenth century important developments occurred in thinking about women. Although earlier writers, such as Allestree, continued to be extremely popular, eighteenth-century writers like Fordyce were articulating a somewhat new vision of sex and gender. Eighteenth-century writers shared with earlier writers the view that women were inferior, and that they should be submissive and obedient. New to the eighteenth-century writers was the grounding of such claims in a "two-sex" model that located difference in women's *bodies.* For a nuanced and astute discussion of this, see Kerrison, *Claiming the Pen,* 42–59.

34. Fordyce, *Sermons to Young Women,* 175–176, 192–198, 205–206, 223.

35. Ibid., 211, 181, 213.

36. See Meyers, "Everyday Life," 251–259.

37. Creffield, *A Good Wife,* 23. On views of Eve, see Kerrison, *Claiming the Pen,* 64–65, 71–73.

38. William Douglas Sermon Collection 2: 185–189.

39. Howell, "'A More Perfect Copy,'" 164–169.

40. *VG,* December 3, 1772, p. 2; Wertenbaker, *Norfolk,* 8, 11, 25, 33; Parramore with Bogger and Stewart, *Norfolk,* 63; Tarter, "Samuel Boush," 125–126.

41. Wertenbaker, *Norfolk,* 6; Burton, *The History of Norfolk, Virginia,* 3; Tarter, "Sam-

uel Boush," 125–126. Ring, *Girlhood Embroidery,* 533. For information on Catherine Ballard's antecedents, see Brewer, *York County, Virginia, Wills, Inventories and Court Orders,* 1–2. See also "Virginia Council Journals, 1726–1753," 49; "Historical Genealogical Notes," 208; Dorman, *Adventures of Purse and Person,* 604–605.

42. *VG,* March 21, 1766, p. 3, col. 3; Ring, "Persons of Fortune," 1–11; Ivey, *Neatest Manner,* 61; *VG,* February 20, 1772, p. 3, col. 2.

43. Ivey, *Neatest Manner,* 60–61; Ring, "Persons of Fortune," 11–13; *VG,* December 3, 1772, p. 2; "Norfolk County Marriage Book," 108; "Travis Family," 143; Ring, *Girlhood Embroidery,* 11; Tyler, *Encyclopedia,* 344. Champion Travis's will, which was recorded in Williamsburg, James City County (a burned record county), August 28, 1810, was re-recorded in Deed Book U of the Kentucky Court of Appeals on April 23, 1821. It is abstracted in Cook and Cook, Kentucky Court of Appeals Deed Books O-U, 524–525. See also Samuel Travis's will in Crozier, Virginia County Records, 54.

44. Ring, "Memorial Embroideries," 80.

45. Since 1977, when needlework historians first began work on Boush's Sacrifice of Isaac, scholars have thought that the pattern Boush used was based on Gerard de Jode's *Thesaurus Veteris Testamenti.* However, Kathleen Staples has recently determined that the print source for Boush's needlework is more likely to have been Egbert van Panderen's engraving, ca. 1600, after Pieter de Jode's painting. Whereas Gerard de Jode's illustration shows Abraham raising his left hand, the van Panderen engraving shows, as does Boush's needlework, Abraham's left hand placed atop Isaac's head. Many thanks to Kathleen Staples for sharing her yet unpublished discovery with me.

46. Robertson quoted in Ivey, *Neatest Manner,* 44.

47. Staples, "'Plain, Fine, and Fancy,'" 36–37; Deutsch, "Needlework Patterns," 373; Ring, "Persons of Fortune," 9–11. See also Ivey, *Neatest Manner,* 75–76. For a discussion of women's choosing patterns, see Parker, *Subversive Stitch,* 12. Richardson, *Clarissa,* 971.

48. On the prevalence of heroic women in needlework, see Jones and Stallybrass, *Renaissance Clothing,* 158. For Jefferson, see Stein, *Thomas Jefferson at Monticello,* 33. For illustrated Bibles, see, e.g., the illustration of Genesis 22 in the Tunstall Bible (1716), University of Virginia Special Collections Library, n.p. On the engraving owned by Mary Byrd, see Will of Mrs. Mary (Willing) Byrd in the *VMHB,* 146. For Jans's sampler, see Bolton and Coe, *American Samplers,* 28, 56. See also Parker, *Subversive Stitch,* 89, 96.

49. Staples, "Tangible Displays," 200.

50. Stein, *Thomas Jefferson at Monticello,* 70.

51. A search through the following sources turned up no instances of contemporaries offering that political reading of Genesis 22: Papers of George Washington; Papers of Thomas Jefferson; Papers of John Adams; Papers of James Madison; *Virginia Gazette;* Early American Imprints Database; Moore, *Patriot Preachers;* Thornton, *Pulpit of the American Revolution;* Jensen, *Tracts;* Bailyn and Garrett, *Pamphlets of the American Revolution;* Noll, *Christians in the American Revolution;* and Bonomi, *Under the Cope of Heaven.*

52. Saxton, *Being Good,* 113–114; Kerrison, *Claiming the Pen,* 40.

53. Kulikoff, *Tobacco and Slaves,* 66–67.

54. Brown, *Good Wives,* 334, 339.

55. EFW, spring 1789.

56. Kulikoff, *Tobacco and Slaves,* 195, 199.

57. Watts, *Plain and Easy.* Although Watts was an English nonconformist, he was read widely by Virginia Anglicans. For example, George Washington gave his wife, Mar-

tha, a volume of Watts's psalms and hymns in 1789. See Mary V. Thompson, "'As if I had Been a Very Great Somebody,'" unpublished essay in author's possession, 120–121. Evidence suggests that Isaac Watts tended to be read and sung more often by those with evangelical leanings. See Gillespie, "1795: Ramsay," 68; Jarratt, *Life,* 46. On the theological breadth of Anglicans' reading more broadly, see Davis, *Intellectual Life,* 2: 507 and passim. Hardwick has found that there was a greater presence of Puritan and Calvinist writings in the seventeenth-century genteel Virginia libraries. "After 1700 the theological collections of Virginia gentlemen strongly emphasized moderate, latitudinarian Anglicanism"; "Mirrors for Their Sons," 242. Kerrison, however, finds "striking . . . the breadth of Virginian taste" in theological and devotional reading, and notes the presence of Puritans, Anglicans, and Catholics all comingled together in Virginia libraries. Kerrison, *Claiming the Pen,* 42. See also Ivey, *Neatest Manner,* 7; Nelson, *Blessed Company,* 193. Allestree, *Ladies Calling,* 225. Tillotson, "A Sermon Preached at White-Hall," *Works,* 50–51. On the popularity and importance of Tillotson in the homiletical and reading lives of Virginia Anglicans, see Bond, *Spreading the Gospel,* 37, 73n23, 114–115, and passim. Bond, "Anglican Theology and Devotion," 318n11; Blosser, "Pursuing Happiness," 75–114, passim; Kerrison, *Claiming the Pen,* 48–49; Byrd, *Commonplace Book,* 5n4; Davis, 581; Hardwick, "Mirrors for Their Sons," 240–271. Maria Carter's copybook, page 14, verso, quotes Tillotson. Carter's copybook also includes on page 20: "Slanderers are like flies, which pass over the good parts of a man's Body, and indulge in his Sores." Though Carter does not offer attribution, this is a slight adaptation of a line—"Slanderers are like flies; they pass over the good parts of a man, and indulge on his sores"—often attributed to Tillotson in eighteenth-century books of aphorisms. Maria Carter's version may be found in *The pleasing instructor; or, entertaining moralist* (1756), as well as *The lady's accomptant and best accomplisher* (1771). On the general use of the Bible in teaching children moral and social lessons, see Bottigheimer, *The Bible for Children,* xi, and passim; for Bottigheimer's insightful treatment of the Sacrifice of Isaac, see ibid., 75–81, 88–90.

58. Stein, *Thomas Jefferson at Monticello,* 33; Parker, *Subversive Stitch,* 89, 96.

59. On how girls might have read the story of Jephthah's daughter, see Bottigheimer, *The Bible for Children,* 72.

60. Chapone, *Improvement of the Mind,* 18–19. On southern women's reading Chapone, see Spruill, *Women's Life and Work,* 224–225; Kerrison, *Claiming the Pen,* 157–164.

61. Jones and Stallybrass, *Renaissance Clothing,* 148–149, 158, 170–171. See also Frye, "Sewing Connections," 165–182.

62. Let us revisit Freud's provocative claim that needlework led to daydreams and induced hysteria in women. His observation about daydreams unwittingly reveals the subtly subversive potential of needlework. Needlework kept girls' hands busy—but needlework also gave girls hours and hours to think. It may be that girls like Elizabeth Boush obediently stitched and at the same time escaped into their own thoughts—needlework had the appearance of genteel propriety and submission but may also have been an undertaking in which girls dreamed. But Freud's reading cuts both ways. He may be read to say that needlework virtually induced a trance; perhaps girls needed practices like needlework —practices designed to discipline—precisely because they were taught, in the hierarchy of their households, to identify with Isaac, the sacrificed. The stories of Isaac and Jephthah's daughter made clear that submission to male direction could have terrifying consequences, especially for daughters. Perhaps needlework fostered a kind of fatalistic obedience, which girls needed because their fate was uncertain and out of their control.

Chapter Three. People of the Book

1. Mrs. Elizabeth Cabell to Dr. William Cabell, May 15, 1739, MSS 9513, Cocke Family Papers, box 1, folder: 1,736 Copies of Sundry Letter to and from Dr. William Cabell, UVA Special Collections. For a discussion of the Cabells' participation in the Anglican church, see Rose, *Diary,* 56, 74, 97, and 287n705.

2. Books of Common Prayer were restricted by patent, and thus not printed in the colonies. See Stiverson and Stiverson, "The Colonial Retail Book Trade," 167. Books of Common Prayer came to Virginia in a number of ways. Parish libraries were stocked by such organizations as the Bray Society and the Society for the Propagation of the Gospel in Foreign Parts, clergy ordered Books of Common Prayer (see, e.g., William Dawson, Letter to unknown, n.d. [1744?], William Dawson Family Papers, Manuscript Division, Library of Congress); individuals ordered them directly from England (see, e.g., Stanard, *Colonial Virginia* [1917], 204). People inherited books from family members (see, e.g., "Books in Colonial Virginia," 389–405), family and friends in England sent them, and colonists brought back prayer books when they traveled to England (see, e.g., William Reynolds to John Norton [London], August 18, 1771, p. 3, Papers of William Reynolds, 1771–1796, LOC Manuscripts, Call Number: MMC-1623, LOC Control Number: mm 82037671, Manuscript Division, Library of Congress). Booksellers imported them from England and sold them in the colonies (see, e.g., Stiverson and Stiverson, "The Colonial Retail Book Trade," 140–141, 146–147; *VG,* October 24, 1745, p. 4; *VG,* July 1, 1768, p. 3; *VG,* November 29, 1770, p. 2; *VG,* December 13, 1770, p. 4).

3. Bond, *Damned Souls,* 264.

4. On religious books in colonial Virginia, see especially Hall, *Cultures of Print,* 119–122; Wright, "Pious Reading," 384–391; Hall, "Chesapeake in the Seventeenth Century," 74; Smart, "Private Libraries," 44–46; Davis, *Intellectual Life,* 499–508, 580. See also Jones, *American Colonial Wealth,* 1295–1403; Butler, "Thomas Teackle's 333 Books," 457; Spruill, *Women's Life and Work,* 208; Patterson, "Private Libraries in Virginia," 11–12; Whiting, "Religious Literature"; Hardwick, "Mirrors for Their Sons," 237–247; Kerrison, *Claiming the Pen,* 34–104. There were practical reasons that books figured so prominently in the religious culture of Virginia: parishioners saw books as a substitute for scarce, overextended, or incompetent ministers, and clergymen themselves believed that "the putting proper books in their hands will . . . be one very good Expedient" for teaching the basic principles of Christianity; St. Stephens Parish, King and Queen response to "Queries to be Answered by every Minister," in Perry, *Papers,* 303; Bond, *Damned Souls,* 295. Religious books were difficult to obtain in the seventeenth century—even ordering them from London was chancy—but in the eighteenth century many avenues for book acquisition opened up. Ordering books directly from England became easier, and, in 1730, William Parks opened Virginia's first printing office in Williamsburg. He printed his own books and sold imports, formally establishing a bookstore around 1742. Later in the century, tobacco merchants began carrying books in their stores, as well. Winton, "Southern Book Trade," 228–232; Hall, "Chesapeake in the Seventeenth Century," 73. On Washington, see Thompson, *"In the Hands,"* 39.

5. Anonymous document about the distribution of religious books, Library of Virginia (Richmond) microfilm, Virginia Miscellany, miscellaneous reel 19, n.p. Though catalogued as anonymous at the Library of Virginia, this letter was probably written by William Dawson; see Dawson to Henry Neuman, 1743, William Dawson Family Papers, vol. 1, f. 16.

6. Ibid.

7. Smith, *Inside the Great House,* 62.

8. James Maury to James Maury, [Jr.], 1762, in Bond, *Spreading the Gospel,* 268–269. Bond notes that the phrase "read, mark & digest" echoes the Book of Common Prayer's collect for the second Sunday of Advent.

9. Page, *Deed of Gift,* 73–79.

10. Griffiths, *Religious Reading,* ix. The metaphors of food, nourishment, and eating that Maury and Page invoked were not original to Virginia Anglicans. Digestive images pervade the pedagogical writings of the ancients, of medieval logicians, and of Renaissance humanists. Writers ranging from Seneca to Johann Sturm described the process of gaining knowledge as one in which people ingest information and make it their own. In particular, the process of selecting, recopying and organizing material in commonplace books was described in gustatory language: in Erasmus's formulation, just as the bee turns nectar "into a liquid by the action of their mouths and digestive organs, and having transformed it into themselves, they then bring it forth from themselves," so too people master knowledge through commonplacing. Moss, *Printed Commonplace-Books,* 1, 18–20, 105, 112, 152. See also Radway, "Reading Is Not Eating." Jews and Christians found the language of eating text in the Bible, in Jeremiah (15:16), Ezekiel (2:8–3:3), and Revelation: "I went to the angel and told him to give me the little scroll; and he said to me, 'Take, it, and eat; it will be bitter to your stomach, but sweet as honey in your mouth.' And I took the little scroll from the hand of the angel and ate it; it was sweet as honey in my mouth, but when I had eaten it my stomach was made bitter" (10:9–10). The twenty-first-century pastoral theologian Eugene Peterson's explication of the passage from Revelation is an apt summary of this gustatory spiritual reading: "He eats the book—not just reads it—he got it into his nerve endings, his reflexes, his imagination"; Peterson, *Eat This Book,* 9. These gustatory images, with their scriptural imprimatur, had polemical meaning when invoked by Protestants; the language of taking and eating the Bible defined Anglicans like Page and Maury over and against Catholics, who took and ate the Eucharist.

11. EFW, September 1788.

12. Hambrick-Stowe, *The Practice of Piety,* 23.

13. For the importance of the Book of Common Prayer to Virginians' devotional lives, and the relationship between the Book of Common Prayer and the Bible, see Bond and Gundersen, "Colonial Origins and Growth," 188; Bond, *Damned Souls,* 264. The relationship between the Bible and the Book of Common Prayer in Anglican Virginia is intriguing. They were the two most numerous books in Virginians' private libraries; Bond, "Anglican Theology and Devotion," 328–329. Bibles outnumbered prayer books in absolute terms. See, e.g., Kulikoff, *Tobacco and Slaves,* 198n64. Still, it is noteworthy that among books sold at the Williamsburg Printing Office, the Book of Common Prayer far outsold the Bible; between 1751 and 1752, the office sold twenty-eight Bibles and seventy-one prayer books; Zambone, "Anglican Enlightenment," chapter 2. Sometimes the two books were bound together, a material suggestion of the extent to which each book read and interpreted the other. Visually and materially, a Bible bound with a prayer book was contextualized by that prayer book, and the prayer book was likewise interpreted by Scripture. In Virginia the Bible was not given the same freestanding status it had among Puritans or Baptists. Indeed, for Anglicans, the prayer book and the Bible were each other's hermeneutical keys. Orthodox doctrine made clear that the Bible took priority over the prayer book. Yet the prayer book itself contained vast quantities of Scripture, and the

prayer book also contained the liturgy that interpreted people's encounters with Scripture. The relationship between the Bible and the Book of Common Prayer is suggested by the aforementioned anonymous cleric who took up a collection to buy religious books for his parish. He declared that of all books, "the Bible ought to have the Preference, because it is the written Word of God, & containes the Terms and Conditions of their Eternal Happiness." But "the Common-Prayer or Liturgy of the Church of England ought to accompany it, because it is the Service of the Church wherein they are obliged frequently to join, & therefore cannot be too well acquainted with it." In an early iteration of an apologetic still heard in Episcopal churches in Virginia today, the cleric noted that "it is a peculiar Advantage of the Members of the Church of England that if they frequent the publick prayers, they constantly hear a considerable Portion of the Holy Scriptures read to them." Anonymous document about the distribution of religious books, Library of Virginia (Richmond) microfilm, Virginia Miscellany, miscellaneous reel 19, n.p. For a helpful and provocative discussion of the relationship between the Bible and the Book of Common Prayer in England, see Rosendale, *Liturgy and Literature*, 4–6.

14. Fifth century: Durston, "By the Book," 51.

15. Duffy, *Marking the Hours*, 4–5 and passim.

16. Branch, *Rituals of Spontaneity*, 35–61, esp. 37, 42–45; Targoff, *Common Prayer*, esp. 36. On Quaker views, see Durston, "By the Book," 65–66, 70.

17. Branch, *Rituals of Spontaneity*, 35–61, esp. 37, 42–45; Targoff, *Common Prayer*, esp. 36.

18. Durston, "By the Book," 58, 62–63, 71; Targoff, *Common Prayer*, 53–56.

19. Indeed, such debates happened in many colonies. See Goodwin, "Anglican Reaction," 354–355.

20. Davies, *Sermons on Important Subjects*, 277–278.

21. James Maury, "First Sermon on Private Prayer," in Bond, *Spreading the Gospel*, 275. Blair, *Our Saviour's Divine Sermon*, 4: 2.

22. Blair, *Our Saviour's Divine Sermon*, 3: 368, 4: 3–4.

23. Ibid., 3: 372, 4: 4, 3: 342. See also Blair, "Vain Repetitions," 210, 211.

24. Blair, *Our Saviour's Divine Sermon*, 3: 359, 369–70. See also ibid., 3: 347, 378–381; 4: 9–10.

25. John Thompson of "Salubria," Culpeper County, Sermons, Library of Virginia (Richmond), miscellaneous microfilm reel 62 (hereafter LVA62), 59. On psalmody in Virginia's Anglican churches, see Nelson, *Blessed Company*, 66.

26. Jones, "Anglican Church," 30, 61, 62.

27. Thrift, *Memoir of the Rev. Jesse Lee*, 3–4.

28. William Dawson, Letter to unknown, n.d. [1744?], William Dawson Family Papers, 16, Manuscript Division of the Library of Congress; "Invoice from Robert Cary and Company," London, 1771, The Papers of George Washington Digital Edition, http://rotunda.upress.virginia.edu/pgwde/print-Colo8d333.

29. Clay, sermon on Romans 12:[1], Charles Clay Papers, Sec. 2, Mss1 C5795 a 34–35, VHS. See also Blosser, "Irreverent Empire."

30. *VG*, March 5, 1752, p. 3; *VG*, February 25, 1768, p. 4.

31. Zambone, "Anglican Influences."

32. Bond, *Damned Souls*, 269.

33. Blair, *Our Saviour's Divine Sermon*, 3: 345.

34. Page, *Deed of Gift*, 210–218. Drawing on Matthew 6:6, contemporaries often

called this kind of individual prayer "closet" prayer. See also Maury, "First Sermon," in Bond, *Spreading the Gospel*, 274; Rambuss, *Closet Devotions*, 122 and passim.

35. Mason, *Recollections*, 65; Lewis quoted in Holmes, *Faiths of the Founding Fathers*, 114; Edmund Randolph, memoir of Elizabeth Nicholas Randolph, March 25, 1810, Daniel Family Papers, Sec. 2, Mss1 D2278b 2, pp. 6–7, VHS. See also Meade, *Old Churches*, 26.

36. Nelson, *Blessed Company*, 190, 66; Byrd, "Biblical Notes, 1728–1729," 109–111; Byrd, *Secret Diary*, 223, 457. This slow process of rewriting Scripture was surely part of how Byrd internalized the biblical story. To translate a text is to go beyond merely annotating or recopying it. Translation requires not just reading but lingering over a text. Byrd had to slow down with the Song of Songs, wrestle with verb tense and word choice. This was a practice of inscription and internalization—in translating he was both memorizing the text and laying claim to it, making it his own. Historians of handwriting have shown that eighteenth-century Americans generally understood "writing" not as original composition but rather as copying texts: to write out a passage was to "reexternalize" a passage that, in reading, one had inscribed "into one's inner being"; Thornton, *Handwriting in America*, 18. See also Stabile, *Memory's Daughters*, 86. In copying and translating biblical passages, Byrd blurred the boundaries between internalizing and reexternalizing a text.

37. On *The Whole Duty of Man*, see Butler, "Knowing the Uncertainties," 68; Byrd, *London Diary*, 293; Kerrison, *Claiming the Pen*, 42; Hardwick, "Mirrors for Their Sons," 242, 244. On similar, contemporaneous practice in England, see Jacob, *Lay People and Religion*, 105. On the Psalm 51 writing, see Byrd, *Commonplace Book*, 63; Byrd, *Secret Diary*, 4, 6, 16, 60, 65, 581.

38. Byrd, *Secret Diary*, 3, 6, 8.

39. Maury, "Sermon Number 12," in Bond, *Spreading the Gospel*, 343.

40. Duffy, *Marking the Hours*, 107.

41. Bond, *Damned Souls*, 264–268; emphasis added.

42. Sparrow, "A Rationale," 143.

43. Rosendale, *Liturgy and Literature*, 108–114.

44. Lockridge, *Diary and Life of William Byrd II*, 2, 52–53.

45. For Byrd's recognition of such indiscretions, see, e.g., Byrd, *Secret Diary*, 442; *Another Secret Diary*, 166.

46. Byrd, *Secret Diary*, 186–187; see also 31, 58. He also saw himself in a biblical framework, as the oft-quoted passage in which he likens himself to Abraham makes clear: "Like one of the Patriarchs, I have my Flocks and my Herds, my Bond-men and Bond-women, and every Soart of trade amongst my own Servants, so that I live in a kind of independence on everyone but Providence." Usually adduced to demonstrate Byrd's unabashed patriarchalism, Byrd's famous statement is also, simply, a reminder that his imagination was shaped by Scripture. For the influence of Scripture, especially the Psalms, in the diary writing of Landon Carter, see Dent, "God and Gentry," 237–238.

47. Maria Carter, Copybook, 22 verso, Armistead-Cocke Papers (1763), Manuscripts and Rare Books Department, Earl Gregg Swem Library, College of William and Mary, ms. 65 Ar6.

48. On the persistence of a magical worldview among white colonists in Virginia, see Sobel, *World They Made Together*, 20, 75–76, 79, 83–84; Horn, *Adapting to a New World*, 411–418; Bond, "Source of Knowledge." See also Jon Butler's discussion of the "folklorization" of magic—and the confining of magic largely to lower-class people in *Awash in a Sea*, 83, 86, 96–97. Amid the voluminous literature on the dichotomy between "religion" and

"magic"—categories scholars cannot seem to escape, despite our recognition of their problems—see, most usefully, Geertz, "An Anthropology of Religion and Magic," 1: 71–89, with a response by Thomas, "An Anthropology of Religion and Magic," 2: 91–109.

49. Cressy, "Books as Totems," 92–106.

50. Byrd, *London Diary,* 456, 469, 476; Hayes, *Library,* 60–61.

51. Flint, *The Rise of Magic,* 291, 232; Wilson, *The Magical Universe,* 146.

52. See, e.g., Dyer, *English Folk-Lore,* 16–17.

53. Wilkie, "Magical Passions," 133.

54. See Opie and Tatum, *Dictionary of Superstitions,* s.v. "Sword and scabbard, divination," 388–389; Lean, *Collectanea,* 2: 379; Pickering, *Cassell's Dictionary of Superstitions,* 456–457.

55. Lean, *Collectanea,* 2: 92.

56. Scribner, "Reformation," 475–494, esp. 484; Thomas, *Religion and the Decline of Magic,* 45, 118, 214; Cressy, "Books as Totems," 93–94, 97, 99. See also Opie and Tatum, *Dictionary of Superstitions,* s.v. "Bible and key, divination," 23–25; Lean, *Collectanea,* 2: 348–349; Daniels and Stevans, *Encyclopedia of Superstitions,* 1: 66.

57. Lean, *Collectanea,* 2: 352.

58. Elizabeth Washington will, Fairfax County, Virginia, will book, k-1, 1812–1816, pp. 1–2. Elizabeth and Lund Washington also at least sometimes used the labor of indentured servants. In 1784, for example, Lund paid fourteen pounds for a two-year term of service from the indentured servant Jerry Murphy, a gardener. "List of Servants & Redemptions," August 2, 1784, RM-545, MS-4193, Library and Special Collections, Mount Vernon.

59. EFW, summer 1784.

60. Elizabeth lived at Mount Vernon for the last four years of the Revolutionary War. During that time, Martha Washington spent more than a year at Mount Vernon. Elizabeth then would have lived with her for roughly another nine months after the war's end before going to Hayfield. For Martha Washington's whereabouts from November 1779 onwards see Thompson, " 'As if I had Been a Very Great Somebody,' " 77–128. On Martha Custis Washington and slavery, see Wiencek, *An Imperfect God,* 67–86, 354–358.

61. EFW, spring 1789.

62. Ibid. See also ibid., summer 1784.

63. EFW, summer 1784, July 1792.

64. Lindman, *Bodies of Belief,* 33–52; Semple, *History of Baptists,* 403, 410.

65. EFW, July 1792, September 1788, summer 1784.

66. Scully, *Nat Turner,* 88–90; Mathews, "Christianizing the South," 87–89; Spangler, "Becoming Baptists," 245; Essig, "A Very Wintry Season"; Najar, " 'Meddling with Emancipation,' " 162–170; Lindman, *Bodies of Belief,* esp. 143–144; Irons, *Origins,* 39–40. For a compelling statement of the "limits of Baptist democracy" vis-à-vis slavery, see Spangler, *Virginians Reborn,* 158–165.

67. Winchester, *Reigning Abominations,* 15–32; Lindman, *Bodies of Belief,* 134–156; Essig, "A Very Wintry Season," 181; Semple, *History of Baptists,* 392; Najar, " 'Meddling with Emancipation,' " 169.

68. EFW, July 1792, spring 1789.

69. This language was not in the Book of Common Prayer until 1789, about a decade into Washington's marriage, five years into her and Lund's setting up housekeeping at Hayfield, and in the middle of the years in which she wrote in the extant diary, 1779–1796. Before that, Washington could have encountered the language in Bishop Edmund Gib-

son's *Family Devotions,* which was available in the colonies (and specifically printed in Williamsburg by William Parks in 1740). On Gibson's book, see Marshall, *Prayer Book Parallels,* 2: 120. See also Brydon, *Virginia's Mother Church,* 2: 7, 9n6, 10n7.

70. Gundersen, "Breaching the Walls," Presentation for the Library of Virginia Symposium, March 19, 2005, copy in author's possession; I am grateful to Dr. Gundersen for sharing this work with me. It is worth noting that women's leading prayer seems to be, for William Douglas, the exception rather than the rule: "Eve[ry] head of a family, even widows, & single persons qo have children or servants under yr care," has an obligation to lead family prayer. This phrasing implies that in a house headed by a man, the man would lead prayers. William Douglas Sermon Collection, 2: 3. The recollections of Richard B. Servant, vestryman in Hampton parish, also suggest that women's leading prayer was not the norm: "My father died when I was sixteen years old," he recalled years later, "and my mother had an aversion to leading in prayer, but she insisted that I should do so"; Meade, *Old Churches,* 1: 238. On Gibson's book, see Marshall, *Prayer Book Parallels,* 120.

71. William Douglas Sermon Collection, 3, 11–13. *A Present for Servants,* n.p. For *A Present for Servants* in Virginia, see William Dawson, Letter to unknown, n.d. [1744?], William Dawson Family Papers, 16, Manuscript Division of the Library of Congress.

72. EFW, spring, 1789, July 1792.

73. Ibid.

74. Ibid., July 1792.

75. Ibid.

76. Elizabeth Foote Washington's fears about her slaves getting a hold of her "little Book" should be read in the context of Washington's recent widowhood—she wrote this strange and fearful entry just months after her husband's death. She was grappling with running Hayfield by herself, and she, like many slaveowning widows, apparently felt in some danger around her slaves. Martha Washington would know this fear most acutely three years later, when George died, leaving a will that freed his slaves upon his widow's death. This gave those slaves, bluntly, an obvious motive to poison her, and Martha "found [it] necessary (for *prudential* reasons) to give them their freedom in one year after the general's decease." On Martha Washington's widowhood and slavery, see Wiencek, *An Imperfect God,* 357–358; on the precarious situation of slaveowning widows more generally, see Saxton, *Being Good,* 165–170.

77. EFW, July 1792, 1796.

Chapter Four. Sarah Foote Stuart's Fish Sauce

1. Mason and Dunn, *Recollections,* 67–68.

2. Kierner, "Hospitality," 455–456.

3. Allestree, *Art of Contentment,* 78. See also Allestree, *Gentleman and Ladies Calling,* vol. 3, 2: 71; Allestree, *Causes of the Decay,* 2: 203–204.

4. On the relationship between power and food, see Laurel Thatcher Ulrich's observation that "because food is a daily source of pleasure (and therefore disappointment), it is also a source of power"; "It 'Went Away Shee Knew not How,'" 94. Indeed, the very structure of the kitchen could communicate lessons about power: many southern elites' kitchens were freestanding outbuildings. Kitchens were detached to maximize the house's coolness and to minimize the chance of a dangerous kitchen fire's consuming the whole estate. Beyond these practical rationales, detached kitchens took on social meaning: part of

what distinguished a gentry's estate from a middling abode was the presence of freestanding outhouses. Kupperman, "Fear of Hot Climates," 234; Wells, "Planter's Prospect," 13–15; Upton, "Vernacular Domestic Architecture," 96, 104; Carson, *Colonial Virginians at Play*, 3–4, 14. See also Beverley, *History and Present State of Virginia*, 290.

5. It is not just the recipes for festival food that suggest reading these cookbooks for their religious cues. As early as the preface to E. Smith's *Compleat Housewife*, the reader understands that she holds a book whose aims are not just culinary but religious; Smith's preface interprets the history of cooking through a biblical scrim. Smith finds evidence in Genesis 14 for the early use of salt; the pottage and meat discussed in Genesis 25 and 27 shows us that as "COOKERY . . . began to become a Science," people turned to "Soops and Savoury Messes" to provide flavor and nourishment late in life when their "digestive Faculty," along with their taste buds, had grown "weak and impotent." The Bible also testified to the development of culinary skill: Abraham merely dressed a fatted calf, but one generation later, Esau became "the first Person mentioned that made any Advances beyond plain Dressing, as boiling, Roasting, &c." He likely learned "the Skill of making savoury Meat" from his mother, Rebecca. Eventually, in the time of kings, the Israelites, having grown more sophisticated, trained "Cooks, Confectioners, &c." From the very preface, cookery texts like Smith's anchored women in domestic identity but overlay the domestic task with religious meaning.

6. Hess, "Historical Notes," in Glasse, *Art of Cookery;* Bullock, *The Williamsburg Art of Cookery*, 208.

7. Yost, *"Compleat Housewife,"* 421. See also Theophano, *Eat My Words*, 193–196; *VG*, May 29, 1752, p. 3, col. 1.

8. The volume at the Library of Virginia is E. Smith, *Compleat Housewife* (Williamsburg[, VA]: Printed and sold by William Hunter, [1752?]), Library of Virginia (Richmond) call no. TX705.S53 1752. This copy of *The Compleat Housewife* is a notable exception to Gilly Lehmann's generally apt lament that most extant eighteenth-century cookbooks inscribed with owners' names belonged to "owners . . . usually unknown to us," thus the inscriptions do little to further our interpretation of published cookbooks; Lehmann, *British Housewife*, 62.

9. To reconstruct this Foote genealogy, see Dorman, *Adventurers of Purse and Person*, 408–426; King, *Register of St. Paul's Parish, 1715–1798, Stafford County, 1715–1776, King George County, Virginia, 1777–1798*, xxii, xxiii, 50, 51; Fairfax County, Virginia, Will Book K-1, 1812–1816, 1–2; Allen, "Equally Their Due"; Fairfax County, Virginia, Will Book G-1, 1794–1799, 213–214; "Lund Family," Lund file, George Harrison Sanford King papers, ms. 1K5823aFA1, VHS; Prentiss Price, Lund Washington ms., 1950 transcription, accession 28353b, Archives and Manuscripts, Library of Virginia; Foote, *Chotankers*, 70–71, 86–99, 128–129.

10. "Unidentified cookbook, c. 1700," VHS, Richmond, ms. 5:5 Un 3:4; Jane (Bolling) Randolph, "Jane Randolph her Cookery Book 1743," VHS, ms. 5:5 1507:1 (copy). Both of these have been published in Harbury, *Cooking Dynasty*, 145–421. For persimmon beer and culinary innovation, see ibid., xviii, 400. On the sources for recipes, see Spencer, "Food in Seventeenth-Century Tidewater Virginia," 29–30.

11. Harbury, *Cooking Dynasty*, 366, 406.

12. Kern, "Jeffersons at Shadwell," 119.

13. Carter, *Diary*, 359; Isaac, *Landon Carter's Uneasy Kingdom*, 271–273. For another example see Eden's discussion of William Byrd: Eden, *The Early American Table*, 122–123.

14. Chew, "Carrying the Keys," 31–32. See also Chew, "Inhabiting the Great Man's House," 231.

15. Kern, "Jeffersons at Shadwell," 49; Wood, *Masterful Women*, 171. See also Mooney, *Prodigy Houses*, 248–255.

16. Carson, "Plantation Housekeeping," 30–43. See also *VG*, June 6, 1745, p. 3, col. 2; December 18, p. 4, col. 1; Shammas, "Black Women's Work," 19–22. On the complex relationship among gender, race, and "women's work" in Virginia's slave society, see Brown, *Good Wives*, esp. 109–116.

17. There is little evidence to suggest that eighteenth-century English cookbook writers were thinking about colonial slaves, but they were very much aware of writing for two English audiences: the gentry women who would purchase their books and the presumably literate servants who would use them. Cookbook authors wrote both for "mistresses of Families" and for "the common Servants generally so ignorant in dressing Meat, and a good cook so hard to be met with." In the first few decades of the eighteenth century, English moralists began to write tracts that seemed to assume that elite women would not themselves cook. In *The Young Ladies Conduct,* John Essex aptly noted that elite women had abandoned "the great Fatigue, or rather slavery, of House-keeping" to servants. Echoing the discourse about needlework that we have already seen, the author of *The Female Spectator* opined that ladies "should learn just as much of cookery . . . as to know when she is imposed on by those she employs . . . but no more." See Mennell, *All Manners of Food,* 96; Raffald, *Experienced English House-keeper,* iii; Lehmann, *British Housewife,* 69–70, 107–108. For a bracing discussion of Virginia cookbooks and enslaved cooks, see Sorensen, "Keeping a Good House," 106–108.

18. Bear, *Jefferson at Monticello,* 3; Chew, "Carrying the Keys," 33.

19. Marshall, *Prayerbook Parallels,* 1: 54; Davies, *Worship and Theology,* 2: 224.

20. Kammen, *A Time to Every Purpose,* 73, 75–76; Isaac, *Landon Carter's Uneasy Kingdom,* 60–71; Byrd, *Secret Diary,* 4, 15, 19.

21. Cressy, *Bonfires and Bells,* 194; Fischer, *Albion's Seed,* 369; Bond, *Damned Souls,* 119–120. Cookery texts also attest to the articulation of ostensibly secular activities in ecclesial time. For example, in *The Art of Cookery Made Plain and Easy,* Hannah Glasse used ecclesial language to detail "the Seasons of the Year for Butchers' Meat, Poultry, Fish, &c." Instead of telling housewives which fish were available in early spring or fall, she spelled out what one could catch during "Candlemas Quarter" (lobsters, crabs, and crawfish) and "Michaelmas Quarter" (cod and haddock, as well as "fine smelts, [which] hold till after Christmas"). During "Christmas quarter," dorey, brile, gudgeons, periwinkles, cockles, and mussels were reliable choices. She explained how to "keep Green Peas" not through winter but "till Christmas" (after shelling, boil the peas with salt for five to six minutes; drain them, and put them in bottles filled and covered with "mutton-fat dried"; when the bottles are cool, cork them, and tie "a bladder and a lath over them"). This language ought not, of course, be overread: the vestigial usage of phrases like "Michaelmas Term" at Oxford and Cambridge today does not imply that the feast of St. Michael and All Angels is the fundamental structure through which Oxbridge students inhabit time. But especially considering the context—Glasse was describing the availability of foods, something indubitably tied not to church seasons but to the natural seasons—Glasse's reflexive use of ecclesial language to calibrate time is striking. She bespoke a way of reckoning time so ingrained in everyday life that it shaped even quotidian details like how to preserve vegetables; Glasse, *Art of Cookery,* frontispiece, 10–12, 218–219; see also 283–284. See also Bond's discussion: descriptions of events that invoke the church calendar

suggest "just how deeply ingrained were notions of religious time to some of the colony's earliest settlers"; Bond, *Damned Souls*, 94.

22. On the relative modesty of Easter celebrations in America before the Victorian era, see Schmidt, *Consumer Rites*, 195. For modest Easter observances in Virginia, see, e.g., Washington, *Diaries*, April 7, 1760, 1: 264. On communion at Easter, see Byrd, *Secret Diary*, 163, 323. Communion was typically celebrated four times a year. In 1724 at least fifteen percent of adult Anglicans took the opportunity to receive communion regularly; Bonomi and Eisenstadt, "Church Adherence," 260–261. On Ascension and wartime, see Maria Taylor Byrd's letter to her son William Byrd II on May 13, 1760: "Mr. Thomas Davis preached at our church on Sunday last & is to give us a sermon again on Thursday"; Tinling, *Correspondence of the Three William Byrds*, 2: 689. Easter that year was April 6; thus Ascension Thursday, forty days from Easter—was May 15 that year. For dates see Cheney and Jones, *A Handbook of Dates for Students of British History*, 231. For another example of an Ascension Day service, see Rose, *Diary*, 57. On Mary Lee's letter, see Mary Lee to "Dear Son," January 16, 1728, Papers of Richard Bland Lee, 1769–1825, in vol. 1, 1922 #353, Manuscript Division, Library of Congress, Custis-Lee Family Papers, box 1, Manuscript Division, Library of Congress. For Candlemas, also see Tyler, "Diary of John Blair," 135.

23. Davies, *Worship and Theology*, 2: 216; Troubetzkoy, "How Virginia Saved the Outlawed English Carols," 198–202; Nissenbaum, *Battle for Christmas*, 4–8; Schmidt, *Consumer Rites*, 176–182; Cressy, *Bonfires and Bells*, 197; Solberg, *Redeem the Time*, 46–47, 114, 158, 169.

24. Davies, "A Christmas-Day Sermon, 1758," 384–385. By the end of the colonial era, John Wesley was inaugurating yet another understanding of holy time. Early on, Wesley declared that "Most of the holy-days (so called) . . . at present [answer] no valuable end," so he erased them from Methodist worship and common life. Wesley vanquished Lent, for example, arguing that because the Holy Spirit was present to the church, an annual season of repentance was not only unnecessary, but ungrateful, an inauthentic expression of God's work among his people in the here and now. Elkins, "'On Borrowed Time,'" 38, 41; Tucker, *Methodist Worship*, 47–49.

25. Charles Clay, sermon "For Christmas Day," Charles Clay Papers, Sec. 2, Mss1 C5795 a 46–47, VHS.

26. Carter, *Diary*, 2: 903; Isaac, *Landon Carter's Uneasy Kingdom*, 282.

27. Bond, *Damned Souls*, 218. Rose, *Diary*, 119, 149. See also responses of Bristol Parish in the Upper Part of the James River; York Hampton Parish; Christ Church Parish, Petsworth; and Bruton Parish to "Queries to be Answered by every Minister," in Perry, *Papers*, 267, 282, 287, 299; Fithian, *Journal and Letters*, 41; Byrd, *Secret Diary*, 122, 276; Fischer finds that the ecclesiastical calendar also influenced the timing of life-cycle celebrations: early Virginians married most often between Christmas and Ash Wednesday, because the penitential seasons of Advent and Lent were not considered appropriate times for nuptial celebrations. Fischer, *Albion's Seed*, 371. John Nelson has found strong evidence that parishioners in one parish (Christ Church, Middlesex) generally avoided Lenten weddings, but his reading of the records of St. James' Northam Parish finds that "Lenten and Advent prohibitions fell away." Nelson, *Blessed Company*, 223–224.

28. Fithian, *Journal and Letters*, 34; Tittle, *Colonial Holidays*, 17; Fairfax, "Diary," 212–213; Carson, *Colonial Virginians at Play*, 9. Carson reads Fairfax to say that her mother cooked this meal herself: "Mrs. Fairfax herself prepared some of the refreshments." I would suggest that this is a misreading of Fairfax; when she says that her mother "herself

prepared" these items, Fairfax means that she oversaw the preparation of them. On this point, see Gordon-Reed, *Hemingses of Monticello,* 130: "When upper-class plantation wives like Martha Jefferson spoke of keeping house—making soap, brewing beer, and the like—what they were really saying is that they supervised the slave women who actually performed the physical labor these tasks entailed."

29. Clay's homiletical emphasis on sin was part of what marked him as an evangelical. On Clay's evangelicalism, see Beliles, "Christian Communities, Religious Revivals," in Sheldon and Dreisbach, *Religion and Political Culture,* 3–40; Brown, *Hills of the Lord,* 134–136; Nelson, "Charles Clay," entry in Kneebone, *Dictionary of Virginia Biography,* 279–280; Meade, *Old Churches,* 2: 48–50; Blosser, "Pursuing Happiness," 188–199; Fithian, *Journal and Letters,* 41; Charles Clay, sermon "For Christmas Day," Charles Clay Papers, Sec. 2, Mss1 C5795 a 46–47, VHS.

30. Sack, *Whitebread Protestants,* 5. On "the secularized Eucharist" in early America, see Stavely and Fitzgerald, *America's Founding Food,* 62, 255.

31. Camp, *American Foodways,* 70–71; Olwell, *Masters, Slaves, and Subjects,* 123; Beasley, *Christian Ritual,* 98–100, 105–108.

32. Henisch, *Cakes and Characters,* 10–11.

33. Ibid., 46. For a detailed Twelfth Night choreography, see May, *Accomplisht Cook,* n.p. For an incisive discussion of the ways such banquets were "paradoxical signs of domestic order," see Hall, "Culinary Spaces," 174–175.

34. Quoted in Henisch, *Cakes and Characters,* 49.

35. Quoted ibid., 207–208.

36. Byrd, *London Diary,* 216.

37. On Byrd's feelings about returning to Virginia, see Lockridge, *Diary and Life of William Byrd II,* 100–110. For the 1721 celebration, see Byrd, *London Diary,* 495.

38. Woodfin, *Another Secret Diary of William Byrd,* 28.

39. Cresswell, *Journal,* 52–53. There was a theological inversion to Twelfth Night as well: as Peter Burke has noted about carnivalesque Christmas festivities in early modern Europe, "the birth of the son of God in a manger was a spectacular example of the world turned upside down." Burke, *Popular Culture in Early Modern Europe,* 193.

40. Dawson, "A Christmas Sermon," 4–5. See also Bond, *Spreading the Gospel,* 485–490; Charles Clay, sermon "For Christmas Day," Charles Clay Papers, Sec. 2, Mss1 C5795 a 46–47, VHS.

41. Gov. William Gooch to Bp. Gibson, June 29, 1729, Fulham Papers, vol. 12, no. 136-7, Lambeth Palace Library. *VG,* September 12, 1755, p. 3; *VG,* January 14, 1746, p. 4; Hawkins, "Imperial 45," 24–47. Many thanks to Al Zambone for helping me think through these fasts.

42. Taylor, *Holy Living,* 1: 268, 273.

43. Virginia women found recipes for pancakes in their cookery texts. See E. Smith, *Compleat Housewife,* 113.

44. Carter, *Diary,* 2: 1075; Isaac, *Landon Carter's Uneasy Kingdom,* 39. See also Carter, *Diary,* 2: 986. On William Beale's larger Anglican participation, see King, *Register of North Farnham Parish,* 13.

45. Mennell, *All Manners of Food,* 27–28; Flandarin, *Arranging the Meal,* 33; Pepys quoted in Fagan, *Fish on Friday,* 241–243.

46. Harbury, *Cooking Dynasty,* 156, 354; Raffald, *Experienced English House-keeper,* 10–11; Moxon, *English Housewifry,* 8; Raffald, *Experienced English House-keeper,* 18–19.

47. Glasse, *Art of Cookery,* 125–131; Harbury, *Cooking Dynasty,* 118; Raffald, *Experienced English House-keeper,* 134; E. Smith, *Compleat Housewife,* 117–118; Martha Bradley, *The British Housewife,* 242; Smith, *Compleat Housewife,* 142, 102, 83, and for fish sauce, 157; Harbury, *Cooking Dynasty,* 210. The Lenten recipes not only conformed to traditional expectations of meatless meals; ironically, they served not to humiliate but to affirm the elite status of practitioners, since abstaining from meat would have meaning principally to those who could afford regularly to eat roasts and duck.

48. Robert Paxton, "On Repentance," Robert Paxton Manuscript Sermon Book, Houghton Library.

Chapter Five. "To Comfort the Living"

1. Mason and Dunn, *Recollections,* 64–65. Mason Family Papers, 481.

2. Life expectancy did increase during the colonial era. In the seventeenth century, adult men lived on average to their mid-forties; by the eighteenth century, they typically reached their mid-fifties. Women, who regularly risked their lives during childbirth, tended to die earlier than men. Smith, *Inside the Great House,* 44–45, 261; Kulikoff, *Tobacco and Slaves,* 61–62, 171–173; Lewis and Lockridge, "'Sally Has Been Sick,'" 5–19; Henretta and Nobles, *Evolution and Revolution,* 87–88.

3. See Maria Carter Cleve copybook, p. 11 verso, p. 13 verso. See also Byrd, *Commonplace Book:* 102, 127, 146, 154, 198, 221–222, 298.

4. Butler, "Knowing the Uncertainties," 175; Fithian, *Journal and Letters,* 61.

5. See especially Miller and Parrott, "Death, Ritual, and Material Culture," 148; Metcalf and Huntington, *Celebrations of Death,* 10–12 and passim.

6. Fischer, *Albion's Seed,* 330–331.

7. Sobel, *World They Made Together,* esp. 218–222.

8. Galpern, *Religions of the People,* 20.

9. Hooker, *Laws of Ecclesiastical Polity,* book 5, chapter 75. It is worth noting that the "funeral duties" that Hooker identified as offering the church's care were, in eighteenth-century Virginia, located in the household. In death as in life, Virginia gentry's religiosity was tied to the church yet was located in the domus.

10. Brown, *Dictionary of the Holy Bible,* 619. Carter's copy is preserved Special Collections, University of Virginia Library, F 229.C28 Z9.D53 1759. See also *The Oxford English Dictionary.*

11. Miller and Parrott, "Death, Ritual, and Material Culture," 148–149; Hallam and Hockey, *Death, Memory, and Material Culture,* 2–5 and passim.

12. Maria Carter Cleve Copy Book, 13; Byrd, *Secret Diary,* 471, 472, 342; Sleeper-Smith, "Dream as a Tool," 49–68; Randolph, Memoir of Elizabeth Nicholas Randolph, March 25, 1810, Daniel Family Papers, ms. 1 D2278b 2 (section 2), p. 11, VHS; Hallam and Hockey, *Death, Memory, and Material Culture,* 8–9, 18 and passim.

13. On the availability of such books in Virginia, see Butler, "Knowing the Uncertainties," 50, 252.

14. Maury/Fontaine memoirs, 398; Stephen Fouace to Philip Ludwell, April 22, 1711, Ludwell Lee Papers, VHS. See also Butler, "Knowing the Uncertainties," 66; William Douglas Sermon Collection, 1: 271, 2: 188.

15. The most astute analysis of colonial Virginians' testamentary practices is found in Patrick Butler's "Knowing the Uncertainties." Butler examined wills from three counties

in colonial Virginia and found that most black freedmen and white indentured servants did not draft wills, and that the wealthier one was, the more likely one was to leave a will. Butler notes that in other instances, the death of a close relative or friend prompted a person to write a will, as the death of Ann Mason so prompted George Mason. Not everyone in Virginia wrote a will—neither slaves, children, nor those deemed mentally incompetent left wills, and many women did not draft wills. Butler, "Knowing the Uncertainties," 80–133, 470–484.

16. John Thompson of "Salubria," Sermons, LVA62, 62, 29, 60–61.

17. Hallam and Hockey, *Death, Memory, and Material Culture*, 162.

18. Butler, "Knowing the Uncertainties," 44–46, 103–109; Byrd, *Secret Diary*, 270, 415, 459; Rose, *Diary*, 236; Boucher, *Reminiscences of an American Loyalist*, 62, 65. The English ars moriendi tradition suggested that attendance at people's deathbeds could and should have good effects in the lives of the survivors; writers like Jeremy Taylor encouraged people to meditate and reflect on deathbed scenes they had witnessed. This reflection would help keep them in the right frame of mind to live a holy life and prepare for a holy death. Vogt, *Patience, Compassion*, 135. See also Taylor, *Holy Living*, 2: 122–123.

19. Sobel, *World They Made Together*, 221; Stanton, *Free Some Day*, 102–103; Bear, *Jefferson at Monticello*, 99–100.

20. *Executive Journals of the Council of Colonial Virginia* (hereafter EJC), 6: 551–552. Charles Smith was the minister of Portsmouth Parish when he wrote his January 24, 1771, will. He freed Mary in an October 30, 1772, codicil. Norfolk County, Virginia, Will Book 2, 1772–1778, p. 23, folio 11 (microfilm) Library of Virginia. See also Wertenbaker, *Norfolk*, 22–23. It was not only Anglicans, of course, who freed slaves in response to deathbed devotion. For example, Dorothy Cartmell, in a will she wrote on her deathbed, manumitted her slave Margaret "as a reward for the extraordinary Diligence and Tenderness with which [Margaret] waited on [Cartmell] during a long and painful Illness." EJC, 6: 450–451. Cartmell was a Quaker (though the early records of the Hopewell meeting in Frederick County have been destroyed, and it is not clear whether she was a practicing Quaker at her death). See O'Dell, *Pioneers of Old Frederick County*, 278–280.

21. Bear, *Jefferson at Monticello*, 99–100; Gordon-Reed, *Hemingses of Monticello*, 144–146; Fitzhugh, *William Fitzhugh and His Chesapeake World*, 334. This analysis follows Seeman, *Pious Persuasions*, 73–77; Maury/Fontaine memoirs, 298.

22. Butler, "Knowing the Uncertainties," 156; Harrower, *Journal*, 87, 184n89. On flannel, see "Old Kecoughtan," 92. On preparing the body as a women's task in England, see Richardson, "Death's Door," 95.

23. Harrower, *Journal*, 87; Butler, 161–162; Ashenburg, *Mourner's Dance*, 11–15; Bondeson, *Buried Alive*, 77–81.

24. Richardson, "Death's Door," 95.

25. See, e.g., Stanard, *Colonial Virginia*, 342.

26. Jones, *Present State of Virginia*, 96–97; Harrison, "With Braddock's Army," 309; Moreau de Saint-Méry, *American Journey*, 68; Blair, April 10, 1719, Proceedings, in Perry, *Papers*, 225; Rose, *Diary*, 44; Butler, "Knowing the Uncertainties," 145–146; Fischer, *Albion's Seed*, 328–329; Sobel, *World They Made Together*, 180.

27. Byrd, *Secret Diary*, 132, 146, 254; Fithian, *Journal and Letters*, 41, 61.

28. Butler, "Knowing the Uncertainties," 145; Fithian, *Journal and Letters*, 41.

29. Butler, "Knowing the Uncertainties," 140–152, 188.

30. Taylor, *Holy Living*, 2: 232; Butler, "Knowing the Uncertainties," 140–152.

31. Tyler, "Old Tombstones in Charles City County," 122; Tombstones in Middlesex County, 170, 172; Peirce, "History of St. Mary's White Chapel," 527; Anderson, "Supplement to Tuckahoe," 404; Stanard, "Major Robert Beverley," 52; "Epitaphs at Brandon," 235; "Tombstones in Warwick County," 167; "Old Tombstones in Westmoreland County," 94.

32. Butler, "Knowing the Uncertainties," 271–278; Allestree, *Whole Duty of Mourning*, 79, 114. This association of buildings and decline was not, of course, unique to Anglican devotional writing. Indeed, in the eighteenth century, the theme of ruin became something of a leitmotif in European decorative arts, architecture, and landscaping. See McCormick, *Ruins as Architecture;* Zucker, *Fascination of Decay*, 195–245.

33. Gittings, *Death, Burial, and the Individual*, 159; Kern, "Jeffersons at Shadwell," 133; "Ward Family," 196; Cochran, "Early Generations of the Newton Family," 180; William Leigh to St. George Tucker, November 3, 1779, quoted in Gundersen, "The Non-Institutional Church," 349; Butler, "Knowing the Uncertainties," 174; Byrd, *Secret Diary*, 188, 549, 165; Brears, "Arvals, Wakes, and Month's Minds," 87–114, esp. 100. Two Virginia women included recipes for a caraway molasses ginger cake in their manuscript cookbooks, and at least one woman wrote a recipe for a ginger molasses caraway cake in the pages of her copy of *Kidder's Receipts of Pastry and Cookery*. These cakes probably would have been prepared for funerary meals. Harbury, *Cooking Dynasty*, 210–211; Weaver, *America Eats*, 106–112; Thursby, *Funeral Festivals*, 82–89; Daniell, *Death and Burial*, 57. See also Davies, who argues that "when alcohol is drunk, as it often is at funerals, it also conduces to an increased feeling of well being"; *Death, Ritual, and Belief*, 41.

34. Kulikoff, "'Throwing the Stocking,'" 517; Tate, "Funerals in Eighteenth-Century Virginia," 9; Butler, "Knowing the Uncertainties," 112, 138, 289–290; Frey, *Water from the Rock*, 38, 40–41, 51, 302–304; Fithian, *Journal and Letters*, 184; Marshall, *Prayerbook Parallels*, 1: 532–558.

35. "Churchill Family," 187; Lee, "Mary Bland's Death," 34–35; Stanard, *Colonial Virginia*, 342; Nelson, *Blessed Company*, 428n96.

36. Clay, sermon on John 16:33b, Charles Clay Papers, Sec. 2. Mss1 C5795 a 26–27, VHS. Sometimes a sermon was not possible because of the aforementioned absence of clergy. Furthermore, not everyone wanted a sermon: Philip Grymes of Middlesex County made clear in his will that he wished to be buried with prayers only, no sermon; Stanard, *Colonial Virginia*, 244. See also, e.g., Courtney, "Will of Colonel Humphrey Hill," 97; George Mason to Mrs. John Moncure, March 12, 1764, Mason Papers, 6: 59; "Schools in Virginia: John Farneffold's Free School," 246. The funeral sermon could be expensive. Some parsons, like the Rev. Devereaux Jarratt, refused to take money for any funeral sermon, but others charged as much as five pounds. Jarratt, *Life*, 70 (page citations are to the reprint edition); Bruce, *Economic History of Virginia*, 70. On funeral sermon costs, see also Lucy Temple Latane, *Parson Latane*, 45; Hening, *Statutes at Large*, 6: 81, 84; Byrd, *Secret Diary*, 165.

37. *VG*, November 29, 1776, p. 2, col. 2; Charles Clay, sermon on 1 Sam 3:18, Charles Clay Papers, Sec. 2, Mss1 C5795 a 58–59, VHS; Charles Clay, sermon on John 16:33, Charles Clay Papers, Sec. 2, Mss1 C5795 a 26–27, VHS, 62, 87; Greene, "A Mirror of Virtue," 183.

38. "Journal of Colonel James Gordon," 226.

39. Charles Clay, sermon fragment, Charles Clay Papers, Sec. 2, Mss1 C5795 a 40–41, VHS; John Thompson of "Salubria," Sermons, LVA62. It is tempting to draw a sharp and dramatic contrast between Puritan and Anglican "attitudes" toward death. Up to a point,

the contrast is a helpful one, for members of Virginia's Anglican gentry appear optimistic and confident about their eternal fate; that confidence is surely linked in part to Anglicanism's more generous soteriology, and it is a confidence that is shown in particularly clear relief when contrasted to Puritan anxiety. And yet such a contrast—Puritans were anxious about death, and Anglicans were confident and optimistic—must be qualified at the outset. First, it is easy to exaggerate Puritans' anxiety. Puritans were not unambiguously anxious about death: they were ambivalent about death, anticipating it both with terror and hope; Hijiya, "American Gravestones," 347. As Erik Seeman's work in particular has shown, Puritan clergy certainly tried to foster anxiety in people, especially about the eternal fate of dead children, but laypeople often disregarded the logical conclusions of Calvinist theology when it came to deaths in their own families, and in fact confidently assumed that dead loved ones were in heaven. Laypeople's adaptations of Puritan belief, Seeman concludes, make it impossible to speak of a singular "Puritan way of death"; *Pious Persuasions,* 52, 45; see also Brekus, "Children of Wrath." Furthermore, the starkest contrasts between Puritan and Anglican deathways defy chronology. Simply put, by the eighteenth century, whatever anxiety about death and damnation Puritans felt had begun to be supplanted by a cautious optimism about eternity that has more in common with Anglican optimism than any simple demarcation of "Puritan anxiety" and "Anglican confidence" would suggest. This can be seen most clearly in Puritan funerary art. As is well known, through the seventeenth century and at the beginning of the eighteenth, images such as death's heads and hourglasses appear on many New England tombstones. These images were meant to turn the thoughts of passers-by to their impending deaths. In the middle of the eighteenth century, these memento mori begin to be replaced by more optimistic cherubs, and by the end of the century, by the sylvan scenes of beautiful morning common to the sentimental religion that pervades all the colonies at the turn of the century; Deetz and Dethlefsen, "Death's Head," 503–505; Hijiya, "American Gravestones," 339–363; Deetz, *In Small Things Forgotten,* 69–72. Deetz's arguments are usefully contextualized and criticized in Hall, "The Gravestone Image as a Puritan Cultural Code," 23–32.

40. John Thompson of "Salubria," Sermons, LVA62, 17–19. See also Charles Clay, sermon fragment, Charles Clay Papers, Sec. 2, Mss1 C5795 a 40–41, VHS; Charles Clay, sermon on John 3:5, Charles Clay Papers, Sec. 2, Mss1 C5795 a 24–25, VHS. Both in warning against deathbed repentance and in their anti-Catholicism, Virginia polemics echo text from the English Anglican ars moriendi tradition; see Taylor, *Holy Living,* 2: 6, 9; Beaty, *Craft of Dying.* A variation on the theme of the dangers and inadequacies of deathbed repentance was found in the *Virginia Gazette,* which, in 1769, ran an article denouncing popular enthusiasm about Messier's comet: "Pretenders to astrology, which only tend to fill the world with ignorance and superstition," had frightened many people into believing that the comet portended natural disaster and widespread death, and had "thought to frighten people into a preparation for death." The comet, this writer said, absolutely did not portend catastrophe, and furthermore, "we would just observe, that a preparation for death, produced from mere fear, instead of love to God and a rational sense of duty, is seldom lasting, if the frightened survive the fear; and that, should they be taken off in their fright, it is much to be doubted, whether a preparation made just at that instant would gain them admission into Heaven." This author's preference for a lifetime of preparation for death, preparation inspired by "love [of] God and a rational sense of duty," is consonant with the Anglican clergy's urging that a life of consistent, faithful holiness is the best preparation for death.

41. On confidence, see Sobel, *World They Made Together,* 223, and Butler, "Knowing the Uncertainties," 123, 128, 509. Susan Kwilecki finds "an attitude of hopeful resignation in the face of . . . death" among wealthy colonists in eighteenth-century Virginia; Kwilecki, "Through the Needle's Eye," 115. Anglican soteriology defies succinct summary, because Anglican theologians and parsons were not altogether consistent in their views of salvation and the afterlife. Anglican theology always had a Calvinist element (e.g., in the 39 Articles of Religion). Yet over the course of the seventeenth and eighteenth centuries, Anglicans became increasingly confident about their eternal prospects. Some Anglican thinkers began to question the teaching that a great number of sinners would burn eternally in hell. This teaching, they reasoned, might seem consistent with the letter of Scripture, but in fact it necessarily proclaimed a falsehood about God, for only an unloving God could assign a vast proportion of humanity to eternal hellfire. To maintain a broadly orthodox notion of biblical authority and yet question what appeared to be a straightforward reading of Scripture required a certain finessing: Tillotson, for example, argued that "God would break his word rather than execute his salutary but cruel threats, being bound by his promises only when he offered rewards." McManners, *Death and the Enlightenment,* 177. On the diversity of approaches to salvation among Virginia clergy, see Gundersen, *The Anglican Ministry in Virginia,* 162–163. On the admixture of Calvinism and Arminianism in Anglican theology, see Butler, "Knowing the Uncertainties," 4–7, 46–50, 121–122, 128–130, and passim.

42. Marshall, *Prayerbook Parallels,* 1: 552. For an astute discussion of the Book of Common Prayer as "the primary source for religious language" in Virginia, especially as pertains to death, see Butler, "Knowing the Uncertainties," 110–133.

43. Gittings, *Death, Burial, and the Individual,* 41.

44. "Will of Benjamin Harrison," 124; Boddie, "Lygon of Madresfield," 310; Tyler, "Old Tombstones in Charles City County," 123. See also "Will of William Armistead," 254–256; Pecquet du Bellet, *Some Prominent Virginia Families,* 716; Meade, *Old Churches,* 1: 352; Branch, *Epitaphs of Gloucester and Mathews Counties,* 38. Deshler, "How the Declaration Was Received," 186–187; Maier, *American Scripture,* 158. Capt. John Washington was one of the vestrymen for Petsworth Parish. See Chamberlayne, *Vestry Book of Petsworth Parish,* 184.

45. Maury/Fontaine memoirs, 398–399; Greene, "A Mirror of Virtue," 186–201. This same point is also made in English Anglican prescriptive literature. See Allestree, *Whole Duty of Mourning,* 150–154. In the most sophisticated recent discussion of the history of grief in early America, Nicole Eustace argues that immoderate grief was read as "rebelling against divine authority," and that, given the connections between divine authority and the authority of "earthly governors," immoderate grief threatened to subvert social order; Eustace, *Passion Is the Gale,* 294–295.

46. John Parke Custis to Martha Custis Washington, July 5, 1773, in Fields, *Papers of Martha Washington,* 152–153; Butler, "Knowing the Uncertainties," 296; EFW, 77.

47. Smith, *Inside the Great House,* 249–280; Lewis, *Pursuits of Happiness,* 69–105.

48. Byrd, *Secret Diary,* 165, 223; Butler, "Knowing the Uncertainties," 296.

49. Byrd, *Secret Diary,* 186–187; Smith, *Inside the Great House,* 261–262; Bloch, "Death, Women, and Power," 226. On the contest between women and men over mourning, see also Eustace, *Passion Is the Gale,* 301–302.

50. See Philippe Ariès's argument that mourning has a double purpose. On the one hand, mourning rites dictate that the family of the deceased demonstrate, at least for a

certain period, sorrow it does not necessarily feel, and on the other hand, the same rites protect the sincerely grieving survivor from the excesses of his grief. "It imposed upon him a certain type of social life, visits from relatives, neighbors and friends . . . and in the course of which the sorrow might be dissipated without allowing its expression to exceed social conventions"; Ariès, *Western Attitudes towards Death*, 66.

51. Moreau de St. Méry, *American Journey*, 68.

52. Taylor, *Mourning Dress*, 70, 92; Llewellyn, *Art of Death*, 89–93. On the symbolism of the color in death rites more broadly, see Metcalf and Huntington, *Celebrations of Death*, 63.

53. "Diary of John Blair," 2; *VG*, January 16, 1761, p. 4; *VG*, April 4, 1768, p. 2, col. 2; *VG*, March 1, 1738, p. 3, col. 2; "Free Schools in Isle of Wight County; King's Moon's and Smith's, with Will of Mrs. Elizabeth Smith-Stith," 116; *VG*, May 27, 1737, p. 4; Butler, "Knowing the Uncertainties," 177–178; Thompson, "Death and Mourning in the Family of George Washington," 27–30; Taylor, *Mourning Dress*, 70–119; Cunnington and Lucas, *Costume for Births, Marriages, and Deaths*, 145–155, 245–252; "Funeral Expenses of Benjamin Harrison, 1745," 329.

54. Though commonplace in the early modern world, mourning jewelry seems quaint or creepy to many people today. When we consider mourning rings in particular, it is worth recalling that although today many rings are purely decorative, for most of Western history, exclusively decorative rings were rare. Most rings—wedding rings, class rings, fraternal rings, engagement rings, friendship rings—had explicit emotional and social meaning; Monfredo, "American Finger Rings," 70–75, and passim. On the history of mourning rings generally, see ibid., 21–31 and passim; Fales, *Jewelry in America*, 23–28. On mourning rings in the Chesapeake, see Gibbs, "Precious Artifacts," 72; Butler, "Knowing the Uncertainties," 179–182, 209–211. On New England mourning rings, see Stannard, *Puritan Way of Death*, 113, 156–157; Deetz, *In Small Things Forgotten*, 64–90. The deep reflexive connection between hair and women is another way in which, through hair jewelry, grief and death become tied to women. The symbolism of hair, which would come to figure more prominently in mourning jewelry in the nineteenth century, is not opaque. Hair has been—at least since Paul made the connection in 1 Corinthians—associated with women, described as their "crowning glory." Captured in a ring, a lock of Ann Eilbeck Mason's hair is evident testimony that she is dead, but, insofar as hair resists the kind if decay to which the rest of the human body, save bone and teeth, is subject, it carries with it a refutation of death. Her hair, contained in a ring, served as a synecdoche not only for Ann herself, but for the practices of dying and mourning, practices that seek to contain death. See Pointon, "Wearing Memory," 65–82, esp. 73; Holm, "Sentimental Cuts," 139–143; DeLorme, *Mourning Art and Jewelry*, 66; Stabile, *Memory's Daughters*, 223–225; Pointon, "Materializing Mourning," 39–57. For details on Sarah Berkeley Wormeley's church affiliation, see Chamberlayne, *Vestry Book of Christ Church Parish*, 138, 89, 145. Wormeley probably worshiped at Christ Church, Christ Church Parish, Middlesex County, which was built halfway between Brandon and Rosegill, the seats of the Wormeleys and Grymeses, not far from the Rappahannock River. See also Meade, *Old Churches*, 1: 357. On the prevalence of memento mei inscriptions in Virginia mourning rings, see Butler, "Knowing the Uncertainties," 212n51. On Stott, see Butler, "Knowing the Uncertainties," 180. On Ann Fox's will, see "Fox Family," 62.

55. Gittings, *Death, Burial, and the Individual*, 159–161. On gift exchange, see also Mauss, *The Gift*; Bourdieu, *Outline of a Theory of Practice*, 72–95; Bell, *Ritual*, 78–79; Daniell, *Death and Burial*, 56.

56. Orr, *Journal of a Young Lady, 1782*, 19–20. On the communicative nature of clothing, see Lurie, *Language of Clothes*, 3–4 and passim.

57. "Free Schools in Isle of Wight County; King's Moon's and Smith's, with Will of Mrs. Elizabeth Smith-Stith," 116.

58. This identification of "Nancy" differs from the identification given in the 1976 edition of Orr's diary. There another Nancy is identified as the daughter of Richard Henry Lee. But that Nancy is identified in the diary just three days later and three days earlier as being quite ill, so it is not in fact logical that she would be the Nancy lumped in with Mrs. Selden and Mrs. Brooke at church. The church in question was probably the Potomac Church (Overwharton Parish), as the marriage of Samuel Selden and his first wife, Mary Thompson Mason, the birth of four of their children, and her death are recorded in the Overwharton Parish Register. Potomac Church was built near the narrows of Potomac Creek, the same creek on which the Selden plantation Salvington was located. See King, *Register of Overwharton Parish*, 106, 192. For the connections of the Selden women see Dorman, *Adventurers of Purse and Person*, 319, 320, 341; and for Mary Mason (Selden) Page Selden's death, see ibid., 115.

59. See Reis, *Death Is a Festival*, 115–116; Thompson, "Lowest Ebb of Misery"; Fields, *Papers of Martha Washington*, 8, 23–25; Harrison, "Will of Charles Carter," 45–47. On the English custom of clothing servants in mourning, see Buck, *Dress in Eighteenth-Century England*, 63.

60. Beasley, *Christian Ritual*, 109–135, esp. 129. See Frey and Wood, *Come Shouting to Zion*, 55; Fischer, *Albion's Seed*, 329; Jones, "Anglican Church," 199; EJC, 1: 86–87, 148; Jones, "The Established Virginia Church," 19; Walsh, *From Calabar to Carter's Grove*, 105; Hening, *Statutes at Large*, 4: 128–129.

61. Stanard, *Colonial Virginia*, 210; Bruce, *Economic History of Virginia*, 195–196; Hilden, "Smiths of Middlesex County," 219; MacFarlane, "Will of Patrick Henry's Mother," 117; Ludwell, "Original Letter," 198; Monfredo, "American Finger Rings," 70–75.

62. Carrington Family Papers, acc. 21333, Personal Papers Collection, Archives and Manuscripts, Library of Virginia.

63. Barnhill, "'Keep Sacred the Memory,'" 60–74; McDannell, *Material Christianity*, 69–84.

64. Indeed, the practice was not unique to either Virginians or Anglicans. In the 1760s and 1770s, for instance, John Carlyle, who was born and raised a Presbyterian—though he also owned a pew at Christ Episcopal Church in Alexandria and was married to an Anglican—chronicled his family genealogy in a leather-bound folio Bible; Carlyle family Bible 75.3.1, Carlyle House, Alexandria, Virginia.

65. Two exceptions are Kern, "Jeffersons at Shadwell," 459–485, and McDannell, *Material Christianity*, 67–102; McDannell's treatment focuses on family Bibles in the Victorian era. See also Wulf's forthcoming study, "Lineage: The Politics and Poetics of Genealogy," in *British America, 1680–1820*.

66. Wulf, "'Of the Old Stock,'" 304–306.

67. On the relative failure of parishes to keep adequate records, see Kulikoff, *Tobacco and Slaves*, 233. Family Bibles were also, more mundanely, tools for literacy—books in which people practiced reading and writing. See, e.g., the Tunstall family Bible; children perfected their hands on its pages. Opposite the table of contents, Richard Gregory Tunstall seems to have practiced his hand, writing, "Richard Gregory Tunstall was born May 1722," and then simply *Richard* several more times. Randolph Jefferson practiced his

writing in the Jefferson family Prayer Book; see Kern, "Jeffersons at Shadwell," 469. In the Custis-Tompkins Bible, someone has doodled all over the margin of the first page of the Book of Ruth. See 1724 Bible, call no. BX5145.A4 1720, Special Collections, University of Virginia Library. This use of Bibles and prayer books as spaces for practicing writing is itself a clue about the religious culture in which they were so used. These books were not sacred, in the sense of being set apart and treated with unique reverence, because *sacred* texts do not double as hornbooks. They were, rather, abundant with meanings both religious and quotidian, and the doodles in the Book of Ruth show how religious texts and objects were pulled into quite everyday activities. In contrast to religious cultures in which religious books are venerated and would never be written in, the handwriting exercises in Virginia family Bibles and prayer books are a reminder that the division between the sacred and the profane did not hold fast in elite Anglican households.

68. On medieval practice, see Anderson, "Family Record-Keeping," 248; Ashley, "Creating Family Identity." On paper, see Kerrison, *Claiming the Pen,* 84–85. For a genealogist's account of the origin of family Bibles, see Fiske, "An Editor's Perspective," 243–245.

69. Some biblical writers turn genealogies into stories, shaping family data into narrative, and others cast genealogical information in terse lists. Different genealogies may appear to give the same information, but in fact, upon closer reading, contradict each other, with different genealogists including or excluding different people. And genealogies have many different tasks in the Bible—they name political and religious relationships as well as familial ones. They establish kinship connections, create ethnic identity, and justify dynastic leadership. They stitch apparent outsiders into the family, and they erase from the story people who seemingly belong. In Genesis, in particular, genealogies testify to people's involvement with God, demonstrating their fulfillment of the command to be fruitful and multiply and showing how multiple generations participate in a God-ordained cycle of day and night, seasons, and birth and death. Early modern readers were intrigued by biblical genealogies. Some commentators worried about the Bible's ubiquitous genealogies. In particular, commentators thought that Old Testament genealogies attested to the Israelites' relentless endogamy. (In fact, some biblical genealogies give proof of exogamy.) This apparent tribalism and clannishness did not square with the kind of enlightened Christianity Anglican writers advocated, and yet elite Virginia families, spelling out in their Bibles the marital connections they forged with other elites, may have sympathized with Hebrew priestly classes whom they believed kept genealogical records in part to ensure that "they never married below themselves"; "Genealogy," in Brown, *Dictionary of the Holy Bible,* 519. Other commentators simply found the long lists tedious: the pious Mrs. Chapone went so far as to advise her readers that they could skip all of 1 Chronicles and the first eleven chapters of 2 Chronicles; Chapone, *Improvement of the Mind,* 29.

70. See, e.g., "The Prayer Book of Frances Bland," 267–268; "The Cocke Family," 77–78; "Genealogical Notes and Queries," 99; Tyler, "Lewis Family," 45; Moore, "Gen. John Hartwell Cocke," 153–154.

71. "Mason Family Bible Entries of Marriages, Births, and Deaths," in *Papers of George Mason,* 1: 481.

72. Ibid., 1: 481–482; Mason and Dunn, *Recollections,* 65; Broadwater, *George Mason,* 58; Rowland, *Life of George Mason,* 164.

73. "Mason Family Bible Entries of Marriages, Births, and Deaths," in *Papers of George Mason,* 1: 482. Within his evocation of the Song of Songs, Mason—perhaps con-

sciously, perhaps not—appears to have made a hermeneutical point. The Song of Songs was the biblical book Anglican commentators were most likely to insist be read metaphorically—that is, read not as what it appears to be, a frankly erotic love poem, but read instead as a metaphor about God's relationship to the church. Yet Mason insisted that when he drew on the Song of Songs to describe his wife, he was speaking almost literally: to describe Ann Mason's complexion as blending roses and lilies is, Mason wrote, to speak "almost without a Metaphor."

74. Ibid.

75. Tunstall Bible (1716), Special Collections, University of Virginia Library.

76. See "Maury Bible Records." Note the statement of James Maury that some of the information came from his mother's Bible.

77. E.g., Genesis 10 mentions no deaths; Genesis 11 traces ten generations, but narrates only two deaths. In tracing the line of Esau, Genesis 36 mentions no deaths until the king list begins (see also 1 Chron 1, which follows a nearly identical pattern). An important exception is Genesis 5, which records the long lives—and deaths—of the patriarchs before the flood.

78. Family Bibles are often referred to with double-barreled names, e.g. Tunstall-Maury Bible. Such terms suggest the ways family Bibles figured into larger discourses about gender, patrilineal descent, and family identity. As Laurel Thatcher Ulrich has noted, genealogies are conventional, not natural; thus to record a list like Ann Hill Tunstall's is to give *social* shape to an utterly complex mass of biology. On one level, the social shape Tunstall gave her family narrative was devoutly patriarchal. She recorded the records in a book that was patriarchal twice over—first, the Bible records patriarchal genealogies about people in relationship to a Father God, and second, the Bibles Virginians read were published with apparatuses that located the Bible and its readers in relationship to the monarch of England (e.g., prayers for the king, publisher's announcement that the Bible was printed "By his Majesty's special Command," etc.; see Wulf, "Lineage," forthcoming. On the relationship between royal imprimatur and Bible publishing in England and the English colonies, see Carpenter, *Imperial Bibles, Domestic Bodies*, xvi, 5). To some extent, Ann Hill Tunstall cut against the patriarchal assumptions of both the biblical text and the monarchical apparatus in which it was embedded. For example, unlike biblical genealogies, which tended to trace descent only through fathers, Ann Tunstall's genealogy names her children as the sons and daughters of both "Richard & Ann Tunstall." Yet Tunstall's records also reinscribe patrilineal assumptions. The records Tunstall wrote begin when a woman leaves her father's house and marries another man. The children born to that couple carry the father's surname. Those surnames—patronyms—define families that are traceable from generation to generation. Bibles were often passed down through female lineage through the "umbilical" line—handed down from mother to daughter to daughter. Yet our genealogical convention has no way to name that pattern of inheritance, no nomenclature for a "family" that handed down this Bible across female lines. To call the book in question here the "Tunstall-Maury Bible" is to risk suggesting that it was owned by two different families, not two generations of the same family. The Carrington Bible, which followed the male line, risks no such confusion. The very pattern of inheritance itself reinscribed normatively patrilineal notions of family. Ann's giving the Bible to her daughter was one small gesture in a system of inheritance in which sons received land and daughters received "movables"—furniture, animals, slaves, pictures, cooking implements, books. As Ulrich has noted, the system of inheritance was reflexive—daughters were

themselves movable, moving their bodies and their identities from their father's house to their husband's house. See Ulrich, "Creating Lineages," 5–11, and Ulrich, "Hannah Barnard's Cupboard," 253–255.

79. The intertwining of births and deaths in family Bible records may subtly refigure a recent debate among theorists of religion about what essentially drives religion: death or birth? Many theorists have argued that religions compete with one another through the stories they tell about death. The religious communities that offer people compelling solutions for the problem of human mortality flourish, and those that do not disappear. In the face of this seemingly compelling argument, some feminist theorists have countered that rather than trading on death, religions more essentially seek to explain birth: the religions that succeed are those that offer practitioners a compelling narrative of the mysteries that obtain at the beginning of life. More than mortality, argue theorists like Grace Janzen, creativity is the great mystery. (For the priority of natality over mortality in theorizing religion, see Jantzen, *Becoming Divine*, 128–155.) The artifacts and practices of death in early Virginia show this to be a false debate, or at least a debate that would not have made any sense before the twentieth century, and still would not make sense in the many places where high infant mortality rates and high puerperal death rates mean that natality and mortality are, especially for mothers, ineluctably intertwined. Thus the records that eighteenth-century Virginians set down in their Bibles—in their copies of the "book of life"—were literally vital. Birth and death twinned, as they did in the minds of eighteenth-century women, for whom to await giving birth was also to fear one's own death in childbirth and to anticipate the possible death of an infant. On mothers' grief over children's death, see Dye and Smith, "Mother Love and Infant Death," 329–330, 335–337, 343, 352, and passim.

80. Wulf, "Bible, King, and Common Law," unpublished essay, copy in author's possession.

81. Jane Jefferson Bible, Special Collections, University of Virginia Library. On the various Jefferson family bibles and prayer books, see Kern, "Jeffersons at Shadwell," 459–485.

Epilogue

1. The term "Protestant Episcopal," to describe the American churches that had been part of the Church of England, was first used in Maryland in 1780, at a convention of clergy and laypeople; four years later, Samuel Seabury became the first American bishop, consecrated in Scotland, for the church in Connecticut; in 1789, at a general convention, delegates from across the country adopted a constitution, and revised the Book of Common Prayer. James Madison, a cousin of the future president, became the first bishop of Virginia in 1790. Concise overviews of the organization of the Episcopal Church in America may be found in Holmes, *Brief History of the Episcopal Church*, 50–59, and Prichard, *History of the Episcopal Church*, 82–103.

2. Meade, *Old Churches*, 1: 369. See also Loth, *Virginia Landmarks*, 310.

3. See, e.g., Meade, *Old Churches*, 1: 250–251.

4. Lewis, *Pursuit of Happiness*, 126–143; Kierner, "Dark and Dense Cloud," 191; Evans, *A "Topping People,"* 192–202 and passim; Evans, "Rise and Decline," 68–78.

5. Rhoden, *Revolutionary Anglicanism*, 102–103; Buckley, "Evangelicals Triumphant"; Waukechon, "The Forgotten Evangelicals," 113–151; Holmes, *Decline and Revival*, 55–60; Bond and Gundersen, "Like a Phoenix," 204–215.

6. Hatch, *Democratization of American Christianity*, 60; Holmes, *Brief History of the Episcopal Church*, 26; Cleaveland et al., *Up from Independence*, 59; Meade, *Old Churches*, 2: 148–149, 154–157, 163–164; 1: 391–392, 454.

7. Holmes, "William Meade," 143.

8. Meade describes not just the decline but also the revival in *Old Churches*. After observing woefully that the church in Middlesex County had "returned to its native dust," he declared in dramatic italics, "*But nature abhors a vacuum*. A sycamore-tree sprung up within [the church's] walls. All know the rapidity of that tree's growth. It filled the void. Its boughs soon rose above and overspread the walls." The tree served nicely as a metaphor. The "tree" that had taken over what was, in Meade's view, a hypocritical, debauched colonial church was the awakened faith of evangelical Episcopalianism. That faith grew, and in 1840 "it pleased God to put it into the hearts of some, in whom the spirit of old Virginia Episcopalians still remained, to seek the revival of the Church's dry bones in Middlesex." That once abandoned church building, Meade proudly declared, "is now one of our best country-churches." (The metaphor broke down at the end as the actual syc-amore tree had to be removed when a congregation returned to the church. Meade, *Old Churches*, 1: 369.) The turnaround was so dramatic that at least three historians have likened the church's reinvention in the early nineteenth century to a phoenix rising from the ashes. Bond and Gundersen, "Like a Phoenix," 201; Brown, *Hills of the Lord*, 35.

9. Bond and Gundersen, "Like a Phoenix"; Bond and Gundersen, "Evangelicals Ascendant"; Holmes, "Decline and Revival," in Cleaveland et al., *Up from Independence*, 85–89; Mathews, *Religion in the Old South*, 129–131; Waukechon, "The Forgotten Evan-gelicals," 186–211.

10. Bond and Gundersen, "Evangelicals Ascendant," 247.

11. Lomax, *Sabbath Journal*, 70; Gundersen, "Breaching the Walls," 4; Lindman, "Beyond the Meetinghouse," 147–149; Meade, *Old Churches*, 1: 409–418; 2: 325; 1: 21–22; Holmes, "William Meade," 54–55; Johns, *Memoir of Meade*, 14.

12. That evangelical Episcopal piety took root, in part, in the home is no surprise. The new affectionate understanding of the home was, as Jan Lewis has noted, a feature of the new emotional and religious landscape Virginia gentry came to inhabit in the early Republic: "Home," writes Lewis, "was where the heart, and consequently—in an age of sentimental religion—piety was"; Lewis, *Pursuit of Happiness*, 58. As we have seen in the present study, the sentimental tone of Virginia gentry's religion was new in the early nineteenth century, as was the sharp break that Lewis finds early Republic Virginia gentry drawing between church and world, but the centrality of the household was not. The gentry Lewis studied gravitate toward a household religious practice not only because their religion was one of the heart, and therefore it belonged at the hearth. They practiced religion in the home in part because that is what they and their families were accustomed to doing. Religious practices such as prayer may have been performed with different emotions or different theologies, but the habit of household piety, the expectation that the household was a significant site of religious expression, was not new.

13. Cunningham, *Velvet Cushion*, passim. On novels narrated by inanimate objects, see Flint, "Speaking Objects," and Carlson, "Vulgar Things." *The Velvet Cushion* was first published in London in 1814 and in America a year later. Based on the third London edition, the American version went through nine printings in 1815. The novel inspired some published replies (including *The Legend of the Velvet Cushion*, published under the pseudonym Jeremiah Ringletub in 1815, and *A New Covering to the Velvet Cushion*, in 1816,

attributed to John Styles), and it earned its author the moniker "The Velvet Cunningham." On the publication and reception history of *The Velvet Cushion*, see Shaw, *American Bibliography*, 15: 86–87; Drummond, *Churches in English Fiction*, 13. See also the entry in the *Oxford Dictionary of National Biography*, "Cunningham, John William."

14. Digges, "My Table and Its History," 1, Smith-Digges Papers.

15. Ibid.

16. Ibid., 2; Kirkham and Boyce, *In Every Generation*, n.p.; Hatch, *Grace Church General Study*, 24.

17. Thomas Nelson's parents, William Nelson and Elizabeth Burwell Nelson, were remembered as being "most strictly pious persons . . . strict Episcopalians." In *Old Churches*, Meade praised Elizabeth Nelson for her "private and public exercises of religion, her well-known and frequent prayers for her children and pious instruction of them." She was "not alone in her personal piety, nor in her wishes and endeavours for the religious welfare of her children." William Nelson "performed his part most faithfully." Digges, "My Table and Its History," 5, Smith-Digges Papers; Meade, *Old Churches*, 1: 206. According to Loth, Springfield was built in 1820. Loth, *Virginia Landmarks*, 221. See also the statement in Digges, "My Table and Its History," 15–16, that the house in Hanover was completed for her after the death of her son Robert.

18. Meade, *Old Churches*, 1: 212–213, 420–421; Mason, "York," 165–166; Kirkham and Boyce, *In Every Generation;* Hatch, *Grace Church General Study*, 9, 21–27; Hawks, *Contributions to the Ecclesiastical History*, 1: 176, 203–204; Micou, "Colonial Churches of York County Virginia," 130; Mason, "New Kent," 261–262; Perry, *Journals of General Conventions*, 1: 600; Lancaster, *Sketch of the Early History*, 17; Evans, "Survey Report."

19. Meade, *Old Churches*, 1: 423–425; Digges, "My Table and Its History," 5, 16, 23–24, Smith-Digges Papers. For the centrality to evangelical Episcopal thought of concepts of human depravity, the atonement of the Cross, and people's inability to achieve salvation on their own, see Holmes, "William Meade," 113, and Waukechon, "The Forgotten Evangelicals," 186 and passim.

20. See Marshall, *Prayerbook Parallels*, 1: 442.

21. Loth, *Virginia Landmarks*, 221.

22. Digges, "My Table and Its History," 5–6, Smith-Digges Papers.

23. Whittingham, *Catalogue of the Liturgies*, 34; Dix, *Shape of the Liturgy*, 14; Brydon, *Virginia's Mother Church*, 2: 7, 9–10. Even when she could no longer read, Lucy Nelson continued to pray by rote. During the last years of her life, Lucy Nelson was blind, and her granddaughter recalled the two of them reciting "the Psalms for the day, each one a verse alternately—while a soft and devout voice would chime in with one, to the other, from the pillow." Lucy's granddaughter, in other words, was reading the Psalm from a book, but Lucy herself had the psalm by heart; so sure and steady was her recitation of the Psalm, said Lucy's granddaughter, that "when the white half folded pocket handkerchief was removed from her eyes we could scarce persuade ourselves, that the intelligent glances that turned from one to the other, conveyed no outward information of our occupation, to the mind within." Digges, "My Table and Its History," 20, Smith-Digges Papers.

24. Tucker, *Methodist Worship*, 227.

25. Digges, "My Table and Its History," 25–28, Smith-Digges Papers.

26. Digges, "My Table and Its History," 2, Smith-Digges Papers.

Bibliography

Some of the primary sources quoted in *A Cheerful and Comfortable Faith* are drawn from edited volumes; in those cases, I have, of course, followed the various editors' choices regarding standardizing spelling, punctuation, and so forth. When quoting from primary sources, I have retained many of the original orthographic features but have sometimes silently corrected the sources for the sake of clarity.

Archival Sources

Colonial Williamsburg
  Digital History Archive, Higgins and Muraca, "Archaeological Data," Shields
    Tavern Archaeological Report
  Margaret Pritchard Research Card File
  Smith-Digges Papers

Gunston Hall
  Monteith File

Houghton Library, Harvard University, Cambridge
  Robert Paxton Sermon Collection

Lambeth Palace Library, London
  Fulham Papers

Library of Congress Manuscript Division, Washington, DC
  Custis-Lee Family Papers
  William Dawson Family Papers

Papers of Richard Bland Lee
Papers of William Reynolds
Journal of Elizabeth Foote Washington

Library of Virginia, Richmond
Carrington Family Papers
Patrick Henry Ledger
Lund Washington Manuscripts
Misc. Microfilm Reel no. 19
Misc. Microfilm Reel no. 62
Norfolk County, Virginia. Will Book 2, 1772–1778
E. Smith, *The Compleat Housewife*
The Will of John Yeates

Museum of Early Southern Decorative Arts, Winston-Salem, NC
Accomack County, Virginia, Wills and Deeds
Will of James Crocker, Isle of Wight County, Virginia, Wills and Accounts

Mount Vernon (VA) Library and Special Collections
"A List of Servants & Redemptions"

Earl Gregg Swem Library, College of William and Mary, Williamsburg, VA
Armistead-Cocke Papers

University of Virginia, Special Collections, Charlottesville
Papers of the Ambler Family
Cocke Family Papers
Tunstall Bible
Virginia Miscellany

Virginia Historical Society (VHS), Richmond
Charles Clay Papers
Daniel Family Papers
George Harrison Sanford King Papers
Ludwell Lee Papers

Virginia Theological Seminary Archives, Bishop Payne Library, Alexandria
William Douglas Sermon Collection

Wilton House Museum, Richmond, VA
Randolph Christening Gown File

Published Primary Sources

Abercrombie, Janice L. *Louisa County, Virginia Judgments, 1766–1790.* Athens, GA: Iberian, 1998.

The Accomplish'd Housewife; or, the Gentlewoman's Companion: Containing Reflections on the education of the fair sex . . . London: J. Newbery, 1745.

Allestree, Richard. *The Art of Contentment, by the Author of the Whole Duty of Man, & c.* Oxford: At the Theater in Oxford, 1705.

———. *The Causes of the Decay of Christian Piety; or, An Impartial Survey of the Ruines of the Christian Religion Undermin'd by* . . . London: R. Norton for Robert Pawlett, 1683.

———. *The Gentleman and Ladies Calling in Two Parts. Written by the Author of The Whole Duty of Man Vol. III.* Edinburgh: W. Ruddiman, J. Richardson, 1765.

———. *The Ladies Calling in Two Parts. By the Author of The Whole Duty of Man, &c. Allestree, Richard.* Oxford, 1720.

———. *The Whole Duty of Man Laid Down in a Plain and Familiar Way for the Use of All,* . . . *With Private Devotions for Several Occasions.* London: R. Norton for E. Pawlet, 1713.

———. *The Whole Duty of Mourning and the Great Concern of Preparing Our Selves for Death, Practically Considered.* London: J. Bach, 1695.

Armistead, Hannah Ellyson, and William Armistead. "Armistead Wills." *William and Mary Quarterly* 12 (1904): 253–256.

Bacon, Thomas. "Second Sermon on Colossians 4:1, 1750." In Bond, *Spreading the Gospel.*

Bailyn, Bernard, and Jane Garrett, eds. *Pamphlets of the American Revolution, 1750–1776.* Cambridge: Belknap Press of Harvard University Press, 1965.

Bear, James Adam. *Jefferson at Monticello.* Ed. Isaac Jefferson and Hamilton W. Pierson. Charlottesville: University Press of Virginia, 1967.

Bell, John C. *Louisa County Records You Probably Never Saw.* Nashville: the author, 1983.

Blair, James. *Our Saviour's Divine Sermon on the Mount.* London: J. Brotherton, 1772.

———. "Vain Repetitions and Length in Prayer." In *Spreading the Gospel in Colonial Virginia: Sermons and Devotional Writings,* ed. Edward L. Bond. Lanham, MD: Lexington, 2004.

Blair, John. "Diary of John Blair." *William and Mary Quarterly* 8 (1899): 1–17.

Bond, Edward L., ed. *Spreading the Gospel in Colonial Virginia: Sermons and Devotional Writings.* Lanham, MD: Lexington, 2004.

Boucher, Jonathan. *Reminiscences of an American Loyalist, 1738–1789; being the Autobiography of the Revd Jonathan Boucher, Rector of Annapolis in Maryland and Afterwards Vicar of Epsom, Surrey, England.* Boston: Houghton Mifflin, 1925.

Bradley, Martha. *The British Housewife; or, The Cook, Housekeeper's and Gardiner's*

Companion. Ed. Gilly Lehmann and Sallie Bingham. Blackawton, Devon: Prospect, 1996.

Branch, Joseph Bryan. *Epitaphs of Gloucester and Mathews Counties in Tidewater, Virginia, through 1865.* Richmond: Association for the Preservation of Virginia Antiquities and Virginia State Library, 1959.

Breuer, Josef, and Sigmund Freud. *Studies in Hysteria.* Ed. A. A. Brill. New York: Nervous and Mental Disease Publishing, 1936.

Brewer, Mary Marshall. *York County, Virginia, Wills, Inventories and Court Orders, 1745–1759.* Lewes, DE: Colonial Roots, 2005.

Brown, John, ed. *A Dictionary of the Holy Bible Containing, an Historical Account of the Persons . . .* Edinburgh: John Gray and Gavin Alston, 1769.

Bullock, Helen. *The Williamsburg Art of Cookery; or, Accomplish'd Gentlewoman's Companion: Being a Collection of Upwards of Five Hundred of the Most Ancient and Approv'd Recipes in Virginia Cookery.* Williamsburg, VA: Colonial Williamsburg, 1949.

Byrd, William. *Another Secret Diary of William Byrd of Westover, 1739–1741; with Letters & Literary Exercises, 1696–1726.* Ed. Marion Tinling and Maude Howlett Woodfin. Richmond, VA: Dietz, 1942.

——. "Biblical Notes, 1728–1729." In Bond, *Spreading the Gospel.*

——. *The Commonplace Book of William Byrd II of Westover.* Ed. Kevin Berland, Jan Kirsten Gilliam, and Kenneth A. Lockridge. Chapel Hill: University of North Carolina Press for the Omohundro Institute of Early American History and Culture, Williamsburg, VA, 2001.

——. *The London Diary (1717–1721) and Other Writings.* Ed. Marion Tinling and Louis Booker Wright. New York: Oxford University Press, 1958.

——. *The Secret Diary of William Byrd of Westover, 1709–1712.* Ed. Louis B. Wright and Marion Tinling. Richmond, VA: Dietz, 1941.

——. *William Byrd's Histories of the Dividing Line Betwixt Virginia and North Carolina.* Raleigh: North Carolina Historical Commission, 1929.

Carter, Landon. *The Diary of Colonel Landon Carter of Sabine Hall, 1752–1778.* Ed. Jack P. Greene. Charlottesville: University Press of Virginia for the Virginia Historical Society, 1965.

Chamberlayne, Churchill, ed. *The Vestry Book and Register of Bristol Parish, Virginia, 1720–1789.* Richmond, VA: W. E. Jones, 1898.

——. *The Vestry Book and Register of St Peter's Parish, New Kent and James City Counties, Virginia, 1684–1786.* Richmond, VA: Division of Purchase and Printing, 1937.

——. *The Vestry Book of Christ Church Parish, Middlesex County, Virginia, 1663–1767.* Richmond, VA: Division of Purchase and Printing, 1927.

——. *The Vestry Book of Kingston Parish, Mathews County, Virginia (Until May 1, 1791, Gloucester County) 1679–1796.* Richmond, VA: Old Dominion, 1929.

——. *The Vestry Book of Petsworth Parish, Gloucester County, Virginia, 1677–1793.* Richmond, VA: Division of Purchase and Printing, 1933.

——. *The Vestry Book of St Paul's Parish, Hanover County, Virginia, 1706–1786.* Richmond, VA: Division of Purchase and Printing, 1940.

Chapone, Hester. *Letters on the Improvement of the Mind, Addressed to a Young Lady.* London: J. Walter and E. and C. Dilly, 1777.

"Churchill Family." *William and Mary Quarterly* 7 (1899): 186–188.

Cochran, Charles F. "Early Generations of the Newton Family of Westmoreland County, Virginia." *Virginia Magazine of History and Biography* 37 (1929): 87–91.

"The Cocke Family of Virginia (Henrico)." *Virginia Magazine of History and Biography* 5 (1897): 71–89.

Cook, Michael L., and Bettie A. Cook. Kentucky Court of Appeals Deed Books O–U, vol. 3. Evansville, Ind.: Cook, 1985.

Courtney, Elizabeth S. "Will of Colonel Humphrey Hill." *William and Mary Quarterly* 16 (1907): 97–99.

Cranmer, Thomas. "On the Sacrament of Baptism." In *Cranmer's Selected Writings,* ed. Carl S. Meyer. London: Society for Promoting Christian Knowledge, 1961.

Creffield, Edward. *A Good Wife a Great Blessing: or, The Honour and Happiness of the Marriage State, in Two Sermons . . .* London: T. Taylor, [1717?].

Cresswell, Nicholas. *The Journal of Nicholas Cresswell, 1774–1777.* London: J. Cape, 1925.

Crozier, William Armstrong. Virginia County Records, vol. 3: Williamsburg Wills Being Transcriptions from the Original Files at the Chancery Court of Williamsburg. 1906; rpt., Baltimore: Genealogical Publishing, 1973.

Cunningham, J. W. *The Velvet Cushion.* London: G. Sidney for T. Cadell and W. Davies, 1815.

Davies, Samuel. "A Christmas-Day Sermon, 1758." In Bond, *Spreading the Gospel.*

——. *Sermons on Important Subjects, by the Late Reverend and Pious Samuel Davies, A.M., Sometime President of the College in New-Jersey.* 2 vols. 6th ed., 1749.

Davis, Rosalie Edith. *Fredericksville Parish Vestry Books, 1742–1787.* Manchester, MO: the author, 1978.

——. *Louisa County Tithables and Census, 1743–1785.* 2nd ed. Manchester, MO: Heritage Trails, 1988.

Dawson, Thomas. "A Confirmation Sermon." In Bond, *Spreading the Gospel.*

Dawson, William. "A Christmas Sermon." In Bond, *Spreading the Gospel.*

Dodd, William. *A common-place-book to the Holy Bible: . . . The fifth edition; carefully revised and improved.* London: T. Osborne; W. Johnston; Hawes, Clarke and Collings, and T. Longman; T. Caslon; B. Law; E. and C. Dilly; and C. and R. Ware, 1766.

"Epitaphs at Brandon, Prince George County, Va." *Virginia Magazine of History and Biography,* 6 (1899): 233–236.

Essex, John. *The Young Ladies Conduct; or, Rules for Education, under Several Heads; with Instructions upon Dress, both Before and After Marriage and Advice to Young Wives.* London: John Brotherton, 1722.

Evans, William, and Thomas Evans, eds. "A Short Account of Alice Hayes, a Minister of the Gospel in the Society of Friends." *Friends Library*. Vol. 2. Philadelphia: Joseph Rakestraw, 1838.

Executive Journals of the Council of Colonial Virginia. 6 vols. Ed. H. R. McIlwaine. Richmond: Virginia State Library, 1925–1966.

Fairfax, Sally Cary. "Diary of a Little Colonial Girl." *Virginia Magazine of History and Biography* 11 (1903–1904): 212–214.

Fields, Joseph, ed. *Worthy Partner: The Papers of Martha Washington.* Westport, CT: Greenwood, 1994.

Fithian, Philip Vickers. *Journal and Letters of Philip Vickers Fithian: A Plantation Tutor of the Old Dominion, 1773–1774.* Ed. Hunter D. Farish. Charlottesville: University Press of Virginia, 1983.

Fitzhugh, William. *William Fitzhugh and His Chesapeake World, 1676–1701: The Fitzhugh Letters and Other Documents.* Ed. Richard Beale Davis. Chapel Hill: University of North Carolina Press for the Virginia Historical Society, 1963.

Fontaine, James, comp. *Memoirs of a Huguenot Family.* New York: Putnam, 1853.

Fordyce, James. *Sermons to Young Women in Two Volumes.* London: D. Payne, 1766.

"Fox Family." *William and Mary Quarterly* 17 (1908): 59–64.

"Free Schools in Isle of Wight County." *William and Mary Quarterly* 5 (1896): 112–113.

Fristoe, William. *A Concise History of the Ketocton Baptist Association.* Staunton, VA, 1808.

"Funeral Expenses of Benjamin Harrison, 1745." *Virginia Magazine of History and Biography* 8 (1901): 329.

Glasse, H. *The Art of Cookery Made Plain and Easy.* Introduction by Karen Hess. Bedford, MA: Applewood, 1997.

Greene, Jack P., ed. "A Mirror of Virtue for a Declining Land: John Camm's Funeral Sermon for William Nelson." In *Essays in Early Virginia Literature Honoring Richard Beale Davis,* ed. J. A. Leo Lamay. New York: Burt Franklin, 1977.

Gregory, John. *A Father's Legacy to His Daughters.* London: G. Robertson, 1792.

Harrison, Fairfax. "With Braddock's Army: Mrs. Browne's Diary in Virginia and Maryland." *Virginia Magazine of History and Biography* 32 (1924): 305–320.

——. ed. "The Will of Charles Carter of Cleve." *Virginia Historical Magazine* 21 (1923): 39–69.

Harrower, John. *The Journal of John Harrower, an Indentured Servant in the Colony of Virginia, 1773–1776.* Ed. Edward M. Riley. New York: Holt, Rinehart and Winston, 1963.

Hartwell, Blair and Chilton, eds. *The Present State of Virginia and the College.* London: John Wyat, 1727.

Hawks, Francis L. *Contributions to the Ecclesiastical History of the United States of America.* New York: Harper, 1836–1839.

Hening, William Waller, ed. *The Statutes at Large; Being a Collection of all the Laws of Virginia, from the First Session of the Legislature, in the Year 1619: Published Pursuant to an Act of the General Assembly of Virginia, Passed on the Fifth Day of February One Thousand Eight Hundred and Eight.* 13 vols. New-York: Bartow, 1823.

Hewlett, Ebenezer. *A Refined Quaker's Remarks on Baptism: in Answer to Mr Caleb Fleming's Pamphlet, intituled, A Defence of Infant Baptism. By Eben. Hewlett.* London: M. Cooper and the author in Sun-street without Bishopsgate, 1745.

Hooker, Richard. *Of the Laws of Ecclesiastical Polity.* In *The Folger Library Edition of the Works of Richard Hooker,* ed. W. Speed Hill, 6 vols. Cambridge: Harvard University Press, 1977–1993.

Ingersoll, Thomas N., ed. "'Releese us out of this Cruell Bondegg': An Appeal from Virginia in 1723." *William and Mary Quarterly* 51 (1994): 777–782.

Jarratt, Devereux. *The Life of the Reverend Devereux Jarratt, Rector of Bath Parish, Dinwiddie County, Virginia.* Baltimore: Warner and Hanna, 1806.

Jensen, Merrill. *Tracts of the American Revolution, 1763–1776.* Indianapolis: Bobbs-Merrill, 1967.

Johns, John. *A Memoir of the Life of the Right Rev William Meade, D.D., Bishop of the Protestant Episcopal Church in the Diocese of Virginia.* Ed. William Sparrow. Baltimore: Innes, 1867.

Jones, Hugh. *The Present State of Virginia; from Whence is Inferred a Short View of Maryland and North Carolina.* Ed. Richard L. Morton. Chapel Hill: University of North Carolina Press for Virginia Historical Society, 1956.

"Journal of Colonel James Gordon." *William and Mary Quarterly* 11 (1902): 98–112.

Kennett, White. *The Excellent Daughter; A Discourse very Necessary to be Given by all Parents to their Children: To which is Added, several Proper Lessons on the Duty of Daughters.* London: F. and C. Rivington, Booksellers to the Society for Promoting Christian Knowledge, 1792.

Kenrick, W. *The Whole Duty of Woman.* New York: W. Borradaile, 1821.

Kidder, E. *E. Kidder's Receipts of Pastry and Cookery, for the Use of his Scholars . . .* London, [1740?].

King, George Harrison Sanford. *The Register of North Farnham Parish, 1663–1814, and Lunenburg Parish, 1783–1800, Richmond County, Virginia.* Fredericksburg, VA: the author, 1966.

——. *The Register of Overwharton Parish, Stafford County, Virginia, 1723–1758, and Sundry Historical and Genealogical Notes.* Fredericksburg, VA: the author, 1961.

——. *Register of St. Paul's Parish, 1715–1798, Stafford County, 1715–1776, King George County, Virginia, 1777–1798.* Fredericksburg, VA: the author, 1960.

The Ladies Library . . . Written by a Lady. London: J. and R. Tonson, 1739.

Lee, Henry. "Mary Bland's Death: Letter of Henry Lee." *William and Mary Quarterly* 8 (1899): 34–35.

Leland, John, "The Virginia Chronicle, 1790." In Bond, *Spreading the Gospel.*

Lomax, Judith. *The Sabbath Journal of Judith Lomax.* Ed. Laura Hobgood-Oster. New York: Oxford University Press, 2000.

Ludwell, Thomas. "Original Letter." *William and Mary Quarterly* 3 (1895): 197–199.

MacDonald, William, ed. *Documentary Source Book of American History, 1606–1926.* New York: B. Franklin, 1968.

MacFarlane, Senner Higginbotham. "Will of Patrick Henry's Mother." *William and Mary Quarterly* 8 (1928): 117–119.

Markham, Gervase. *The English Hus-Wife, Contayning, the Inward and Outward Vertues which Ought to be in a Compleat Woman.* London: John Beale for Roger Jackson, 1615.

"Marriage Bonds of Norfolk County." *William and Mary Quarterly* 8 (1928): 99–110.

Marshall, Paul V., ed. *Prayer Book Parallels: The Public Services of the Church Arranged for Comparative Study.* New York: Church Hymnal, 1989–1990.

Mason, George. *The Papers of George Mason, 1725–1792.* Ed. Robert Allen Rutland. Chapel Hill: University of North Carolina Press, 1970.

Mason, John. *The Recollections of John Mason: George Mason's Son Remembers His Father and Life at Gunston Hall.* Ed. Terry K. Dunn. Marshall, VA: EPM, 2004.

"Maury Bible Records." *Virginia Magazine of History and Biography* 27 (1919): 375–376.

Maury, James. "First Sermon." In Bond, *Spreading the Gospel.*

———. "Sermon Number 12." In Bond, *Spreading the Gospel.*

May, Robert. *The Accomplisht Cook; or, The Art and Mystery of Cookery: Wherein the Whole Art is Revealed in a More Easie and Perfect Method than Hath been Publisht in any Language.* London: R.W. for Nath. Brooke, 1660.

Meade, William. *Old Churches, Ministers, and Families of Virginia.* Philadelphia: Lippincott, 1861.

Moreau de Saint-Méry, M. L. E. *Moreau de Saint-Méry's American Journey, 1793–1798.* Trans. and ed. Kenneth Roberts and Anna M. Roberts. Garden City, NY: Doubleday, 1947.

Moxon, Elizabeth. *English Housewifry improved; or, A Suppleent to Moxon's cookery. Containing upwards of sixty modern and valuable receipts.* 8th ed. Leeds: Griffith Wright for George Copperthwaite, 1758.

"Old Kecoughtan." *William and Mary Quarterly* 9 (1900): 83–131.

"Old Tombstones in Westmoreland County." *William and Mary Quarterly,* 7 (1898): 93–98.

Orr, Lucinda Lee. *Journal of a Young Lady of Virginia, 1782.* Baltimore: J. Murphy, 1871.

Page, John. *A Deed of Gift to My Dear Son, Captain Matt Page, One of His Majesty's Justices for New Kent County, in Virginia. 1687.* Ed. Bryan Fairfax, William Meade, and Matthew Page. Philadelphia: H. B. Ashmead, 1856.

Perry, William Stevens, ed. *Papers Relating to the History of the Church in Virginia, A.D. 1650–1776.* N.p., 1870.

"The Prayerbook of Frances Bland, the Mother of John Randolph, of Roanoke." *William and Mary Quarterly* 17 (1909): 267–268.

A Present for Servants, from their Ministers, Masters, Or Other Friends. London: J. F. and C. Rivington, 1787.

Raffald, Elizabeth. *The Experienced English House-keeper for the use of ladies, housekeepers, cooks, &c . . . Consisting of several hundred original receipts.* Manchester, 1769.

Read, Helen Calvert Maxwell. *Memoirs of Helen Calvert Maxwell Read.* Ed. Charles Brinson Cross. Chesapeake: Norfolk County Historical Society of Chesapeake, Virginia, 1970.

Richardson, Samuel. *Clarissa; or, The History of a Young Lady.* Ed. Angus Ross. 3rd ed. London: Penguin, 1985.

Rose, Robert. *The Diary of Robert Rose: A View of Virginia by a Scottish Colonial Parson, 1746–1751.* Ed. Ralph Emmett Fall. Verona, VA: McClure, 1977.

"Schools in Virginia: John Farneffold's Free School." *William and Mary Quarterly* 17 (1909): 244–247.

Slaughter, Philip. *Memoir of the Life of the Rt Rev. William Meade, D.D., Bishop of the Protestant Episcopal Church of the Diocese of Virginia.* Cambridge: J. Wilson, 1885.

Stith, William. *The History of the First Discovery and Settlement of Virginia.* New York: Rpt. for Joseph Sabin, 1865.

Taylor, Jeremy. *Holy Living and Holy Dying.* 2 vols., ed. P. G. Stanwood. Oxford: Clarendon, 1989.

Thomas, David. *The Virginian Baptist; or, A view and defence of the Christian religion, as it is professed by the Baptists of Virginia..* Baltimore: Enoch Story, 1774.

Thornton, John Wingate. *The Pulpit of the American Revolution; or, The Political Sermons of the Period of 1776 with a Historical Introduction, Notes, and Illustrations.* Boston: Gould and Lincoln; New York: Sheldon, 1860.

Thrift, Minton. *Memoir of the Rev. Jesse Lee with Extracts from His Journals.* New York: N. Bangs and T. Mason, for the Methodist Episcopal Church, 1823.

Tillotson, John. *The Works of the Most Reverend Dr. John Tillotson.* London: William Rogers, 1712.

Tinling, Marion, ed. *The Correspondence of the Three William Byrds of Westover, Virginia, 1684–1776.* Charlottesville: University Press of Virginia for the Virginia Historical Society, 1977.

Tittle, Walter. *Colonial Holidays; Being a Collection of Contemporary Accounts of Holiday Celebrations in Colonial Times.* New York: Doubleday, Page, 1910.

"Tombstones in Middlesex County: Urbanna." *William and Mary Quarterly* 12 (1904): 170–174.

"Tombstones in Warwick County." *William and Mary Quarterly* 14 (1906): 163–167.

Tyler, Lyon G. "Diary of John Blair." *William and Mary Quarterly* 7 (1899): 133–153.

——. "Lewis Family." *William and Mary Quarterly* 11 (1902): 39–47.

——. "Old Tombstones in Charles City County." *William and Mary Quarterly* 4 (1895): 122–125.

——. "Old Tombstones in Charles City County." *William and Mary Quarterly* 4 (1896): 143–150.

"The Use and Design of Scriptural Prints." *Universal Magazine,* December 1748.

Van Horne, John C., ed. *Religious Philanthropy and Colonial Slavery: The American Correspondence of the Associates of Dr Bray, 1717–1777.* Urbana: University of Illinois Press, 1985.

"Virginia Council Journals, 1726–1753." *Virginia Magazine of History and Biography* 35 (1927): 27–54, 405–418.

Wakelyn, Jon., ed. *America's Founding Charters: Primary Documents of Colonial and Revolutionary Era Governance.* Westport, CT: Greenwood, 2006.

"Ward Family." *William and Mary Quarterly* 27 (1919): 185–199.

Washington, George. *The Diaries of George Washington.* Ed. Donald Dean Jackson and Dorothy Twohig. Charlottesville: University Press of Virginia, 1976–1979.

Watts, Isaac. *Dr Watts' Plain and Easy Catechisms for Children: To which is Added some Verses and Short Prayers.* Canandaigua, NY: J. D. Bemis, 1822.

"Will of Benjamin Harrison." *Virginia Magazine of History and Biography* 3 (1895): 124–131.

Winchester, Elnathan. *The Reigning Abominations, Especially the Slave Trade, Considered as Causes of Lamentation: Being the substance of a Discourse Delivered in Fairfax County, Virginia, December 30, 1774.* London: H. Trapp for the author, 1788.

Secondary Sources

Allen, Gloria Seaman. "Equally Their Due: Female Education in Antebellum Alexandria." *Historic Alexandria Quarterly* (1996): 1–11.

Anderson, Jefferson Randolph. "Supplement to Tuckahoe and the Tuckahoe Randolphs." *Virginia Magazine of History and Biography* 45 (1937): 392–405.

Anderson, Jerome E. "Family Record-Keeping: A Rich and Diverse Heritage." *National Genealogical Society Quarterly* 90 (2002): 247–256.

Ariès, Philippe. *Western Attitudes towards Death, from the Middle Ages to the Present.* Baltimore: Johns Hopkins University Press, 1975.

Ashenburg, Katherine. *The Mourner's Dance: What We Do when People Die.* New York: North Point, 2004.

Ashley, Kathleen. "Creating Family Identity in Books of Hours." *Journal of Medieval and Early Modern Studies* 32 (2002): 145–165.

Austin, John C., and Colonial Williamsburg Foundation. *British Delft at Wil-*

liamsburg. Williamsburg, VA: Colonial Williamsburg Foundation in association with Jonathan Horne, 1994.

Bailey, Derrick Sherwin. *Sponsors at Baptism and Confirmation: An Historical Introduction to Anglican Practice*. London: Society for Promoting Christian Knowledge, 1952.

Barbour, Hugh, and J. William Frost. *The Quakers*. New York: Greenwood, 1988.

Barnhill, Georgia Brady. " 'Keep Sacred the Memory of Your Ancestors': Family Registers and Memorial Prints." In *The Art of Family: Genealogical Artifacts in New England*, ed. D. Brenton Simons and Peter Benes. Boston: Northeastern University Press for New England Historic Genealogical Society, 2002.

Baumgarten, Linda. *What Clothes Reveal: The Language of Clothing in Colonial and Federal America: The Colonial Williamsburg Collection*. Williamsburg, VA: Colonial Williamsburg Foundation; New Haven: Yale University Press, 2002.

Beasley, Nicholas M. *Christian Ritual and the Creation of British Slave Societies, 1650–1780*. Athens: University of Georgia Press, 2009.

Beaty, Nancy Lee. *The Craft of Dying: A Study in the Literary Tradition of the Ars Moriendi in England*. New Haven: Yale University Press, 1970.

Beaudry, Mary C. " 'Or What Else You Please to Call It': Folk Semantic Domains in Early Virginia Probate Inventories." Ph.D. diss., Brown University, 1980.

Beeth, Howard. "Outside Agitators in Southern History: The Society of Friends, 1656–1800." Ph.D. diss., University of Houston, 1984.

Beliles, Mark A. "The Christian Communities, Religious Revivals, and Political Culture of the Central Virginia Piedmont, 1737–1813." In *Religion and Political Culture in Jefferson's Virginia*, ed. Garrett Ward Sheldon and Daniel L. Dreisbach. Lanham, MD: Rowman and Littlefield, 2000.

Bell, Catherine M. *Ritual: Perspectives and Dimensions*. New York: Oxford University Press, 1997.

Bennett, J. H. "English Bishops and Imperial Jurisdiction, 1660–1725." *Historical Magazine of the Protestant Episcopal Church* 32 (1963): 175–188.

Beverley, Robert. *The History and Present State of Virginia*. Ed. Louis B. Wright. Chapel Hill: University of North Carolina Press, 1947.

Bloch, Maurice. "Death, Women, and Power." In *Death and the Regeneration of Life*, ed. Maurice Bloch and Jonathan Perry. Cambridge: Cambridge University Press, 1982.

Blosser, Jacob M. "Irreverent Empire: Anglican Inattention in an Atlantic World." *Church History* 77 (2008): 596–628.

———. "Pursuing Happiness: Cultural Discourse and Popular Religion in Anglican Virginia, 1700–1770." Ph.D. diss., University of South Carolina, 2006.

Boddie, John Bennett. "Lygon of Madresfield, Worcester, England, and Henrico, Virginia." *William and Mary Quarterly* 16 (1936): 289–315.

Bolton, Ethel Stanwood, and Eva Johnston Coe. *American Samplers*. Boston: Massachusetts Society of the Colonial Dames of America, 1921.

Bond, Edward L. "Anglican Theology and Devotion in James Blair's Virginia, 1685–1743." *Virginia Magazine of History and Biography* 104 (1996): 313–340.

———. *Damned Souls in a Tobacco Colony: Religion in Seventeenth-Century Virginia.* Macon, GA: Mercer University Press, 2000.

———. "Prologue to the Biography of the Reverend James Blair." *Anglican and Episcopal History* 76 (2007): 12–28.

———. "Source of Knowledge, Source of Power: The Supernatural World of English Virginia, 1607–1624." *Virginia Magazine of History and Biography* 108 (2000): 105–138.

Bond, Edward L., and Joan R. Gundersen. "Colonial Origins and Growth: The Church of England Adapts to North America, 1607–1760." *Virginia Magazine of History and Biography* 115 (2007): 165–199.

———. "Evangelicals Ascendant: Bishop Meade and the High Tide of Evangelical Episcopalianism, 1840–1865." *Virginia Magazine of History and Biography* 115 (2007): 243–275.

———. "Like a Phoenix from the Ashes: The Reinvention of the Church in Virginia, 1760–1840." *Virginia Magazine of History and Biography* 115 (2007): 201–241.

Bondeson, Jan. *Buried Alive: The Terrifying History of Our Most Primal Fear.* New York: Norton, 2001.

Bonomi, Patricia U. *Under the Cope of Heaven: Religion, Society, and Politics in Colonial America.* New York: Oxford University Press, 2003.

Bonomi, Patricia U., and Peter R. Eisenstadt, "Church Adherence in the Eighteenth-Century British American Colonies." *William and Mary Quarterly* 39 (1982): 245–286.

Booty, John E. *William Meade: Evangelical Churchman.* Alexandria, VA: Protestant Episcopal Seminary in Virginia, 1962.

Bossy, John. *Christianity in the West, 1400–1700.* New York: Oxford University Press, 1985.

Bottigheimer, Ruth B. *The Bible for Children: From the Age of Gutenberg to the Present.* New Haven: Yale University Press, 1996.

Bourdieu, Pierre. *Outline of a Theory of Practice.* Cambridge: Cambridge University Press, 1977.

Braithwaite, William C. *The Beginnings of Quakerism.* Ed. and rev. Henry Joel Cadbury. York: William Sessions in association with the Joseph Rowntree Charitable Trust, 1981.

Branch, Lori. *Rituals of Spontaneity: Sentiment and Secularism from Free Prayer to Wordsworth.* Waco: Baylor University Press, 2006.

Brears, Peter. "Arvals, Wakes, and Month's Minds: Food for Funerals." In *Food and the Rites of Passage,* ed. Laura Mason. Totnes, Devon: Prospect, 2002.

Breen, T. H. *Puritans and Adventurers: Change and Persistence in Early America.* New York: Oxford University Press, 1980.

Brekus, Catherine A. "Children of Wrath, Children of Grace: Jonathan Edwards and the Puritan Culture of Child Rearing." In *The Child in Christian Thought,* ed. Marcia J. Bunge. Grand Rapids, MI: Eerdmans, 2001.

———. "Writing as a Protestant Practice: Devotional Diaries in Early New England." In *Practicing Protestants,* ed. Laurie F. Maffly-Kipp, Leigh E. Schmidt, and Mark Valeri. Baltimore: Johns Hopkins University Press, 2006.

Bridenbaugh, Carl. *Myths and Realities: Societies of the Colonial South.* New York: Atheneum, 1963.

Broadwater, Jeff. *George Mason, Forgotten Founder.* Chapel Hill: University of North Carolina Press, 2006.

Brown, Anne S. "Bound Up in a Bundle of Life: The Social Meaning of Religious Practice in Northeastern Massachusetts, 1700–1765." Ph.D. diss., Boston University, 1995.

Brown, Johanna. "Such Luxuries as a Sofa: An Introduction to North Carolina Moravian Upholstered Furniture." *Journal of Early Southern Decorative Arts* 25 (2001): 1–50.

Brown, Katharine L. *Hills of the Lord: Background of the Episcopal Church in Southwestern Virginia, 1738–1938.* Roanoke: Diocese of Southwestern Virginia, 1979.

Brown, Kathleen M. *Good Wives, Nasty Wenches, and Anxious Patriarchs: Gender, Race, and Power in Colonial Virginia.* Chapel Hill: University of North Carolina Press for the Institute of Early American History and Culture, 1996.

Bruce, Philip Alexander. *Economic History of Virginia in the Seventeenth Century: An Inquiry into the Material Condition of the People, Based upon Original and Contemporaneous Records.* New York: P. Smith, 1935.

Brydon, G. M. *Virginia's Mother Church and the Political Conditions under which it Grew.* Richmond: Virginia Historical Society, 1952.

Buck, Anne. *Dress in Eighteenth-Century England.* New York: Holmes and Meier, 1979.

Buckley, Thomas. "Evangelicals Triumphant: The Baptists' Assault on the Virginia Glebes, 1789–1801." *William and Mary Quarterly* 45 (1988): 33–69.

Burke, Peter. *Popular Culture in Early Modern Europe.* Aldershot, England: Scolar; Brookfield, VT: Ashgate, 1994.

Burton, H. W. *The History of Norfolk, Virginia: A Review of Important Events and Incidents Which Occurred from 1736–1877; also a Record of Personal Reminiscences and Political, Commercial, and Curious Facts.* Norfolk: Norfolk Virginian, 1877.

Bushman, Richard L. "The Complexity of Silver." In *New England Silver and Silversmithing, 1620–1815,* ed. Jeannine Falino and Gerald W. R. Ward. Boston: Colonial Society of Massachusetts, 2002.

———. *The Refinement of America: Persons, Houses, Cities.* New York: Knopf, 1992.

Butler, Jon. *Awash in a Sea of Faith: Christianizing the American People.* Cambridge: Harvard University Press, 1990.

———. "Thomas Teackle's 333 Books: A Great Library on Virginia's Eastern Shore, 1697." *William and Mary Quarterly* 49 (1992): 449–491.

———. "Transatlantic Pieties: Connections and Disconnections." *Journal of British Studies* 28 (1989): 411–418.

Butler, Patrick Henry, III. "Knowing the Uncertainties of this Life: Death and

Society in Colonial Tidewater Virginia." Ph.D. diss., Johns Hopkins University, 1998.

Calabresi, Bianca. " 'You sow, Ile read': Letters and Literacies in Early Modern Samplers." In Hackel and Kelly, *Reading Women*.

Calvert, Karin. "The Function of Fashion." In *Of Consuming Interests: The Style of Life in the Eighteenth Century*, eds. Cary Carson et al. Charlottesville: University Press of Virginia, 1994.

Carlson, Hannah. "Vulgar Things." *Common-Place* 7 (2007): http://www.com mon-place.org/vol-07/no-02/carlson/.

Carpenter, Mary Wilson. *Imperial Bibles, Domestic Bodies: Women, Sexuality, and Religion in the Victorian Market*. Athens: Ohio University Press, 2003.

Carson, Jane. *Colonial Virginians at Play*. Williamsburg: University Press of Virginia for Colonial Williamsburg, 1965.

Cheney, C. R., and Michael Jones, eds. *A Handbook of Dates: For Students of British History*. Cambridge: Cambridge University Press, 2000.

Chew, Elizabeth V. "Carrying the Keys: Women and Housekeeping at Monticello." In *Dining at Monticello: In Good Taste and Abundance*, ed. Damon Lee Fowler. Chapel Hill: University of North Carolina Press for Thomas Jefferson Foundation, 2005.

——. "Inhabiting the Great Man's House: Women and Space at Monticello." In *Structures and Subjectivities: Attending to the Early Modern Woman*, ed. Joan Hartman and Adele Seeff. Newark: University of Delaware Press, 2007.

Cleaveland, George, et al., eds. *Up from Independence: The Episcopal Church in Virginia: Articles*. Orange, VA: Interdiocesan Bicentennial Committee of the Virginias, 1976.

Clifford, Mary Louise. *From Slavery to Freetown: Black Loyalists after the American Revolution*. Jefferson, NC: McFarland, 1999.

Clinton, Catherine, and Michele Gillespie, eds. *The Devil's Lane: Sex and Race in the Early South*. New York: Oxford University Press, 1997.

Cobb, Sanford H. *The Rise of Religious Liberty in America: A History*. New York: Macmillan, 1902.

Colonial Churches in the Original Colony of Virginia: A Series of Sketches by Especially Qualified Writers. Richmond, VA: Southern Churchman, 1908.

Cornelius, Charles O. "An Important Loan of American Silver." *Metropolitan Museum of Art Bulletin* 20 (1925): 152–154.

Cornelius, Janet Duitsman. *"When I Can Read My Title Clear": Literacy, Slavery, and Religion in the Antebellum South*. Columbia: University of South Carolina Press, 1991.

Coster, Will. *Baptism and Spiritual Kinship in Early Modern England*. Aldershot, England: Ashgate, 2002.

Cowden, Gerald Steffens. "The Randolphs of Turkey Island: A Prosopography of the First Three Generations, 1650–1806." Ph.D. diss., College of William and Mary, 1977.

Cressy, David. *Birth, Marriage, and Death: Ritual, Religion, and the Life-Cycle in Tudor and Stuart England.* Oxford: Oxford University Press, 1997.

——. *Bonfires and Bells: National Memory and the Protestant Calendar in Elizabethan and Stuart England.* Berkeley: University of California Press, 1989.

——. "Books as Totems in Seventeenth-Century England and New England." *Journal of Library History* 21 (1986): 92–106.

——. "Purification, Thanksgiving, and the Churching of Women in Post-Reformation England." *Past and Present* 141 (1993): 106–146.

Cross, Arthur Lyon. *The Anglican Episcopate and the American Colonies.* Norwood, MA: Norwood, 1902.

Crowley, John E. "The Sensibility of Comfort." *American Historical Review* 104 (1999): 749–782.

Cunnington, C. Willett, and Phillis Emily Cunnington. *Handbook of English Costume in the Eighteenth Century.* Philadelphia: Dufour, 1957.

Cunnington, Phillis, and Catherine Lucas. *Costume for Births, Marriages, and Deaths.* London: A and C Black, 1972.

Daniell, Christopher. *Death and Burial in Medieval England, 1066–1550.* London: Routledge, 1997.

Daniels, Cora Linn, and C. N. Stevans, eds. *Encyclopedia of Superstitions, Folklore, and the Occult Sciences of the World.* 3 vols. Detroit: Gale, 1971.

Davidson, Mary M. *Plimoth Colony Samplers.* Marion, MA: The Channings, 1974.

Davies, Adrian. *The Quakers in English Society, 1655–1725.* Oxford: Clarendon; New York: Oxford University Press, 2000.

Davies, Douglas James. *Death, Ritual, and Belief: The Rhetoric of Funerary Rites.* London: Continuum, 2002.

Davies, Horton. *Worship and Theology in England.* Grand Rapids, MI: Eerdmans, 1996.

Davis, Edward Morris, III. "Historical Silver in the Commonwealth of Virginia." *Virginia Magazine of History and Biography* 49 (1941): 105–124.

Davis, John D. *English Silver at Williamsburg.* Williamsburg: University Press of Virginia for Colonial Williamsburg Foundation, 1976.

Davis, Richard Beale. *Intellectual Life in the Colonial South, 1585–1763.* Knoxville: University of Tennessee Press, 1978.

Deetz, James. *In Small Things Forgotten: An Archaeology of Early American Life.* New York: Anchor/Doubleday, 1996.

Deetz, James, and Edwin S. Dethlefsen. "Death's Head, Cherub, Urn, and Willow." *Natural History* 76, no. 3 (1967): 29–37.

DeLorme, Maureen. *Mourning Art and Jewelry.* Atglen, PA: Schiffer, 2004.

Dent, Anne Sorrell. "God and Gentry: Public and Private Religion in Tidewater Virginia, 1607–1800." Ph.D. diss., University of Kentucky, 2001.

Deshler, Charles D. "How the Declaration Was Received in the Old Thirteen." *Harper's New Monthly Magazine* 85, no. 506 (1892): 165–187.

Deutsch, Davida Tenenbaum. "Needlework Patterns and Their Use in America." *Antiques* 139 (1991): 368–381.

——. "The Polite Lady: Portraits of American Schoolgirls and Their Accomplishments, 1725–1830." *Antiques* 135 (1989): 742–753.

Dierks, Konstantin. *In My Power: Letter Writing and Communications in Early America.* Philadelphia: University of Pennsylvania Press, 2009.

Dix, Dom Gregory. *The Shape of the Liturgy.* 2nd ed. New York: Continuum, 2005.

Dorman, John Frederick. *Adventures of Purse and Person, Virginia, 1602–1624/5.* 3 vols. Baltimore: Genealogical Publishing, 2004–2007.

Drummond, Andrew. *The Churches in English Fiction: A Literary and Historical Study from the Regency to the Present Time of British and American Fiction.* Leicester: Backus, 1950.

Duffy, Eamon. *Marking the Hours: English People and Their Prayers, 1240–1570.* New Haven: Yale University Press, 2006.

Durston, Christopher. "By the Book or with the Spirit: The Debate over Liturgical Prayer during the English Revolution." *Historical Research* 79, no. 203 (2006): 50–73.

Dye, Nancy Schrom, and Daniel Blake Smith. "Mother Love and Infant Death, 1750–1920." *Journal of American History* 73 (1986): 329–353.

Dyer, T. F. T. *English Folk-Lore.* London: Bogue, 1880.

Eden, Trudy. *The Early American Table: Food and Society in the New World.* DeKalb: Northern Illinois University Press, 2008.

Elkins, Heather Murray. "'On Borrowed Time': The Christian Year in American Methodism, 1784–1960." Ph.D. diss., Drew University, 1991.

Essig, James David. "A Very Wintry Season: Virginia Baptists and Slavery, 1785–1797." *Virginia Magazine of History and Biography* 88 (1980): 170–185.

Eustace, Nicole. *Passion Is the Gale: Emotion, Power, and the Coming of the American Revolution.* Chapel Hill: University of North Carolina Press for the Omohundro Institute of Early American History and Culture, Williamsburg, VA, 2008.

Evans, Emory G. "The Rise and Decline of the Virginia Aristocracy in the Eighteenth Century: The Nelsons." In *The Old Dominion: Essays for Thomas Perkins Abernathy,* ed. Darrett B. Rutman. Charlottesville: University Press of Virginia, 1964.

——. *A "Topping People": The Rise and Decline of Virginia's Old Political Elite, 1680–1790.* Charlottesville: University of Virginia Press, 2009.

Evans, James Archer. "Survey Report." Library of Virginia (Richmond). http://lvaimage.lib.va.us/VHI/html/13/0274.html.

Fagan, Brian M. *Fish on Friday: Feasting, Fasting, and the Discovery of the New World.* New York: Basic, 2006.

Fales, Martha Gandy. *Jewelry in America, 1600–1900.* Woodbridge, Suffolk, England: Antique Collectors' Club, 1995.

Finkleman, Paul. "Colonial Charters and Codes." In *Encyclopedia of American Civil Liberties,* ed. Paul Finkleman. New York: Routledge, 2006.

Fischer, David Hackett. *Albion's Seed: Four British Folkways in America.* New York: Oxford University Press, 1989.

Fiske, Jane Fletcher. "An Editor's Perspective: The Plight of the Family Bible." *National Genealogical Society Quarterly* 90 (2002): 243–245.

Flandarin, Jean-Louis. *Arranging the Meal: A History of Table Service in France.* Trans. Julie E. Johnson, Antonio Roder, and Sylvia Roder. Berkeley: University of California Press, 2007.

Flint, Christopher. "Speaking Objects: The Circulation of Stories in Eighteenth Century Prose Fiction." *PMLA* 113 (1998): 212–226.

Flint, Valerie I. J. *The Rise of Magic in Early Medieval Europe.* Princeton: Princeton University Press, 1991.

Foote, A. Edward. *Chotankers, a Family History.* Florence, AL: Thornwood, 1982.

Frey, Sylvia. *Water from the Rock: Black Resistance in a Revolutionary Age.* Princeton: Princeton University Press, 1991.

Frey, Sylvia R., and Betty Wood. *Come Shouting to Zion: African American Protestantism in the American South and British Caribbean to 1830.* Chapel Hill: University of North Carolina Press, 1998.

Frost, William J. "From Plainness to Simplicity: Changing Quaker Ideals for Material Culture." In *Quaker Aesthetics,* ed. Emma Jones Lapsansky and Anne E. Verplanck. Philadelphia: University of Pennsylvania Press, 2003.

Frye, Susan. "Sewing Connections: Elizabeth Tudor, Mary Stuart, Elizabeth Talbot, and Seventeenth-Century Anonymous Needleworkers." In *Maids and Mistresses, Cousins and Queens: Women's Alliances in Early Modern England,* ed. Susan Frye and Karen Robertson. New York: Oxford University Press, 1999.

Galpern, A. N. *The Religions of the People in Sixteenth-Century Champagne.* Cambridge: Harvard University Press, 1976.

Gardner, John Starkie. "Silver Plate in the Collection of the Duke of Newcastle at Clumber." *Burlington Magazine for Connoisseurs* 8 (1905): 120–127.

Garrett, Elisabeth Donaghy. "American Samplers and Needlework Pictures in the DAR Museum, Part I: 1739–1806." In *Needlework: An Historical Survey,* ed. Betty Ring. New York: Main Street/Universe, 1975.

"Genealogical Notes and Queries." *William and Mary Quarterly* 16 (1936): 95–102.

Gibbs, M. J. "Precious Artifacts: Women's Jewelry in the Chesapeake, 1750–1799." *Journal of Early Southern Decorative Arts* 13 (1987): 53–103.

Gillespie, Joanna Bowen. "1795: Martha Laurens Ramsay's 'Dark Night of the Soul.'" *William and Mary Quarterly* 48 (1991): 68–92.

Gittings, Clare. *Death, Burial, and the Individual in Early Modern England.* London: Croom Helm, 1984.

Glassie, Henry H. *Art and Life in Bangladesh.* Bloomington: Indiana University Press, 1997.

Goetz, Rebecca Anne. "From Potential Christians to Hereditary Heathens: Religion and Race in the Early Chesapeake, 1590–1740." Ph.D. diss., Harvard University, 2006.

Goggin, Maureen Daly. "An 'Essamplaire Essai' on the Rhetoricity of Needlework Sampler-Making: A Contribution to Theorizing and Historicizing Rhetorical Praxis." *Rhetoric Review* 21 (2002): 309–388.

Gomez, Michael. *Exchanging Our Country Marks: The Transformation of African Identities in the Colonial and Antebellum South.* Chapel Hill: University of North Carolina Press, 1998.

Goodwin, Edward Lewis. *The Colonial Church in Virginia, with Biographical Sketches of the First Six Bishops of the Diocese of Virginia, and Other Historical Papers, Together with Brief Biographical Sketches of the Colonial Clergy of Virginia.* Milwaukee: Morehouse, 1927.

Goodwin, Gerald J. "The Anglican Reaction to the Great Awakening." *Historical Magazine of the Protestant Episcopal Church* 35 (1966): 343–371.

Gordon-Reed, Annette. *The Hemingses of Monticello: An American Family.* New York: Norton, 2008.

Gorman, Frederick J. E., and Michael DiBlasi. "Gravestone Iconography and Mortuary Ideology." *Ethnohistory* 28 (1981): 79–98.

Green, I. M. *The Christian's ABC: Catechisms and Catechizing in England c. 1530–1740.* Oxford: Clarendon; New York: Oxford University Press, 1996.

Greene, Jack P. *Landon Carter: An Inquiry into the Personal Values and Social Imperatives of Eighteenth-Century Virginia Gentry.* Charlottesville: University Press of Virginia, 1967.

———. *Pursuits of Happiness: The Social Development of Early Modern British Colonies and the Formation of American Culture.* Chapel Hill: University of North Carolina Press, 1988.

Greven, Philip J. *The Protestant Temperament: Patterns of Child-Rearing, Religious Experience, and the Self in Early America.* New York: Knopf, 1977.

Griffiths, Paul J. *Religious Reading: The Place of Reading in the Practice of Religion.* New York: Oxford University Press, 1999.

Gundersen, Joan R. *The Anglican Ministry in Virginia, 1723–1766: A Study of a Social Class.* New York: Garland, 1989.

———. "Breaching the Walls of the Enclosed Garden." Presentation for the Library of Virginia Symposium, March 19, 2005.

———. "The Double Bonds of Race and Sex: Black and White Women in a Colonial Virginia Parish." *Journal of Southern History* 52 (1986): 351–372.

———. "Kith and Kin: Women's Networks in Colonial Virginia." In *The Devil's Lane: Sex and Race in the Early South,* ed. Catherine Clinton and Michele Gillespie. New York: Oxford University Press, 1997.

———. "The Myth of the Independent Virginia Vestry." *Historical Magazine of the Protestant Episcopal Church* 44 (1975): 133–141.

———. "The Non-Institutional Church: The Religious Role of Women in

Eighteenth-Century Virginia." *Historical Magazine of the Protestant Episcopal Church* 51 (1982): 347–357.

——. "The Search for Good Men: Recruiting Ministers in Colonial Virginia." *Historical Magazine of the Protestant Episcopal Church* 48 (1979): 453–464.

——. *To Be Useful to the World: Women in Revolutionary America, 1740–1790.* Chapel Hill: University of North Carolina Press, 2006.

Hackel, Heidi Brayman, and Catherine E. Kelly, eds. *Reading Women: Literacy, Authorship, and Culture in the Atlantic World, 1500–1800.* Philadelphia: University of Pennsylvania Press, 2008.

Hall, David D. "The Chesapeake in the Seventeenth Century." In *The Colonial Book in the Atlantic World,* ed. Hugh Armory and David D. Hall. New York: Cambridge University Press, 2000.

——. *Cultures of Print: Essays in the History of the Book.* Amherst: University of Massachusetts Press, 1996.

——. "From 'Religion and Society' to Practices: The New Religious History." In *Possible Pasts: Becoming Colonial in Early America,* ed. Robert Blair St. George. Ithaca: Cornell University Press, 2000.

——. "The Gravestone Image as a Puritan Cultural Code." *Dublin Seminar for New England Folk Life Annual Proceedings,* Boston University, 1976, 23–32.

——, ed. *Lived Religion in America: Toward a History of Practice.* Princeton: Princeton University Press, 1997.

Hall, Kim F. "Culinary Spaces, Colonial Spaces: The Gendering of Sugar in the Seventeenth Century." In *Feminist Readings of Early Modern Culture,* ed. Valerie Traub et al. New York: Cambridge University Press, 1996.

Hallam, Elizabeth, and Jenny Hockey. *Death, Memory, and Material Culture.* Oxford: Berg, 2001.

Hallman, Clive Raymond, Jr. "The Vestry as a Unit of Local Government in Colonial America." Ph.D. diss., University of Georgia, 1987.

Hambrick-Stowe, Charles. *The Practice of Piety: Puritan Devotional Disciplines in Seventeenth-Century New England.* Chapel Hill: University of North Carolina Press for the Institute of Early American History and Culture, Williamsburg, Virginia, 1982.

Hamm, Thomas D. *The Transformation of American Quakerism: Orthodox Friends, 1800–1907.* Bloomington: Indiana University Press, 1988.

Harbury, Katharine E. *Colonial Virginia's Cooking Dynasty.* Columbia: University of South Carolina Press, 2004.

Hardwick, Kevin R. "Mirrors for Their Sons: A History of Genteel Ethics in England and Virginia 1500–1750." Ph.D. diss., University of Maryland, 1996.

Hatch, Charles E. *Grace Church: General Study.* Washington, DC: Office of History and Historic Architecture, Eastern Service Center, 1970.

Hatch, Nathan. *Democratization of American Christianity.* New Haven: Yale University Press, 1989.

Hatchett, Marion J. *Commentary on the American Prayer Book.* New York: Seabury, 1981.

Hatfield, April Lee. *Atlantic Virginia: Intercolonial Relations in the Seventeenth Century.* Philadelphia: University of Pennsylvania Press, 2004.

Hawkins, Jonathan. "Imperial 45: The Jacobite Rebellion in Transatlantic Context." *Journal of Imperial and Commonwealth History* 24 (1996): 24–47.

Hayes, Kevin J. *A Colonial Woman's Bookshelf.* Knoxville: University of Tennessee Press, 1996.

——. *The Library of William Byrd of Westover.* Madison, WI: Madison House, 1997.

Henisch, Bridget Ann. *Cakes and Characters: An English Christmas Tradition.* London: Prospect; Charlottesville: University Press of Virginia, 1984.

Henretta, James A., and Gregory H. Nobles. *Evolution and Revolution: American Society, 1600–1820.* Lexington, MA: D. C. Heath, 1987.

Heyrman, Christine Leigh. *Southern Cross: The Beginnings of the Bible Belt.* New York: Knopf, 1997.

Hiden, Mrs. P. W. "Smiths of Middlesex County, Virginia." *William and Mary Quarterly* 10 (1930): 214–220.

Hijiya, James A. "American Gravestones and Attitudes toward Death: A Brief History." *Proceedings of the American Philosophical Society* 127 (1983): 339–363.

"Historical Genealogical Notes." *William and Mary Quarterly* 3 (1895): 202–209.

Holm, Christiane. "Sentimental Cuts: Eighteenth-Century Mourning Jewelry with Hair." *Eighteenth-Century Studies* 38 (2004): 139–143.

Holmes, David L. "The Anglican Tradition in Colonial Virginia." In *Perspectives on American Religion and Culture,* ed. Peter W. Williams. Malden, MA: Blackwell, 1999.

——. *A Brief History of the Episcopal Church.* Valley Forge, PA: Trinity, 1993.

——. "The Decline and Revival of the Church of Virginia." In *Up from Independence: The Episcopal Church in Virginia: Articles,* ed. George Cleaveland et al. Orange, VA: Interdiocesan Bicentennial Committee of the Virginias, 1976.

——. *The Faiths of the Founding Fathers.* Oxford: Oxford University Press, 2006.

——. "William Meade and the Church of Virginia, 1789–1829." Ph.D. diss., Princeton University, 1971.

Horn, James P. P. *Adapting to a New World: English Society in the Seventeenth-Century Chesapeake.* Chapel Hill: University of North Carolina Press for the Institute of Early American History and Culture, Williamsburg, VA, 1994.

Howell, William Hunting. "'A More Perfect Copy than Heretofore': Imitation, Emulation, and Early American Literacy Culture." Ph.D. diss., Northwestern University, 2005.

Irons, Charles F. *The Origins of Proslavery Christianity: White and Black Evangelicals in Colonial and Antebellum Virginia.* Chapel Hill: University of North Carolina Press, 2008.

Isaac, Rhys. *Landon Carter's Uneasy Kingdom: Revolution and Rebellion on a Virginia Plantation.* New York: Oxford University Press, 2004.

——. *The Transformation of Virginia, 1740–1790.* Chapel Hill: University of

North Carolina Press for the Institute of Early American History and Culture, Williamsburg, VA, 1982.

Ivey, Kimberly Smith. *In the Neatest Manner: The Making of the Virginia Sampler Tradition.* Austin: Curious Works Press; Williamsburg, VA: Colonial Williamsburg Foundation, 1997.

Jacob, W. M. *Lay People and Religion in the Early Eighteenth Century.* New York: Cambridge University Press, 1996.

James, Edward W. "Libraries in Colonial Virginia." *William and Mary College Quarterly Historical Magazine* 4 (1895): 15–17.

Jantzen, Grace. *Becoming Divine: Toward a Feminist Philosophy of Religion.* Bloomington: Indiana University Press, 1999.

Jensen, Robin Margaret. "Living Water: Images, Settings, and Symbols of Early Christian Baptism in the West." Ph.D. diss., Columbia University, 1991.

Jones, Alice Hanson. *American Colonial Wealth: Documents and Methods.* New York: Arno, 1977.

Jones, Ann Rosalind, and Peter Stallybrass. *Renaissance Clothing and the Materials of Memory.* Cambridge: Cambridge University Press, 2000.

Jones, Jerome Walker. "The Anglican Church in Colonial Virginia, 1690–1760." Ph.D. diss., Harvard University, 1960.

——. "The Established Virginia Church and the Conversion of Negroes and Indians, 1620–1760." *Journal of Negro History* 46 (1961): 12–23.

Jonge, Caroline Henriette de. *Dutch Tiles.* New York: Praeger, 1971.

Juster, Susan. *Disorderly Women: Sexual Politics and Evangelicalism in Revolutionary New England.* Ithaca, NY: Cornell University Press, 1994.

——. "'In a Different Voice': Male and Female Narratives of Religious Conversion in Post-Revolutionary America." *American Quarterly* 41 (1989): 34–62.

Kammen, Michael G. *A Time to Every Purpose: The Four Seasons in American Culture.* Chapel Hill: University of North Carolina Press, 2004.

Karant-Nunn, Susan. *The Reformation of Ritual: An Interpretation of Early Modern Germany.* London: Routledge, 1997.

Kelley, Mary. "Crafting Subjectivities: Women, Reading, and Self-Imagining." In Hackel and Kelly, *Reading Women.*

Kelly, Catherine E. "Reading and the Problem of Accomplishment." In Hackel and Kelly, *Reading Women.*

Kern, Susan A. "The Jeffersons at Shadwell: The Social and Material World of a Virginia Plantation." Ph.D. diss., College of William and Mary, 2006.

Kerrison, Catherine. *Claiming the Pen: Women and Intellectual Life in the Early American South.* Ithaca, NY: Cornell University Press, 2006.

Kidd, Thomas S. *The Great Awakening: The Roots of Evangelical Christianity in Colonial America.* New Haven: Yale University Press, 2007.

Kierner, Cynthia A. *Beyond the Household: Women's Place in the Early South, 1700–1835.* Ithaca, NY: Cornell University Press, 1998.

——. "'The Dark and Dense Cloud Perpetually Lowering over Us': Gender and the Decline of the Gentry in Postrevolutionary Virginia." *Journal of the Early Republic* 20 (2000): 185–217.

———. "Hospitality, Sociability, and Gender in the Southern Colonies." *Journal of Southern History* 62 (1996): 449–480.

Kieschnick, John. "Material Culture." In *The Oxford Handbook of Religion and Emotion*, ed. John Corrigan. New York: Oxford University Press, 2008.

Kirkham, Jean, and Debra Boyce. *In Every Generation: A Celebratory History of Grace Episcopal Church, Yorktown, Virginia, 1697–1997*. Yorktown, VA: Grace Episcopal Church, 1997.

Kneebone, John T., et al., eds. *Dictionary of Virginia Biography*. Richmond: Library of Virginia, 1998.

Kroll-Smith, J. Stephen. "Transmitting a Revival Culture: The Organizational Dynamic of the Baptist Movement in Colonial Virginia, 1760–1777." *Journal of Southern History* 50 (1984): 551–568.

Kross, Jessica. "Mansions, Men, Women, and the Creation of Multiple Publics in Eighteenth-Century British North America." *Journal of Social History* 33 (1999): 385–408.

Kulikoff, Allan. "'Throwing the Stocking': A Gentry Marriage in Provincial Maryland." *Maryland Historical Magazine* 71 (1976): 516–521.

———. *Tobacco and Slaves: The Development of Southern Cultures in the Chesapeake, 1680–1800*. Chapel Hill: University of North Carolina Press for the Institute of Early American History and Culture, Williamsburg, Virginia, 1986.

Kupperman, Karen Ordahl. "Fear of Hot Climates in the Anglo-American Colonial Experience." *William and Mary Quarterly* 41 (1984): 213–240.

Kwilecki, Susan E. "Through the Needle's Eye: Religion in the Lives of Wealthy Colonial Americans." Ph.D. diss., Stanford University, 1982.

Laing, Annette. "Heathens and Infidels? African Christianization and Anglicanism in the South Carolina Low Country, 1700–1750." *Religion and American Culture* 12 (2002): 197–228.

Lancaster, Robert B. *A Sketch of the Early History of Hanover County, Virginia, and Its Large and Important Contributions to the American Revolution*. Richmond: Whittet and Shepperson, 1976.

Latane, Lucy Temple. *Parson Latane, 1672–1732*. Charlottesville, VA: Michie, 1936.

Lean, Vincent Stuckey. *Lean's Collectanea*. Vol. 2. Bristol: Arrowsmith, 1903.

Lehmann, Gilly. *The British Housewife: Cookery-Books, Cooking, and Society in Eighteenth-Century Britain*. Totnes: Prospect, 2003.

Lewis, Jan. *The Pursuit of Happiness: Family and Values in Jefferson's Virginia*. New York: Cambridge University Press, 1983.

Lewis, Jan, and Kenneth A. Lockridge. "'Sally Has Been Sick': Pregnancy and Family Limitation among Virginia Gentry Women, 1780–1830." *Journal of Social History* 22 (1988): 5–19.

Lindman, Janet. "Beyond the Meetinghouse." In *The Religious History of Ameri-*

can Women: Reimagining the Past, ed. Catherine A. Brekus. Chapel Hill: University of North Carolina Press, 2007.

———. *Bodies of Belief: Baptist Community in Early America.* Philadelphia: University of Pennsylvania Press, 2008.

———. "A World of Baptists: Gender, Race, and Religious Community in Pennsylvania and Virginia, 1689–1825." Ph.D. diss. University of Minnesota, 1994.

Llewellyn, Nigel. *The Art of Death: Visual Culture in the English Death Ritual, c. 1500–c. 1800.* London: Reaktion, in association with the Victoria and Albert Museum, 1991.

Locklair, Paula. " 'The Beautiful Embroidery . . .': Fine Needlework from the Salem Girls' Boarding School." *Sampler and Antique Needlework Quarterly* 34 (2004): 14–20.

Lockridge, Kenneth A. *The Diary, and Life, of William Byrd II of Virginia, 1674–1744.* Chapel Hill: University of North Carolina Press, 1987.

Lomax, James. *British Silver at Temple Newsam and Lotherton Hall.* Leeds: W. S. Maney, 1992.

Loth, Calder, ed. *The Virginia Landmarks Register.* Charlottesville: University Press of Virginia for the Virginia Department of Historic Resources, 1999.

Lurie, Alison. *The Language of Clothes.* New York: Random House, 1981.

Lyerly, Cynthia Lynn. *Methodism and the Southern Mind, 1770–1810.* New York: Oxford University Press, 1998.

———. "Passion, Desire, and Ecstasy: The Experiential Religion of Southern Methodist Women." In *The Devil's Lane: Sex and Race in the Early South,* ed. Catherine Clinton and Michele Gillespie. New York: Oxford University Press, 1997.

Maffly-Kipp, Laurie F., Leigh E. Schmidt, and Mark Valeri, eds. *Practicing Protestants: Histories of Christian Life in America, 1630–1965.* Baltimore: Johns Hopkins University Press, 2006.

Maier, Pauline. *American Scripture: Making the Declaration of Independence.* New York: Knopf, 1997.

Marshall, Peter. "Angels around the Deathbed: Variations on a Theme in the English Art of Dying." In *Angels in the Early Modern World,* ed. Peter Marshall and Alexandra Walsham. New York: Cambridge University Press, 2006.

Martin, Ann Smart. *Buying into the World of Goods: Early Consumers in Backcountry Virginia.* Baltimore: Johns Hopkins University Press, 2008.

Martin, Maureen M. " 'Boys Who Will Be Men': Desire in 'Tom Brown's Schooldays.' " *Victorian Literature and Culture* 30 (2002): 483–502.

Martin, Peter. *The Pleasure Gardens of Virginia: From Jamestown to Jefferson.* Princeton: Princeton University Press, 1991.

Mason, George Carrington. "The Colonial Churches of Christ Church Parish, Middlesex County, Virginia." *William and Mary Quarterly* 19 (1939): 8–24.

———. "The Colonial Churches of Gloucester County, Virginia." *William and Mary Quarterly* 19 (1939): 325–346.

——. "The Colonial Churches of King and Queen and King William Counties, Virginia." *William and Mary Quarterly* 23 (1943): 440–464.

——. "The Colonial Churches of New Kent and Hanover Counties, Virginia." *Virginia Magazine of History and Biography* 53 (1945): 243–264.

——. "The Colonial Churches of Northumberland and Lancaster Counties, Virginia (Concluded)." *Virginia Magazine of History and Biography* 54 (1946): 233–243.

——. "The Colonial Churches of Sussex and Surrey Counties, Virginia." *William and Mary Quarterly* 20 (1940): 285–305.

——. "The Colonial Churches of Warwick and Elizabeth City Counties." *William and Mary Quarterly* 21 (1941): 371–396.

——. "The Colonial Churches of Westmoreland and King George Counties, Virginia, Part I." *Virginia Magazine of History and Biography* 56 (1948): 154–172.

——. "The Colonial Churches of Westmoreland and King George Counties, Virginia, Part II." *Virginia Magazine of History and Biography* 56 (1948): 280–293.

——. "The Colonial Churches of York County." *William and Mary Quarterly* 19 (1939): 159–280.

Mathews, Donald G. "Christianizing the South." In *New Directions in American Religious History,* ed. Harry S. Stout and Daryl G. Hart. Oxford: Oxford University Press, 1997.

——. *Religion in the Old South.* Chicago: University of Chicago Press, 1977.

Mauss, Marcel. *The Gift: The Form and Reason for Exchange in Archaic Societies.* Trans. W. D. Halls. New York: Norton, 2000.

McCormick, Thomas J. *Ruins as Architecture: Architecture as Ruins.* Dublin, NH: William L. Bauhan, 1999.

McDannell, Colleen. *Material Christianity: Religion and Popular Culture in America.* New Haven: Yale University Press, 1995.

McDougall, Walter A. *Freedom Just Around the Corner: A New American History, 1585–1828.* New York: HarperCollins, 2004.

McFadden, David Revere. *Pricked: Extreme Embroidery.* New York: Museum of Arts and Design, 2007.

McGroaty, William Buckner. "Elizabeth Washington of Hayfield." *Virginia Magazine of History and Biography* 33 (1925): 154–165.

McKeon, Michael. *The Secret History of Domesticity: Public, Private, and the Division of Knowledge.* Baltimore: Johns Hopkins University Press, 2005.

McManners, John. *Death and the Enlightenment: Changing Attitudes to Death among Christians and Unbelievers in Eigtheenth-Century France.* Oxford: Clarendon; New York: Oxford University Press, 1981.

McNab, Jessie. "The Legacy of a Fantastical Scot." *Metropolitan Museum of Art Bulletin* 19 (1961): 172–180.

Mennell, Stephen. *All Manners of Food: Eating and Taste in England and France from the Middle Ages to the Present.* Urbana: University of Illinois Press, 1996.

Metcalf, Peter, and Richard Huntington. *Celebrations of Death: The Anthropology of Mortuary Ritual.* Cambridge: Cambridge University Press, 1991.

Meyers, Carol L. "Everyday Life: Women in the Period of the Hebrew Bible." In *The Women's Bible Commentary,* ed. Carol A. Newsom and Sharon H. Ringe. London: Society for Promoting Christian Knowledge, 1998.

Micou, Mary D. "The Colonial Churches of York County, Virginia." In *Colonial Churches in the Original Colony of Virginia: A Series of Sketches by Especially Qualified Writers.* Richmond, VA: Southern Churchman, 1908.

Middleton, Arthur Pierce. "The Colonial Virginia Parson." *William and Mary Quarterly* 26 (1969): 425–440.

Miller, Daniel, and Fiona Parrott. "Death, Ritual, and Material Culture in South London." In *Death Rites and Rights,* ed. Belinda Brooks-Gordon et al. Oxford: Hart, 2007.

Miller, Perry. "Religion and Society in the Early Literature of Virginia." In *Errand into the Wilderness.* New York: Harper and Row, 1964.

Miller, Susan. *Assuming the Positions: Cultural Pedagogy and the Politics of Commonplace Writing.* Pittsburgh: University of Pittsburgh Press, 1998.

Monaghan, E. Jennifer. *Learning to Read and Write in Colonial America.* Amherst: University of Massachusetts Press, 2005.

Monfredo, Rachel Jean. "American Finger Rings: Representing Bonds of Relationships." M.A. thesis, University of Delaware, 1990.

Montgomery, Florence M. *Textiles in America, 1650–1870.* New York: Norton, 1984.

Mooney, Barbara Burlison. *Prodigy Houses of Virginia: Architecture and the Native Elite.* Charlottesville: University of Virginia Press, 2008.

Moore, Frank. *The Patriot Preachers of the American Revolution with Biographical Sketches, 1776–1783.* New York: Printed for the Subscribers, 1860.

Moore, John Hammond. *Albemarle, Jefferson's County, 1727–1976.* Charlottesville: University Press of Virginia, 1976.

Moore, William Cabell. "Gen. John Hartwell Cocke of Bremo, 1780–1866: A Brief Biography and Genealogical Review with a Short History of Old Bremo." *William and Mary Quarterly* 13 (1933): 143–154.

Morall, Andrew. "Protestant Pots: Morality and Social Ritual in the Early Modern Home." *Journal of Design History* 15 (2002): 263–273.

Morgan, Edmund Sears. *American Slavery, American Freedom: The Ordeal of Colonial Virginia.* New York: Norton, 2003.

——. *Virginians at Home: Family Life in the Eighteenth Century.* Charlottesville, VA: Dominion, 1963.

Morgan, Philip D. *Slave Counterpoint: Black Culture in the Eighteenth-Century Chesapeake and Lowcountry.* Chapel Hill: University of North Carolina Press, 1998.

Moss, Ann. *Printed Commonplace-Books and the Structuring of Renaissance Thought.* Oxford: Clarendon; New York: Oxford University Press, 1996.

Muir, Edward. *Ritual in Early Modern Europe.* Cambridge: Cambridge University Press, 2005.

Najar, Monica. "'Meddling with Emancipation': Baptists, Authority, and the Rift over Slavery in the Upper South." *Journal of the Early Republic* 25 (2005): 162–170.

Nelson, John K. *A Blessed Company: Parishes, Parsons, and Parishioners in Anglican Virginia, 1690–1776.* Chapel Hill: University of North Carolina Press, 2001.

——. "Charles Clay." In *Dictionary of Virginia Biography,* vol. 3, ed. Sara B. Bearss. Richmond: Library of Virginia, 2006.

Nelson, Louis P. *The Beauty of Holiness: Anglicanism and Architecture in Colonial South Carolina.* Chapel Hill: University of North Carolina Press, 2008.

——. "Sensing the Sacred: Anglican Material Religion in Early South Carolina." *Winterthur Portfolio* 41 (2007): 203–235.

Nichols, Frederick D., and Joan R. Gundersen. Review of Upton, *Holy Things and Profane. William and Mary Quarterly* 46 (1989): 378–382.

Nissenbaum, Stephen. *The Battle for Christmas.* New York: Vintage, 1997.

Noll, Mark A. *Christians in the American Revolution.* Grand Rapids, MI: Christian University Press, 1977.

Ochs, Vanessa L. *Inventing Jewish Ritual.* Philadelphia: Jewish Publication Society, 2007.

O'Dell, Cecil. *Pioneers of Old Frederick County, Virginia.* Marceline, MO: Walsworth, 1995.

Olwell, Robert. *Masters, Slaves, and Subjects: The Culture of Power in the South Carolina Low Country, 1740–1790.* Ithaca, NY: Cornell University Press, 1998.

Opie, Iona, and Moira Tatem, eds. *A Dictionary of Superstitions.* New York: Oxford University Press, 1989.

Orsi, Robert. "Everyday Miracles: The Study of Religion." In *Lived Religion in America: Toward a History of Practice,* ed. David D. Hall. Princeton: Princeton University Press, 1997.

The Oxford English Dictionary, 2nd ed., 1989; Oxford English Dictionary Online, Oxford University Press, http://dictionary.oed.com/cgi/entry/50107934.

Painter, Borden W. "The Anglican Vestry in Colonial America." Ph.D. diss., Yale University, 1965.

Parent, Anthony S. *Foul Means: The Formation of a Slave Society in Virginia, 1660–1740.* Chapel Hill: University of North Carolina Press, 2003.

Parker, Rozsika. *The Subversive Stitch: Embroidery and the Making of the Feminine.* London: Women's Press, 1984.

Parmal, Pamela A. *Samplers from A to Z.* Boston: MFA Publications; New York: D.A.P./Distributed Art Publishers, 2000.

Parramore, Thomas C., with Tommy L. Bogger and Peter C. Stewart. *Norfolk: The First Four Centuries.* Charlottesville: University Press of Virginia, 1994.

Parris, Linda Eileen. "'A Dutiful Obedient Wife': The Journal of Elizabeth Foote Washington of Virginia, 1779–1796." M.A. thesis, William and Mary University, 1984.

Patterson, J. M. "Private Libraries in Virginia in the Eighteenth Century." M.A. thesis, University of Virginia, 1935.

Pecquet du Bellet, Louise. *Some Prominent Virginia Families.* Ed. Edward Jaquelin and Martha Cary Jaquelin. Lynchburg, VA: J. P. Bell, 1907.

Peirce, Elizabeth Combs. "History of St. Mary's White Chapel." *William and Mary Quarterly* 16 (1936): 522–533.

Pennell, Sara. "'Pots and Pans History': The Material Culture of the Kitchen in Early Modern England." *Journal of Design History* 11 (1998): 201–216.

Peterson, Eugene H. *Eat This Book: A Conversation in the Art of Spiritual Reading.* Grand Rapids, MI: Eerdmans, 2006.

Peterson, Mark. "Puritanism and Refinement in Early New England: Reflections on Communion Silver." *William and Mary Quarterly* 58 (2001): 307–346.

———. "The Significance of Silver." *William and Mary Quarterly* 59 (2002): 728–736.

Pickering, David. *Cassell's Dictionary of Superstitions.* New York: Sterling, 2002.

Pointon, Marcia. "Materializing Mourning: Hair, Jewellery, and the Body." In *Material Memories,* ed. Marius Kwint, Christopher Breward, and Jeremy Aynsley. Oxford: Berg, 1999.

———. "Wearing Memory: Mourning Jewellry and the Body." In *Trauer Tragen-Trauer Zeigen: Inszeierungen der Geschlechter,* ed. Gisela Ecker. Munich: Wilhelm Fink Verlag, 1999.

Prichard, Robert. *A History of the Episcopal Church.* Harrisburg, PA: Morehouse, 1999.

Raboteau, Albert J. *Slave Religion: The "Invisible Institution" in the Antebellum South.* New York: Oxford University Press, 2004.

Radway, J. A. "Reading Is Not Eating: Mass-Produced Literature and the Theoretical, Methodological, and Political Consequences of a Metaphor." *Book Research Quarterly* 2 (1986): 7–29.

Rambuss, Richard. *Closet Devotions.* Durham, NC: Duke University Press, 1998.

Reis, João José. *Death Is a Festival: Funeral Rites and Rebellion in Nineteenth-Century Brazil.* Chapel Hill: University of North Carolina Press, 2003.

Rhoden, Nancy L. *Revolutionary Anglicanism: The Colonial Church of England Clergy during the American Revolution.* New York: New York University Press, 1999.

Richardson, Ruth. "Death's Door: Thresholds and Boundaries in British Funeral Customs." In *Boundaries and Thresholds: Papers from a Colloquium of the Katherine Briggs Club,* ed. Hilda Ellis Davidson. Stroud, Gloucestershire: Thimble, 1993.

Rieder, Paula M. *On the Purification of Women: Churching in Northern France, 1100–1500.* New York: Palgrave Macmillan, 2006.

Ring, Betty. "For Persons of Fortune Who Have Taste: An Elegant Schoolgirl Embroidery." *Journal of Early Southern Decorative Arts* 3, no. 2 (1977): 1–11.

———. *Girlhood Embroidery: American Samplers and Pictorial Needlework, 1650–1850.* New York: Knopf, 1993.

——. "Memorial Embroideries by American Schoolgirls." In *Needlework: An Historical Survey*, ed. Betty Ring. New York: Main Street/Universe, 1975.

Roche, Daniel. *The Culture of Clothing: Dress and Fashion in the Ancien Régime.* Cambridge: Cambridge University Press, 1994.

Roeber, A. G. *Faithful Magistrates and Republican Lawyers: Creators of Virginia Legal Culture, 1680–1810.* Chapel Hill: University of North Carolina Press, 1981.

Rosendale, Timothy. *Liturgy and Literature in the Making of Protestant England.* Cambridge: Cambridge University Press, 2007.

Rowland, Kate Mason. *The Life of George Mason, 1725–1792; Including His Speeches, Public Papers, and Correspondence.* New York: Putnam, 1896; rpt., New York: Russell and Russell, 1964.

Rutman, Darrett Bruce, and Anita H. Rutman. *A Place in Time: Middlesex County, Virginia, 1650–1750.* New York: Norton, 1984.

Rutman, Darrett Bruce, with Anita H. Rutman. *Small Worlds, Large Questions: Explorations in Early American Social History, 1600–1850.* Charlottesville: University Press of Virginia, 1994.

Sack, Daniel. *Whitebread Protestants: Food and Religion in American Culture.* New York: St. Martin's, 2000.

Saxton, Martha. *Being Good: Women's Moral Values in Early America.* New York: Hill and Wang, 2003.

Schmidt, Leigh Eric. "'A Church-Going People Are a Dress-Loving People': Clothes, Communication, and Religious Culture in America." *Church History* 58 (1989): 36–51.

——. *Consumer Rites: The Buying and Selling of American Holidays.* Princeton: Princeton University Press, 1995.

——. "Practices of Exchange: From Market Culture to Gift Economy in the Interpretation of American Religion." In *Lived Religion in America: Toward a History of Practice*, ed. Donald D. Hall. Princeton: Princeton University Press, 1997.

Scribner, Robert W. "The Reformation, Popular Magic, and the 'Disenchantment of the World.'" *Journal of Interdisciplinary History* 23 (1993): 475–494.

Scully, Randolph Ferguson. *Religion and the Making of Nat Turner's Virginia: Baptist Community and Conflict, 1740–1840.* Charlottesville: University of Virginia Press, 2008.

Sebba, Anne. *Samplers: Five Centuries of a Gentle Craft.* New York: Thames and Hudson, 1979.

Seeman, Erik R. *Pious Persuasions: Laity and Clergy in Eighteenth-Century New England.* Baltimore: Johns Hopkins University Press, 1999.

Seiler, William H. "The Anglican Parish Vestry in Colonial Virginia." *Journal of Southern History* 22 (1956): 310–337.

——. "The Church of England as the Established Church in Seventeenth-Century Virginia." *Journal of Southern History* 15 (1949): 478–508.

——. "Land Processioning in Colonial Virginia." *William and Mary Quarterly* 6 (1949): 416–436.

Semple, Robert B. *A History of the Rise and Progress of the Baptists in Virginia.* Richmond: Published by the author, 1810.

Shammas, Carole. "Black Women's Work and the Evolution of Plantation Society in Virginia." *Labor History* 26 (1985): 5–28.

Shaw, Ralph. *American Bibliography: A Preliminary Checklist, 1801–1819.* Vol. 15. New York: Scarecrow, 1958–1966.

Sheldon, Garrett Ward, and Daniel L. Dreisbach. *Religion and Political Culture in Jefferson's Virginia.* Lanham, MD: Rowman and Littlefield, 2000.

Simons, D. Brenton and Peter Benes, eds. *The Art of Family: Genealogical Artifacts in New England.* Boston: Northeastern University Press for New England Historic Genealogical Society, 2002.

Slater, Peter Gregg. *Children in the New England Mind: In Death and in Life.* Hamden: Archon, 1977.

Sleeper-Smith, Susan. "The Dream as a Tool for Historical Research: Reexamining Life in Eighteenth Century Virginia through the Dreams of a Gentleman, William Byrd, II, 1674–1744." *Journal of the Association for the Study of Dreams* 3 (1993): 49–68.

Smart, George K. "Private Libraries in Colonial Virginia." *American Literature* 10 (1938): 24–52.

Smith, Daniel Blake. "'Autonomy and Affection': Parents and Children in Eighteenth-Century Virginia Families." In *Growing Up in America: Children in Historical Perspective,* ed. N. Ray Hiner and Joseph M. Hawes. Urbana: University of Illinois Press, 1985.

——. *Inside the Great House: Planter Family Life in Eighteenth-Century Chesapeake Society.* Ithaca, NY: Cornell University Press, 1980.

Smith, Jonathan Z. *Imagining Religion: From Babylon to Jonestown.* Chicago: University of Chicago Press, 1982.

Smith, Kimberly. "'The First Effort of an Infant Hand': An Introduction to Virginia Schoolgirl Embroideries, 1742–1850." *Journal of Early Southern Decorative Arts* 16 (1990): 89–98.

Smith, Mark M. *How Race Is Made: Slavery, Segregation, and the Senses.* Chapel Hill, NC: University of North Carolina Press, 2006.

Snyder, Terri L. *Brabbling Women: Disorderly Speech and the Law in Early Virginia.* Ithaca, NY: Cornell University Press, 2003.

Sobel, Mechal. *Trabelin' On: The Slave Journey to an Afro-Baptist Faith.* Westport, CT: Greenwood, 1979.

——. *The World They Made Together: Black and White Values in Eighteenth-Century Virginia.* Princeton: Princeton University Press, 1987.

Solberg, Winton U. *Redeem the Time: The Puritan Sabbath in Early America.* Cambridge: Harvard University Press, 1977.

Sorensen, Leni. "Keeping a Good House." *Gastronomica* 5 (2005): 106–108.

Spacks, Patricia Ann Meyer. *Privacy: Concealing the Eighteenth-Century Self.* Chicago: University of Chicago Press, 2003.

Spangler, Jewel L. "Becoming Baptists: Conversion in Colonial and Early National Virginia." *Journal of Southern History* 67 (2001): 243–286.

——. *Virginians Reborn: Anglican Monopoly, Evangelical Dissent, and the Rise of the Baptists in the Late Eighteenth Century.* Charlottesville: University of Virginia Press, 2008.

Spencer, Maryellen. "Food in Seventeenth-Century Tidewater Virginia: A Method for Studying Historical Cuisines." Ph.D. diss., Virginia Polytechnic Institute and State University, 1982.

Spinks, Bryan D. *Early and Medieval Rituals and Theologies of Baptism: From the New Testament to the Council of Trent.* Aldershot, England: Ashgate, 2006.

Spruill, Julia Cherry. *Women's Life and Work in the Southern Colonies.* New York: Norton, 1998.

Stabile, Susan M. *Memory's Daughters: The Material Culture of Remembrance in Eighteenth-Century America.* Ithaca, NY: Cornell University Press, 2004.

Stanard, Mary Newton. *Colonial Virginia, Its People and Customs.* Philadelphia: Lippincott, 1917.

Stanard, W. G. "Major Robert Beverley and His Descendants." *William and Mary Quarterly* 2 (1895): 405–413.

Stannard, David E. *The Puritan Way of Death: A Study in Religion, Culture, and Social Change.* New York: Oxford University Press, 1977.

Stanton, Lucia. *Free Some Day: The African-American Families of Monticello.* Charlottesville: Thomas Jefferson Foundation, 2000.

Staples, Kathleen. "'The Advantages of Religious Instruction': Girlhood Embroidery and Religious Diversity." *Sampler and Antique Needlework* 42 (2006): 27–34.

——. "Girlhood Embroidery: The African-American Experience." *Sampler and Antique Needlework* 42 (2006): 15–18.

——. "'Plain, Fine, and Fancy': Materials, Patterns, Projects, Techniques and Stitches." *Sampler and Antique Needlework* 42 (2006): 35–42.

——. "Tangible Displays of Refinements: Southern Needlework at MESDA." *Antiques* 171 (2007): 198–203.

Stavely, Keith W. F., and Kathleen Fitzgerald. *America's Founding Food: The Story of New England Cooking.* Chapel Hill: University of North Carolina Press, 2004.

Stein, Susan. *The Worlds of Thomas Jefferson at Monticello.* New York: Abrams, in association with the Thomas Jefferson Memorial Foundation, 1993.

Stitt, Sue. *Museum of Early Southern Decorative Arts.* Winston-Salem, NC: Hunter, 1970.

Stiverson, Cynthia Z., and Gregory A. Stiverson. *Books Both Useful and Entertaining: A Study of Book Purchases and Reading Habits of Virginians in the Mid-Eighteenth Century.* Charlottesville: University Press of Virginia for Colonial Williamsburg Foundation, 1977.

——. "The Colonial Retail Book Trade: Availability and Affordability of Reading Material in Mid-Eighteenth-Century Virginia." In *Printing and Society in Early America,* ed. William L. Joyce et al. Worcester, MA: American Antiquarian Society Program in the History of the Book in American Culture, 1983.

Strong, Rowan. *Anglicanism and the British Empire, c. 1700–1850.* Oxford: Oxford University Press, 2007.

Sturtz, Linda L. *Within Her Power: Propertied Women in Colonial America.* New York: Routledge, 2002.

Swan, Susan Burrows. *A Winterthur Guide to American Needlework.* New York: Crown, 1976.

Swinburne, Layinka, and Laura Mason. "'She Came from a Groaning Very Cheerful . . .': Food in Pregnancy, Childbirth, and Christening Ritual." In *Food and the Rites of Passage,* ed. Laura Mason. Devon: Prospect, 2002.

Sykas, P. "Fustians in Englishmen's Dress: From Cloth to Emblem." *Costume,* 43 (2009). http://www.ingentaconnect.com/content/maney/cos/2009/00000043/00000001/art00002.

Targoff, Ramie. *Common Prayer: The Language of Public Devotion in Early Modern England.* Chicago: University of Chicago Press, 2001.

Tarter, Brent. "Reflections on the Church of England in Colonial Virginia." *Virginia Magazine of History and Biography* 112 (2004): 338–371.

———. "Samuel Boush." In *Dictionary of Virginia Biography,* vol. 2, ed. Sara B. Bearss et al. Richmond: Library of Virginia, 2001.

Tarter, Michele Lise. "'Varied Trials, Dippings, and Strippings': Quaker Women's Irresistible Call to the Early South." In *Feminist Interventions in Early American Studies,* ed. Mary Carruth. Tuscaloosa: University of Alabama Press, 2006.

Tate, Thad W. "The Colonial College." In *The College of William and Mary: A History,* ed. Susan H. Godson et al. Williamsburg: King and Queen Press, 1982.

———. "Funerals in Eighteenth Century Virginia a Research Report." Williamsburg, VA: Colonial Williamsburg, 1956.

———. "James Blair." In *Dictionary of Virginia Biography,* vol. 1, ed. John T. Kneebone et al. Richmond: Library of Virginia, 1998.

Taylor, Lou. *Mourning Dress: A Costume and Social History.* London: Allen and Unwin, 1983.

———. *The Study of Dress History.* Manchester: Manchester University Press, 2002.

Theophano, Janet. *Eat My Words: Reading Women's Lives through the Cookbooks They Wrote.* New York: Palgrave, 2002.

Thomas, Keith. "An Anthropology of Religion and Magic, II." *Journal of Interdisciplinary History* 1 (1975): 91–109.

———. *Religion and the Decline of Magic.* New York: Scribner's, 1971.

Thompson, Mary V. "'As if I had Been a Very Great Somebody.'" Unpublished essay in author's possession.

———. "Death and Mourning in the Family of George Washington." Unpublished essay in author's possession.

——. "In the Hands of a Good Providence": Religion in the Life of George Washington. Charlottesville: University of Virginia Press, 2008.

——. "The Lowest Ebb of Misery: Death and Mourning in the Family of George Washington." Historic Alexandria Quarterly (2001): 1–14.

Thornton, Martin. English Spirituality: An Outline of Ascetical Theology According to the English Pastoral Tradition. Cambridge, MA: Cowley, 1986.

Thornton, Tamara Plakins. Handwriting in America: A Cultural History. New Haven: Yale University Press, 1996.

Thursby, Jacqueline. Funeral Festivals in America: Rituals for the Living. Lexington: University Press of Kentucky, 2006.

Traub, Valerie, et al., eds. Feminist Readings of Early Modern Culture: Emerging Subjects. Cambridge: Cambridge University Press, 1996.

"Travis Family." William and Mary Quarterly 18 (1909): 141–144.

Troubetzkoy, Ulrich. "How Virginia Saved the Outlawed English Carols." Historical Magazine of the Protestant Episcopal Church 30 (1961): 198–202.

Tucker, Karen B. Westerfield. American Methodist Worship. New York: Oxford University Press, 2001.

Turpin, John B. A Brief History of the Albemarle Baptist Association: A Discourse Delivered before the Body at Its Centennial Session, Chestnut Grove Church, August 19th, 1891. Ed. W. W. Landrum. Richmond: Virginia Baptist Historical Society, [1891?].

Tweed, Thomas A. Our Lady of the Exile: Diasporic Religion at a Cuban Catholic Shrine in Miami. New York: Oxford University Press, 1997.

Tyler, Lyon Gardiner, ed. Encyclopedia of Virginia Biography, vol. 1. New York: Lewis Historical Publishing, 1915.

Ulrich, Laurel Thatcher. The Age of Homespun: Objects and Stories in the Creation of an American Myth. New York: Knopf, 2001.

——. "Creating Lineages." In The Art of Family, ed. D. Brenton Simons and Peter Benes. Boston: New England Historic Genealogical Society, 2002.

——. "Hannah Barnard's Cupboard: Female Property and Identity in Eighteenth-Century New England." In Through a Glass Darkly: Reflections on Personal Identity in Early America, ed. Ronald Hoffman, Mechal Sobel, and Fredrika J. Teute. Chapel Hill: University of North Carolina Press, 1997.

——. " 'It Went Away Shee Knew Not How': Food Theft and Domestic Conflict in Seventeenth Century Essex County." In Foodways in the Northeast, ed. Peter Benes. The Dublin Seminar for New England Folklife: Annual Proceedings, 1982. Boston: Boston University, 1984.

——. "Of Pens and Needles: Sources in Early American Women's History." Journal of American History 77 (1990): 200–207.

Upton, Dell. Holy Things and Profane: Anglican Parish Churches in Colonial Virginia. New Haven: Yale University Press, 1997.

——. "Vernacular Domestic Architecture in Eighteenth-Century Virginia." Winterthur Portfolio 17 (1982): 95–119.

van Keuren, Louise. "The American Girl at Her Sampler, ca. 1633–1850: Inspiring a Feminine Ideal." In *Rituals and Patterns in Children's Lives*, ed. Kathy Murdock Jackson. Madison: University of Wisconsin Press, 2005.

Vogt, Christopher P. *Patience, Compassion, Hope, and the Christian Art of Dying Well.* Lanham, MD: Rowman and Littlefield, 2004.

Walsh, Lorena S. *From Calabar to Carter's Grove: The History of a Virginia Slave Community.* Charlottesville: University Press of Virginia, 1997.

Waukechon, John Frank. "The Forgotten Evangelicals: Virginia Episcopalians, 1790–1876." Ph.D. diss., University of Texas at Austin, 2000.

Weaver, William Woys. *America Eats: Forms of Edible Folk Art.* New York: Harper and Row, 1989.

Webster, Tom. "Writing to Redundancy: Approaches to Spiritual Journals and Early Modern Spirituality." *Historical Journal* 39 (1996): 33–56.

Weir, David A. *Early New England: A Covenanted Society.* Grand Rapids, MI: Eerdmans, 2005.

Wells, Camille. "Dower Play/Power Play: Menokin and the Ordeal of Elite House Building in Colonial Virginia." *Perspectives in Vernacular Architecture* 9 (2003): 2–21.

———. "The Planter's Prospect: Houses, Outbuildings, and Rural Landscapes in Eighteenth-Century Virginia." *Winterthur Portfolio* 28 (1993): 1–31.

Wenger, Mark R. "The Central Passage in Virginia: Evolution of an Eighteenth-Century Living Space." *Perspectives in Vernacular Architecture* 2 (1986): 137–149.

———. "The Dining Room in Early Virginia." *Perspectives in Vernacular Architecture* 3 (1989): 149–159.

Wertenbaker, Thomas Jefferson. *Norfolk: Historic Southern Port.* Ed. Marvin W. Schlegel. Durham, NC: Duke University Press, 1962.

Wertz, Richard W., and Dorothy C. Wertz. *Lying-in: A History of Childbirth in America.* New Haven: Yale University Press, 1989.

Whiting, Marvin. "Religious Literature in Virginia: A Preface to a Study in the History of Ideas." M.A. thesis, Emory University, 1975.

Whittingham, William R., ed. *A Catalogue of Liturgies, Liturgical Works, Books of Private Devotion, Hymnals and Collections of Hymns . . .* Baltimore: privately printed, 1881.

Wiencek, Henry. *An Imperfect God: George Washington, His Slaves, and the Creation of America.* New York: Farrar, Straus and Giroux, 2003.

Wilkie, Laurie A. "Magical Passions: Sexuality and African-American Archaeology." In *Archaeologies of Sexuality*, ed. Robert A. Schmidt and Barbara L. Voss. London: Routledge, 2000.

Wilson, Adrian. "The Ceremony of Childbirth and Its Interpretation." In *Women as Mothers in Pre-Industrial England: Essays in Memory of Dorothy McLaren*, ed. Valerie Fildes. London: Routledge, 1990.

Wilson, Stephen. *The Magical Universe: Everyday Ritual and Magic in Pre-Modern Europe.* London: Hambledon and London, 2000.

Wingate, Isabel B., ed. *Fairchild's Dictionary of Textiles.* New York: Fairchild, 1967.

Winton, Calhoun. "The Southern Book Trade in the Eighteenth Century." In *A History of the Book in America,* I: *The Colonial Book in the Atlantic World,* ed. Hugh Amory and David D. Hall. Chapel Hill: University of North Carolina Press, 2007.

Wood, Kirsten E. *Masterful Women: Slaveholding Widows from the American Revolution through the Civil War.* Chapel Hill: University of North Carolina Press, 2004.

Woolverton, John Frederick. *Colonial Anglicanism in North America.* Detroit: Wayne State University Press, 1984.

Worrall, Jay. *The Friendly Virginians: America's First Quakers.* Athens, GA: Iberian, 1994.

Wright, Louis B. "Pious Reading in Colonial Virginia." *Journal of Southern History* 6 (1940): 383–392.

Wulf, Karin. "Bible, King, and Common Law: Family History Practices and Genealogical Literacies in Colonial British America." Unpublished essay in author's possession.

——. "Lineage: The Politics and Poetics of Genealogy in British America, 1680–1820," forthcoming.

——. "'Of the Old Stock': Quakerism and Transatlantic Genealogies in Colonial British America." In *The Creation of the British Atlantic World,* ed. Elizabeth Mancke and Carole Shammas. Baltimore: Johns Hopkins University Press, 2005.

Yost, Genevieve. "*The Compleat Housewife* or *Accomplish'd Gentlewoman's Companion:* A Bibliographical Study." *William and Mary Quarterly* 18 (1938): 419–435.

Zambone, Albert. "Anglican Enlightenment: Intellectual Culture in Virginia, 1690–1750." Ph.D. diss., Oxford University, forthcoming.

Zucker, Paul. *Fascination of Decay: Ruins: Relic, Symbol, Ornament.* Ridgewood, NJ: Gregg, 1968.

Acknowledgments

This book could not have been written without the help of countless archivists, curators, and museum staff members. I am enormously thankful for the staffs of the Museum of Early Southern Decorative Arts (especially Johanna Brown, Sally Gant, Robert Leath, June Lucas, and Martha Rowe), Colonial Williamsburg (especially Linda Baumgarten, Suzanne Hood, Carl Lounsbury, Margaret Pritchard, Janine Skerry, and George Yetter), Stratford Hall (especially Gretchen Goodell and Judy Hynson), Mount Vernon (especially Sherry Birk, Joan Stahl, and Mary V. Thompson), Carlyle House (especially Erin Adams), Wilton House (especially Dana Hand Evans), the Textile Museum of Canada (especially Erinn Langille), the Victoria and Albert Museum (especially Susan North), the Association for the Preservation of Virginia Antiquities (especially Catharine Dean), Winterthur (especially Linda Eaton and Tom Savage), the Jefferson Library at Monticello (especially Anna Berkes and Eric Johnson), Gunston Hall (especially Michele Lee and Caroline M. Riley), the Albert and Shirley Small Special Collections Library at the University of Virginia (especially Gayle Cooper and Eileen O'Toole), the Library of Virginia (especially David Feinberg and Brent Tarter), the Swem Library at the College of William and Mary (especially Susan Riggs), the Virginia Historical Society (especially Heather Beattie and Jeffrey Ruggles), and the Bishop Payne Library of Virginia Theological Seminary (especially Julia Randle). For research assistance along the way, I am grateful to Molly Bosscher Davis, Rebekah Eklund, Barbara Vines Little, Kim May, Abby Love Smith, Megan Stubbendeck, and Timothy Wardle and, near the end of the project, the heroic and unstinting efforts of Donyelle McCray.

The visual images in this book also represent the cooperation and generosity of many people. I am grateful to Mike Adamo (Duke University), Gary Albert (MESDA), Dawn Bonner (Mount Vernon), Rob Cardillo (Rob Cardillo Photography), Jamison Davis (Virginia Historical Society), Christina Deane (University of Virginia Library), R. Douglas Geddes and Kingston Episcopal Parish, Torrance Harman and the vestry of St. Mary's White

Chapel, Audrey Johnson (Library of Virginia), Iris Labeur (Rijksmuseum), Charles Lawson (Highlander Studios/Quantum Imaging), Marianne Martin (Colonial Williamsburg Foundation), Howell Perkins (Virginia Museum of Fine Arts), Robert Teagle (Foundation for Historic Christ Church), William Woys Weaver (Drexel University), and Lisa Williams (Virginia Department of Historic Resources).

A Cheerful and Comfortable Faith began as a dissertation at Columbia University, where I was very lucky to be cheered on and challenged by wonderful fellow students, especially Jonathon Kahn, Kim Philips-Fein, Jana Riess, and Ellen Stroud. Catherine Randall, who served as an external reader on the dissertation, offered characteristically astute insights. The other members of the committee were Randall Balmer, Richard Bushman, Eric Foner, and Martha Saxton. Since I was a college student, these four scholars have been treasured mentors, unstinting in the time and energy they have devoted to teaching me the historian's craft. I am not quite sure how to thank them, or even to begin to accurately describe the impact they have had on my intellectual, moral, and political imagination. I am also grateful to Barbara Fields, who taught the first southern history course I took, during my sophomore year of college, and whose intellectual standards continue to guide me today.

Beyond Columbia, I was privileged to undertake revisions as a fellow at the Center for the Study of Religion at Princeton University. I am grateful for the hospitality extended to me there by Robert Wuthnow and David Michelson, and for the responses to chapters offered by the members of the Religion and Culture workshop and the American religion workshop. At Princeton, Marie Griffith, Ryan Harper, Leigh Schmidt, Judith Weisenfeld, and my two beloved fellow fellows, Darren Dochuk and Matthew Hedstrom, all read the manuscript, and each offered probing questions and crucial encouragement. Also at Princeton, two conversations with Jeff Stout were enormously helpful.

I finished writing *A Cheerful and Comfortable Faith* as a new faculty member at Duke Divinity School. I am daily grateful for the goodwill of my colleagues. This book has benefited enormously from conversations—some more directly related to Virginia's Anglicans, some less directly related—with numerous students and colleagues, especially Charles Campbell, J. Kameron Carter, Stephen Chapman, Susan Eastman, Paul Griffiths, Amy Laura Hall, Stanley Hauerwas, Randy Maddox, Joel Marcus, Thea Portier-Young, Warren Smith, Laceye Warner, and Jo Bailey Wells. Diane Decker and Ron Mimnaugh helped in ways large and small. Judith Heyhoe rescued me from disorganization and despair. The library staff has been unflaggingly cheerful, in both senses of the term. (I knew I needed to wrap up this book when a librarian called me and said, "We have an Interlibrary Loan book with no label on it; we assume it's yours." He was correct.) The junior faculty reading group, chaired by Ellen Davis (associate dean for faculty development), read a portion of the manuscript. Grant Wacker read the entire book, as did students in his Interpretations of American Religion class; Grant's comments were predictably insightful, and discussion with the class was invaluable. The collegiality in these halls would be unthinkable without the leadership of Dean L. Gregory Jones, and I am thankful each day for his support.

Many additional friends and colleagues read drafts of chapters or of the entire manuscript: deepest thanks to Julie Byrne, Grace Hale, Paul Harvey, Kathryn Lofton, Mary E. Lyons, Donald Mathews, David Morgan, W. David Myers, Vanessa Ochs, Ted Ownby, Randi Rashkover, Kevin Seidel, Kathleen Staples, and Mark Valeri. Susan Wise Bauer, Richard Bushman, Sarah Johnson, Stephen Prothero, and Martha Saxton went especially beyond the call of duty in reading draft after draft. The trenchant comments of the anonymous readers for Yale University Press were also quite helpful. I have been most fortunate to have Al Zambone as an Anglican Virginia partner-in-crime. His gimlet eye and his devotion to Clio provide constant inspiration.

Two research fellowships—the Madelyn Moeller Research Fellowship in Southern Material Culture at the Museum of Early Southern Decorative Arts and a short-term fellowship at the Robert H. Smith International Center for Jefferson Studies at Monticello (ICJS)—provided not only funding and access to crucial sources but also an opportunity to share sections of my work. At MESDA, in addition to the staff members, I was lucky to meet Rick Pardue, who shared his knowledge of Dutch tiles, and Kathleen Staples, who has generously answered all my questions about Virginia needlework. At the ICJS, I benefited from conversations with Andrew O'Shaughnessy, Leni Sorensen, and especially Elizabeth Chew. During my presentation at the ICJS, feedback from Susan Stein was particularly helpful. I also benefited from the opportunity to present portions of this book to faculty and students at Eastern Nazarene College in Quincy, Massachusetts, where I was welcomed by the generous hospitality of Randall Stephens, and at the "Reading and Writing Recipe Books, 1600–1800" conference at the University of Warwick; I am grateful for the vision of conference organizers Michelle DiMeo and Sara Pennell, and for particularly stimulating conversation with Amanda E. Herbert.

When I traveled to do research, countless friends have opened their homes to me, especially Susan and Peter Bauer, Lil Copan, Grace Hale, and Mary E. Lyons and Paul Collinge. Much of this book was written in the upstairs bedroom of the Hull family of Princeton, New Jersey, and for their bountiful generosity, I remain grateful.

I have been bowled over by the willingness of colleagues whom I do not know well, many of whom I have never met, to answer questions about sources and method. I particularly appreciate the scholarly generosity of Edward L. Bond, Lori Branch, Christopher Densmore, Joan R. Gundersen, Kevin Hayes, Susan Kern, Emma Lapsansky-Werner, Ann Smart Martin, Robert Bruce Mullin, John K. Nelson, Louis Nelson, Robert Prichard, and Karin Wulf.

At Yale University Press, I have been keenly thankful for Laura Davulis, Dan Heaton, and Chris Rogers. As ever, I remain grateful for the support of my agent, Carol Mann.

My family has provided encouragement during the many years of my education. I am grateful especially for the support of Bob Winner, Leslie Winner, and my father, Dennis Winner. My mother, Linda C. Winner, lived to see *A Cheerful and Comfortable Faith* only at the most embryonic stage; her teaching me to work hard and follow my passions is this book's sine qua non.

Thirteen years after beginning to think about Anglicanism in colonial Virginia, I am thrilled to thank the many people who helped me with this book. I am doubtless accidentally omitting some people from this list; I regret those omissions, which are only a mark of my addled brain, and of the length of the list of people who have extended themselves to me as I have worked on *A Cheerful and Comfortable Faith*.

Thank you.

Index